HAPPENINGS AND OTHER ACTS

Edited by Mariellen R. Sandford

Routledge
Taylor & Francis Group

LONDON AND NEW YORK

First published 1995
by Routledge
2 Park Square, Milton Park, Abingdon, Oxon, OX14 4RN

Simultaneously published in the USA and Canada
by Routledge
270 Madison Ave, New York NY 10016

Transferred to Digital Printing 2005

Routledge is an imprint of the Taylor & Francis Group

Typeset in Times by Solidus (Bristol) Limited

British Library Cataloguing in Publication Data
A catalogue record for this book is available from the British Library

Library of Congress Cataloging in Publication Data
Happenings and Other Acts / edited by Mariellen R. Sandford.
       p.   cm. — (Worlds of performance)
   Includes bibliographical references (p.   ) and index.
   1. Happening (Art)   I. Sandford, Mariellen R.
   II. Series.
   PN3203.H34   1994
   792'.022–dc20   94–681

ISBN 0-415-09935-8 (hbk)
ISBN 0-415-09936-6 (pbk)

Printed and bound by Antony Rowe Ltd, Eastbourne

For my mother,
     Ann D. Rokosny

CONTENTS

ILLUSTRATIONS

CONTRIBUTORS

Editor's note: Most contributors have two entries, one after "1965" and one after "1994." The 1965 entry is taken from *TDR* 10, 2 (T30). If the contributor's essay is from a subsequent issue of *TDR*, the early entry is from the *TDR* in which their article first appeared. The 1994 entry is an update. In some cases we were unable to reach or find out about a contributor, and no update was possible.

Robert Ashley. 1965: A composer-musician and an organizer of the Cooperative Studio for Electronic Music. Ashley is coordinator of the ONCE Group's activities, including its annual festival in Ann Arbor, Michigan.
1994: Ashley's quartet of short operas, *Now Eleanor's Idea*, premiered at the Festivale d'Avignon in July.

Günter Berghaus. Not in the 1965 volume, his contribution was written especially for this collection.
1994: A Reader in Theatre History in the Drama Department, Bristol University, Berghaus has studied theatre, film, and art history in Cologne and Berlin.

George Brecht. 1965: No entry.
1994: Lives and works as an artist in Cologne. Brecht's early "Note-books" are being published by Walther Köning. The first of the series, *George Brecht: Notebooks I, II, III*, was released in 1991.

John Cage. 1965: Music Director for Merce Cunningham and Dance Company. His most recent contributions (and performances) are *Rozart Mix*, done at Brandeis University with six performers and thirteen tape machines, *Variations V* at Lincoln Center and *Talk I* at the ONCE Festival in Ann Arbor.
1994: Cage died in 1992. Among his later books are *X: Writing '79–82* (1983, Wesleyan University Press) and *I–VI* (1990, Harvard University Press), collected lectures delivered at Harvard 1988–89. Works composed since the late 1960s include *Hpschd* (1969), *Etudes Australes* (1974–75), *Roratorio* (1979), and five *Europa* works (1987–91).

Ken Dewey. 1965: Formed Action Theatre, Inc., in New York City. Dewey died in 1972.

Letty Eisenhauer. 1965: Teaches art history at New York Community College. She has exhibited paintings and sculpture in New York and Los Angeles, and was a performer in many early Happenings.

1994: Continues to paint and sculpt. She is active as a psychotherapist and children's art therapist.

Anna Halprin. 1965: The director of the Dancers' Workshop of San Francisco and has appeared with her company in contemporary art festivals throughout the United States and Canada, as well as in European festivals and TV programs. (At this time Halprin was known as Ann Halprin and the original articles refer to her by that name.)
1994: Halprin is currently involved in developing rituals of healing, personally and collectively.

Dick Higgins. 1965: Studied composition with John Cage and Henry Cowell. Higgins has made movies, written Happening-type pieces, an electronic opera, and plays, and published several books.
1994: Higgins is painting, lecturing, and making performance works. His *Buster Keaton Enters into Paradise* was published in 1994 by Left Hand Books.

Joe Jones. 1965: No entry.
1994: Jones created mechanical instruments and musical objects and, in 1982, a solar orchestra with solar-powered motors that produced sounds. He moved to Germany in 1972 and died in 1993.

Allan Kaprow. 1965: No entry.
1994: Kaprow, coiner of the term "Happening," recently retired from forty years as a professor of art to completely devote his time to the making of un-art.

Michael Kirby. 1965: Co-editor of the Happenings issue of *TDR*, Kirby teaches at Saint Francis College, Brooklyn, directs off-Broadway, and exhibits sculpture in several New York galleries. His book, *Happenings*, was published in 1965.
1994: After more than 20 years on the faculty of the Department of Performance Studies, Tisch School of the Arts, NYU, and fifteen years as editor of *TDR* (1971–86), Kirby retired in 1991 to the rank of professor emeritus. He acts in films and writes screenplays.

Alison Knowles. 1965: No entry.
1994: *Bread and Water*, a radio performance done in Cologne, which exists as print graphics adapted for radio. Knowles published *Event Scores* and *Spoken Text* in 1994 and continues to do performance work and installations. A large exhibition is scheduled for Warsaw and Saarbrucken in 1995.

Jean-Jacques Lebel. Lebel's essay is from *TDR* 13, 1, (T41) 1968. At that time, he was France's leading Happener and Happenings theorist.

1994: Continues to make Happenings, events, and actions. He is the author of nine books and many articles including poetry, art history, sociology, and politics.

George Maciunas. 1965: Designed the cover for the 1965 *TDR* issue as well as the Fluxus fold-out, weighs 148 lbs., is 5' 11⅛" tall. Social security #106-24-6003, driver's license #7996134, bank account #112-008360, blood type 0 …
Maciunas died in 1978.

Jackson Mac Low. 1965: A poet, playwright, and composer whose work has been published/performed in the United States, Japan, Mexico, and several European countries. He will have three books published in 1965–66.
1994: Mac Low is the author of 26 books, writes poems, performance works, essays, plays, and radio works, and is a composer, painter, and multimedia performance artist.

Anthony Martin. 1965: No entry.
1994: In February 1994, Martin had a one-person show of his paintings at the Painting Center, New York.

Robert Morris. 1965: Has had one-man shows of painting and sculpture in San Francisco, New York, and Germany. He began choreographing dances in 1962 and his work has been performed here and in Europe.
1994: Morris was featured in a retrospective exhibit of his sculpture at the Guggenheim Museum in New York.

Claes Oldenberg. 1965: A leading Pop artist who has shown his work throughout the country and, recently, in the Venice Bienalle, Oldenberg has also done many Happenings and Environments.
1994: Now an internationally known visual artist who occasionally does performances.

Benjamin Patterson. 1965: No entry.
1994: Does art works and performances.

Yvonne Rainer. 1965: Studied with Martha Graham, Merce Cunningham, and Ann Halprin. She first performed her own dances at the Living Theatre in New York and has appeared frequently here and in Europe.
1994: A filmmaker and performance theorist, Rainer is finishing her newest film, *Murder and Murder*.

Richard Schechner. 1965: No entry.
1994: Editor of *TDR*; general editor of the Routledge Worlds of Performance series; University Professor and Professor of Performance Studies, Tisch School of the Arts, NYU; artistic director East Coast Artist; and the author of books and articles.

Carolee Schneemann. Not in the 1965 volume, her contribution is from her book, *More Than Meat Joy* (1979).
1994: Among Schneemann's recent installations is *Mortal Coils* at the Penine Hart Gallery in New York. Other installations are upcoming in Paris, Vienna, and Linz. Two books about her writings and work are due out in 1995.

Ramon Sender. 1965: A Composer and Studio Director of the San Francisco Tape Music Center.
1994: The Executive Director of the Peregrine Foundation, an organization which assists families who are exiting from experimental social groups (ex-cult members). Sender is also Chief Editor of Carrier Pigeon Press.

Paul Sills. 1965: Director of the Chicago 43rd Ward Game Theatre and a founder of Second City, Inc.
1994: In his own words, Sills is "more or less retired." He does yearly story theatre shows at the New Actors Workshop in New York and yearly one-week summer workshops on improvisation near his home in Wisconsin. He is also involved in community theatre.

Darko Suvin. Suvin's essay is from *TDR* 14, 3 (T47) 1970. Another article, on the Paris Commune, was published in *TDR* 13, 4 (T44) 1969.
1994: Professor of English, McGill University, where he teaches theory and history of dramaturgy, as well as modern European and Japanese theatre, genre theory, and utopian and science fiction.

Robert Watts. 1965: No entry.
1994: Watts continued multimedia artworks, with numerous solo and group exhibitions in Europe and the United States throughout the 1960s, 1970s and 1980s. Selected exhibitions include: *American supermarket*, Bianchini Gallery, NYC (1964); *Documenta V,* Kassel (1972); *Soho/Berlin*, Academie der Kunst, Berlin (1976); and *Blam*, The Whitney Museum of American Art, NYC (1984).Watts died in 1988.

Robert Whitman. 1965: No entry.
1994: No entry.

Kelly Yeaton. 1965: Is best known as a specialist on arena theatre and author of many articles on that subject. He is Associate Professor of Theatre Arts at Pennsylvania State University.

1994: What was printed in *TDR* was only a "precis" of The Great Gaming House. The whole text appeared in *Co-Evolution Quarterly* 4, 21, December 1974. The event was staged for one night only in San Francisco. Yeaton, now retired, writes that his most recent book, co-authored with his brother Samuel, is *The Story of the Shanghai Fighting Knife*.

La Monte Young. 1965: Is connected with The Theatre of Eternal Music in New York City.

1994: Continues to make music and large-scale performance environments with Marian Zazeela. His magnum opus, *The Well-Tuned Piano* (1964–present), premiered live in Rome in 1974. In 1987 at the MELA Foundation La Monte Young 30-Year Retrospective, he played the work for 6 hours and 24 minutes continuously. In 1990, he formed The Forever Bad Blues Band.

PREFACE

> There is a prevalent mythology about Happenings. It has been said, for example, that they
> are theatrical performances in which there is no script and "things just happen." It has
> been said that there is little or no planning, control, or purpose.
>
> **Michael Kirby**

These myths, Michael Kirby went on to say, "are entirely false." Written
nearly thirty years ago as the introduction to his *Happenings* anthology
(E.P. Dutton, 1965), Kirby's essay set about dispelling the myths and the
"titillating" yet false impressions that most people seem to have
gathered from the popular press. These misconceptions are still with us,
especially among those who were born in the decades since Happenings made the private process of art-making public and performative.

Kirby's clear and carefully crafted essay pulls together the various
historical threads that tangled to form the art world of the late 1950s and
contributed to the moment that produced the first Happenings, including: the Futurist-Dada tradition of nonmatrixed performance; the theatre
of the Bauhaus; the progression from collage to Environment; action
painting; developments in dance, from modern to postmodern; experiments in visual literature and sound poetry; and the influential investi-
gations of John Cage. With his kind permission, I have used Kirby's
historical and theoretical treatise on Happenings to introduce the
material that forms the bulk of this volume: the special *TDR* issue on
Happenings and Fluxus which Kirby co-edited with Richard Schechner in
1965 (T30). As he did for his own *Happenings* anthology, Kirby gathered
together for this *TDR* issue reflective and analytical essays, photos,
drawings, interviews, performance descriptions, and performance texts
which reveal the range of styles and forms that – largely for the sake of
convenience and despite differing labels used by some of the artists
themselves – have been categorized as "Happenings." I am grateful to
Kirby for documenting this work and pleased to have the opportunity to
put it into print again.

Ideally, I would have liked to replicate all the material in the 1965 *TDR*
but, unfortunately, have been unable to reproduce all of the artwork.
Conspicuously absent are the two fold-outs from the original volume.
Thanks to the efforts of Anthony Martin, the *City Scale* performance
"map" has been broken down and printed on consecutive pages. And,
for the sake of making available in this anthology the documentation of
Events depicted in George Maciunas's "FLUXUS" fold-out, the photos
– which Maciunas had cropped for his original design – have been
printed uncropped and separately, each with the text from the fold-out.

While there has been little discussion recently regarding the historical significance of Happenings, there has been a renewed interest in the work of the Fluxus artists. In the U.S. there have been several exhibitions in the past few years, notably "In the Spirit of Fluxus" from the Walker Art Center, as well as several publications, including the book produced in conjunction with the Walker show (Walker Art Center, 1993) and articles in *Performing Arts Journal* and elsewhere. In his 1993 *PAJ* article, Michael Oren claims Fluxartist Harry Flynt attributes this "spasm of interest" to "commercialization spiced with nostalgia." I don't know how profitable it is, but if it is nostalgia that turns our heads back to the revolutions of the 1960s, perhaps rumbling beneath the vacuous sentiment is a healthy need for inspiration – the inspiration to break free of a decade that in many ways rivaled the conservatism of the years preceding the Fluxus and Happenings movements.

In Günter Berghaus's interview with Happenings and Fluxus artist Tomas Schmit (for *TDR*'s Spring 1994 issue), Schmit says he "shudders" when he hears Happenings and Fluxus lumped together, emphasizing the asceticism of Fluxus Events as opposed to the "bombastic and Wagnerian character" of the "material intensive" Happenings. While Fluxus was determinedly undefinable and unaligned with the Happenings movement, Kristine Stiles, in her article on Fluxus performance for the Walker catalog, points out some of the similarities – as well as the differences – between the two. She also notes archivist Barbara Moore's comment that the Fluxus nonmovement was indeed distinctive enough for artists to know if they wanted to "associate with or disassociate from it." Still, Berghaus wonders if perhaps they weren't "two sides of the same coin." Certainly there was a crossover of artists between the two forms, which shared a point in time as well as a revolutionary spirit that questioned the assumptions, boundaries, and definitions of the art that came before. Most significantly, and the reason Happenings and Fluxus Events both found space on the pages of the 1965 *TDR*, they were both performance arts.

In addition to the T30 articles and performance texts is a follow-up letter from Allan Kaprow to the editors of that issue, taking exception to the emphasis given to John Cage and Marshall McLuhan as "germinal influences" on Happenings. A few years later, in an interview published in a 1968 issue of *TDR* on theatrical architecture and environments (T39), Kaprow talks further about McLuhan in relation to Happenings, about the beginnings of his Happenings work, and how the genre had developed. Kaprow's *Self-Service: A Happening*, was printed with the interview, and is described by Kaprow as a "piece without spectators." It took place in three cities over the span of four months and incorporates found environments and Fluxus-like Events.

Adding to the material Kaprow contributed to *TDR*, I have included excerpts from his lengthy essay "Assemblages, Environments & Happenings," which is at the center of his book by the same name (Harry N. Abrams, Inc., 1966). The oversized, burlap-covered edition is an invaluable resource as well as a work of art. It is illustrated with photos of Assemblages, Installations, Environments, and Happenings by such artists as Jean Follett, Clarence Schmidt, Robert Rauschenberg, Jean Tinguely, Red Grooms, the Gutai group, Wolf Vostell, and Claes Oldenburg, in addition to many of Kaprow's works. Beginning with developments in architecture beyond the conventions of the inorganic squared room, and the relation to advances in twentieth-century painting, Kaprow leads us step by step from cave painting to rectangular bounded picture space to Assemblages and Environments. The materials and properties of various forms of Assemblages are detailed, and the "extension" of the Assemblage to an Environment. As Environments began to include perishable components and environmental variables – specifically, the weather and other sounds and effects of nature – the artist was no longer the only one "responsible for a creative action." Again by extension, other people, as expectant "observers, listeners, or intellectual participants," contributed meaning to the artwork. By amplifying this one previously subordinate element – the presence of people – Environments, by extension, became Happenings. The section excerpted here lists Kaprow's "rules-of-thumb" for creating a Happening.

In contrast to the straightforward reportage of most of the early *TDR* material and the practical nature of the Kaprow excerpt, Darko Suvin's "Reflections on Happenings" offers a typological analysis and attempts to define the genre and its aesthetics. Whereas Kaprow insisted that Happenings avoid all performance conventions to break free of comparisons to theatrical forms, Suvin asserts that Happenings should be "discussed within a proper theory of theatre based on a sociology of spectacle forms" and goes on to draw comparisons with the English Masque and finally with the work of Brecht. Suvin, who wrote this essay for a 1970 issue of *TDR* (T47) attributes the demise of Happenings to their "magico-religious stance," which rendered them incapable of outlasting their "sociopolitical moment." In a brief retort published in *TDR* later that year (T49), Lee Baxandall, whose 1966 article on Brecht and Happenings is cited by Suvin, takes issue with Suvin on several points, including his conclusions regarding the fate of the genre. Baxandall locates the "downturn of the Happenings trend in 1967," noting the presence of "at least two major practitioners (Carolee Schneemann and Ken Dewey)" at the Siege of the Pentagon. "I have a hunch," wrote Baxandall, "that the development of political struggle and also the *dramaturgical character* of the struggle have perhaps been chiefly responsible for the eclipse of Happenings."

Günter Berghaus, in an essay on Happenings in Europe written for this anthology, cites this same time frame – the 1967/68 student uprisings – as having "brought about a profound and pervasive politicization of the Happenings genre." But for Berghaus, it was the overtly political nature of European Happenings that from the beginning distinguished them from their U.S. counterparts. One of the artists discussed by Berghaus whose work became more and more politically explicit was Jean-Jacques Lebel.

TDR published two articles by the influential French Happenings artist. The first, which I have included in this anthology, appeared in *TDR* in the Fall of 1968 (T41). Here, Lebel discusses the theoretical underpinnings of his work and addresses the differences between the Happenings of his colleagues in Europe and the work of American artists, specifically Kaprow and Claes Oldenburg. For Lebel, Happenings were the new language of art, a new language engaged in a struggle to "force a complete re-examination of the cultural and historical situation of art." This battle, according to Lebel, was "concentrated around political and sexual themes – taboo above all others." Berghaus writes that Lebel delighted in shocking the bourgeois press by using nudity and radical political slogans, and that his simple and spectacular techniques and ideas were what attracted the attention of a generation of young artists. In his essay, Berghaus follows Lebel's career to the stage Lebel called "Political Street Theatre" in a 1969 *TDR* article.

For his extensive and insightful contribution to this volume, Berghaus has gathered information on numerous key figures in the European Happenings movement and descriptions of some of their most important works. It is the first such overview of the European Happenings movement in English and its comprehensive bibliography will prove invaluable to those wishing to do further research in this area.

Here I'd like to acknowledge what was missing from the early *TDR* material. In much of the literature on Happenings and Fluxus, there is a regrettable underrepresentation of women artists and the back issues of *TDR* are no exception. It is unfortunate that readers of the 1965 issue may have been left with the impression that most of the women participants were those ubiquitous "naked girls." We do briefly hear from Letty Eisenhauer; a few of Alison Knowles' Events are recorded; and Yvonne Rainer interviewed Ann (now Anna) Halprin. The most obvious omission was Carolee Schneemann, who continues to fight for her place in the male-dominated art world. I have filled in this gap with some of Schneemann's theoretical notes and two performance texts, all published in her out-of-print book *More Than Meat Joy* (Documentext,

1979). Her poem from "The Notebooks 1963–1968" is a warning and word of advice to other women struggling to do their own work, art or otherwise. While Schneemann is perhaps best known for her sensual, sexual, visceral performance works, such as *Meat Joy*, she was also at the forefront of the 1967/68 movement that led to the "politicization of the Happenings genre," as Berghaus puts it. *Snows* was, as Schneemann noted in her 1979 preface to the *More Than Meat Joy* edition of the play, "built out of my anger, outrage, fury and sorrow for the Vietnamese." It was first performed as early as January 1967.

As for those ubiquitous "girls" . . . They presented another problem. While preparing this material for publication, I was faced with a dilemma. Upon rereading the 1960s articles, I couldn't get past the gender-exclusive pronouns and nouns and the recurrent descriptions of women performers as "girls," who were usually at some stage of undress. What should I do? Should I rescue them from eternal adolescence? I decided to revise the texts so that readers would not get stuck on the sexist language as I had. But I changed my mind. The issues raised by the sexist language shouldn't be swept under the editorial rug. The second-class status of women was an important aspect of that historical period, both in the art world and in society at large. I think it is critical that we maintain an awareness of the situation as it really was in order to keep what came after in historical perspective. Reacting to their exclusion, objectification, and infantilization, women performance artists subsequently went off on their own to do work that was predominantly solo and autobiographical, work that comprised the bulk of the perform-ance art done during the 1970s – the ten years Moira Roth called the *Amazing Decade* (Astro Artz, 1983). I am grateful to Rebecca Schneider for pointing out that if you neutralize the language in the documentary material, you erase the evidence of what these women were respond-ing to, making artworks such as Schneemann's 1964 *Meat Joy* sound like hysterical ravings rather than genuine outcries of frustration and anger.

Some progress has been made. But don't be fooled. Just because people now are more conscientious about their pronouns doesn't mean the underlying problems have been solved. Women still don't get equal pay – for art work or any other kind. Nor do they get their fair share of attention in the art market. Smoothing over the rough edges in historical documentation further obfuscates the problem and lets the past off the hook as well. My intention is not to point a finger at the artists represented here, but merely to allow the material to speak for itself, for the time in which it was written, and for the art world that fostered the work.

• • •

A few technical matters: "Editor's notes" in the *TDR* reprints are from the first printing, written by the T30 editors; the editor's note for the Kaprow excerpts is mine, as is the one preceding *Snows*. The latter was taken from Schneemann's introductory notes to the 1979 publication. Changes in spelling and punctuation and insertions of first names have been made for the sake of consistency. I have also added some missing performance dates where available and references with as much bibliographical information as possible. Deletions in Michael Kirby's "Introduction" to his *Happenings* book are indicated by ellipses. For the most part deleted material referred to the specific performance texts included in the original E.P. Dutton edition. Mention of these Happenings has been retained where performance descriptions are used as vital examples of points made in the text. While some information is duplicated in Kirby's two introductory essays, significant new issues are raised in each; every effort has been made to maintain the integrity of the essays as originally published. For the T30 material, I have retained the ordering of the original table of contents.

I want to thank my co-workers at *TDR*, past and present, for their hard work and good company. And on behalf of *TDR*, I'd like to express my appreciation to the staff of the Performance Studies Department, to the Dean of the Tisch School of the Arts at NYU, Dr. Mary Schmidt Campbell, and to her predecessor, David Oppenheim, who was very supportive of *TDR* during his years at TSOA.

Special thanks and love to Richard Schechner.

More love to my kids – Annie, Phoebe Rose, and Grace.

And, as always, Danny Sandford, thank you for your patience.

Mariellen R. Sandford

ACKNOWLEDGMENTS

TEXT ACKNOWLEDGMENTS

"Happenings: An Introduction" by Michael Kirby (© 1965, Michael Kirby) was originally published as the "Introduction" to *Happenings* (New York: E.P. Dutton, 1965) and is reprinted with permission of the author.

The following were first published in the *Tulane Drama Review* 10, 2 (T30) 1965, and are reprinted with permission of *TDR*: "The New Theatre" by Michael Kirby; "Allan Kaprow's *Eat*" by Michael Kirby; "An Interview with John Cage" by Michael Kirby and Richard Schechner; "Lecture 1960" by La Monte Young; "*Fotodeath*" by Claes Oldenburg; "*The First and Second Wilderness*" by Michael Kirby; "*The Night Time Sky*" by Robert Whitman; "*Washes*" by Claes Oldenburg; "*Verdurous Sanguinaria*: Act I" by Jackson Mac Low; "*Graphis*" by Dick Higgins and Letty Eisenhauer; "Yvonne Rainer Interviews Ann Halprin"; "Some retrospective notes on a dance for 10 people and 12 mattresses called *Parts of Some Sextets*, performed at the Wadsworth Atheneum, Hartford, Connecticut, and Judson Memorial Church, New York, in March, 1965." by Yvonne Rainer; "Notes on Dance" by Robert Morris; "*City Scale*" by Ken Dewey, Anthony Martin, and Ramon Sender; "Three Pieces" by The ONCE Group; "*Calling*" by Allan Kaprow; "*The Great Gaming House*: A Précis" by Kelly Yeaton; "X-ings" by Ken Dewey; "A Monster Model Fun House" by Paul Sills; "Happenings" by Richard Schechner.

"*The Tart, or Miss America*" by Dick Higgins (© 1964, Richard C. Higgins) was first published in *Jefferson's Birthday* (New York: Something Else Press, 1964) and is reprinted with permission of the author.

"In Response" a letter from Allan Kaprow was first published as a letter to the editor in the *Tulane Drama Review* 10, 4 (T32) 1966, and is reprinted with permission of *TDR*.

"Extensions in Time and Space: An Interview with Allan Kaprow" by Richard Schechner; and "*Self-Service*: A Happening" by Allan Kaprow were first published in *The Drama Review* 12, 3 (T39) 1968, and are reprinted with permission of *TDR*.

The selections from "*More Than Meat Joy*" by Carolee Schneemann (Kingston, NY: Documentext/MacPherson and Company, 1979; © 1979, Carolee Schneemann) are reprinted with permission of the author.

The excerpts from "Assemblages, Environments & Happenings" by Allan Kaprow (© Allan Kaprow, 1966) from the book by the same name (New York: Harry N. Abrams Inc., 1966) are reprinted with permission of the author.

"On the Necessity of Violation" by Jean-Jacques Lebel was first published in *TDR/The Drama Review* 13, 1 (T41) 1968 and is reprinted with permission of *TDR*.

"Reflections on Happenings" by Darko Suvin was first published in *The Drama Review* 14, 3 (T47) 1970, and is reprinted with permission of *TDR*.

PHOTOGRAPH ACKNOWLEDGMENTS

I would like to thank Scott Hyde (p. 2); Robert R. McElroy (p. 83); the Gilbert and Lila Silverman Fluxus Collection Foundation (pp. 83 and 103); Anna Halprin (pp. 124 and 134, 147, 155); Princeton University Libraries (pp. 278, 349); Charlotte Victoria (p. 266); Francois Massal, courtesy of J.J. Lebel (pp. 274, 354, 355); Jacques Prayer, courtesy of J.J. Lebel (p. 281); Dr Thelan (p. 321); and Happening Archiv Vostell, Berlin (pp. 322, 327) for permission to reproduce their photographs.

I am especially grateful to Barbara Moore for her kind assistance and permission to reproduce Peter Moore's photographs in this book. All photographs by Peter Moore © 1994 the estate of Peter Moore.

HAPPENINGS

An Introduction

Michael Kirby

There is a prevalent mythology about Happenings. It has been said, for example, that they are theatrical performances in which there is no script and "things just happen." It has been said that there is little or no planning, control, or purpose. It has been said that there are no rehearsals. Titillating to some, the object of easy scorn to others, provocative and mysterious to a few, these myths are widely known and believed. But they are entirely false.

It is not difficult to see why these spurious concepts developed. Myths naturally arise where facts are scarce. Those people who have actually attended even one performance of a Happening and have what might be considered firsthand information are relatively few. Individual audiences have generally been small – they have rarely exceeded one hundred and are usually close to forty or fifty. Productions have been limited to a few performances, and almost all of the artists would reject the idea of "revivals."

Many spectators attended Happenings merely as entertainment. Without concern for the work as art, they noticed only the superficial qualities. In others, the tendency to view everything in terms of traditional categories, making no allowance for significant change, made evaluation difficult. Thus, even among the limited number of people who have been able to see Happenings, a primary distortion has taken place.

Secondary distortion has occurred in the dissemination of information about Happenings. Once people have heard about Happenings, there is the problem of finding one to see. In this atmosphere where facts are scarce, any information takes on much greater significance. The name itself is striking and provocative: it seems to explain so much to someone who knows nothing about the works themselves. And, intentionally or by accident, there have been incorrect and misleading statements in newspapers and magazines. Writing about the Happenings in Claes Oldenburg's store, for example, the *New York Times* stated that, "Mr. Oldenburg and his actors do not follow a script or rehearse." Such a

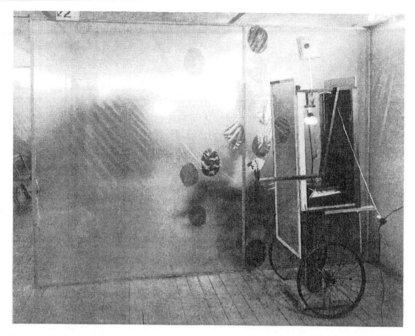

The "sandwich man" from Allan Kaprow's *18 Happenings in 6 Parts* (1959). Despite Kaprow's initial protestations and the objections of other artists, the media picked up on the title as a label for the emerging genre. (Photo by Scott Hyde.)

statement naturally has a much wider audience than the works themselves. When a motionless nude appeared on a balcony behind the audience in a Happening at the Edinburgh Drama Festival, all other details of the work were lost in a welter of news items that mentioned only the girl. Although the peculiar, bizarre, and titillating may be more worthy of space in the mass media by their own standards than are serious creative works whose originality makes them difficult or even obscure for many people, this commercial emphasis functions as an instrument of distortion.

But if Happenings are not improvisations by a group of people deciding to exhibit themselves at a party; if they are not sophisticated buffoonery designed to give a deceitful impression of profundity nor uncontrolled orgies of audience participation, what are they?

Not all were called Happenings by their creators. The poster for Red Grooms' *The Burning Building* (1959) called it "a play"; Robert Whitman refers to his works as "theatre pieces," and Oldenburg uses Ray Gun Theater. Even Allan Kaprow's earliest public work, from which the name originated, was not called *a* Happening but *18 Happenings in 6 Parts* (1959). Each has attempted to defend the unique and personal qualities of his work from the destructive, leveling influences of superficial categorization and misleading comparisons, but the word

"Happening" has been used long enough by a sufficient number of knowledgeable people to give it a certain validity.

[...] The germinal development of the Happening was in New York, and, although they have since been presented in other parts of the country and in Europe, this formative propinquity is another reason to treat these works as a formal entity.

Happenings did not develop out of clear-cut, intellectual theory about theatre and what it should or should not be. No commonly held definition of a Happening existed before the creation of these particular works. If a definition is to be arrived at now, it must be inclusive enough to take in all of these works and rigorous enough to exclude works that, although they might have a certain resemblance, are not commonly referred to as Happenings.

Although some of their advocates claim they are not, Happenings, like musicals and plays, are a form of theatre. Happenings are a new form of theatre, just as collage is a new form of visual art, and they can be created in various styles just as collages (and plays) are.

On the surface, the Happenings had certain similarities of stylistic detail in production. As can be seen from the photographs, Happenings have had in common a physical crudeness and roughness that frequently trod an uncomfortable borderline between the genuinely primitive and the merely amateurish. This was partly intentional, due to their relationship with action painting and so-called junk sculpture, and partly the inevitable result of extremely limited finances. All of the Happenings – except, of course, the later ones presented outdoors – were put on in lofts and stores, in limited spaces for limited audiences. But such similarities are not important: they do not define the essence of the work. If more money, larger spaces, or more elaborate equipment had been available, the productions would have been changed somewhat, but the defining characteristics are to be found beneath these superficialities.

[...] The fact that the first Happening in New York and many succeeding ones were presented in the Reuben Gallery – sometimes on the same three- or four-week rotation schedule that is common with art galleries – serves to emphasize the fundamental connection of Happenings with painting and sculpture. Could Happenings be called a *visual* form of theatre?

Certainly they are not *exclusively* visual. Happenings contain auditory material and some have even used odor. To say that they are *primarily* visual, which is true, loses its importance when it is realized that sight has dominated much of traditional theatre. Pantomime and dance are obvious examples, but many individual directors of verbal drama have stressed, like Gordon Craig, "the priority of the eye." Nor, like the Munich Artists' Theatre of 1908 that learned from painters and sculptors how to turn a play into something resembling a bas-relief that moved, can Happenings be called "pictorial." They have rejected the proscenium stage and the conceit that everyone in the auditorium sees the same "picture." In many Happenings there is a great difference, in both amount and quality, in *what* is seen by different spectators.

But Happenings do have a nonverbal character. While words are used, they are not used in the traditional way and are seldom of primary importance. [...] In *18 Happenings in 6 Parts* and *The Burning Building* stream-of-consciousness monologs in the more-or-less traditional sense are used. Although they are repetitious and discursive, these verbal structures make use of associations and accumulative meaning in addition to affective tone. But some of the monologs in *18 Happenings in 6 Parts* are merely random lists of words and phrases, sometimes chosen and arranged completely by chance methods, and an abstract "conversation" occurred in *The Burning Building* when two performers alternately uttered staccato words and phrases. Here the word "structure" has completely abandoned the power of syntax. It is separated from the usual progressive associations and accumulative meaning and functions as a vocal entity in which pure sound values tend to predominate.

Sound values do predominate in preverbal material [...]. Used quite frequently, it can most significantly be understood as verbal *effect*. Thus it obviously cannot be said that Happenings do not make any use of language. Although noise and music predominate, they are far from being pantomime. But Happenings are essentially nonverbal, especially when compared to traditional theatre whose substance is vocal exchange between characters.

Of even greater importance is the fact that Happenings have abandoned the plot or story structure that is the foundation of our traditional theatre. Gone are the clichés of exposition, development, climax, and conclusion, of love and ambition, the conflicts of personality, the revelatory monolog of character. Gone are all elements needed for the presentation of a cause-and-effect plot or even the simple sequence of events that would tell a story. In their place, Happenings employ a structure that could be called insular or *compartmented*.

Traditional theatre makes use of an *information structure*. There we need information in order to understand the situation, to know who the people are, to know what is happening, or what might happen; we need information to "follow" the play, to apprehend it at all. Much of this information is visual, conveyed by the set, the lights, the expressions and movements of the actors, and much of it is contained in spoken words. This information is essentially cumulative. Although "exposition" conventionally is placed early in the play, additional information is provided by each element. But information structure also functions reflexively, explaining and clarifying material that has already been presented.

Compartmented structure is based on the arrangement and contiguity of theatrical units that are completely self-contained and hermetic. No information is passed from one discrete theatrical unit – or "compartment" – to another. The compartments may be arranged sequentially [...] or simultaneously [...]. *18 Happenings in 6 Parts* is a clear example of both simultaneous and sequential compartmentalization: the physical structure of the three separate rooms emphasizing the isolation of units functioning at the same moment, and the six separate "parts" underline the disjunction in continuity.

This does not mean that Happenings have no structure. A three-ring circus, using both simultaneous and sequential "compartmentalization," exists as an experiential entity with its own character and overall quality. A well-arranged variety show has a unity of style and a cohesiveness that makes it *a* show. But beyond this it has been demonstrated in other fields of art that a work does not require information structure. Although each of the photographs and objects in a Robert Rauschenberg "combine," for example, conveys information, they do not relate to each other in any logical way: they exist in simultaneous compartments. Ignoring "program music" and intellectual "explanations," a unity exists in the separate movements of a symphony even though the formal differences between them may be large. [...]

It should be noted that the terms "scene," or even "hermetic scene," and "compartment" are not the same. "Scene" has primary reference to people and to place. A scene is "played" between actors and by an actor. A "French scene" begins and ends with the entrance or exit of a major character. But many units in Happenings contain only sounds or physical elements, and not performers. Frequently, although performers are in physical proximity, there is no interplay between them, and an imaginary place [...] is seldom established.

It is when we look within the compartments in this manner and study the various theatrical elements – principally the behavior of the performers themselves – that another essential characteristic of Happenings becomes clear. In traditional theatre, the performer always functions within (and creates) a matrix of time, place, and character. Indeed, a brief definition of acting as we have traditionally known it might be the creation of, and operation within, this artificial, imaginary, interlocking structure. When an actor steps onstage, he brings with him an intentionally created and consciously possessed world, or matrix, and it is precisely the disparities between this manufactured reality and the spectators' reality that make the play potentially significant to the audience. This is not a question of style. Time-place-character matrices exist equally in Shakespeare, Molière, and Chekhov. Nor is it equivalent to the classic "suspension of disbelief," although the matrix becomes obvious when pressure is applied to it. (This pressure can be intentional, as in *Six Characters in Search of an Author*, where we seem to be asked to *believe* that these new people onstage are not actors inside of characters but characters without actors; or unintentional, as when Bert Lahr loses his place in the confusingly similar lines of *Waiting for Godot* and, starkly out of character, confides to the audience, "I said that before.") Presentational acting and devices designed to establish the reality of the stage-as-a-stage and the play-as-a-play do not eliminate matrix. Nor do certain characters who function in the same time and place as the audience rather than that of the other roles: the Stage Manager in *Our Town*, Tom in *The Glass Menagerie*, Quentin in *After the Fall*. Even in musical comedies, which interrupt the story line with little logical justification for a song or dance in which the personality of the performer himself predominates, the relationship of mood and atmosphere to situation and plot is retained, and the emotions and ideas expressed are obviously not those of the singer or dancer himself.

Time-place matrices are frequently external to the performer. They are given tangible representation by the sets and lighting. They are described to the audience in words. Character matrices can also be external. For example, the stagehands rearranging the set of *Six Characters in Search of an Author* may be dressed like real stagehands and function like real stagehands (they may even *be* real stagehands), and yet, because of the nature of the play that provides their context, they are seen as "characters." As part of the place-time continuum of the play, which happens to include a stage and the actual time, they "play roles" without needing to "act." They cannot escape the matrix provided by the work. Even when one of the actors in *The Connection* approaches you during the intermission to ask for a handout (as he has promised to do from the stage during the first act), he is still matrixed by character. He is no longer in the physical setting of the play, and he is wearing ordinary clothes that seem disreputable but not unreal in the lobby, but neither these facts nor any amount of improvised conversation will remove him from the character-matrix that has been produced.

Since time and place may be ambiguous or eliminated completely without eliminating character (i.e., time and place both as external, physical, "environmental" factors and as elements that may be subjectively acted by a performer), role-playing becomes primary in determining matrix. By returning from the lobby too soon or sitting through the intermission of a production performed on a platform stage with no curtain to conceal the set changes, one can see the stagehands rearranging props and furniture. Although some productions might rehearse mimes or costumed bit players for these changes, most would just expect you to realize that this was not part of the play. The matrices are neither acted nor imposed by the context: the stagehands are "nonmatrixed." This is exactly what much of the "acting" in Happenings is like. It is *nonmatrixed* performing.

A great variety of nonmatrixed performances take place outside of theatre. In the classroom, at sporting events, at any number of private gatherings and public presentations there is a "performer-audience" relationship. The public speaker can function in front of an audience without creating and projecting an artificial context of personality. The athlete is functioning as himself in the same time-place as the spectators. Obviously, meaning and significance are not absent from these situations, and even symbolism can exist without a matrix – as exemplified in religious or traditional ritual or a "ceremony" such as a bullfight. In circuses and rodeos, however, the picture becomes more complex. Here clowns who are strongly matrixed by character and situation function alternately with the nonmatrixed performances of the acrobat and the broncobuster. The distinction between matrixed and nonmatrixed behavior becomes blurred in nightclubs, among other places. The stand-up comedian, for example, may briefly assume a character for a short monolog and at other times present his real offstage personality. From the clearly nonmatrixed public speaker to the absolutely matrixed performer delivering a "routine," there is a complete continuum. Yet the concept of the nonmatrixed performer is still valid, as in the case of the football player making a tackle, the train conductor calling out stops, even the construction worker with his audience of sidewalk supervisors. A difference of opinion has traditionally existed between the "monists" such as Stanislavsky, who felt that the performer should be unseen within his character, and "dualists" such as Vakhtanghov and Brecht, who felt that the performer should be perceived simultaneously with the character so that the one could comment on the other. Now a new category exists in drama, making no use of time, place, or character and no use of the performer's comments.

Let us compare a performer sweeping in a Happening and a performer sweeping in traditional theatre. The performer in the Happening merely carries out a task. The actor in the traditional play or musical might add character detail: lethargy, vigor, precision, carelessness. He might act "place": a freezing garret, the deck of a rolling ship, a windy patio. He might convey aspects of the imaginary time situation: how long the character has been sweeping, whether it is early or late. (Even if the traditional performer had only a bit part and was not required to be concerned with these things, he would be externally matrixed by the set and lights and by the information structure.)

If a nonmatrixed performer in a Happening does not have to function in an imaginary time and place created primarily in his own mind, if he does not have to respond to often-imaginary stimuli in terms of an alien and artificial personality, if he is not expected either to project the subrational and unconscious elements in the character he is playing or to inflect and color the ideas implicit in his words and actions, what is required of him? Only the execution of a generally simple and undemanding act. He walks with boxes on his feet, rides a bicycle, empties a suspended bucket of milk on his head. If the action is to sweep, it does not matter whether the performer begins over there and sweeps around here or begins here and works over there. Variations and differences simply do not matter – within, of course, the limits of the particular action and omitting additional action. The choices are up to him, but he does not work to create anything. The creation was done by the artist when he formulated the idea of the action. The performer merely embodies and makes concrete the idea.

Nonmatrixed performing does not eliminate the factor of ability, however. [...] Nor is all performing in Happenings nonmatrixed. Character and interpretation have sometimes been important and traditional acting ability has been required. This was especially true in Oldenburg's productions at his store when he employed a "stock company" of himself, his wife Pat, and Lucas Samaras in every performance. On the other hand, Whitman, in an attempt to prevent "interpretation," prefers not to explain "meanings" to his performers.

Although entrances and exits may occasionally be closely cued, the performer's activities are very seldom controlled as precisely as they are in the traditional theatre, and he generally has a comparatively high degree of freedom. It is this freedom that has given Happenings the reputation of being improvised. "Improvised" means "composed or performed on the spur of the moment without preparation," and it should be obvious that this definition would not fit the Happening as an artistic whole. Its composition and performance are always prepared. The few Happenings that had no rehearsal were intentionally composed of such simple elements that individual performers would have no difficulty in carrying them out, and in many of the works the creators themselves took the major roles.

Nor would it be accurate or precise to say that even the small units or details of Happenings are improvised. For one thing, the word already has specific references – primarily to the commedia dell'arte, various actor-training techniques connected with the Stanislavsky method, and certain "improvisational theatres" (such as Second City and The Premise) – which have no significant relationship to the freedom of the performer in Happenings. All of these uses of improvisation are concerned with accurate and successful functioning within the traditional matrices. In both commedia dell'arte and improvisational theatre, character, time, and place are given: details within, and in terms of, the matrix are invented. Although Stanislavsky's techniques are diverse enough to find use in ordinary nonmatrixed behavior, the actual application in countless acting classes and study groups is on the specific control of various aspects of personality and of imaginary time-place orientation. Secondly, in improvisational theatre and in jazz improvisation, one performer reacts to and adjusts his own work to that of another. There is a constant qualitative crisis of choice. But in Happenings, there is no momentary challenge. One performer reacts only functionally, and not aesthetically or creatively, to the actions of another. If involved in a movement pattern, for example, he may get out of another's way or fall down if bumped by him, but he does not consciously adjust the qualities of his movement in order to fuse it visually with that of the other performers. The action in Happenings is often *indeterminate* but not improvised.

Even the most rigid acting technique will show variation from performance to performance if measured carefully, but these small differences are overlooked as presenting no artistic problem. Because of indeterminacy, the differences in detail are greater between two successive performances of a Happening than between two successive performances of a traditional play, but, again, these variations are not significant. (This does not mean that one performance of a Happening cannot be much better than another, but, just as in traditional theatre, this entails discussion of essential performance qualities rather than technique and method.)

Thus in many Happenings the "acting" tends to exist on the same level as the physical aspects of the production. While allowing for his unique qualities, the performer frequently is treated in the same fashion as a prop or a stage effect. When there is no need for continuity of character or statement of personality, the same performer will appear many times, carrying out a variety of tasks. As the individual creativity and technical subtlety of the human operation decreases, the importance of the inanimate "actor" increases. Occasional compartments in Happenings contain nothing but performers; more frequently they work with props, and the balance between the human and the mechanical varies with each work and each artist. But there are numerous examples of entire compartments dominated by physical effects [...]. Performers become things and things become performers. The frequently used shadow sequence perfectly symbolizes this blending of person into thing, this animation and vitalization of the object. From this point of view, Happenings might simply be called a "theatre of effect."

Functioning in terms of an information structure, the elements in traditional theatre are used in either logical or, as in the Theatre of the Absurd, illogical ways. It can be seen that the elements of a Happening have an *alogical* function. This does not mean that either structure or detail does not have an intellectual clarity to the artist, but rather that any private idea structure used in creation is not transformed into a public information structure.

Abstract significance would be one possible alternative for alogical theatre. Particular colors, shapes, and movements might be used in a pure manner with no relevance beyond their own special qualities and physical characteristics. Although sensory qualities are always funda-mental to Happenings, there is rarely any tendency toward idealization or pure abstraction. Green is not just an optical sensation, or a circle a form without any implications or associations. The materials of Happen-ings – performer, physical element, or mechanical effect – tend to be *concrete*. That is, they are taken from and related to the experiential world of everyday life. Within the overall context and structure, the details in Happenings relate to things (or classes of things: note the already conventional one-word titles) and function as direct experience.

This does not mean that the concrete details may not also function as symbols. They often do. But the symbols are of a private, nonrational, polyvalent character rather than intellectual. [. . . They] do not have any one rational public meaning as symbols. Although they may, like everything else, be interpreted, they are intended to stir the observer on an unconscious, alogical level. These unconscious symbols compare with rational symbols only in their aura of "importance": we are aware of a significance and a "meaning," but our minds cannot discover it through the usual channels. Logical associations and unambiguous details that would help to establish a rational context are not available. There is no relevant framework of reason to which impressions may be referred.

There are two contemporary forms of theatre that might become confused with Happenings and must be considered before arriving at a definition. Chance theatre is any theatre work whose elements are derived or assembled by chance methods. For example, in *Motor Vehicle Sundown (Event)* (1960) by George Brecht an unspecified number of performers each uses, but does not drive, a motor vehicle; the perform-ance directions ("Sound horn," "Strike a window with knuckles," "Pause," etc.), written on cards, are shuffled and distributed equally to each performer. Although chance structure may exist within the compart-ments of a Happening, the relationship of the compartments is intentional rather than fortuitous.

Events are short, uncomplicated theatre pieces with the same alogical qualities as details of Happenings. For example, Brecht places three glasses on the floor of the "playing area" and then fills them with water from a pitcher: it is his *Three Aqueous Events*. An Event is not compartmented. Formally, if not expressively, it is equivalent to a single compartment of a Happening.

Based upon the general characteristics and the specific terms that have been mentioned above, a definition can now be formulated. Happenings might be described as a *purposefully composed form of theatre in which diverse alogical elements, including nonmatrixed performing, are organized in a compartmented structure.*

This definition successfully differentiates Happenings from all other forms of theatre, but, unfortunately, it eliminates one of the works used as examples. *The Burning Building* does not fulfil the requirements of nonmatrixed performing or compartmented structure. Although the alternation of quasi-realistic movement and dance gives the superficial impression of compartmentalization, any hermetic tendency is destroyed by the fact that the same characters exist in contiguous units. Character and place are important: the "dance" of the firemen, for example, establishes their characters which in turn will heighten the sense of danger and suspense during "The Pasty Man's" search and flight. In order to be absolutely correct, it would be best to consider *The Burning Building*, as Grooms himself did, a play. [. . .]

Every work of art is formed in a historical context of attitudes and influences that make the work possible. No new art form springs fully grown into existence. By investigating the historical sources of Happenings it may be possible to fit Happenings into proper perspective in terms of artistic and cultural development and to clarify further the nature of Happenings themselves.

Writing in 1961, soon after the presentation of the first Happening in New York, William Seitz stated that, "Although the connection is far too dispersive to make precise, the productions known as 'happenings' . . . had their origin in painting and collage" and placed the works within a detailed and authoritative analysis of "juxtaposition" in the arts (1961: 91). The following year Harriet Janis and Rudi Blesh also traced a historical progression from painting to Happenings (1962).

Although the latter treatment of Happenings is frequently inaccurate and generally superficial, the development documented by these writers has a certain significance.

In 1911 Boccioni used part of a wooden window frame in a piece of Futurist sculpture, and ever since 1911 or 1912 when Braque or Picasso, depending on which authority you follow, glued the first piece of real material to the canvas and originated collage, actual elements have been incorporated into painting.

The picture – transformed into "combines," assemblages or constructions which hang on the wall – moved out into the real space of the room.

As an Environment the painting took over the room itself, and finally, as sort of an Environment-with-action, became a Happening. The simplicity of this theory is one of its strong points, and, if it does not completely explain Happenings, at least it does relate them intellectually to some of their most important precedents.

Kurt Schwitters, the greater master of collage, almost completed the whole cycle in his own work. In about 1924, he transformed his house in Hanover, Germany, into a *Merzbau* – into an Environment or series of Environments. Called *Column* or *Cathedral of Erotic Misery*, its walls and ceilings were covered solidly with angled and protruding abstract shapes. There were recessed lights, secret sliding panels, and, in one of the cave rooms, the "blood"-splattered figure of a nude female mannequin. The house was destroyed by bombs in 1943, and the partly completed *Merzbarn* in Ambleside, England, is the only existing example of Schwitters' work on Environments, but he did not stop there.

Schwitters himself was a writer and a performer. He had read his own poetry with great success (one "poem" was only the letter *W* shown to the audience on a large card and recited with continuously varied vocal dynamics). It seems natural that he thought of theatre. *Merz*, a word derived from a fragment of the word *Kommerz* which Schwitters had used in a collage, was applied by its originator to all his art, and he wrote in 1921 of the "Merz composite work of art" or the Merz theatre:

> In contrast to the drama or the opera, all parts of the Merz stagework are inseparably bound up together; it cannot be written, read or listened to, it can only be produced in the theatre. Up until now, a distinction was made between stage-set, text, and score in theatrical performances. Each factor was separately enjoyed. The Merz stage knows only the fusing of all factors into a composite work. Materials for the stage-set are all solid, liquid and gaseous bodies, such as white wall, man, barbed wire entanglement, blue distance [...]. The stage-set can be conceived in approximately the same terms as a Merz picture. [...]
>
> [...] Take the dentist's drill, a meat grinder, a car-truck scraper, take buses and pleasure cars, bicycles, tandems and their tires, also wartime ersatz tires and deform them. Take lights and deform them as brutally as you can. Make locomotives crash into one another, curtains and portieres make threads of spider webs dance with window frames and break whimpering glass. Explode steam boilers to make railroad mist. Take petticoats and other kindred articles, shoes and false hair, also ice skates and throw them into place where they belong, and always at the right time. For all I care, take man-traps, automatic pistols, infernal machines, the tinfish and the funnel, all of course in an artistically deformed condition. Inner tubes are highly recommended. Take in short everything from the

hairnet of the high class lady to the propeller of the S.S. Leviathan, always
bearing in mind the dimensions required by the work.

Even people can be used.

People can even be tied to backdrops.

People can even appear actively, even in their everyday position.

(in Motherwell 1951: 62–3)

Schwitters might have been describing certain aspects of Happenings,
and, although he never actually produced an example of Merz theatre, he
apparently documents the progression from painting to collage to
Environment to Happening. Since he was primarily an artist and only
secondarily a poet, this would also support the relationship between
Happenings and their artist-creators on the most obvious level. It is not
that simple, however.

In the first place, it is based on a misunderstanding of the actual
development of Happenings and of their environmental aspect. In the
second place, there is a historical progression to Happenings that is
basically unrelated to painting, collage, or assemblage. And in the third
place, the diversity of the "composite work of art," which Happenings as
well as almost all theatre represent, is, by its nature, susceptible to a
much wider range of influences than the collage theory allows, and the
only complete explanation of Happenings lies in a total picture of all
developmental factors.

Any collage theory of the development of Happenings must include a
clear definition of an Environment. As applied to nontheatrical art, an
Environment is usually considered to be a work of art or creation that
surrounds or encloses the viewer on all sides. Thus a "found environment" [...] cannot be considered artistically equivalent to the Environment that apparently developed out of collage. The "found environment"
has its own history and has even been used in traditional theatre.
Eisenstein, for example, produced *Gas Masks* (1923/24), a play about a
gas factory, in an actual gas factory. If the definition of Environment is
strictly applied to Happenings, it can be seen that many Happenings do
not make use of an Environment.

Nor are the spectators *within* an environment in all cases. Although
Oldenburg's first presentation, *Snapshots from the City* (1960), was
performed in a work of art that had its own independent life as an
Environment, the spectators watched it from a doorway. This is not
significantly different from the viewing experience of a realistic play
with an "environmental" set enclosing it on three sides. The Happenings
in Oldenburg's store did not make use of expressive elements that
surrounded the audience. [...]

Actually the environmental factor is one aspect of an attempt in almost all Happenings to alter the audience-presentation relationship, as we have generally known it, and to use this relationship artistically. This manipulation of the physical relationship between the spectator and the theatre elements that he perceives is broader than, and includes, environmental considerations. [. . .]

Whether or not the works include environmental factors, the intimacy of the audience-presentation relationship has been exploited to increase the immediacy of the theatrical material. The painters in *18 Happenings in 6 Parts* could have walked in from the control room rather than getting up from their places among the audience; the final chase in *The Burning Building* could have occurred behind the proscenium rather than almost in the laps of the spectators. These fairly conventional attempts to "get through" to the audience by "breaking the fourth wall" are certainly not from the collage tradition, and later Happenings developed more inventive and insistent methods of forcing themselves into the awareness of the spectator in ways that could not be avoided or dismissed. [. . .]

The tendency to change the audience-presentation relationship by entirely re-creating the overall physical context of the performance is most apparent in Kaprow's *A Spring Happening* (1961) in which the manner of perception is controlled. At first glance the unique transformation of the viewing experience might not seem incompatible with traditional theatre. Spectators inside a tunnel similar to that of *A Spring Happening*, for example, might look out the slots to watch a play by Shakespeare or Genet. Although this might not hurt the play – theatregoers have been forced to use awkward viewing positions and angles before – it certainly would not add anything significant. But once a presentation becomes concrete, the direction of the presented elements and its distance become integral expressive elements in their own right. The content of *A Spring Happening* lies in the comparisons and contrasts that are made between right and left, loud and soft, immediate and remote. Without this particular and exact physical arrangement, the work could not exist. It would be utterly impossible to transfer it to any other physical setup. The viewing situation has become an organic part of the work itself. [. . .]

Environmental factors and other attempts to expressively alter the audience-presentation relationship are so common in Happenings that they might easily be mistaken for part of the form itself. Each of the examples included here manipulates the relationship in one way or another. But Happenings presented on a stage with the traditional audience-presentation relationship (and with no environmental aspects) are still Happenings. It must be concluded that spatial arrangement and control and active contact with the spectators are matters of style rather than form.

The collage theory parallels, but does not explain, the psychological reasons why New York artists began working in theatre.

Although Kaprow himself progressed from painting and sculpture to assemblages, to Environment, and, finally, to Happenings, the aesthetic possibility for Happenings had existed at least since Schwitters' time. Additional factors outside of the collage-Environment aesthetic apparently were necessary.

In the late 1940s and early 1950s in New York, certain artists began to shift the emphasis in painting upon the act itself. Influenced by Surrealist theories and experiments in automatic creation, Jackson Pollock produced his famous "drip" paintings. The unpremeditated slashing brushstrokes of Willem de Kooning became the ideal of many younger artists. The painter's hand was directed by intuition and emotion, and the "happy accident" was treasured. Swirls and spatters of paint were dynamic traces of the significant gesture. Paintings became records of movement rather than merely visual compositions. "Action painting" was born. Although critical judgment operated after the fact, it could not make a painting, and the crucial moments were those when the painter was "acting" in front of the canvas.

With the success of action painting (better known as Abstract Expressionism), New York artists received attention that they did not expect and that they were not experienced at handling. America finally had an art it could brag a little about, and the artists became internationally known. Not only did their work bring increasingly higher prices, but the mass media devoted more and more time and space to art and to the men who made it. The traditional "opening" of an exhibition changed from a gathering of artists and friends into a cosmopolitan party. Within little more than a decade the artist was thrown from the relative anonymity of WPA arts projects into the celebrity spotlight. All of these internal and external factors focused attention on the artists themselves and helped to create a performance mentality.

In March of 1959 *Art News* quoted "Woks," an ex-Russian abstract painter, as saying:

> I believe that we are living a critical moment in the history of painting. Since Cézanne, it has become evident that, for the painter, what counts is no longer the painting but the process of creation. Tachism, or whatever you call it, has drawn the lesson. Whether you regard painting as a means of penetrating the self or the world, it is creation. When Pollock painted, his situation, his inner behavior as an artist, were certainly more complex than the painting, for he was living the process. Why should this creation be pinned down, shut up in a rectangle, hung on the wall? I believe that when an "automatist" paints, there are actually two painters in him: the

one who wants to act, the other who wants to create an object. That is why the most precious goal of painting cannot be attained completely. Henceforth, the essential aim of painting must be the process of creation; the viewer must no longer be made to look at the painting alone, but the very process of making it.

(Woks 1959: 62)

He went on to describe one way of achieving this goal – a hall in which spectators would watch two painters working simultaneously on opposite sides of a screen lit by spotlights. Each painter "imagines that everything is going on on his side of the screen." (Except for the limited number and type of brushstrokes in the Happening, this is almost exactly the procedure followed in *18 Happenings in 6 Parts*.)

Georges Mathieu, the French action painter, dramatized the painting of a picture until the creation reached theatrical proportions. When he re-enacted the thirteenth-century Battle of Bouvines on canvas, he wore a costume made up of black trousers, a black silk jacket, white cross-leggings, and a white helmet that tied under his chin. Friends represented the opposing Counts of Flanders and Toulouse. The creation of the painting, which was based upon detailed historical research and executed during the same hours of the day that the battle itself was fought, was filmed. When Mathieu was invited to Japan, he appeared on television, rushing furiously up various ladders in costume to paint a huge mural. He was a tremendous popular success.

When Jim Dine exhibited constructions at the Reuben Gallery, he attended his opening in costume. Red Grooms' first theatrical work was to paint a painting in front of an audience at the Sun Gallery in Provincetown in 1958. Announced as "a play" called *Fire*, the action lasted about twenty-five minutes. The finished work, in free brush-strokes, included the helmeted heads of several firemen.

The Gutai is a group of Japanese artists in Osaka under the leadership of Jiro Yoshihara. Influenced by painters such as Mathieu and well aware of contemporary directions in Western art, they expanded the means used in the action of painting. One artist tied a paintbrush to a toy tank and exhibited the marks it left on the canvas; others painted with their feet, with boxing gloves made of rags and dipped in paint, or by throwing bottles filled with paint at a canvas with rocks under it.

In 1957 the Gutai presented more formal theatre works for an audience. A large plastic bag filled with red smoke was pushed through a hole at the back of the stage and inflated. Smoke puffed out through holes in the side. Another presentation employed a large box with three transparent plastic walls and one opaque white wall. Performers inside the box dipped balls of paper into buckets of paint and threw them against the white wall, coloring the surface. Then colored water was thrown against the plastic walls that separated the spectators from the performers. (The activities of the Gutai were described in an article on the front page of the art section of the *New York Times* on Sunday, 8 December 1957, and might, therefore, have had some influence on the origins of Happenings.)

Thus it would seem that performances by artists are more closely related to the tradition of action painting than to collage-Environment. Secondly, all of the defining characteristics (and many of the stylistic ones) were in existence by 1924 when Schwitters and the collage progression produced an Environment.

It is in Dada that we find the origin of the nonmatrixed performing and compartmented structure that are so basic to Happenings. Dada was officially born with the 1916 performances at the Cabaret Voltaire in Zurich. In a small room that could seat thirty-five to fifty guests at fifteen or twenty tables, there were lectures, concerts, readings, sound poems, and dances in bizarre costumes. Diverse activities were presented at the same time, and simultaneous poems were common. (Simultaneity, a concept that went back to the Futurist F.T. Marinetti was part of Dada theory.) Everyday life was brought onto the stage. Announcing the title of a poem, Tristan Tzara read an article from the newspaper. Although many of the performers were artists, the actual confrontation of the public was the vital focus of Dada at that time, and, in addition to the café, theatre stages in Zurich were utilized.

Under the pressure of absolute theories that applied to life rather than to a specific art, the distinction between performing and not performing began to break down for the Dadaists. Schwitters not only read his poetry to audiences, but visitors to his home in Hanover found him seated in a tree in his front yard speaking a "bird language" of pure sounds that he and Raoul Hausmann had invented.

The "found environment" was used in many Dada activities. In April 1920, an exhibition of works by Jean Arp, Johannes T. Baargeld, and Max Ernst was held in a small court behind a café in Cologne. It could be reached only through the public urinal. At the opening a young girl in a communion dress recited obscene poetry. (Ernst exploited spectator-presentation relationship by exhibiting a wooden object to which a hatchet was chained.)

The inclination toward the "found environment" was given impetus in April 1921, when André Breton suggested that the Dadaists meet the public in the streets rather than in the theatres and exhibition halls, and a series of "excursions and visits" was planned. Breton and Tzara lectured in the garden of the church of St. Julien-le-Pauvre, and Georges Ribemont-Dessaignes conducted a tour, now and then reading random definitions from a dictionary, but the succeeding visits and walks – to the Louvre, the Saint-Lazare station, and the Canal de l'Ourcq, among other places – were abandoned.

In May 1921, the Dadaists turned an exhibition of collages by Max Ernst at the Galerie Au Sans Pareil into a theatrical performance. Wearing white gloves but without ties, they walked among the visitors. Benjamin Péret and Serge Charchoune shook hands repeatedly. Louis Aragon miaowed. Breton chewed matches. Philippe Soupault and Tzara played hide-and-seek. A voice from the closet called out insults. Over and over, Ribemont-Dessaignes yelled, "It's raining on a skull!" while Jacques Rigaut stood at the door, loudly counting the arriving cars and the pearls of the ladies who entered the exhibition. Simultaneous presentation of nonmatrixed performances was typical of the Dadaists, but in this case they not only altered the usual spectator-presentation relationship by mixing with the guests but made use of a space not intended for theatre.

Relâche by Francis Picabia with a score by Erik Satie, performed at the Théâtre de Champs-Élysées in 1924, was apparently nothing more than a ballet with Dada additions. Spotlights were beamed directly into the eyes of the spectators, making it difficult to see what was taking place on the stage. Upstage, the dancers went through their movements. A naked man and woman, standing motionless in the poses of Cranach's *Adam and Eve*, were intermittently illuminated, while downstage, a man dressed as a fireman constantly poured water from one bucket to another. Man Ray, also unrelated to the dancers or the other performers, was sitting on a chair near the edge of the stage, and occasionally he would stand and walk back and forth. Not only were indeterminacy, non-matrixed performing, and simultaneously compartmented structure used in a theatrical presentation, but the motion picture *Entr'acte*, shown between the two parts of the program, increased the traditional range of functional elements.

Unique and expressive physical relationship between the spectators and the presentation was not attempted by *Relâche*, but the composer, Erik Satie, who had also composed the partially *bruitist* score for *Parade*, had already made a striking investigation of that area in his own work. In 1920 a play by Max Jacob, a concert of music by les Six, and songs by Stravinsky were presented at the Barbazange gallery in Paris. An exhibition of children's paintings was held at the same time. During the intermission of the play, a trombone in the balcony and a piano and three clarinets, one in each corner of the room, played a piece by Satie. This was the introduction of *musique d'ameublement* or "furnishing music," but the important point regarding the development of Happenings was the purposeful investigation of audience-performance relationship by a man who was later to be held in high regard by John Cage.

John Cage, the composer, integrated various dominant strains in the Futurist–Dada tradition into his own work. Speaking along with tape recordings of his own voice, Cage was able to give "simultaneous lectures" reminiscent of the activities in the Cabaret Voltaire. He proposed the "simultaneous presentation of unrelated events" – a theoretical position clearly derived from Dada activities. And in a single presentation at Black Mountain College in the summer of 1952 (the authoritative anthology on Dada which included, among other things, Kurt Schwitters' description of Merz theatre had been published the preceding year), he was able to combine a variety of expressive elements including indeterminate nonmatrixed performing in a compartmented structure that made use of an expressive spectator-performance relationship.

The chairs, all facing the center, were arranged in the middle of the dining hall, leaving open space between the audience and the walls of the room. Timed to the second as in a musical composition, the various performances took place in and around the audience. Cage, dressed in a black suit and tie, read a lecture on Meister Eckhart from a raised lectern at one side. (The Dadaists, similarly dressed, had solemnly declaimed from Jakob Böhme and Lao-tzu.) M.C. Richards recited from a ladder. Charles Olsen and other performers "planted" in the audience each stood up when their time came and said a line or two. David Tudor played the piano. Movies were projected on the ceiling: at first they showed the school cook, then the sun, and, as the image moved from the ceiling down the wall, the sun sank. Robert Rauschenberg operated old records on a hand-wound phonograph, and Merce Cunningham improvised a dance around the audience. A dog began to follow Cunningham and was accepted into the presentation.

John Cage's ideas have had a profound influence on all the arts. Perhaps his greatest contribution has been through his teaching, both formal and informal. From 1956 to 1958 Kaprow studied with Cage at the New School in New York. The subject was music composition, but Cage saw no reason why the limits could not be stretched to include visual material as well. Kaprow composed short pieces that, in addition to using concrete sounds, contained movements and purely visual images. There is no question that much of the material and structure of *18 Happenings in 6 Parts* resulted directly from this work.

Thus a clear progression which has little to do with collage-Environment aesthetics can be traced from Dada activities to the first New York Happening. But another group of artists, quite different from the Dadaists in inclination, also developed performances that were formally identical with Happenings although stylistically quite different.

The German Bauhaus of the 1920s was involved with actual and theoretical work in every field of art, including theatre (see Schlemmer *et al.* 1961) The artists of the Bauhaus were well aware of the Dada theatre and of Schwitters' Merz theories, but, although they endorsed the rejection of logical and "literary encumbrance," they considered these earlier approaches to be structurally and stylistically arbitrary. Their theatre was based on rationally determined "laws."

At its practical core the theatre of the Bauhaus, directed by Oskar Schlemmer, who had enlarged the scope of his sculpture workshop to include the stage, was a dance theatre. Space, form, and gesture (emotional expression) were studied separately, and independent dances of each type were composed. But Schlemmer merely saw Man as Dancer (*Tänzermensch*) as the focus for transition to the absolute visual stage (*Schaubühne*), and in both theory and accomplishment the theatre of the Bauhaus progressed far beyond dance.

In accordance with the basic principles of abstraction and mechanization, the Bauhaus tended to dehumanize its human performers, frequently hiding them under elaborate costumes and masks. This led, on one hand, to marionette plays such as *The Adventures of the Little Hunchback*, where the wooden "actors" were matrixed by character and place, and, on the other, to productions in which physical effects dominated the action or took it over completely. "Light plays" combined human forms, shadow effects, and projection. Heinz Loew built a model for a totally mechanical stage in which various circles, columns, panels, volumes, and geometric shapes could be spun, turned, raised, lowered, and moved across a proscenium stage by machinery that was visible to the audience.

Laszlo Moholy-Nagy made a colorful sketch for a "score" for a "Mechanized Eccentric," a "synthesis of form, motion, sound, light (color) and odor" (Schlemmer *et al.* 1961: 48). Three stages were to be arranged more or less above each other and used simultaneously. The effects on the upper and lower stages included moving arrows, spinning discs, shifting grids, "gigantic apparatus," odors, and "mechanized men" (apparently wrestlers). Rear projection of films and moving, variable, colored lights played an important part. On the middle stage, mechanical instruments, sound effects, and noisemakers would play in view of the audience.

The stage designed in 1926 by Walter Gropius for the Dessau Bauhaus was a platform located between the assembly hall and the dining room. It could be used as a proscenium stage, as it almost always was, or opened so that spectators faced it from both sides. But again theory went far beyond practice, and the artists of the Bauhaus proposed to change the spectator-presentation relationship by changing the design of the theatre itself. Gropius designed a "Total Theatre" in which projection screens completely surrounded the audience. (Its construction in Berlin for Erwin Piscator was halted in 1926 by the Nazi rise to power.) Andreas Weininger designed a "Spherical Theatre" in which the audience would sit against the walls of a huge sphere and watch mechanical presentations in the central space.

Although the theatre of the Bauhaus had no direct influence on Happenings, and only *Coca Cola, Shirley Cannonball?* (Kaprow, 1960) bears any resemblance to their work, a very important formative factor deriving from theatre was the publication in 1958 of an English translation of *The Theater and Its Double* by Antonin Artaud. The single spectacle that is described (*The Conquest of Mexico*) is not a Happening, but the general theory propounded in the book is almost a text for Happenings. For example, Artaud writes in *The Theater of Cruelty (First Manifesto)*:

> instead of continuing to rely upon texts considered definitive and sacred, it is essential to put an end to the subjugation of the theatre to the text, and to recover the notion of a kind of unique language half-way between gesture and thought.
>
> This language cannot be defined except by its possibilities for dynamic expression in space as opposed to the expressive possibilities of spoken dialogue. And what the theatre can still take over from speech are its possibilities for extension beyond words, for development in space, for dissociative and vibratory action upon the sensibility. This is the hour of intonations, of a word's particular pronunciation. Here too intervenes (besides the auditory language of sounds) the visual language of objects, movements, attitudes and gestures, but on condition that their meanings, their physiognomies, their combinations be carried to the point of becoming signs, making a kind of alphabet out of these signs. Once aware of this language in space, language of sounds, cries, lights, onomatopoeia, the theatre must organize it into veritable hieroglyphs, with the help of characters and objects, and make use of their symbolism and inter-connections in relation to all organs and on all levels. [...]
>
> It would be meaningless to say that [this language] includes music, dance, pantomime, or mimicry. Obviously it uses movement, harmonies, rhythms, but only to the point that they can concur in a sort of central expression without advantage for any one particular art.
>
> (1958: 89–90)

In addition to proposing the rejection of the "supremacy of speech" and the creation of a pure theatrical language based on the mise en scène in which representation would be secondary to the sensory knowledge of the elements, Artaud wished to change the traditional spectator-presentation relationship by placing the audience within the spectacle, and he asked for the elimination of the "duality between author and director" and the combination of both functions in a single "Creator."

Artraud, an actor-director-playwright-poet, was essentially a man of the theatre. Although his scripts make use of Surrealist dream matrices and, like Schwitters, he was never able to realize his theories in production, the impact of his thought was entirely independent from collage and construction considerations. Some Happenings are the best examples of Artaud's Theatre of Cruelty that have yet been produced.

Of course there are stylistic similarities between particular Happenings and certain constructions, assemblages, and Environments. Since the men who originated Happenings in New York all worked in other art forms, resemblance between their work in various forms is to be expected, but stylistic detail must not be mistaken for defining characteristics which predated the arrival of the Happening in New York.

With the consideration of the style of the New York Happenings we are faced with the relevance of many different art forms. Since theatre has duration – it exists in time – it is susceptible to influence from arts such as literature and music which have duration. Since it may make use of both visual and auditory material, it is open to influence from all other arts. If the development of Happenings is approached exclusively from the point of view of painting and sculpture, the basic relationship of theatre to all other arts is overlooked and the possibility of influence from other areas is ignored.

Several of the stylistic tendencies in Happenings can also be related to Dada and to John Cage. Methodical use of Chance method began with Dada. According to one version of the story, the movement's name itself was chosen by chance from a German-French dictionary. In 1916/17 Jean Arp made a collage of colored squares of paper arranged according to "the law of chance." (He also repeated exactly the same drawing each morning in order to illustrate the significant differences resulting from the human, technical factor in art, and, although this is not Chance method, it helps to illustrate the type of thought and is certainly pertinent to the performance techniques used in Happenings.) Marcel Duchamp dropped three threads, each exactly one meter long, onto three sheets of glass from a height of one meter. Fastening them down, he used the sinuous lines arrived at by chance (that is, gravity, etc.) to make three measuring sticks, the varying curved edges of which are each exactly one meter in length. The six pieces are called *Trois Stoppages-Etalon* or *Three Standard Needle Weavings* (1913/14). Picabia, Man Ray, and others were preoccupied by chance in various forms. Tristan Tzara recited poems "composed" from the individual words on slips of paper drawn at random from a hat.

Bruitisme (or "Noise Music") was originated by Luigi Russolo, the great Italian Futurist, and explained in his 1913 manifesto *The Art of Noise*. In keeping with general Futurist beliefs, he called for a music of noise, of machines, of the industrial and commercial city, and he conducted noise concerts in Milan and London in 1914 on *Intonarumori* (or "Noise Intoners") that he had constructed. The new approach to music was adopted by the Dadaists: noise by bells, rattles, cans, keys, sirens, falling objects, etc., would often accompany, and perhaps drown out, "poetry" readings in the Cabaret Voltaire. Hugo Ball, who opened the cabaret in 1916, composed a complete "concert Bruitisme" which was performed behind a white screen.

According to the theory, traditional music with its discrete notes, scales, and harmonies is *abstract*. Noise, on the other hand, since it is part of everyday life and experience, is *concrete*. Sirens, motors, typewriters, and other concrete elements were blended with both popular tunes and music of a more classical feeling in Erik Satie's score for *Parade*, a ballet performed in 1917 in Paris.

John Cage has accepted, enriched, and promulgated both of these relatively young traditions. He has made extensive use of "noise" (and silence) in his work. He has systematically investigated and employed Chance methods – dice, the flipping of coins, random number tables, the use of imperfections in the paper to determine notes – in his compositions. Some of his pieces are indeterminate, limiting but not setting the number and type of instruments, for example, while any part or the whole may be performed. Indeterminacy and bruitisme are both very commonly used in Happenings.

One of the most direct influences on Happenings has been from the dance. Classical ballet was, of course, entirely matrixed in character and place. It told stories. But since its origins in Germany before the First World War, modern dance has tended to eliminate matrix. Although the *Tanzgymnastik*, or gymnastic exercises, apparently were used only for conditioning, they influenced a certain kind of thought that began to consider movement for its own sake rather than as a means of artistically conveying character information. A Hungarian, Rudolf von Laban, attempted to set down laws of movement based on everyday life. In order to study movement, he built a glass-faced icosahedron within which a person could stand and move. In Zurich during World War I the Laban-Wigman troupe, of which Sophie Taeuber was a member, danced during Dada performances.

Mary Wigman, once a pupil of von Laban, was perhaps the most influential figure in modern dance during the early 1920s. Although she often told stories in her dances and almost always concentrated on an emotional core that turned her works into character studies, she did away with music and even rhythm as necessities in dance.

The emphasis in modern dance in general has been away from the two-dimensional picture-frame approach of classical dancing and into a dynamic three-dimensional use of space that might be related to the dominant tendency in Happenings to reject the traditional stage, but most modern dance retained a matrix. The plot turned inward and dance became a representation of subjective emotional states and stories.

Merce Cunningham, who was a soloist with Martha Graham's company from 1940 until 1945, felt that such emotional continuity was unimportant. Forming his own group in 1950 with John Cage as musical director, he created works with neither story nor consistent characters. Sometimes he organized the dance movements by chance methods in order to ensure objectivity of development. It was Cunningham who danced in Cage's "Happening" (the name would not be coined for several years yet) in 1952 at Black Mountain College.

Paul Taylor moved away even farther from accepted views of dance. One of the numbers on a program given at Rutgers University in 1957/58, for example, consisted of Taylor, alone onstage, making movements to ten-second time signals such as those heard on the telephone. A girl's voice would announce the actual time, and at each time tone Taylor, standing erect and facing the audience, would move – turn his head, raise his arm, crouch, or twist, etc. – and return to the "neutral" position. The dance itself was compartmented, and a series of such relatively brief dances (in another "dance" on the program, the curtain opened and closed on motionless figures) would give the effect, if not the overall aesthetic unity of sequential compartmentalization. Kaprow and Whitman both saw this performance, and Kaprow has stated that Taylor, as well as Cage, influenced his work on *18 Happenings in 6 Parts*. James Waring and Ann Halprin, who found stimulation in many of Cage's concepts, also influenced the style of Happenings. Although Happenings as complete works cannot be confused with dances, many of them contain compartments that are basically dances or indeterminate systems of movement.

In spite of their formal indebtedness, Happenings on the whole cannot be considered to be Dadaist works. In the New York performances with which we are concerned here, Dada lost its stylistic dominance after *18 Happenings in 6 Parts*. With *The Burning Building* Surrealism, in the broadest use of the term, became the most obvious precedent. [...]

Of course the parallel may be drawn between the Surrealist device for joining disparate images in order to create a new reality (Comte de Lautréamont's famous "possibility of a sewing machine and an umbrella meeting on a dissecting table") and the relationship of logically unrelated compartments in Happenings, but often the material within the compartments has also been in the Surrealist tradition.

Surrealism was concerned with dreams and the products of the unconscious. *The Burning Building* with its passage of unnaturally slow movement, its grotesque characters, its distorted shadows and frequently dim illumination had a kinship to dream. All of Oldenburg's works have contained nightmare images: it is not surprising, since for years he diligently recorded all his dreams. [...] The revelation of repressed sexual material, often in symbolical ways, is a common characteristic of dreams; the symbolical or oblique treatment of sexual material, a frequent Surrealist concern, is central to many Happenings.

(Similarity in the type of images only helps to make obvious the difference between Happenings and plays, however. Dada, Surrealist, and Expressionist plays by Tzara, Ribemont-Dessaignes, Aragon, Artaud, Federico García Lorca, and Oskar Kokoschka are similar in many details to some Happenings, but in the plays the dream elements and distortions always exist in a matrix. They follow a distorted continuity: time, place, and character change with the fluidity of thought, but they are always present, and a continuous information structure exists. They cling to story chronology. *The Burning Building* and Oldenburg's *Injun I* (1962) very closely resemble the dream story of Expressionist-Surrealist theatre and this sets them apart from true Happenings.)

In Happenings as in Surrealism we find a frequent blending, metamorphosis, and interpenetration of the animate and the inanimate. Ernst's plants assume the forms of birds and men. Dali fuses man and object. Arp gives stone and wood vitality of organisms. [...] A cardboard box comes alive in Kaprow's *A Spring Happening*. [...]

The Environmental aspect of Happenings also relates most directly to the Surrealist tradition. Since at least 1938, major Surrealist exhibitions have tended to become single or multiple Environments. Marcel Duchamp, who was the "generator-referee" of the 1938 exhibition at the Galerie Beaux Arts in Paris, designed a great central hall with a pool surrounded by real grass. Four large comfortable beds stood among the greenery. Twelve hundred sacks of coal hung from the ceiling. In order to illuminate the paintings which hung on the walls, Duchamp planned to use electric eyes that would switch on lights for the individual works when a beam was broken. Because of technical difficulties this project was abandoned, and flashlights were loaned to the visitors (they were all stolen, and more traditional lighting was finally employed). At the opening of the exhibition, the odor of roasting coffee filled the hall. A recording of a German army marching song was broadcast, and a girl performed a dance around the pool.

Duchamp transformed the 1942 Surrealist Exhibition, held in New

York, into an Environment by crisscrossing the space with a complicated network of twine. The 1947 exhibition, which was again held in Paris, included a room where rain constantly fell onto artificial grass, and another attempt to involve the visitors failed when all of the balls were stolen from a billiard table in the room.

When a Surrealist exhibition was held in early 1960 in Paris, it was made up of several connected Environments. The first room, which had oval doorways, was lined with pink velvet. The velvet ceiling moved, and recorded sighs and murmurs could be heard. Another room was covered with green padding and there was the suggestion of stalactites and stalagmites. At the end of a narrow corridor lined with black was a black Fetish Chamber. During the opening, Surrealists enacted a homage to de Sade there, using a naked girl as a banquet table. Later, wax figures replaced the real ones.

Finally the Surrealist tradition is stylistically related to Happenings through Abstract Expressionist painting and the "combines" of Robert Rauschenberg. Abstract Expressionism was, theoretically, the purist form of Surrealist painting, although its practitioners did not consider themselves Surrealists. Influenced by Surrealist thought and practice, it was in essence the "pure psychic automatism" demanded by Breton in the *Surrealist Manifesto* of 1924. The emotional energy and spontaneous use of materials of Abstract Expressionism have been echoed in many Happenings.

Rauschenberg has been closely associated with John Cage. He designed lighting and sets for dance concerts by Merce Cunningham and Paul Taylor. Although his handling of paint in his assemblages of the late 1950s was roughly Abstract Expressionist, he also incorporated a wide variety of objects and images from everyday life into his work, creating pieces that seem to be personal journals filled with emotionally weighted statements that are not intended to have an explicit meaning or a logical clarity to the observer. This balance between private and public has also been struck in many Happenings.

Motion pictures have also had a broad and diffuse influence on Happenings. Surrealist films and those making use of hallucinatory images are more readily available than productions of Surrealist plays: *Entr'acte* by Picabia and René Clair (1924: first screened during the intermission of *Relâche*), *An Andalusian Dog* (1929) by Luis Buñuel and Salvador Dali, *The Blood of a Poet* (with its four distinct parts tending toward compartmentalization), *Beauty and the Beast* and *Orpheus* by Cocteau, *Dreams That Money Can Buy* (1944) by Hans Richter (in six parts). But beyond questions of form, use of symbols, and the character of images, some of these works had a homemade, unsophisticated technical quality. *The Cabinet of Dr. Caligari* (1919) with its crudely painted sets and grotesque makeup and *8 × 8* (1956/57) by Richter with its backyard locations, ingenuous costumes, and cast of nonactor friends are good examples. (Arp, Ernst, Duchamp, Calder, Cocteau, Tanguy, and Hülsenbeck appeared in the latter film in which eight parts continued the minor convention of dividing a Surrealist film into sections.) This "nonprofessional" approach has often been apparent in Happenings.

The primitive quality of early films was also provocative. Red Grooms was so impressed by Georges Méliès' 1902 film, *A Trip to the Moon*, that he and Rudy Burckhardt made their own version called *Shoot the Moon* (1962). *A Trip to the Moon* handled fantastic material – the inhabitants of the moon, for example, are part bird, part man, and part lobster – in a style which now seems very naïve, childlike, and homemade. As in his other works, Méliès wrote, designed, directed, and acted in the film.

Many of the people who produced Happenings found stimulation in American comedy films: Chaplin, W.C. Fields, the Marx Brothers (for whom the Surrealists showed so much enthusiasm) with their deadpan fantasy, sequences of frantic activity, and emphasis on the visual. Although Oldenburg never saw the stage version of *Hellzapoppin'*, he did see the Olsen and Johnson movie.

Certain types of literature, especially poetry, also must be recognized for their formative influence on Happenings. Certainly the general tendency in much modern poetry to base structure on association and implication rather than on traditional formal patterns and sequential logic is a precedent for Happenings. Kaprow's published script which later became the partial basis for *18 Happenings in 6 Parts* bears a resemblance to Mallarmé's *A Throw of the Dice Never Will Abolish Chance* (1897) in its use of various typefaces and the special composition of words and word groups on the page. Oldenburg published three poems in *Exodus* (spring/summer 1960), a small review. (Behind a cover photograph of Jim Dine the issue also included correspondence between Antonin Artaud and Jacques Rivière, drawings by Red Grooms of *The Burning Building*, and drawings by Oldenburg. [...]

Mention might also be made of the stream-of-consciousness monolog that has been used in several Happenings and of its literary tradition. But detailed analysis of stylistic detail on this level is not of primary importance. It is enough to emphasize the fact that every field of art (not just painting and sculpture) has had some formative influence on Happenings. Since the Happenings with which we are concerned here were produced by educated and perceptive men living in what, at the moment, is the greatest cultural center in the world, the use of diverse stimuli should not be surprising.

Nor is discussion of historical influence intended to minimize the important accomplishments of the men who created Happenings. For a good number of years many people have felt that theatre was not functioning at the profound aesthetic level of the other arts. Over half a century ago, in 1905, Konstantin Stanislavsky wrote:

> realism, and (depicting) the way of life have outlived their age. The time has come to stage the unreal. Not life itself, as it occurs in reality, must be depicted, but rather life as it is vaguely perceived in fantasies and visions at moments of lofty emotion. This is the spiritual situation that must be transmitted scenically, in the way that painters of the new school use cloth, musicians of the new trend write music, and the new poets, poetry. The works of these painters, musicians, and poets have no clear outlines, definite and finished melodies, or precisely expressed ideas. The power of the new art lies in its combinations of colors, lines, musical notes, and the rhyming of words. They create general moods that carry over to the public unconsciously. They create hints that make the most unobservant person create with his own imagination.
>
> (in Gerchakov 1957: 44)

At the time he wrote, the first collage had not yet been made and the arts were beginning to move in unprecedented new directions. Stanislavsky could not have guessed that painters, musicians, and poets would have to make their own theatre before theatre began to approach the level of the other arts.

REFERENCES

Artaud, Antonin (1958) *The Theater and Its Double*. Translated by Mary Caroline Richards. New York: Grove Press, Inc.

Gerchakov, Nikolai A. (1957) *The Theatre in Soviet Russia*. Translated by Edgar Lehrman. New York: Columbia University Press.

Janis, Harriet, and Rudi Blesh (1962) *Collage*. Philadelphia and New York: Chilton, Co.

Motherwell, Robert, ed. (1951) *The Dada Painters and Poets*. New York: George Wittenborn, Inc.

Schlemmer, O., L. Moholy-Nagy, and F. Molnar (1961) *The Theatre of the Bauhaus*. Middletown, CT: Wesleyan University Press.

Seitz, William G. (1961) *The Art of Assemblage*. New York: The Museum of Modern Art.

Woks (1959) *Art News*, March:62.

THE NEW THEATRE

Michael Kirby

Since the turn of the century, most art forms have vastly expanded their materials and scope. Totally abstract or nonobjective painting and sculpture, unheard of in 1900, is practiced by many major artists today. Composers tend to discard traditional Western scales and harmonies, and atonal music is relatively common. Poetry has abandoned rhyme, meter, and syntax. Almost alone among the arts, theatre has lagged. But during the last few years there have been a number of performances that begin to bring theatre into some relation with the other arts. These works, as well as productions in other performance-oriented fields, force us to examine theatre in a new light and raise questions about the meaning of the word "theatre" itself.

In discussing this new theatre, new terms are needed. A few have already been provided by public usage, although they need clarification and standardization. Others will have to be created. Accurate nomen-clature is important – not for the sake of limitation but to facilitate easy, accurate, and creative exchange among those concerned with the work and its concepts. If my own approach seems too serious, it may be justified as a reaction against those who take the new theatre very lightly and thus dismiss, without seeing them, theatrical developments of real importance.

It is clear, however, that perfect definitions are almost impossible to derive from actual recent theatrical productions. Just as no *formal* distinctions between poetry and prose can be made in some cases, and passages of "prose" are published in anthologies of "poetry," and as traditional categories of "painting" and "sculpture" grow less and less applicable to much modern work, so theatre exists not as an entity but as a continuum blending into other arts. Each name and term refers only to a significant point on this continuum. Definitions apply to *central tendency*, but cannot set precise limits.

For example, we find that theatre blends at one extreme into painting and sculpture. Traditionally these arts did not structure the time dimension as theatre does, but in recent years paintings and sculptures have begun to move and give off sound. They have become "performers." Some of the works of Rauschenberg and Tinguely are obvious examples, and pieces of kinetic sculpture by Len Lye have been exhibited to an audience from the stage in New York's Museum of Modern Art. Art displays, such as the large Surrealist exhibitions and the recent "labyrinths" of the Groupe de Recherche d'Art Visuel de Paris, are turned into environmental mazes through which the spectator wanders, creating a loose time structure. The Environment which completely surrounds the viewer has become an accepted art form.

Although almost all Environments have made use of light, sound, and movement, *Eat* by Allan Kaprow (1964) went one step further by employing human beings as the "mechanized" elements. The people involved functioned within narrow and well-defined limits of behavior. Their tasks, which had no development or progression, were repeated without variation. They responded only to particular actions on the part of the spectators – only when their "switch was turned on." It may be easy to keep "performing" paintings and sculptures within the categories of those arts, but does Kaprow's use of the human performer make his *Eat* "theatre"? Certainly *Eat* is at the dividing line between forms. My own opinion is that the very strong emphasis upon static environmental elements outweighs the performance elements. *Eat* is not quite theatre. It is just this kind of weighing, this evaluation guided by dominant characteristics and central tendency, which must be used in assigning works of the new theatre to a category.

• • •

The most convenient beginning for a discussion of the new theatre is John Cage. Cage's thought, in his teaching, writing, lectures, and works, is the backbone of the new theatre. In the first place, Cage refuses as a composer to accept any limits for music. Traditional sound-producers did not satisfy him, and he created his own instruments: the prepared piano, in which various materials were placed on the strings of a piano to change the qualities of the sounds; the water gong, which was lowered into water while vibrating to produce a change in tone; etc. Not only did he equate sound and silence so that long passages of silence were integral parts of his compositions, but he pointed out that absolute silence does not exist. (He is fond of describing his experience in a theoretically soundproof research room in which he heard two sounds: the circulation of his blood and the functioning of his nervous system.) If sound is ever-present, so are the other senses, and Cage has gone so far as to deny the existence of music itself, if music is considered as hearing isolated from sight, touch, smell, etc.

These considerations led to a shift of emphasis in Cage's concerts toward nonauditory elements. Of course the performance of music for an audience is never entirely auditory. Rituals of tuning up, the appearance of the conductor, and the attitudes, behavior, and dress of the musicians are important parts of the experience. Although we enjoy watching performances on traditional instruments (at a piano recital, for example, seats on the keyboard side are preferred), the visual aspects are relatively easy to take for granted (and those who cannot see the keyboard do not feel cheated). A new instrument, such as a water gong, or a new way of playing, such as reaching inside the piano to pluck the strings, calls attention to itself: *how* the sound is produced becomes as significant a part of the experience as the *quality* of the sound itself. This theatricalization of a musical performance exists on an entirely different level from the emotional dramatizations of a Bernstein.

If any kind of sound-producer may be used to make music, and if silence is also music (because true silence does not exist), it follows that any activity or event may be presented as part of a music concert. La Monte Young may use a butterfly as his sound source; the ONCE group can refer to the performance of a piece which includes the broadcast narration of a horse race (the only primarily auditory element), the projected image of rolling marbles, and a series of people moving in various ways (on roller skates, etc.) as "music."

This emphasis upon performance, which is one result of a refusal to place limits upon music, draws attention to the performer himself. But the musician is not acting. Acting might be defined as the creation of character and/or place: details of "who" and "where" the performer is are necessary to the performance. The actor functions within subjective or objective person-place matrices. The musician, on the other hand, is *nonmatrixed*. He attempts to be no one other than himself, nor does he function in a place other than that which physically contains him and the audience.

Nonmatrixed performances are not uncommon. Although the audience-performer relationship which is the basis of theatre exists in sporting events, for example, the athlete does not create character or place. Nor is such imaginary information a part of the halftime spectacle of a football game, religious or secular rituals, political conventions, or many other activities in "real life." The tendency, however is to deny the performers in these situations serious consideration either because, like the musician, they are not a "legitimate" and accepted part of the formal experience, or because the works in which they appear are not art. My point is not to change our view of these "common" events but to suggest the profound possibilities and potentialities of nonmatrixed performing for the theatre.

Since acting is, by definition, matrixed performing, why not simply use the terms "acting" and "nonacting" rather than suggesting new and fairly awkward terms? The fact is that "nonacting" would be equally awkward and less meaningful. Matrix is a larger and more inclusive concept than the activity of the performer, and a person may be matrixed without acting. Acting is something that a performer does; matrix can be externally imposed upon his behavior. The context of place, for example, as determined by the physical setting and the information provided verbally and visually by the production, is frequently so strong that it makes an "actor" out of any person, such as an extra, who walks upon the stage. In many cases nothing needs to be done in order to "act." The priest in church performing part of the service, the football player warming up and playing the game, the sign painter being raised on a scaffold while passersby watch, are not matrixed by character or place. Even their specific, identifying clothing does not make them "characters." Yet the same people might do exactly the same things in a play involving a scene of worship, a football game, or the creation of a large sign, and become "actors" because of the context.[1]

This does not mean that there is always a clear line between matrixed and nonmatrixed performing. The terms refer to polar conceptions which are quite obvious in their pure forms, but a continuum exists between them, and it is possible that this or that performance might be difficult to categorize. In other words, the strength of character-place matrices may be described as "strong" or "weak" and the exact point at which a weak matrix becomes nonmatrix is not easy to perceive. But even in the extreme case in which both the work of the performer and the information provided by his context are so vague and nonspecific that we could not explain "who" he was or "where" he was supposed to be, we often feel that he is someone other than himself or in some place other than the actual place of performance. We know when we are suspending disbelief or being asked to suspend it.

Nonmatrixed performances which are complete in themselves are referred to as Events. A piano is destroyed. The orchestra conductor walks onstage, bows to the audience, raises his baton, and the curtain falls. A formally dressed man appears with a French horn under his arm; when he bows, ball bearings pour from the bell of the horn in a noisy cascade. A person asks if La Monte Young is in the audience; when there is no answer, he leaves. A man sets a balloon onstage, carefully estimates the distance as he walks away from it, then does a backward flip, landing on the balloon and breaking it. Since Events are usually short, they are frequently performed as parts of longer programs. The Fluxus group, a fairly loose organization which includes most of the people working in the form in New York, has presented many "concerts" composed entirely of Events. The form demonstrates a type of performing that is widely used in the new theatre and which is one of its most important contributions.

● ● ●

In his music Cage abandoned harmony, the traditional means of structuring a composition, and replaced it with duration. This was logically consistent, since duration was the only dimension of music which applied to silence as well as to sounds. Duration could also be used to structure spoken material, and Cage built lectures with these same techniques. Indeed, duration is the one dimension which exists in *all* performance, and in the summer of 1952, stimulated no doubt by his awareness of the performance aspects of music and by his programmatic refusal to place limits upon the sounds used or the manner in which they were produced. Cage presented a work at Black Mountain College which combined dance, motion pictures, poetry and prose readings, and recorded music. These materials were handled exactly as if they had been sounds. The musical and nonmusical elements were all precisely scored for points of entry into the piece and duration – a wide variety of performance materials was "orchestrated."

Theatre as we have generally known it is based primarily upon *information structure.* Not only do the individual elements of a presentation generate meaning, but each conveys meaning to and receives it from the other elements. This was not true of the piece which Cage presented at Black Mountain College. Although some of the elements contained information, the performance units did not pass information back and forth or "explain" each other. The film, for example, which was of the cook at the school and later of a sunset, did not help the spectator to "understand" the dance any more clearly than if the dance had been presented by itself. The ideas expressed in the poetry had no intentional relationship to the ideas contained in the prose. The elements remained intellectually discrete. Each was a separate compartment. The structure was *alogical.*

The information structure of traditional theatre is not alogical but either logical or illogical. Information is built and interrelated in both the logical well-made play and the "illogical" dream, surreal, or absurd play. Illogic depends upon an awareness of what is logical. Alogical structure stands completely outside of these relationships.

Of course the structure of all music (overlooking the "waterfalls" and "twittering birds" of program music and the written program itself, which adds its own information structure to the composition) and of abstract or nonobjective painting and sculpture is alogical. It depends upon sensory rather than intellectual relationships. Literature, on the other hand, depends primarily upon information structure. It is this fact rather than a reliance upon written script material or the use of words which makes it so easy and so correct to call traditional theatre "*literary* theatre." As Cage's piece demonstrated, "verbal" should not be confused with "literary." Nor is the nonverbal necessarily alogical. Information is conveyed by movement, setting, and lighting as well as by words, and a mime play, although more limited in its technical means, constructs the same web of information that a dialog play does. Both are literary. The spectator "reads" the performance.[2]

A performance using a variety of materials (films, dance, readings, music, etc.) in a compartmented structure, and making use of essentially nonmatrixed performance, is a Happening. Thus the distinction between Happenings and Events can be made on the basis of compartments or logically discrete elements. The Event is limited to one compartment, while the Happening contains several, most often sequential, compartments, and a variety of primary materials.

The name "Happening" was taken by the public from *18 Happenings in 6 Parts* by Allan Kaprow (who had studied with Cage), which was presented in 1959. Since then it has been applied indiscriminately to many performances ranging from plays to parlor games. It has been a fad word, although the small attendance at presentations prevents Happenings themselves from being called a fad. Nobody seems to like the word except the public. Since the name was first applied to a piece by Kaprow, it tends to be his word, and some other artists, not caring for the slightest implication that their work is not at least 100 percent original, do not publicly apply the name "Happening" to their productions. (I am reminded of the person who said he did not want to go to a particular Happening because he had seen a Happening already. It was as if he were saying that he did not want to read a particular novel because he had read a novel once.) Names are beginning to proliferate: Theatre Piece (Robert Whitman), Action Theatre (Ken Dewey), Ray Gun Theatre (Claes Oldenburg), Kinetic Theatre (Carolee Schneemann), etc. The ONCE group and Ann Halprin perform works which I would call Happenings, but they refer to them as "music," "dance," or by no generic name. Because nothing better has been coined to replace it, I will use the term "Happening."

A dominant aspect of Cage's thought has been his concern with the environmental or directional aspects of performance. In addition to the frequent use of extremely loud sounds which have a high density and fill the space, he often distributes the sound sources or loudspeakers around the spectators so that the music comes to them from various angles and distances. In his presentation at Black Mountain College, the audience sat in the center of the space while some performers stood up among them to read, other readings were done from ladders at either end, Merce

Cunningham danced around the outer space, and a film was projected on the ceiling and walls.

This manipulation and creative use of the relationship between the presented performance material and the spectator has been developed extensively in Happenings. Spectators are frequently placed in unconventional seating arrangements so that a performance element which is close to some is far from others and stimuli reach the observer from many different directions. In some arrangements the spectators are free to move and, in selecting their own vantage points, control the spatial relationship themselves. At other times they are led through or past spatially separated performance units much as medieval audiences passed from one station to another.

A major aspect of directional and environmental manipulations is not merely that different spectators experience stimuli at different intensities but that they may not experience some of the material at all. This is intentional, and unavoidable in a situation that is much like a three-ring circus.

If a circus were a work of art, it would be an excellent example of a Happening. Except for the clowns (and perhaps the man with the lions who pretends that they are vicious), the performances are nonmatrixed. The acrobats, jugglers, and animal trainers are "merely" carrying out their activities. The grips or stagehands become performers, too, as they dismantle and rig the equipment – demonstrating that nonmatrixed performing exists at all levels of difficulty. The structure of a three-ring circus makes use of simultaneous as well as sequential compartments. There is no information structure: the acts do not add meaning to one another, and one can be fully "understood" without any of the others. At the same time the circus is a total performance and not just the sum of its parts. The flow of processions alternates with focused activity in the rings. Animal acts or acrobatic acts are presented at the same time. Sometimes all but one of the simultaneous acts end at the same moment, concentrating the spectators' previously scattered attention on a single image. Perhaps tumblers and riders are presented early in the program, and a spatial progression is achieved by ending the program with the high wire and trapeze artists. And the circus, even without its traditional tent, has strong environmental aspects. The exhibits of the side show, the menagerie, and the uniformed vendors in the aisles are all part of the show. Sometimes small flashlights with cords attached are hawked to the children: whenever the lights are dimmed, the whole space is filled with hundreds of tiny lights being swung in circles.

But although the acrobat may be seen as an archetypal example of nonmatrixed performing, he can be something else. In Vsevolod Meyerhold's biomechanics, actors were trained as acrobats and gymnasts. The actor functioned as a machine, and the constructivist set was merely an arrangement of platforms, ramps, swings, ladders, and other nonrepresentational elements that the performer could use. But the performers were still matrixed by place and character. Although the set did not indicate a particular place, the dialog and situations made it clear. Biomechanics was used merely as a way of projecting the characters of the story. An actor turned a somersault to express rage or performed a salto-mortale to show exaltation. Calm and unrest could both be signified on the high wire rather than in the usual ways. Determination could be projected from a trapeze. Although biomechanics used movements which, out of context, were nonmatrixed acrobatics, it used them within place and character matrices created by an information structure.

The nonmatrixed performing in Happenings is of several types. Occasionally people are used somewhat as inanimate objects. In *Washes* by Claes Oldenburg (1965), for example, a motionless girl covered with balloons floated on her back in the swimming pool where the piece was being presented while a man bit the balloons and exploded them. At other times the simple operation of theatrical machinery becomes part of the performance: in *Washes* a record player and a motion-picture projector were turned on and off in plain view of the audience; the "lifeguard" merely walked around the pool and helped with certain props. Most nonmatrixed performing is more complicated, however. It might be thought of as combining the image quality of the first type with the purposeful functioning of the second. At one point in *Washes*, for example, four men dove into the pool and pushed sections of silver flue pipe back and forth along a red clothesline. There was no practical purpose in shoving and twisting the pipes, but it was real activity. Manufactured character or situation had nothing to do with it. The men did not pretend to be anyone other than themselves, nor did they pretend – unlike the swimmers in *Dead End* or *Wish You Were Here* – that the water they were in was anything other than what it actually was: in this case a health-club pool with spectators standing around the edge.

When acting is called for in a Happening, it almost always exists in a rudimentary form. Because of the absence of an information structure, the job of acting tends to fall into its basic elements. Perhaps an emotion is created and projected as it was by the exaggerated frenzy with which the man in *Washes* bit the balloons attached to the floating girl. Although the rate or tempo of this action had no necessary connection with character, and the activity could have been carried out in a nonmatrixed manner, it could not be denied that the agitated and mock-ferocious quality that was dominant was acting. The acted qualities stood out and remained isolated because they did not fit into a character matrix or into a larger situation. Other facets of acting – "playing an attitude," place, details of characterization, etc. – are also found in Happenings, but they are usually isolated and function as a very weak matrix.

This is not to say that emotion of any sort during a performance is necessarily acted. Although much nonmatrixed performance is comparatively expressionless, it would be erroneous to think that this type of performing is without emotion. Certainly feelings are expressed in the "nonmatrixed performing" of everyday life: in the runner's face as he breaks the tape, in the professor's intonation and stress during his lecture, in the owner's attitude as he handles his dog in a dog show. The important point is that emotions apparent during a nonmatrixed performance are those of the performer himself. They are not intentionally created, and they are the natural result of the individual's attitude toward the piece, of the particular task being performed, or of the particular situation of being in front of an audience. Without acted emotions to mask their own feelings, the performers' own attitudes are more apt to become manifest than they are in traditional theatre.

Of course acting and nonmatrixed performing have certain elements in common. When the production of various kinds of information is eliminated from the actor's task, certain requirements still remain. They are the same requirements which exist for performers of any kind. Concentration, for example, is as important to athletes and Happeners as it is to actors, and stage-presence – the degree to which a person can mask or control feelings of nervousness, shyness, uncertainty, etc. – is equally useful to actors, public speakers, and musicians.[3]

One final point about performance in the new theatre concerns the question of improvisation and indeterminacy. Indeterminacy means that limits within which the performers are free to make choices are provided by the creator of the piece: a range of alternatives is made available from which the performer may select. Thus in a musical composition the number of notes to be played within a given time period may be given but not the notes themselves; the pitch ranges may be indicated for given durations but specific notes not required. Indeterminacy is used in the new theatre when, for example, the number of steps a performer should take is limited but the direction is optional; when the type of action is designated but no specific action is given; etc. The choices involved in indeterminacy may be made before the actual performance, but they are most frequently left until the moment of presentation in an attempt to insure spontaneity.

Indeterminacy is not the same as improvisation. Although spontaneity may be a goal of both, it is also the goal of much precisely detailed acting. The primary difference between indeterminacy and improvisation is the amount of momentary, on-the-spot creativity which is involved. Not only is the detail – the apt comment, the *bon mot*, the unexpected or unusual reaction – central to improvisation, but the form and structure of a scene may also be changed. Even when, as was common in commedia dell'arte, the general outline of the scene is set, the performer is responding to unfamiliar material and providing in return his inventions, which require a response. As evidenced by the so-called "improvisational theatres" such as Second City, an improvisation loses these values once it has been repeated a few times. It no longer is an improvisation, and most of these groups make no pretense among themselves that it is. In indeterminacy the alternatives are quite clear, although the exact choice may not be made until performance. And the alternatives *do not matter*: one is as good as another. Since the performers usually function independently and do not respond to the choices made by the other performers, no give-and-take is involved. The situation is not "open-ended" as it is in improvisation.

Thus the four men who manipulated the sections of pipe in *Washes*, for example, did no creative work although the details of their actions and procedure were different during each performance. They merely embod-ied the image of man-and-pipe which Oldenburg had created. They were not, in the true sense, improvising. Only the type of behavior mattered and not the details. Whether they swam for a while rather than "working," whether they twisted this length of pipe rather than that one, whether they worked together or individually, did not matter provided they kept within the directed limits. The image was the same each night.

A somewhat related attitude is the acceptance of incidental aspects of audience reaction and environmental occurrences as *part* of the produc-tion. One of Cage's most notorious musical compositions is *4' 33"* (1952) – four minutes and thirty-three seconds of silence by the musician or musicians performing it. The nonplaying (in addition to focusing the "performer" aspects of the piece) allows any "incidental" sounds – perhaps traffic noises or crickets outside the auditorium, the creak of seats, coughing and whispering in the audience – to become "music." This exploitation and integration of happenstance occurrences unique to each performance into the performance itself is another common, but not universal, trait of the new theatre.

• • •

One method of assuring completely alogical structure in a work is to use chance methods. Beginning in about 1951 Cage used chance operations such as a system of coin tossing derived from *I Ching*, the Chinese *Book of Changes*. In a method close to pure chance, he determined the placement of notes in certain compositions by marking the imperfections in the score paper. In the Happening which he presented during the summer of 1952 at Black Mountain College, the point of entry and the duration of the various performance elements were fixed by chance techniques. Cage's *Theatre Piece* of 1960 can be performed by one to eight musicians, singers, actors, dancers, and is unusual in that it provides an elaborate *method* (including the use of plastic overlays) of determining individual "scores," but it does not designate the actions, sounds, phrases, etc. – several groups of which are selected to be the raw material for the chance operations.

The use of chance and indeterminacy in composition are aspects of a wide concern with methods and procedure in the new theatre. Another approach to the question of method is illustrated by a *Graphis* by Dick Higgins (who also studied with Cage) in which a linear pattern is marked out on the floor of the performance space with words written at various points. Performers may move only along the lines, and they perform preselected actions corresponding to each word when they arrive at that word. Thus the repeated actions and limited lines of movement create visual and rhythmic patterns which freely structure the work in an alogical way.

Jackson Mac Low, another of Cage's students, applied chance methods to the materials of the traditional drama. For *The Marrying Maiden*, for example, he selected characters and speeches from the *I Ching*. The order and duration of speeches and the directions for rate, volume, inflection, and manner of speaking were all independently ascribed to the material by chance techniques. Five different tempos ranging from "Very Slow" to "Very Fast" and five different amplitudes ranging from "Very Soft" to "Very Loud" were used. The attitudes to be acted were selected and placed into the script by the application of random number methods to a list of 500 adverbs or adverbial phrases ("smugly," "religiously," "apingly," etc.) compiled by Mac Low. Although the delivery of the lines in *The Marrying Maiden* is more closely controlled than in a traditional script, no movements, business, or actions are given. Staging is left to the director or actors. When the play was presented by The Living Theatre in 1960 and 1961, the physical activity worked out by Judith Malina, the director, was fixed. Other actions were inserted at random intervals by the use of an "action pack" of about 1,200 cards containing stage directions ("scratch yourself," "kiss the nearest woman," "use any three objects in an action") which were given to the performers by a visible stage manager who rolled dice to determine his own behavior.

In many of the works by Dick Higgins the operations of chance shift emphatically onto the performance. In *The Tart* (1965), for example, selection by chance or taste is made from among the given characters, speeches, and cues by the performer or director, who then decides on actions to supplement the chosen material. Since at least some of the behavior or effects which cue the speeches and actions are provided by one or more "special performers," a complicated cueing situation exists, creating a performance *pattern* which is different each time, although the performance *materials* remain constant.

Since the chance performances of Mac Low and Higgins make basic use of acting, the fundamental material of traditional theatre, there is some justification for retaining them in the "play" or "drama" category. They can be called *chance plays* or *alogical drama*. They are not Happenings. As with other definitions in the new theatre, however, these terms can only be applied by measuring central tendency. Plays obviously use materials other than acting; Happenings may use acting as part of the performance. It then becomes a question of whether acting is the *primary* element, as in a play, or whether the emphasis is on nonmatrixed performing, physical effect, or a balance between several components, as in a Happening.

The recent production of *The Tart* is an example of the difficulty that can result when one tries to categorize a particular performance without making up pointless terms. Reading the script, there seems to be no question that the basic performance element is supposed to be acting and that it is a chance play. In the actual production at the Sunnyside Garden boxing arena in Queens, however, acting was used much less than it could have been, and physical effects were added. Because of this, the emphasis was shifted past the borderline between Happenings and chance theatre. This, in itself, is not important, but the way in which it came about makes clearer how to apply the terms I have been using.

In order to understand the apparent shift away from acting in the performance of *The Tart*, two things must be remembered. In the first place, distinctions between matrixed and nonmatrixed performing are not made on the basis of acting style or on the basis of good or bad acting. Both naturalistic acting, in which the performer disappears within the character, and formalized acting, which makes use of "artificial" gesture and speech, develop equally strong matrices. The acrobatic performers in *Le Cocu Magnifique* were acting. And the poor actor – unless he gives up completely and drops out of character to ask for a line – is, like the good actor, providing a supply of character-place data. The work may be more obvious in one case and the matrices demonstrated or indicated rather than implied, but this is basically an aesthetic question rather than a formal one.

In the second place, neither costumes nor dialog have any necessary relationship to acting. A costume or a line of dialog is – like a prop, a particular kind of light, or the setting – merely another piece of information. It may be related to character material which is acted or to other information and thus helps to form a strong matrix, but a nonmatrixed performer may also wear a costume or speak.

The Tart makes great demands upon actors. The performers do not speak to each other and "play scenes" in the way possible, for example, with the alogical verbal material of Jackson Mac Low's *Verdurous Sanguinaria* (1961). The dialog of *The Tart* usually consists of speeches attributed to some other character, and something of that character is supposed to be superimposed upon the base character when the line is given. Obviously, in order to keep "in character," highly skilled actors are needed, and when the performers cannot sustain the base character, as happened in this case, acting disintegrates into disparate lines and actions. Although the performers are required to select their own actions, which can strengthen the character matrix and ease the complicated and difficult acting task, many of them in this production chose to use arbitrary or meaningless movement, which only destroyed any character matrix they might have established. One or two of the performers, experienced in Happenings, made no attempt to act. Thus the final effect was one in which acting was subordinate to effect and to nonmatrixed performing. In performance *The Tart* turned from a chance play into a Happening.

Just as the words "play" and "drama" have a historical usage which should not be replaced with "Happening" or "Event" unless the fundamental elements are different, the word "dance" has an accepted meaning which takes precedence over any new terminology. And certain contemporary developments in dance are a very important part of the new theatre. Although these developments are the result of progressive aesthetic changes within the field, the form has been brought to that point where many formal and stylistic similarities exist between contemporary dance works and pieces presented by nondancers that are not referred to as "dance." Significant creative exchange has become possible between disciplines which have been thought of as isolated. One pronounced and important characteristic of the new theatre is the tendency to reduce or eliminate the traditionally strong divisions of drama, dance, opera, etc.

The changes in dance which give it a place in the new theatre parallel those which are exemplified by Events, Happenings, and chance theatre, but did not necessarily derive from them. For example, Merce Cunningham created *16 Dances* by chance method in 1951 – the year before Cage's presentation at Black Mountain College. The order of passages and even the order of movements within one passage were determined by tossing coins. (Cage, who has worked closely with Cunningham for many years and was working with chance techniques at that time, composed the music for the piece by setting a fixed procedure for moving on a chart containing the noises, tones, and aggregates of sound that would be used in the composition.) Since Cunningham's early work, much investigation into chance, game, and indeterminacy methods and various other alogical structures has been undertaken by dancers, especially by Ann Halprin's Dancers' Workshop and by Robert Dunn, whose classes at Cunningham's studio in 1960–1962 eventually developed into the Judson Dance Theatre. '

As structure in dance became alogical and made use of simultaneous performances that were not interrelated (except that they were concurrently presented to the spectator), the manner of performance has also changed. Of course certain types of dancing have always been nonmatrixed. No character or place is created and projected in ballroom dancing (which, it might be pointed out, almost always has an audience, although that is not its orientation), and acrobatic dancing, tap dancing, soft-shoe dancing, and the like are all nonmatrixed – unless, of course, they appear as part of the action in a play. But, from the stories of ballet to the psychological projections of modern dance, the dance as an art form has generally made use of character and place matrices. In recent years, however, story, plot, character, situation, "ecstasy," personal expression, and self-dramatization have all dropped away, and dance has made use of nonmatrixed performing.

The separation of dance from music is perhaps one of the factors responsible for the shift. Musical accompaniment functions in part as an emotional matrix which "explains" dancers. Think, for example, of how much expression and character can be given to the film image of a blank face or even the back of a head by the music on the sound track. In John Cage's scores for many of Merce Cunningham's dances, music and movement merely fill the same time period without relationship. Some of Mary Wigman's dances just after the First World War and almost all of the dances in the new theatre entirely eliminated music; thus "interpretation" is no longer a factor, and the possibility of nonmatrixed performing is increased.

As character, emotional continuity, and a sense of created locale have been eliminated from dance, walking, running, falling, doing calisthenics, and other simple activities from everyday life have become dance elements. No attempt is made to embellish these actions, and it does not take years of training to "dance" them. Merce Cunningham did a piece called *Collage* at Brandeis University in 1953 in which he used fifteen untrained "dancers" who performed simple, ordinary movements and activities such as running and hair combing. A number of "nondancers" are performing members of the Judson Dance Theatre[4] in New York City.

The concern for activity with its concomitant movement rather than for movement in itself – for *what* is done rather than *how* it is done –

brings much new dance very close to Happenings and Events. And just as any performance may be called "music" with the justification that sound is involved, almost any performance may be referred to as "dance" when human movement is involved. Works which are not formally distinguishable from Happenings have been called dance pieces. Actually the most important differences among many of the performances in the new theatre – whether done by painters, sculptors, musicians, dancers, or professional theatre people – exist on stylistic rather than formal grounds. One wonders what difference it would make if *Check* by Robert Morris, for example, were called a Happening, and Claes Oldenburg's *Washes* were referred to as a dance.

• • •

Certain works have come out of the new theatre and out of the creative climate fostered by Cage which have pushed "performance" beyond the limits of theatre and offer new insights into the nature of performing and of theatre. Cage advocated the elimination of boundaries between art and life. The acceptance of chance is an acceptance of the laws of nature; and life, as illustrated in *4' 33"*, always participates in the totality of the perceived work of art. (This way of thinking means, for example, that a painting or sculpture is not the same in the gallery as it is in the studio.)

Performance and audience are both necessary to have theatre. But it might be thought that it is this very separation of spectator and work which is responsible for an "artificiality" of the form, and many Happenings and related pieces have attempted to "break down" the "barrier" between presentation and spectator and to make the passive viewer a more active participator. At any rate, works have recently been conceived which, since they are to be performed without an audience – a totally original and unprecedented development in art – might be called Activities.

In some of George Brecht's pieces the question of an audience seems ambiguous. Brecht's work implies that any performance piece has an aesthetic value for its performer or creator which is distinct from its value for an audience: the performance of *any* piece without an audience is a certain kind of art. Some of his things, such as the untitled child-thermometer-clock piece, are so intimate that spectators are obviously not intended or required.

Activities make it possible to work with time and space dimensions that would be very difficult or impossible in theatre. In *Chair* by Robert Ashley, for example, a wooden chair is variously transformed on each of six successive days. The lines in Stanley Brouwn's *Phonedrawings* exist only in the mind of the performer, who is aware that if the locations he has called on the telephone were connected (in the same way the child connects numbered dots to make a picture appear) the image he has chosen would actually exist on a vast scale. These works emphasize the private, proprioceptive, and cerebral aspects of Activities.

Allan Kaprow has performed pieces which also eliminate the audience but function on a much larger scale. Some of them, using many performers, resembled his Happenings except for the absence of spectators. The more recent pieces, although involving sizable numbers of performers, are more widely distributed through space and time so that the participants are frequently entirely separated from each other. Ken Dewey's recent works have mixed both Activity sections and units in which the assembled people functioned in the traditional passive manner of spectators.

Although these works, like Kaprow's *Eat* Environment, are outside the limits of theatre, they are related to the performance mentality, and they help to clarify some of the attitudes and concepts of the new theatre as well as providing fresh theoretical positions from which to evaluate theatre as a whole.

• • •

John Cage is emphasized as the touchstone of the new theatre for at least two reasons. In the first place, the body of his work – writings and lectures as well as musical compositions and performance pieces – gives clear precedents for many later developments. Secondly, many of the younger artists in the new theatre actually studied with Cage, although each creates in his own manner.

But there are at least as many reasons why the formulation I have presented is not wholly true or valid. As a simplification, it glosses over the exceptions and degrees of shading that any complete account should have. Actually, the new theatre has been in existence long enough for widening aesthetic ripples to spread far from the source. Each artist changes it. It has moved in various directions, making use of established techniques as well as the most recent developments in other fields and disciplines. Many of the artists producing Happenings, for example, are not fundamentally in sympathy with Cage's views, and their work is stylistically very different.

The emphasis on Cage may have implied that he is a completely original artist. This of course is not true. Completely original artists – like Dylan Thomas' "eggs laid by tigers" – do not exist. Actually each of the dimensions of Cage's work was prefigured in the work of the Futurists and the Dadaists, in Marinetti, Duchamp, and others. (Of course, much of this material had been available to everyone for a good number of years. It is to Cage's credit that he saw what was in it while others apparently did not.)

A sketch of the earlier history and origins of the new theatre would have to begin at least with the Italian Futurists, whose *bruitisme*, the use of everyday sounds and noises rather than those produced by traditional musical instruments, can be traced through Dada, the compositions of Erik Satie and Edgar Varése, and, finally, electronic music, which has as its material a sound spectrum of unprecedented width and variety. Although the Futurists apparently did not add nonmusical elements to their performances, their theoretical position provided the basis for the later expansion of music into performance.

In addition to their own "noise music" performed by "instruments" such as baby rattles and jangled keys and tin cans, the Dadaists in Zurich during the First World War and later in Paris read and recited simultaneous poems and manifestoes which were an early form of compartmentalization. (These and the Dada distortion of the lecture into a work of art prefigure certain aspects of Cage's lectures.) Unrelated "acts" were often performed at the same time, and the Dadaists presented what would now be referred to as Events: Philippe Soupault in his *Le célèbre illusioniste* (The Famous Magician) released balloons of various colors, each bearing the name of a famous man; Walter Serner, instead of reading a poem, placed a bouquet of flowers at the feet of a dressmaker's dummy; in their *Noir Cacadou* Richard Huelsenbeck and Tristan Tzara waddled around in a sack with their heads in a piece of pipe; Jean Arp recited his poems from inside a huge hat; and Georges Ribemont-Dessaignes danced inside a giant funnel. The Dadaists even staged a mock trial in front of an audience with "witnesses" called for the prosecution and the defense.

The intentional use of chance so important to Cage and some of the new theatre was also used by the Dadaists. Tristan Tzara composed and recited poems by mixing cards with words on them in a hat and drawing out the cards one at a time. Arp and Duchamp used chance in making paintings and constructions.

Surrealism also had its impact on the new theatre. It proposed the irrational as the material of art and stressed the dream, the obsessive act, the psychic accident; it supported automatism and chance as creative techniques and thus – after being driven from Europe to this country by the Second World War – provided the basis for Abstract Expressionism. (Although Cage accepted this concern with method, he differed sharply with later creators of Happenings such as Oldenburg and Whitman who stressed the unconscious affective aspects in their work.)

The Abstract Expressionist mentality which pervaded the New York art world in the late 1950s was one of the contributing factors in bringing painters into the performing arts. The *act* of painting rather than the completed composition had become the creative focus. At the same time painting and sculpture had a long tradition, in which Dada and Surrealism played their parts, of assemblage – the fabricating of a work from disparate objects and materials. Thus the artists found nothing strange about assembling a theatrical work from various types of alogically related performance material.

• • •

The new theatre is not important merely because it is new. But if it is agreed that a work of art may be important if only it is new – an aesthetic position which cannot be elaborated or defended here – then these works deserve serious consideration. Not only should they suggest to any practicing theatre artist new directions in which his work may go, but they represent several of the most significant developments in the history of theatre art.

In this theatre "suspension of disbelief" is not operative, and the absence of character and situation precludes identification. Thus the traditional mode of experiencing theatre, which has dominated both players and spectators for thousands of years, is altered.

As I have tried to show, structure and, almost always, the manner of performing are radically different in the new theatre. These innovations place theatre – in a very limited way – in some equivalency with the other arts. If painting and sculpture, for example, have not yet exhausted the possibilities of their nonobjective breakthrough (which occurred only three years after the start of this century), and if music has not yet begun to assimilate all the implications of its new-found electronic materials, there is every reason to feel that there will also be a fruitful aesthetic future for the new theatre.

NOTES

1. Of course the behavior in "real life" and onstage might not be exactly the same. A particular emotional reaction to facing an audience in the theatre situation could be expected. But while *created* or acted emotions are part of character matrix, *real* emotions are not. The question of emotion will be touched on again below.

2. Thus it is not essentially the degree of correlation between the written script and the performance which makes a theatre piece "literary." Whether or not it began from written material, any production, no matter how alogical, may be described in words, and the description could then be used as the literary basis for another production. On the other hand, there is the additional question of the latitude of interpretation allowed by a printed script – e.g., George Brecht's *Exit*, the "score" of which consists in its entirety of the single word with no directions or suggestions for interpretation and realization. *Any* written material, and even nonverbal material, may serve as the "script" for a performance.

3. The *use* of stage presence is an aesthetic question. Some performances place a high degree of emphasis upon it, while in others it is intentionally excluded or performers are employed *because* they are somewhat ill at ease.

4. Although traditional dance movements and techniques are not excluded, this emphasis on relatively simple kinds of movement has led to the style being labeled "anti-dance." In lieu of a more accurate term, the name has some usefulness, but the intent of the dancers is not to oppose or destroy dance but to eliminate what seems to be unnecessary conventions and restrictions, to approach movement in a fresh way, and to open new formal areas.

3

ALLAN KAPROW'S *EAT*

Michael Kirby

Eat, an Environment by Allan Kaprow, was presented during the mornings and afternoons of the two last weekends in January 1964. Prospective visitors made reservations through the Smolin Gallery and were given directions on getting to the caves in the Bronx in which the Environment was created. Only twenty reservations were made for each one-hour period in an attempt – almost always successful – to forestall overcrowding and keep free circulation in the space.

After entering an old building that fronted low cliffs, the visitor walked through several corridors and doorways and finally came to the Environment. The rock from which the caves were carved had been somewhat incompletely covered with white paint – the place had once been used by the Ebling Brewery – and age and seeping water had created a sense of decay. Black charred wooden beams stood propped against the walls in several places. Here and there water collected in depressions in the floor and trickled in rivulets through the dirt. Soft but steady ticking noises could be heard from several spots in the cave where battery-operated window-display devices had been hidden, and a man's voice called out, "Get 'em! Get 'em! Get 'em! . . ."

As the visitor moved from the antechamber through a stone arch and into the cave itself, he faced several wooden steps that led up to a low platform. At the far end of the platform more steps led down again to the cave floor. (This entrance to the main part of the cave was not mandatory. An unobstructed passage was possible along one wall.) At right angles to the entrance platform and crossing just under it was another platform, at either end of which stood a rectangular wooden tower about seven feet high. On each of these towers a girl sat motionless on a chair facing away from the entrance. The girl on the left had a gallon of red wine and the girl on the right had a gallon of white wine. If a visitor specifically asked her for wine, she poured some into a paper cup and handed it to him. The girls did not speak and seldom moved, except to pour.

Directly in front of the entrance, apples hung on rough strings from the ceiling. If the visitor wished, he could remove one of the apples and eat

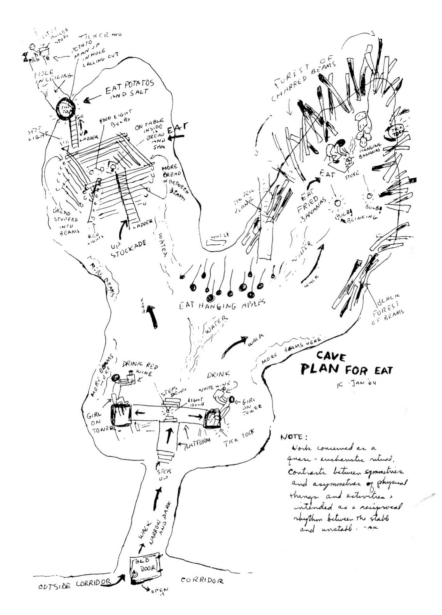

it or, if he was not very hungry, merely take a bite from it and leave it dangling.

To the right and left of the hanging apples, the cave divided into two large branches or bays of equal size. At the far end of the bay on the right, which contained many charred wooden beams, a girl sat at a small electric hot plate frying sliced bananas in brown sugar. If a spectator asked for some, she gave them to him, but she did not speak. Nearby, whole bunches of bananas wrapped in transparent plastic hung from the ceiling. If he wished (although no suggestions or instructions were ever

A view into the right bay of the cave Environment for Allan Kaprow's *Eat* (1964). The performer seated at left is serving fried bananas to two visitors. (Photo by Peter Moore.)

given) the visitor could take a banana and eat it.

In the left bay a square structure about eight feet high had been built of wooden beams. In the spaces between the beams and on a table inside the enclosure were loaves of sliced bread, jars of strawberry jam, and a few table knives. The only way to get inside the structure – and to get at most of the food – was to climb a tall ladder propped against the side.

At the rear of the bay another ladder leaned against the stone. It led to a small cave high in the wall, in which a man sat with a large pot. "Get 'em! Get 'em! Get 'em! . . .," he called out mechanically over and over, pausing occasionally for a while and then continuing again. If a visitor climbed the ladder, the man cut a piece of boiled potato, salted it, and gave it to him.

The visitors were free to wander about through the cave. Some ate and drank; others did not. At the end of the hour the remaining people were ushered out, the "performers" were replaced by fresh volunteers, and new visitors were allowed to enter.

4

AN INTERVIEW WITH JOHN CAGE

Michael Kirby and Richard Schechner

KIRBY: What's your definition of theatre?

CAGE: I try to make definitions that won't exclude. I would simply say that theatre is something which engages both the eye and the ear. The two public senses are seeing and hearing; the senses of taste, touch, and odor are more proper to intimate, nonpublic, situations. The reason I want to make my definition of theatre that simple is so one could view everyday life itself as theatre.

SCHECHNER: Is a concert a theatrical activity?

CAGE: Yes, even a conventional piece played by a conventional symphony orchestra: horn players, for example, from time to time empty the spit out of their horns. And this frequently engages my attention more than the melodies, harmonies, etc.

SCHECHNER: What about a mime troupe or dancers where sound is incidental? Their sound is silence. Would that be a theatrical activity also?

CAGE: Yes.

KIRBY: You say that absolute silence doesn't exist, so you wouldn't be able to separate seeing from hearing, right?

CAGE: Hearing would always be there and seeing too, if you have your eyes open.

KIRBY: How about listening to recorded music?

CAGE: I find that most interesting when one finds something in the environment to look at. If you're in a room and a record is playing and the window is open and there's some breeze and a curtain is blowing, that's sufficient, it seems to me, to produce a theatrical experience.

SCHECHNER: When I listen to recorded music – I'm really hung up on *The Messiah* –

CAGE: Hallelujah.

SCHECHNER: – I lie down and I close my eyes and I fantasize along with the music. That's how I get the most enjoyment out of music. I don't like concerts because I have to sit up.

CAGE: When you're lying down and listening you're having an intimate, interiorly realized theatre which I would – if I were going to exclude anything – exclude from my definition of theatre as a public occasion. In other words you're doing something by yourself that's extremely difficult to describe or relate to anyone accurately. I think of theatre as an occasion involving any number of people, but not just one.

KIRBY: You said once, "I try to get it so that people realize that they themselves are doing their experience and that it's not being *done* to them." Isn't all art done to you?

CAGE: It has been, but I think we're changing that. When you have the proscenium stage and the audience arranged in such a way that they all look in the same direction – even though those on the extreme right and left are said to be in "bad seats" and those in the center are in "good seats" – the assumption is that people will see *it* if they all look in one direction. But our experience nowadays is not so focused at one point. We live in, and are more and more aware of living in, the space around us. Current developments in theatre are changing architecture from the Renaissance notion to something else which relates to our lives. That was the case with the theatre in the round. But that never seemed to me any real change from the proscenium, because it again focused people's attention and the only thing that changed was that some people were seeing one side of the thing and the other people the other side.

It could of course produce more interesting conversation afterward or during intermission, because people didn't see the same side. It was like the story of the blind men with the elephant. More pertinent to our daily experience is a theatre in which we ourselves are in the round ... in which the activity takes place around us. The seating arrangement I had at Black Mountain in 1952 was a square composed of four triangles with the apexes of the triangles merging towards the center, but not meeting. The center was a larger space that could take movement, and the aisles between these four triangles also admitted movement. The audience could see itself, which is of course the advantage of any theatre in the round. The larger part of the action took place *outside* of that square. In each one of the seats was a cup, and it wasn't explained to the audience what to do with this cup –

some used it as an ashtray – but the performance was concluded by a kind of ritual of
pouring coffee into each cup.

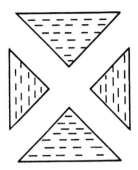

Black Mountain
performance (1952)
seating and stage space.

KIRBY: Could you describe the whole performance?

CAGE: At one end of the rectangular hall, the
long end, was a movie and at the other end
were slides. I was up on a ladder delivering a
lecture which included silences and there was
another ladder which M.C. Richards and
Charles Olsen went up at different times.
During periods that I called time brackets, the
performers were free within limitations – I think you would call them
compartments – compartments which they didn't have to fill, like a
green light in traffic. Until this compartment began, they were not free
to act, but once it had begun they could act as long as they wanted to
during it. Robert Rauschenberg was playing an old-fashioned phonograph that had a horn and a dog on the side listening, and David Tudor
was playing a piano, and Merce Cunningham and other dancers were
moving through the audience and around the audience. Rauschenberg's pictures were suspended above the audience –

KIRBY: Those were the "white paintings"?

CAGE: Right. He was also painting black ones at the time, but I think
we used only the white ones. They were suspended at various angles,
a canopy of painting above the audience. I don't recall anything else
except the ritual with the coffee cup. I remember a lady coming in at
the beginning who was the widow of the man who had formerly
headed the music department. She had made a point of coming very
early in order to get the best seat. And she asked me where the best
seat was and I said they were all equally good.

SCHECHNER: Did she believe you?

CAGE: Well, she saw that she wasn't getting a reply in relation to her
question so she simply sat down where she chose. She had no way, nor
did I, of telling where the best seat was, since from every seat you
would see something different.

SCHECHNER: One of the consequences of eliminating central focus is
that you do away with all the usual texts because they depend on
central focus. Let's take a very classical play, something like the

Oresteia ... in the multifocus thing do we no longer attempt the *Oresteia*, or do we have to restructure it?

CAGE: Our situation as artists is that we have all this work that was done before we came along. We have the opportunity to do work now. I would not present things from the past, but I would approach them as materials available to something else which we were going to do now. They could enter, in terms of collage, into any play. One extremely interesting theatrical thing that hasn't been done is a collage made from various plays.

Let me explain to you why I think of past literature as material rather than as art. There are oodles of people who are going to think of the past as a museum and be faithful to it, but that's not my attitude. Now as material it can be put together with other things. They could be things that don't connect with art as we conventionally understand it. Ordinary occurrences in a city, or ordinary occurrences in the country, or technological occurrences – things that are now practical simply because techniques have changed. This is altering the nature of music and I'm sure it's altering your theatre, say through the employment of color television, or multiple movie projectors, photo-electric devices that will set off relays when an actor moves through a certain area. I would have to analyze theatre to see what are the things that make it up in order, when we later make a synthesis, to let those things come in. Now in terms of music I thought of something manually produced, and then of something vocally produced, wind, etc. This includes all the literature. And then I thought of sounds we cannot hear because they're too small, but through new techniques we can enlarge them, sounds like ants walking in the grass. Other sounds are city sounds, country sounds, and synthetic sounds. I haven't analyzed all the things that go into theatre, but I think one could.

SCHECHNER: What are some of them?

CAGE: It's extremely complex because it involves, as I said earlier, seeing and hearing. We know, or think we know, what the aspects of sound are, what we can hear and how to produce sounds. But when you're involved with sight the situation becomes more complex. It involves color, light, shapes that are not moving, shapes that are moving; it involves what in Buddhism is called "nonsentient" being and then goes again in relation to what is called "sentient being" – animals, etc. I would refer back to Artaud's thinking about theatre. He made lists that could give ideas about what goes into theatre. And one should search constantly to see if something that could take place in theatre has escaped one's notice.

KIRBY: Do you believe that we'll ever get to a point where there won't be any unknowns left?

CAGE: I've been reading Buckminster Fuller lately and he said that we live in a finite world, and that the part we see as being relevant to our experience is "de-finite" and he sees two areas outside of that definite one which are still finite but which are either too big or too interior – too small – for us yet to have noticed and related to our daily experience.

KIRBY: We end up the same way, always with some unknowns left.

SCHECHNER: One of the consequences of this line of thinking is that the basic structure of theatre necessarily becomes altered. Once you remove action-focus you change the structure all the way up and down the line: modes of rehearsal to modes of production. In all the work of yours that I have read or heard there is a great feeling for structure. I wonder what kind of structure replaces the focus-structure?

CAGE: The structure we should think about is that of each person in the audience. In other words, his consciousness is structuring the experience differently from anybody else's in the audience. So the less we structure the theatrical occasion and the more it is like unstructured daily life the greater will be the stimulus to the structuring faculty of each person in the audience. If we have done nothing, he then will have everything to do.

SCHECHNER: Theatre before this time has depended upon a space structure, of which the focus was the most important thing. Kirby would call it an information structure, though I'm not sure that I would agree. Let's say an information-space structure. Are you suggesting that a duration structure replace the space-information structure?

CAGE: I did formerly. In 1952 we had a duration structure with compartments which had been arrived at by chance operations. But in my more recent work I'm concerned rather with what I call process – setting a process going which has no necessary beginning, no middle, no end, and no sections. Beginnings and endings can be given things but I try to obscure that fact, rather than to do anything like what I used to do, which was to measure it. The notion of measurement and the notion of structure are not notions with which I am presently concerned. I try to discover what one needs to do in art by observations from my daily life. I think daily life is excellent and that art introduces us to it and to its excellence the more it begins to be like it.

SCHECHNER: Is there a difference between a group of people deciding to go to the beach and watching what happens on the beach, and a group of people deciding to go to an Event or an Activity and watching or participating in it?

CAGE: If a person assumes that the beach is theatre and experiences it in those terms I don't see that there's much difference. It is possible for him to take that attitude. This is very useful because you often find yourself, in your daily life, in irritating circumstances. They won't be irritating if you see them in terms of theatre.

KIRBY: In other words, if you remove yourself from them?

CAGE: Can we say remove, or: use your faculties in such a way that you are truly the center? We've been speaking of the central factor being each person in the audience.

SCHECHNER: Let's take a hypothetical but possible event. I'm involved in an auto wreck in which I'm not hurt but in which my best friend is killed. Well, I imagine that's a few steps above irritating – but if I look at it as theatre, as happening to another but not to me, I can learn from the experience, respond to it but not be in it; then perhaps I can remove the irritants.

CAGE: I didn't mean by putting the person at the center that he wasn't in it, I meant rather to show him that he was at the very center of it.

SCHECHNER: I don't see how this can remove the irritation then.

CAGE: Do you know the Zen story of the mother who has just lost her only son? She is sitting by the road weeping and the monk comes along and asks her why she's weeping, and she says she's lost her only son, and he hits her on the head and says, "There, that'll give you something to cry about." Isn't there something of that same insistence in Artaud, in the business of the plague and of cruelty? Doesn't he want people to see themselves not in a pleasant world but in something that is the clue to all the things that we normally try to protect ourselves from?

SCHECHNER: Sure. My only quarrel is whether one really enjoys it or not. When the mother gets hit over the head she has two things to cry about.

Another thing about the structure. Isn't the difference between the beach and the theatre that the beach is not rehearsed and the theatre is? The thing that bothered me about the Happenings I've seen is that they were obviously rehearsed but badly done. Either they shouldn't have been rehearsed, or they shouldn't have gone halfway. In one

Happening there was a man choking another and it became very theatrical for me in a bad way, because I knew that they weren't really choking each other . . .

CAGE: And you knew what that word "theatrical" should mean . . .

SCHECHNER: Convincingly. Either they should have done it well or not at all.

CAGE: I couldn't be in greater agreement. If there are intentions, then there should be every effort made to realize those intentions. Otherwise carelessness takes over. However, if one is able to act in a way that doesn't have intention in it, then there is no need for rehearsal. This is what I'm working on now: to do something without benefit of measurement, without benefit of the sense that now that this is finished we can go on to the next thing.

Let me give you one example. In those two boxes over there are some ninety loops on tape. They vary from small loops that are just long enough for a tape machine, to ones which are, say, forty feet long. We gave a performance, last week, at Brandeis, with six performers – the number that turned up at the time that the set-up was made – and thirteen tape machines. The performance simply consisted of putting the loops on the various machines and taking them off. Doing this, a complex stage situation developed because we had to set up stands around which the tapes would go, and these things were overlapping. The number of loops made it fairly certain that there was no intention involved in putting on one rather than another loop. The number of people and the number of machines also created a situation that was somewhat free of intentions. Another way is by making use of electronic circuits to involve the performers in manipulating the amplifiers. Somebody might be working at a microphone or a cartridge point when another person is at the amplifier altering it. Both people are prevented from successfully putting through any intentions.

SCHECHNER: Both these cases depend upon the use of a machine which will short circuit human intention.

CAGE: If you have a number of people, then a nonknowledge on the part of each of what the other is going to do would be useful. Even if one of them was full of intentions, if none of them knew what the others' intentions were . . .

SCHECHNER: Even though each individual thing may be very structured? The combination would . . .

CAGE: ... tend in a nonintentional, unstructured direction, and would resemble what I referred to as daily life. If you go down the street in the city you can see that people are moving about with intention but you don't know what those intentions are. Many, many things happen which can be viewed in purposeless ways.

SCHECHNER: How do you take into account the fact that people, as soon as they become an audience, demand structure and impose it even if it's not there?

CAGE: Those people coming together to see a play come as it were to a salvation. If there is this lack of distinction between art and life, then one could say: Well, why have the arts when we already have it in life? A suitable answer from my point of view is that we thereby celebrate. We have a history in our culture of special occasions, and I don't see anything wrong with that, and I don't see anything wrong with doing something that's unnecessary.

KIRBY: Why didn't you go on doing the 1952 Black Mountain piece? It was given only once. It seems that you were somewhat disappointed with this piece and went in other directions ...

CAGE: No. One does what one does largely due to circumstances. When I was at Black Mountain I was working on a very time-consuming task – part of a project which involved the making of tape music by other composers: Morton Feldman, Christian Wolff, and Earle Brown. My piece alone took nine months of work, for composing and splicing. While I was working on those tape pieces I received a commission from Donaueschingen in Germany to make a piece for two prepared pianos. I wrote those *Timelength Pieces* for two pianos, and that interested me very much. Then I wrote a part for a percussion player and a part for a string player. My time was much taken up by work with Merce Cunningham and his dancers, by the tours and concerts, and lectures. So the interest in doing a specifically theatrical work was satisfied by the work with Cunningham, and then later by the *Theatre Piece* [1960].

SCHECHNER: How have all these things come together in your mind and work? You work in music, theatre, writing, lecturing, dance ...

CAGE: Mushrooms ...

SCHECHNER: That kind of range is very unusual today.

CAGE: Don't you think again we would have to trace circumstances? When I was just beginning I wrote a piece for a clarinet solo. Since I knew it was difficult to play I called up the first clarinetist of the Los

ST HELENS COLLEGE
Self Service Station

Demi-leigh Foster

RENEWAL   19/04/2017 15:20:14

1. 118665   Check-in: **17/05/2017**
   Happenings and other acts

2. 125000   Check-in: **17/05/2017**
   Avant-garde performance:

Angeles Philharmonic Orchestra. And when he looked at it he said, "That's not the way to write music." He thought I should write like most writers, so he was not going to play it, and advised me not to do the sort of thing that I was committed to doing. Then I made another stab at getting this piece done, and it failed again. That time not because the clarinetist wasn't willing to play it but because he didn't have the time to devote to learning to overcome its difficulties, and didn't choose to overcome them. The circumstances again. Then at just about that time I was called up by some modern dancers at UCLA, who actually wanted me to do something . . . and so I did it, and in that way I soon learned that if you were writing music that orchestras just weren't interested in – or string quartets, I made several attempts, I didn't give up immediately – that you could get things done very easily by modern dance groups. At the time I was interested in structure because I was fresh from working with Schoenberg. I thought that dealing with noises, as I was, I'd need another structure so I found this time structure and immediately was able to give it to the dancers to work with. Time was a common denominator between dance and music, rather than being specific to music as harmony and tonality were. I freed the dancers from the necessity to interpret music on the level of feeling; they could make a dance in the same structure that a musician was using. They could do it independently of one another, bringing their results together as pure hypothetical meaning. And we were always delighted to see that what we brought together worked. We thought it worked because we had a common structure, as if you, I, and Kirby decided to write a sonnet. We could do it two ways: we could write three sonnets and see that they were related to one another, or we could assign six lines to each, and find the results stimulating on an irrational level. Nevertheless these things do go together and we thought that they were together because of the structure. But then in circumstances that I recounted in a lecture called *Changes* [1958], which is in my book, and also in the *Lecture on Nothing* [1949; printed 1959], we discovered that more and more things we thought were necessary were not necessary. Things can be done without those precautions.

SCHECHNER: How did you move into the theatre thing?

CAGE: Experience with the dance led me there. The reflection that a human being isn't just ears, but has these eyes, I think it was this: around 1945/46/47 I became concerned about music – I think you know this story – and I determined not to continue with this activity unless it was useful, and unless I found answers that struck me as being sufficient reason to devote one's life to it. I found through

Oriental philosophy, my work with Suzuki, that what we are doing is living, and that we are not moving toward a goal, but are, so to speak, at the goal constantly and changing with it, and that art, if it is going to do anything useful, should open our eyes to this fact. Before the *Theatre Piece* I did two pieces for television. One was called *Water Walk* [1959] and one was called *Sounds of Venice* [1959]. I called it *Water Walk* because of the *Music Walk* [1958], and the *Music Walk*, I think you would agree, is a theatrical work. Before the *Music Walk* was the *Water Music*. Those titles wish to show that all those works are connected. The *Water Music* comes from 1952, I believe – the same year as the Black Mountain show – and was my immediate reaction to that event.

KIRBY: Could you describe it briefly?

CAGE: The *Water Music* wishes to be a piece of music, but to introduce visual elements in such a way that it can be experienced as theatre. That is, it moves towards theatre from music. The first thing that could be theatrical is what the pianist is looking at – the score. Normally nobody sees it but him, and since we're involved with seeing now, we make it large enough so that the audience can see it. I was working at the time on chance operations and a chart which enabled me to determine what sound pops up at what time and how loud, etc. So I simply put into the chart things that not only would produce sounds but that would produce actions that were interesting to see. I had somewhere gotten the notion that the world is made up of water, earth, fire, etc., and I thought that water was a useful thing to concentrate on. So the possibilities that I put into the chart involved, not exclusively, but largely, water.

KIRBY: What were some of these?

CAGE: Well, pouring water from one cup into another, using a whistle that requires water to produce sound, making that whistle descend into the water and come out of it.

KIRBY: Do you remember any of the nonwater images?

CAGE: There was a glissando on the keyboard, also a dominant 7th chord. I was already interested at that time in avoiding the exclusion of banal elements. In the development of twelve-tone music there was an emphasis on dissonance, to the exclusion, or very careful treatment, of consonances. Octaves as well as 5ths and particularly dominant 7ths and cadences became things that one shouldn't do. I've always been on the side of the things one shouldn't do and searching for ways of bringing the refused elements back into play. So I included sounds that were, just from a musical point of view, forbidden at that time. You could talk to any modern composer at the time and no matter how enlightened he was he would refuse to include banal musical sounds.

SCHECHNER: When you came to the *Theatre Piece* in 1960 . . .

CAGE: Before that came a time-length piece, which is thirty-four minutes for a pianist predominantly. I had been commissioned to write a piece for two prepared pianos, but I introduced an "x" concept of auxiliary noises. Thus I had other groups of noises: one was produced inside the piano, one was produced outside the piano but on it, and then there were noises separated from the piano – whistles. The parts are not in a scored relation, they are independent of one another. Then I wrote a lecture to go with them, involving combing the hair and kiss sounds and gestures that made the lecture theatrical. So I think you could find the theatrical continuing in my work.

In Milan, when I was invited to perform on a quiz show, the first performance was of *Amores* [1943], an early piece for prepared piano, and the next two especially for television. I used the *Fontana Mix* [1958]. They are overlaying transparencies involving points and curvy lines which don't cross over themselves. A given line doesn't cross over itself but it goes in curving, meandering ways from one side of the page to another. These curving lines are six in number and are differentiated by thickness (three are dotted) and you simply place them over the sheet with points – one sheet with points and one sheet with curved lines – and then a graph which is a hundred units in one direction and twenty in the other. There is a straight line used to connect a point that is outside the graph with one that is inside, and one measures the intersection of the curved lines with this straight line with reference to the graph vertically, to determine the kind of thing that would happen. The horizontal measurement gives the time. I used the *Fontana Mix* to make a tape piece, and I used it to make television pieces. I don't think I used all six of the lines. I used as many as I thought were necessary. And then I made lists of actions that I was willing to involve myself in. Then through the intersection of those curved lines and the straight line I could see within what amount of time I had, for instance, to put a rose in a bathtub, if that came up. If at the same time playing a particular note – or not a particular note – on the piano came up, those two things had to get done within the time allotted. I ended up with six parts which I then rehearsed very carefully, over and over and over again with people watching me and correcting me, because I had to do it within three minutes. It had many actions in it and it demanded what you might call virtuosity. I was unwilling to perform it until I was certain that I could do it well.

KIRBY: You say there were many things you had to do within the three-minute time; could you mention a few of them?

CAGE: They're all listed in the score. What is more interesting, I think, is that my chart included far more activity than came up through the measurements, so that a lot of my preparatory planning and thinking was, from a normal point of view, wasted.

SCHECHNER: Have the charts been published?

CAGE: You can buy them, you can buy the *Fontana Mix*, and you can also buy the *Theatre Piece*. The *Theatre Piece* carries this kind of activity up to an abstract point, because none of the things to be done are verbalized. But what an actor will do in a given time space is up to him. He follows my directions – and I think many people perform that piece without following my directions – and puts verbs and nouns on cards. He conceals the order from himself by shuffling the cards. Then he lays them out so he can tell which is one and which is two, up to twenty. Reading the numbers, which are the only things which are in my score, he will be able to make a program of action just as I made one for the *Water Walk*. And if he did it as I did it he would, I know, arrive at a complex situation. But what people tend to do is to get ideas of what they think will be interesting and these, of course, are a limited number of things, because their imaginations are lazy, and they do fewer things rather than more and they are satisfied to do one thing over an inordinately long duration.

SCHECHNER: Did you originally perform the *Theatre Piece* yourself?

CAGE: No. I might be said to have conducted it. I acted as a clock simply because we couldn't lay our hands on a large enough clock for everyone to see.

SCHECHNER: How many people does it involve?

CAGE: Eight. And I think it says in my directions that if you want more material you can apply to me for it, or you could take those eight, divide them in half and get sixteen, etc.

SCHECHNER: That was 1960, and that's still a highly structured piece of work . . .

CAGE: No. It has what Kirby would call "compartments," but these overlap in a way that is quite complex. The notion of an overall structure is not in the work.

SCHECHNER: But there is on each card a thing, there is a word.

CAGE: Each sheet takes up many of these compartments and can amount to as much time as a performer chooses.

SCHECHNER: There's a development from *Water Walk* to this, and during the next five years from this to the position we talked about at the beginning . . .

CAGE: *Theatre Piece* was composed in terms of what I would call process rather than structure. When we do anything and bring it to a performance, it reaches to a point that becomes realization. At that realization point it can be viewed, as we said earlier, as structured, though it wasn't.

SCHECHNER: So the structure is the observer's and not the piece's.

CAGE: When I was writing the *Theatre Piece* I started out in terms of process, just overlaying these things and taking measurements, and I went far enough with that concept to put it on paper, but not to specify verbally. I left that up to the performer. I stopped the process before it was realized, leaving the realization up to the individual. This is why: I had a conversation earlier that year with Karlheinz Stockhausen and he asked, "If you were writing a song would you write for the singer or would you write music?" I said I would write for the singer. He said, "That's the difference between us, I would write music." He was at the time thinking about writing a song for Cathy Berberian and he wanted to make use of as many ways of vocal production as he could think of. He was interested in African clicking, and she was able to do that, so he put it in. He was also interested in whistling. It didn't occur to him that she couldn't whistle. She's absolutely incapable of whistling. So he gave her things to do which she was unable to do. That was why I left the *Theatre Piece* unspecified. I didn't want to ask anyone to do something he couldn't do.

KIRBY: The words could be taken by chance from a dictionary . . .

CAGE: Right.

KIRBY: Yet they're supposed to be the basis of the action.

CAGE: Right. I wanted to leave the performer free. I didn't want him to get involved in a situation that he wasn't willing to carry through.

SCHECHNER: What happened after the *Theatre Piece*?

CAGE: At about that time my music was published, and it took a long time to make up a catalog for it. In 1958 I began some pieces called *Variations*. The first one was involved with the parameters of sound, the transparencies overlaid, and each performer making measurements that would locate sounds in space. Then, while I was at Wesleyan, in this first piece I had had five lines on a single transparent sheet, though I had had no intention of putting them the way I did, I just drew them quickly. At Wesleyan while talking to some students it suddenly occurred to me that there would be much more freedom if I put only a single line or a single notation on a single sheet. So I did that, but it still involved measurement. *Variations III* came along [1963]. I had been working very early with structure, with this process which could be seen as structure; it always involved space, which struck me as distinguishing what we now call neo-Dada from earlier Dada. I admired most modern architecture with all its open space. I admired those Japanese gardens with just a few stones. I had been committed to the notion of activity and nonactivity, just as earlier I had been committed to sound and silence.

Just as I came to see that there was no such thing as silence, and so wrote the *Silent Piece*, I was now coming to the realization that there was no such thing as nonactivity. In other words the sand in which the stones in a Japanese garden lie is also something. Why that had not been evident to me before, I don't know. There isn't any nonactivity. Or, as Jasper Johns says, looking at the world, "It appears to be very busy." And so I made *Variations III*, which leaves no space between one thing and the next and posits that we are constantly active, that these actions can be of any kind, and all I ask the performer to do is to be aware as much as he can of how many actions he is performing. I ask him, in other words, to count. That's all I ask him to do. I ask him even to count passive actions, such as noticing that there is a noise in the environment. We move through our activity without any space between one action and the next, and with many overlapping actions. The thing I don't like about *Variations III* is that it requires counting, and I'm now trying to get rid of that. But I thought that performance was simply getting up and then doing it.

SCHECHNER: There is a contradiction here.

CAGE: You won't find me logical.

SCHECHNER: No, not that kind of contradiction. You say that these things should be somehow like everyday life. And yet in hearing you talk, or listening to the composition, they're anything but like everyday life. The action may be as random as everyday life, but the visual and aural effect is most unusual and strange.

CAGE: Yes, but I think that when nonintention underlies it – even though it is strange and special, and for that reason suitable for a celebration – it does relate to daily life. Many people have told me after a concert that they notice changes in perception of everyday life.

SCHECHNER: Sure it is related and sharpens one's perceptions – simply because it makes one pay attention. But . . .

CAGE: The attitude that I take is that everyday life is more interesting than forms of celebration, when we become aware of it. That *when* is when our intentions go down to zero. Then suddenly you notice that the world is magical.

From a musical point of view, and I'm sure from the visual point of view, one thing makes everyday life far more fascinating and special than, say, concert life. That is the variety of sound with respect to all the other things, including space. When we make electronic music, we have to flood the hall with sound from a few loudspeakers. But in our everyday life sounds are popping up, just as visual things and moving things are popping up, everywhere around us. I would like to imitate that – to present fantastic architectural and technological problems. That's how the theatre will be. We have in America two or three loudspeakers in a theatre, in Europe they have them up in the teens, and I think in the hundreds in Russia, so that sounds can move or appear to come from any point in space, generally around the shell. I would also like it to appear, as I think it will with transistor means, in the center of the space. And then there's mobility too. When a fly buzzes past me now I have, from an artistic point of view, a frightful problem. But it's quite reasonable to imagine that we will have a loudspeaker that will be able to fly through space.

SCHECHNER: Amplifications of sounds are so very un-everyday-life-ish simply because they're so amplified.

CAGE: I agree with you. I only said what I said in order to show that one needn't agree with you. Alan Watts came to a concert once, and left very shortly because, as he said, "I can hear this sort of thing outside, I don't need to be here."

SCHECHNER: It would be a good thing to take people to watch something out there, to create in the "out-there" a celebratory situation, if not a play.

CAGE: That was so touching in *Miracle in Milan*: people seated in rows to look at the sunset. What is so interesting about modern art and Pop Art in this country is that it has more and more trained our eyes not on the most noticeable things, but on the things generally overlooked.

SCHECHNER: Which are very much there; when we are asked to look at them, they are translated into something they were not intended for. These Madison Avenue images were intended to engage us, and the result of Pop Art is to disengage us. So that when we face them again in reality we're looking at them as themselves and not as what they're luring us to do. The painting separates us from the intention of the billboard. When you see the face or the can or the girl the first time you are moved to do something; you see the painting and then see her again on the billboard, you're moved just to look at her but not do what the sign tells you to do. A very interesting basic freedom is involved in Pop Art . . . you're no longer compelled to go out and buy. Do these theatre experiences have a similar thrust?

CAGE: Yes. We can become more aware and furthermore we can become more curious.

KIRBY: When you taught at the New School, around 1956, you worked with performance material as well as with music. What kind of assignments did you give?

CAGE: The course generally began with my trying to bring the students to the point of knowing who I was, that is, what my concerns and activities were, and I wanted them to find out who they were and what they were doing. I wasn't concerned with a teaching situation that involved a body of material to be transmitted by me to them. I would, when it was necessary, give them a survey of earlier works, by me and by others, in terms of composition, but mostly I emphasized what I was doing at that time and would show them what I was doing and why I was interested in it. Then I warned them that if they didn't want to change their ways of doing things, they ought to leave the class, that it would be my function, if I had any, to stimulate them to change.

SCHECHNER: Did many leave?

CAGE: Well there never were many and they mostly stayed. Eight or ten at the most. Some people did quite conventional musical work, they knew that I would try to get them to budge a bit. And some of them did. After this basic introduction, the classes consisted simply in their showing what they had done. And if I had anything to say I would say it. I also got them to say things about their work . . . but this is a common progressive education practice isn't it? We had very little to work with: a closet full of percussion instruments, a broken-down piano, and things that people brought with them. The room was very small, so we simply did what we could do in that room.

I reminded them that because we had so little they had to do things that would nevertheless work. I didn't want them making things that couldn't be done. Practicality has always seemed to me to be of the essence. I hate the image of an artist who makes things that can't be done.

KIRBY: Wasn't it surprising to have painters in a music class like that?

CAGE: It wasn't surprising to me because I had, before that, in the late 1940s and the early 1950s, been part and parcel of the Artists Club. I had early seen that musicians were the people who didn't like me. But the painters did. The people who came to the concerts which I organized were very rarely musicians – either performing or composing. The audience was made up of people interested in painting and sculpture.

SCHECHNER: What kind of dialog came out of your class?

CAGE: You mean what could a painter do with this kind of situation?

SCHECHNER: What *did* they do?

CAGE: But you know that. It's a matter of history now. Allan Kaprow introduced the element of time more and more into his work. Normally a musician writes in measures, and then assigns to the unit of those measures a metronomic figure. So we have *andante* and *largo* and all those things. In a piece called the *Music of Changes* [1951], which I composed for the *Book of Changes*, all the things I could discern in a piece of music were subjected to chance operation. Among the things I noticed and subjected to chance operation was tempo. If you look at the *Music of Changes* you see that every few measures, at every structural point, things were speeding up or slowing down or remaining constant. How much these things varied was chance determined. David Tudor learned a form of mathematics which he didn't know before in order to translate those tempo indications into actual time. It was a very difficult process and very time-consuming for him. After that I altered my way of composing; I didn't write in tempos but always in times. By the time I was teaching at the New School this was one of the facts of my work, and they caught on readily because it gives one enormous facility in the field of time to know by means of a clock when something's got to start.

SCHECHNER: Why do you think this kind of thing turns painters on?

CAGE: I think that Kirby has indicated that in his introduction to the book on Happenings.

SCHECHNER: A lot of your own work seems to be very different in substance, if not in underlying theory, from Happenings.

CAGE: In Kirby's introduction he searches to do something fairly precisely which I've said I don't like myself to do, namely to make a definition. In making that definition he was brought to excluding the *Motor Vehicle Sundown (Event)* of George Brecht [1960] from the category of Happenings simply because it didn't involve intention. Am I right?

KIRBY: I think at the time I made the definition I was thinking of another category of Chance Theatre. I've changed my opinion somewhat since then.

CAGE: And you wanted in the case of Happenings to set up a notion of an intentional theatre that was alogical and nonmatrixed?

KIRBY: Yes.

CAGE: I have felt the presence of intention in an alogical continuity to be something that doesn't interest me, for this reason: does not the term "alogical" mean that anything can happen?

KIRBY: I was thinking that there weren't any intellectual relationships; it wasn't either logical or illogical.

CAGE: That will be very hard to prove. In Kaprow's Happening with the mountain, he says that there is this symbol business about the girl . . .

KIRBY: I agree with you about that piece, as I tried to explain in the introduction to *Happenings*. Most of *The Courtyard* [Kaprow, 1962] I consider an allegorical play rather than a Happening.

CAGE: And the Earth Mother. That strikes me as drawing relationships between things, in accord with an intention. If we do that, I think then we have to do it better than people in history did it. Happenings don't do it better because they have this thing we've spoken of as carelessness in them. Carelessness comes about through – to use your words – "nonmatrixed activity." The only way you're going to get a good performance of an intentional piece, that furthermore involves symbols and other relationships which the artist has drawn in his mind, is to have lots of rehearsals, and you're going to have to do it as well as you can; rather than using one symbol you might find another more effective symbol. You're involved in a whole thing that we have been familiar with since the Renaissance and before.

I think what we're doing is something else and not that. So when I go to a Happening that seems to me to have intention in it I go away saying that I'm not interested. I also did not like to be told, in the *18 Happenings in 6 Parts* [Kaprow, 1959], to move from one room to another. Though I don't actively engage in politics I do as an artist have some awareness of art's political content, and it doesn't include policemen.

I think we all realize that anarchy is not practical; the lovely movement of philosophical anarchism in the United States that did quite a lot in the nineteenth century finally busted up because in the large population centers its ideas were not practical. We look at our lives, at the anarchist moments, or spaces, or times, or whatever you want to call them, and there these things that I'm so interested in – awareness, curiosity, etc. – have play. It is not during organized or policed moments that these things happen. I admit that in a policed circumstance I can take an aesthetic attitude and enjoy it, just as I can listen to Beethoven in a way other than he intended and enjoy it on my terms. But why do you think that so many Happenings have become intentional?

I think that those people for one reason or another are interested in themselves. I came to be interested in anything but myself. This is the difference. When I say that anything can happen I don't mean anything that *I want* to have happen.

SCHECHNER: But don't you in some way structure your work?

CAGE: You're aiming now at a purity which we are never going to achieve. When we say "purposelessness" we add "purposeful purpose-lessness." You'll find this more and more being recognized not as double talk, but as truth. That's why I don't like definition; when you succeed in defining and cutting things off from something, you thereby take the life out of it. It isn't any longer as true as it was when it was incapable of being defined.

KIRBY: But some people can't do things unless you define them for them.

CAGE: That kind of sight is not going to enable them to see. The whole desire for definitions has to do with the Renaissance in which we demanded clarity and got it. Now we are not in such a period and such definitions are no longer of use to us.

The difficulty with the theatre, as I see it, is that it has – because of the complexity involved and probably because of the economics – tended to close the circle around it rather than to open it out. This is true also of the symphony orchestra. Whether or not people inside the circle are going to enter into the dialog is very much an open question. Occasions will arise when dialogs will occur, but in the case of theatre it's extremely difficult. I was up at Wesleyan University for discussions about the performing arts. There was a man who had performed Hamlet at the Tyrone Guthrie ...

SCHECHNER: George Grizzard?

CAGE: Yes. And a director associated with him.

SCHECHNER: Alan Schneider?

CAGE: Alan Schneider. I certainly wouldn't have gone had I known what was going to take place. It was a warm evening and they began by taking their coats off, and trying to give the feeling of informality, and they went so far as not to use the chairs but to sit on the table which had been placed in front of them. They proceeded to say that they had nothing to tell the audience, that what they wanted were ideas from the audience, in other words they wanted to have a discussion. Of course there were no questions. So they had to chat and supplement one another's loss of knowledge of what to do next. The whole thing was absolutely disgusting: the kind of ideas and the kinds of objectives, the vulgarity of it, was almost incomprehensible. The chairman of the meeting was also disgusted and at one point he interrupted Schneider and Grizzard and knowing that I was in the audience, asked me to speak my piece. I asked them what they thought of Happenings, and learned that they had no knowledge of them whatsoever. They don't go. They weren't interested. They were concerned with the *Hamlet* situation.

SCHECHNER: This is the difficulty. When a painter comes to a Happening he brings a painting tradition, when a musician comes he brings with him a music tradition, but no one in the theatre brings anything –

CAGE: Except a quality of mind, namely a tremendous ego. You could see that in Grizzard. He kept being humble in order to show that he wasn't so stuck up. But it was clear that he was as stuck on himself as he could be, and that he wanted the best thing to happen to him that could happen. He thought it was nice and ethical of him to have preferred to do *Hamlet* instead of something on Broadway. That kind of shoddy ethic is just intolerable.

I said this sort of thing. I was quite heated, I normally don't like to talk against things, but I had been asked to. When we couldn't discuss Happenings because they had no knowledge nor interest and didn't think it was as serious as *Hamlet* and thought they were being virtuous, then I said, "Well, what do you think about TV?" They weren't interested in TV. And yet they're living in an electronic world where TV is of far more relevance than the legitimate theatre.

Why don't we think of those theatre people as what they are? They're a form of museum. And we are going to have museums and we should just be grateful to them for doing what they're doing and not bother them.

Let me add something that I think might illuminate this. What is the primary concern of the dramatist and the actor? It is content, in any way that you interpret content. But Marshall McLuhan in his work on mass media, begins by saying that content is of no importance. He says "the medium is the message." And he says you can only come to this conclusion and this awareness if you divorce yourself from thoughts of content. This is very similar to my statement about divorcing oneself from thoughts of intention, they go very well together. What does McLuhan see as activity for an artist? It's perfectly beautiful, and every time we see it now we enjoy it: he says all we have to do is brush information against information, and it doesn't matter what. By that brushing we will be made aware of the world which itself is doing that.

5

LECTURE 1960

La Monte Young

Author's Note: This lecture was written in the summer of 1960. I first
delivered it simultaneously with a performance of a tape recording of my
Trio for Strings during a course in contemporary music that Terry Riley
and I gave at the Ann Halprin Dancers' Workshop in Kentfield, California,
summer session 1960. In the fall of 1960, I delivered *Lecture 1960*
simultaneously with Robert Dunn's tape realization of my *Poem for
Chairs, Tables and Benches, etc.* utilizing The Piano Sound from *Vision*
as the sound source, at one of Richard Maxfield's 340 West 88th Street,
Manhattan, studio sessions of his New School for Social Research
Seminar in Electronic Music.

    The lecture is written in sections which are separated below. Each
section originally was one page or a group of pages stapled together. Any
number of them may be read in any order. The order and selection are
determined by chance, thereby bringing about new relationships between
parts and consequently new meanings. Three sections of the lecture were
first published in KULCHUR 10, Summer 1963. Below is the entire
lecture as it was published in the 1965 *TDR* Happenings issue.

La Monte Young, 1994

My *Composition 1960 #9* consists of a straight line drawn on a piece of
paper. It is to be performed and comes with no instructions. The night I
met Jackson Mac Low we went down to my apartment and he read some
of his poems for us. Later, when he was going to go home, he said he'd
write out directions to get to his place so we could come and visit him
sometime. He happened to pick up *Composition 1960 #9* and said, "Can
I write it here?" I said, "No, wait, that's a piece. Don't write on that." He
said, "Whadaya mean a piece? That's just a line."

While Dennis Johnson was preparing *Avalanche #1* in Los Angeles he
sent me a letter describing parts of the concert. The last piece on the

program was to be his composition, *Din*. In *Din* the performers (he hoped for at least forty) are placed in the audience ahead of time. The composition is performed in the dark. The performers have various noises to articulate. There are solo noises, noises produced by small groups, and noises produced by the entire ensemble. Some of the noises are shouting, clapping, screaming, talking about anything, whispering about anything, stamping of feet, shuffling of feet, and various combinations of these. Most of the solo sounds are unique and not easily described. Some of the sound textures in the piece are two and three minutes long, and there are often long silences between them. The spectators, of course, were not to be told that the performers were among them. As I mentioned, this piece was to end the program. Dennis wrote, "After clap piece," (he had not then named it *Din*) "is over (and the concert over also) the people will remain in the dark and silence forever or at least until they decide to leave as we will not prompt them with any more lights or any kind of please leave signal." When we performed *Avalanche #1* it was an intense and very new situation. *Din* was glorious. After it was over we sneaked out of the auditorium to watch and see if and when the audience would ever come out. One of the few readable sentences on the programs we had distributed at the doors read, "Concert is three hours long Concert is three hours long Concert is thr" written all the way across the page. There was at least half an hour left. We waited. What little of the audience still remained finally came out a few at a time. At last two enraged critics from the UCLA paper came over to us and asked if we had any statement to make about the concert before they crucified us in Monday's edition. I looked around and found a paper in my pocket. It was the performing instructions for *Din*. I said, "Yes, I would like to say something." I read, "Shuffle feet for 260." They said, "Is that all?" I said, "Yes." They went away. Then somebody asked, "Are you a part of Zen?" Dennis said, "No, but Zen is a part of us."

❀❀❀❀❀❀

One night, Diane[1] said, "Maybe the butterfly piece should begin when a butterfly happens to fly into the auditorium."

Often I hear somebody say that the most important thing about a work of art is not that it be new but that it be good. But if we define good as what we like, which is the only definition of good I find useful when discussing art, and then say that we are interested in what is good, it seems to me that we will always be interested in the same things (that is, the same things that we already like).

I am not interested in good; I am interested in new – even if this includes the possibility of its being evil.

●

Diane suggested that perhaps the reason the director of the noon concerts at the University would not allow me to perform *Composition 1960 #5* on the third concert of contemporary music that we gave was that he thought it wasn't music. *Composition 1960 #5* is the piece in which the butterfly or any number of butterflies is turned loose in the performance area. I asked her if she thought the butterfly piece was music to any less degree than *Composition 1960 #2* which consists of simply building a fire in front of the audience. She said, "Yes, because in the fire piece at least there are some sounds." I said that I felt certain the butterfly made sounds, not only with the motion of its wings but also with the functioning of its body and that unless one was going to dictate how loud or soft the sounds had to be before they could be allowed into the realms of music that the butterfly piece was music as much as the fire piece. She said she thought that at least one ought to be able to hear the sounds. I said that this was the usual attitude of human beings that everything in the world should exist for them and that I disagreed. I said it didn't seem to me at all necessary that anyone or anything should have to hear sounds and that it is enough that they exist for themselves. When I wrote this story out for this lecture I added, "If you think this attitude is too extreme, do you think sounds should be able to hear people?"

●

When I sent *Compositions 1960 Numbers 2–5* to some of my friends, I received different comments from all of them concerning which ones they liked or disliked with one exception. Almost all of them wrote back to me saying they liked "Number 5" which consists, quite simply, of turning a butterfly or any number of butterflies loose in the auditorium. Diane agreed that it was a very lovely piece and said it would seem almost impossible for anyone not to like it. At any rate, I had hoped to perform either *Composition 1960 #2*, which consists of building a fire in front of the audience, or *Composition 1960 #5*, the butterfly piece, on whatever program came up next. Thus, when the time arrived to do another noon concert of contemporary music at the University in Berkeley, I told a friend who was communicating with the director of the noon concerts that I would like to do either *Composition 1960 #2* or *#5*. The next day he phoned and said he had asked the director. The director had said that both pieces were absolutely out of the question. I was shocked. I could easily understand anyone's concern for a fire in the auditorium, but what could be wrong with a butterfly? Well, *Composi-*

tions 1960 Numbers 2 and 5 were banned from the auditorium and we performed *Composition 1960 #4* instead.

Sometime afterward Diane received a letter from Susan, who was visiting in New York. At the end of the letter she wrote, "I saw a boy in the park today running, quite terrified, from a small yellow butterfly."

When Dennis Johnson and I were staying at Richard Maxfield's apartment in New York, we discussed the amount of choice that a composer retained in a composition that used chance or indeterminacy. We generally agreed that the composer was always left with some choices of one sort or another. At the very least, he had to decide what chances he would take or what he would leave to indeterminacy in his composition. Some time after Dennis and I had both left New York he visited me from Los Angeles. He brought me a copy of his then new composition, *The Second Machine*, which we were going to do on a program of contemporary music at the University in Berkeley along with Cage's *Imaginary Landscapes #4 For Twelve Radios* (which Dennis was conducting), Richard Maxfield's *Cough Music*, and *Vision*, a piece of my own. A short time after he had arrived at my apartment in Berkeley Dennis mentioned that he had been thinking of what we had discussed in New York and that he had discovered a piece which was entirely indeterminacy and left the composer out of it. I asked, "What is it?" He tore off a piece of paper and wrote something on it. Then he handed it to me. It said, "LISTEN."

I recently completed *Compositions 1960 Numbers 2 Through 5. Composition 1960 #2* reads:

> Build a fire in front of the audience. Preferably, use wood although other combustibles may be used as necessary for starting the fire or controlling the smoke. The fire may be of any size, but it should not be the kind which is associated with another object, such as a candle or a cigarette lighter. The lights may be turned out.

> After the fire is burning, the builder(s) may sit by and watch it for the duration of the composition; however, he (they) should not sit between the fire and the audience in order that its members will be able to see and enjoy the fire.

> The composition may be of any duration.

In the event that the performance is broadcast, the microphone may be brought up close to the fire.

Composition 1960 #5 reads:

Turn a butterfly (or any number of butterflies) loose in the performance area.

When the composition is over, be sure to allow the butterfly to fly away outside.

The composition may be any length, but if an unlimited amount of time is available, the doors and windows may be opened before the butterfly is turned loose and the composition may be considered finished when the butterfly flies away.

Some time after the pieces were finished I sent copies around to some of my friends. After a few weeks, Tony Conrad wrote back from Denmark that he enjoyed the fire music very much, that he thought the sounds of a fire were very lovely and that he had even, himself, once considered using the sounds of fire in a composition although he had not at that time been prepared to write anything like *Composition 1960 #2*. He said, however, that he didn't understand *Composition 1960 #5*. In my answering letter I wrote, "Isn't it wonderful if someone listens to something he is ordinarily supposed to look at?"

In another letter Terry Jennings wrote, "the cat is in the middle of time. his tail sometimes hits the sky (just the low parts below the branches.) he lies down a lot"

I have finally begun to hear from Dennis Johnson again. Terry Riley wrote me from San Francisco: "guess what? ———— dennis is here ———— he came in new years eve ———— we went out to ann halprins yesterday and dennis did some real good things like take a shower in her shower while her little girls looked on and went down the road and borrowed an onion from a neighbor and stuff like that . . ."

Every word I say contributes to the lie of art.

Once when Richard Maxfield, Dennis Johnson, and I were talking about Christian Wolff at Richard's apartment in New York Dennis said, "He's only a wolf in a gilded cage." More recently, Richard and I were discussing how original Christian Wolff had been and how many of his ideas had been ahead of everybody. Richard said, "Perhaps what Dennis should have said was that John is only a cage around a gilded wolf." When I told these stories to Diane she said, "They both seem to be wrong. Dennis should have said, 'He's only a gilded wolf in a cage,' and Maxfield should have said, 'John is only a gilded cage around a wolf.'" After Diane and I had decided what everybody meant and should have said, I concluded it didn't really matter anyway since the whole series of stories simply amounted to a study in tarnish.

It is often necessary that one be able to ask, "Who is John Cage?"

Before we gave the first noon concert of contemporary music which I conducted at the University of California at Berkeley, I asked Dennis Johnson if he would write something about his composition, *The Second Machine*, which we were doing on the program because I planned to comment on each piece. Dennis wrote:

> Spin the needle three times. If it ever falls off, don't bother. Cheating is all right, as much as comfortable. I don't know how many possibilities and see if I care. The scores are fire and water proof. Play on either side or the edge, if you get tired, and don't call me for information while I'm burning old scores. May be played under water.

At the end he signed his name, Dennis Johnson.

Last year on one of the occasions I was in Los Angeles, several of us were at my grandmother's house listening to electronic music by Richard Maxfield which he had just sent me from New York. As we were listening my grandmother, who has never been particularly good at keeping things straight, asked Dennis Johnson, "Did you write this?" referring to Maxfield's composition, *Sine Music*. Dennis replied "Oh, many times."

When Karlheinz Stockhausen gave a lecture at the University in Berkeley he talked of some work he had been doing with television. He said he tried to let the new medium, the television machine, inspire the form of the composition. At this point someone in the audience said to his neighbor, "But I thought music was supposed to be for people."

*One of my favourite poets is Po Chu-i. He lived from 772–846. This poem
is translated by Ching Ti.*

The Harp
I lay my harp on the curved table,
Sitting there idly, filled only with emotions.
Why should I trouble to play?
A breeze will come and sweep the strings.

I wish I could remember what Terry Jennings told us about that spider
that is found in Antarctica. It was when Terry visited New York. We were
having dinner and I started asking him about what kinds of animals and
plants lived in Antarctica. He said that the scientists had discovered a
spider that stays frozen most of the year around. It seems like he said,
"About eleven months of the year." Then, when the warmer weather
comes, the spider thaws out and comes to life – for about a month. He
also said that maybe the spider lives to be many years old. I think he said,
"Maybe a hundred or a hundred and sixty years old."

•

When I asked Diane to write down Dennis' statement about his having
written Maxfield's *Sine Music* many times, Dennis said, "What for? Are
you going to give another concert?"

Anarchy

The trouble with most of the music of the past is that man has tried to
make the sounds do what he wants them to do. If we are really interested
in learning about sounds, it seems to me that we should allow the sounds
to be sounds instead of trying to force them to do things that are mainly
pertinent to human existence. If we try to enslave some of the sounds and
force them to obey our will, they become useless. We can learn nothing
or little from them because they will simply reflect our own ideas. If,
however, we go to the sounds as they exist and try to experience them
for what they are – that is, a different kind of existence – then we may
be able to learn something new. A while back, when Terry Riley and I
first met Ann Halprin, we worked with her many times doing improvisations. It was very enjoyable. I remember one night when it took one
of the dancers, who was hanging from the wall, at least half an hour to
work his way around the room. These evenings were especially

conducive to the discovery of new sounds. We found many we had never heard before. Along with the new sounds, of course, we found new ways of producing them, and we also reconsidered sounds we had never previously listened to so closely. Sometimes we produced sounds that lasted over an hour. If it was a loud sound my ears would often not regain their normal hearing for several hours, and when my hearing slowly did come back it was almost as much a new experience as when I had first begun to hear the sound. These experiences were very rewarding and perhaps help to explain what I mean when I say, as I often do, that I like to get inside of a sound. When the sounds are very long, as many of those we made at Ann Halprin's were, it can be easier to get inside of them. Sometimes when I was making a long sound, I began to notice that I was looking at the dancers and the room from the sound instead of hearing the sound from some position in the room. I began to feel the parts and motions of the sound more, and I began to see how each sound was its own world and that this world was only similar to our world in that we experienced it through our own bodies, that is, in our own terms. I could see that sounds and all other things in the world were just as important as human beings and that if we could to some degree give ourselves up to them, the sounds and other things that is, we enjoyed the possibility of learning something new. By giving ourselves up to them, I mean getting inside of them to some extent so that we can experience another world. This is not so easily explained but more easily experienced. Of course if one is not willing to give a part of himself to the sound, that is to reach out to the sound, but insists on approaching it in human terms, then he will probably experience little new but instead find only what he already knows defined within the terms with which he approached the experience. But if one can give up a part of himself to the sound, and approach the sound as a sound, and enter the world of the sound, then the experience need not stop there but may be continued much further, and the only limits are the limits each individual sets for himself. When we go into the world of a sound, it is new. When we prepare to leave the world of the sound, we expect to return to the world we previously left. We find, however, that when the sound stops, or we leave the area in which the sound is being made, or we just plain leave the world of the sound to some degree, that the world into which we enter is not the old world we left but another new one. This is partly because we experienced what was the old world with the added ingredient of the world of the sound. Perhaps it is safe for me to mention now that once you enter a new world, of a sound, or any other world, you will never really leave it. Still, the fact that one carries some parts of previous worlds with him does not in the least prevent one from entering new ones. In fact, if one considers a new combination of old ingredients to be something new, these carried parts of previous worlds may enhance new ones although they (the new combinations) need by no means be the main substance of a new world.

When I told Richard Brautigan that I liked to get inside of sounds, he said that he didn't really understand what I meant because he didn't visualize a shape when he heard a sound, and he imagined that one must conceive of a shape is he is to speak of getting inside of something. Then he asked, "Is it like being alone?" I said, "Yes."

❧

I used to talk about *the new eating*. One time Terry Riley said, "Yeah, even the cooks'll get rebellious. We'll walk into a hamburger stand and order something to eat. In a few minutes the cook'll give us some salt. Just salt. Then one of us will say, 'What? Is this all?' And the cook'll answer, 'Whatsamatter, don't cha like static eating?'"

❧

In his lecture, *Indeterminacy*, John Cage mentions going to a concert and finding that one of the composers had written in the program notes that he felt there was too much suffering in the world. After the concert John Cage said to the composer that he had enjoyed the music but he didn't agree with his statement about too much suffering in the world. The composer said "What? Don't you think there is enough?" to which Cage replied that he thought there was just the right amount. Later, in a letter, Dennis Johnson wrote to me, "Do you think there is too much Evil in the world? John Cage thinks there is just the right amount. I think there is too much world in the Evil." Some time after Dennis' letter I remembered that Richard Huelsenbeck had contributed another permutation to that sentence. At one of those Dada lectures he gave in Berlin, he had made the statement that the war had not been bloody enough.

●

The summer I lived in San Francisco Terry Jennings wrote me in one of his letters, "Have you ever seen any pictures of Antarctica? I saw a book of color pictures of the sea and ice and mountains and cliffs. Colors I hadn't seen before for water and ice. Down there the explorers (in certain places above hidden crevasses) could hear ice breaking and falling underneath their tents all the time and the sounds would get louder during the day and softer at night."

Once I tried lots of mustard on a raw turnip. I liked it better than any Beethoven I had ever heard.

NOTE

1.   The poet Diana Wakoski.

6

FOTODEATH

Claes Oldenburg

NOTES ON THE PERFORMANCE *Fotodeath (Circus)*

The original title of the piece was *Circus* (referring to its structure, resembling the multiple simultaneous action of a circus). In two parts: *Ironworks* and *Fotodeath*, with an intermission feature: a set of slides, photos, and type, called *Pickpocket*.

Circus was given six times in the Reuben Gallery during February 1961. The Reuben Gallery is a deep and wide store on Manhattan's East Third Street. The audience was seated as in a conventional theatre (and stood, when there were not enough chairs) facing a deep square stage. Over the stage were hung four strings of weak lightbulbs, producing when lit the sort of dingy light one remembers from circus tents.

In addition there were three individual lightbulbs over different areas of the stage, and a line of lights over a wall which marked the back of the stage, built across the store for the performance. There were thirty-four events in *Circus*, divided into seven sets. *Ironworks* was made up of four sets, *Fotodeath* of three sets. Excepting one set in *Ironworks*, there were five events in each set. Each event was assigned a zone onstage corresponding to a lightbulb or a string of bulbs. Turning on of the light cued the entrance of the event. The sets were separated by periods of darkness, during which colored lightbulbs placed around the theatre blinked.

The effect (from the audience's point of view) when all events of a set were in action was one of overlapping, superimposition. The wall at the back of the stage area was about seven feet high, having two entrances, one at either side. The entrances were hung with strips of muslin. Muslin was bunched and draped along the top of the wall. The wall and muslin were sprayed red, yellow, and blue in abstract patterns, giving a foggy color effect.

Behind the wall, on a perch to the left, in view of the audience, sat the Operator (Max Baker), controlling lights and phonograph records and

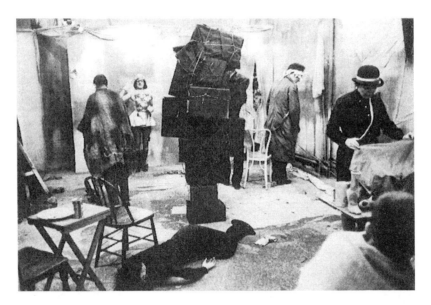

A rehearsal photo of Claes Oldenburg's 1961 *Fotodeath*, Part III. (Photo by Robert R. McElroy.)

projecting the slide sequence during intermission. Above the wall, the store receded into darkness. Dressing rooms were behind the wall. Excepting the entrance of a man with a bag in *Ironworks* I.5, all the players entered from behind the wall. The floor of the stage was of tile, broken in spots and repaired with cement (the store had once been a restaurant and the stage area corresponded to the kitchen).

The left side of the stage, called "the masculine," was painted a flat black and dominated by blacks, grays, and neutrals. At the meeting of the left wall and the wall across the stage was a muslin screen on which a shadow effect was projected (*Fotodeath* I.2). In front of the screen was a large construction of wood and burlap, called the "chimney."

The right side of the stage, called "the feminine," was by contrast brightly colored in dominating pinks and reds. A pink form, made of muslin around a hoop resembling a windsock, jutted out of the wall and hung from the ceiling.

A black wooden settee stood on the left side against the wall and a hat rack and long mirror hung on the right. Other furniture and objects were brought onstage.

Exits of events were cued by a Timer in each set. His departure from the stage was followed by the turning off of the lights over the other events in a determined sequence. When the light over an event was extinguished, the players either went backstage or helped in the darkness to set up props for the next event.

A scrim was hung across the front of the stage and so lit that the actions of preparation for the performance were dimly seen by the entering audience. Music was played before and after the performance. When the piece was ready to begin, the scrim was taken down and slowly rolled on a long bamboo pole in a deliberate action functioning as an event in itself.

THE SCRIPT

I   Fotodeath

1   Pat's light   Zone 1
A man, Lucas, enters from L. in a plain tight   Drum record:
fastidious suit. He admires himself in many   Chavez, all way thru
mirrors he takes from his pockets. He lies
down with a tall mirror, posing himself in
different ways, projecting himself upside
down, etc.

2   Scrim lights   Zone 2
A scrim is illuminated in pink and purple
from behind. A girl in a military cap saluting
and taking various patriotic poses in a
shadow dance. Olga.

3   Light bank 3   Zone 3
Cliff, a wrestler, enters from R. in black   Bugle sound
tights, nude to the waist, with a pink soft
baglike object, a wrestler with which he
wrestles fiercely.

4   Light bank 4   TIMER   Zone 4 L.
A woman dressed as a man in hat, shirt, tie,
and baggy suit, Judy, enters from L., goes to
dresser and undresses in front of mirror. She
wears extremely feminine clothes underneath. She admires herself as a woman then
redresses as a man. She leaves L. taking
mirror with her.

5   Henry's light   Zone 4 R.
A photographer, Carl, in a shiny black
smock and a top hat brings out a camera and
leads in a family of three to be photo-
graphed: Henry, Chippie, and Marilyn. Sets
them on a bench and then shows them

several landscape samples. They disapprove. Finally he finds one they will accept. He hangs it behind them, gets under the fotocloth but the family collapses. The photographer sets them up again, gets under the cloth. Again they collapse, and so on.

When Timer leaves stage, the lights go out in the following sequence: 4—H—3—Pat's—Scrim, *but let scrim lights and record play a while at end.*

In blackout all leave stage or take new positions.

II Fotodeath

1 Light bank 4   Zone 4
A woman enters L., Pat, in long dragging plumage and wings, very colorful and bizarrely made up. She walks slowly and artificially, only interested in herself. She pulls herself up and down the ladder in R. center taking poses, sticking her leg out slowly, etc.

2 Light bank 2   Zone 2
Two girls in summer white costumes suggesting 1913 and a summer day on the ferry in the bay, Claire and Judy enter from R. One has a parasol. They walk slowly laughing and chatting to each other. There are bells on their ankles or under their skirts which jingle as they walk.

3 Light bank 1 TIMER is Gloria   Zone 1
A man in a coat and a woman in a coat with a happy birthday tiara. She carrying a piece of fresh ice and one arm in a black sling. Enter R. Henry and Gloria. She remains in the center, looking blankly. He knocks on door L. It opens showing a packed party in progress. Squeals and talk, etc. He retreats. He reconsiders. He knocks again. Again the view into the party. He does this again and

again. Finally he enters without knocking. The woman then leaves the stage.

4 Light bank 3   Zone 3

Two men stumble in from L. Lucas and Edgar. They are drunk and make foul noises. One falls, the other picks him up. Then he in turn falls. They go back and forth then both fall and remain still. Another man enters from R. corner Zone 4 with a bag of black cans. He falls over the fallen men and the cans are thrown out on the floor. A fourth man enters with an empty bag and slowly picks up the cans. The other men lie still. The picker makes noises with the cans.

When timer gets backstage, the lights are cut in the following sequence: 4—3—2—1 slowly so as to emphasize silhouettes. Actors stop when lights go out. Blackout. All leave or take new positions.

III Fotodeath

1 Strip lights   Zone 1

Lights begin moving. After a while Majorette steps out from R. and saluting approximately at same rhythm moves by single steps back and forth across the stage. She does this throughout, always smiling. Chippie.

2 Light bank 2   Zone 2

A man with a bandaged head and a white chair comes out from wall L. Lucas. He sits down gingerly but it hurts. He grimaces. He picks up the chair, moves it, tries sitting again. But it still hurts. He grimaces, etc., back and forth across stage.

3 Light bank 4   Zone 4 L.

A woman in a Derby hat, mannish, dressed all in black with a patriotic band across bodice something like a Salvation Army woman. Gloria. Enters from R. She carries a black bag like a sample bag and a big can full of viscous liquid. She stops behind table center Zone 4, and takes out of the bag one by one, putting them on the table, numerous different objects of many colors but all marked clearly USA. It is as if she is demonstrating a product, but she has no expression on her face and says nothing. After piling up the objects, she pours from a huge can marked USA a viscous liquid which runs over the objects and on the floor. This she covers with a cloth marked USA. She remains standing over her work until blackout and forms a silhouette.

4 Henry's light   Zone 4 R.

A man, Cliff, informally dressed, shirt open but wearing a jacket drags in as if dead a woman, Olga, dressed in sweater and skirt. He sits her in a chair by a table on which a meal is set. He props her up. He sits down to eat. She falls forward on the table and keeps doing this until the eater loses his patience. Each time he props her up. Finally he reverses the chair so that she will not fall into his food. But now she slides down on the floor. He ignores her and having finished his meal he wipes his mouth and leaves R.

5 Light bank 3   TIMER   Zone 3

Two men bring out – from behind the audience, down the aisle – a topheavy, tied together, mass of boxes painted black. It is a big object which they manipulate with some difficulty into the center of action and leave there. Carl and Edgar. Then they exit, like movers.

Billboard march begins quietly

When Timers come off, the lights go out in this sequence: 4—Henry's—3—2—Strip.

But very slowly, silhouetting first Gloria then object and finally on all alone the strip lights for a time. The music continues softly until strips off, then off abruptly.

Blackout and all leave stage

Light bank 3 on, over object.

House light.

NOTES ON AND CHANGES IN THE EXISTING SCRIPT:

Fotodeath

I   1. Drum record was Carlos Chavez' "Concerto for Percussion."
   2. The "scrim" referred to in script was the above-mentioned screen of muslin at stage left.
   3. The bugle sound was eliminated. Cliff wrestled with a white stuffed laundry bag.
   4. There was no dresser. Judy hung her clothes on the hat rack. Under the men's clothing she wore cotton stockings and an old-fashioned baggy frilly yellow slip.
   5. The landscape samples were fragments edged in black, ripped from a large photomural of the Battery (which appears whole in rehearsal photographs).

II   1. The plumage was made of long tinted strips of muslin. The wings were eliminated. A sound-effect record of cannonfire was played by the Operator.

III   1. The "strip" lights were the above-mentioned lights above the wall across the stage. They were wired to a knob, the turning of which lit one bulb then another in traveling effect such as in electric signs.
   2. Lucas also wore an oversize G.I. raincoat.
   3. The "viscous liquid" used was wheat paste.

7

THE FIRST AND SECOND WILDERNESS

Michael Kirby

During May 1963, the Smolin Gallery sponsored a month-long program of Happenings, Events, music, dance, chance theatre, etc. called the Yam Festival ("Yam" is "May" spelled backward). One of the many performances listed on the published calendar was *The First and Second Wilderness*, subtitled *A Civil War Game*. It was presented for one evening only – 27 May.

When the spectator climbed four flights of stairs to the loft where the piece was being done, he found himself in a clean, freshly painted room about ninety feet long and twenty feet wide. Near the center of the space, the squares of a large game board had been laid out on the floor with tape. The usual rectangular grid pattern was extended by pyramids of squares at each end which ended in single squares marked "Washington" and "Richmond." Blue and gray cardboard soldiers about two feet tall stood near the opposite ends of the board. Representing infantry and cavalry, the figures were formed of intersecting front and profile silhouettes. Chairs had been placed close to the board at both ends, and leaning against one wall at the side of the game grid was a large spinner. To the right of the spinner, under a sign reading "scoreboard," stood a white ladder. Brightly colored Union and Confederate flags hung on the walls, and behind the rows of chairs, about ten feet from either end of the board, were "horses" built from tables and sawhorses, with wooden saddles and heads made, like huge toys, of stuffed plush. To one side and to the rear of each horse a white sheet hung from the ceiling. Illumination was provided by two bulbs with conical shades that hung over the center of the playing area.

As he entered, each spectator was given two sheets of paper. On one the performers and technicians were listed and the rules of the game were explained, while the other gave the words for several cheers. The rules were very simple: infantry could be moved one space at a time, cavalry could be moved two spaces; not more than five markers could be placed on a square at a time, and all on a square could be moved at once; when

Michael Kirby tosses the coin to see who will "kick off" and who will "receive" in his *First and Second Wilderness: A Civil War Game*. The performance was part of the month-long YAM Festival in May 1963. (Photo by Peter Moore)

opposing markers occupied the same square, the spinner would indicate how many men were "killed" or "taken prisoner"; the side which first moved an infantry marker into the opposing "capital" (the final square) was the winner. (The signs on the spinner were in terms of thousands of men – each marker represented a thousand men. An inner ring on the spinner was to be used if each side had an equal number of markers on a square, while an outer ring was to be read if one side had a numerical advantage.)

Four men in blue and gray uniforms – a Union "General" and "Lieutenant" and Confederates of the same ranks – stood talking to each other and to the spectators. The Confederate lieutenant placed small bets on the game with members of the audience. When the chairs were filled, people sat along the wall opposite the spinner and stood at both ends of the board.

A tape-recorded bugle call quieted the room. The generals climbed onto the horses on their respective sides, and the lieutenants moved out onto the board. The four men began to recite short statements about the Civil War: that two battles had been fought in Virginia at a place called The Wilderness (the first better known as the battle of Chancellorsville); that the woods caught fire during the first engagement, burning to death many of the wounded on both sides; that General Stonewall Jackson was mistakenly killed by his own men during the second battle, etc. (Each man had been given three statements to say as often and in whatever order he chose. They were directed to think of the mixture of voices as "word jazz," and to try to say each line once when no one else was speaking.) The four voices grew loud and soft, overlapped, were briefly quiet, and spoke out clearly.

Another bugle call was heard on the dual speakers of the sound system (operated by a girl at a table just behind the audience in one corner), and the performers fell silent. A small procession moved onto the board: a girl in a bathing suit held the arm of a tall man dressed entirely in black and wearing sunglasses; they were followed by two girls in cheerleading costume. When they reached the wall where the spinner stood, the girl in the bathing suit climbed the ladder at the right, and the cheerleaders sat on a small bench to the left.

The lieutenants lifted painted flags down from the opposite wall and carried them briskly to the center. The opposing generals walked forward, saluted each other, and shook hands. Nodding to one of the generals to "call" it, the man in black tossed a silver dollar in the air and caught it. The winners and losers of the toss were indicated by the "receiving" and "kicking off" signals performed by football referees, and the performers returned quickly to their places. Civil War songs blared out on the loudspeakers, the mounted generals called orders down to their lieutenants about which markers should be moved, the "referee" placed "mountains" and a "swamp" on the board (making those squares unusable), and the cheerleaders rushed out to lead a cheer. (The cheers were written by Letty Eisenhauer, one of the cheerleaders. Although they had printed copies of the cheers and were frequently quite noisy, the spectators never joined in the formal cheering, preferring merely to watch the acrobatics of the two girls.)

When both "armies" were arranged on the board, the "war" began. The generals shouted orders and comments over the heads of the spectators to their lieutenants, who actually moved the pieces. Their distance from the board hampered the generals' visibility, and the lieutenants tried to keep them informed about enemy movements, offered suggestions, and made comments. (Touches of "characterization" were sometimes used – the terminology of rank, for example, was frequent – but the pervasive impression was one of men in uniform playing a game.)

Soon opposing markers were moved onto the same square, and the man in black whirled the spinner, removed the indicated marker or markers from the board, held them up so that the girl on the ladder could see them clearly, separated the silhouettes, and threw the pieces onto the floor. The scorekeeper in the bathing suit fastened the appropriate number of small blue or gray figures to the wall with transparent tape. The roar of Civil War cannons and rifles and the sound of galloping horses (from a record of a battle recently "refought" with authentic equipment) now alternated with the songs that were coming from the sound system. At times the volume was almost deafening and at other times faded away, according to the taste of the operator. The cheerleaders ran out with paper megaphones to lead a cheer. (They had been told to cheer for "whomever is winning.") "Prisoners" were placed in "stockades" and, at times, exchanges were formally negotiated.

When he felt like it, the man in black blew a police whistle hanging from a cord around his neck, made one of the signals from the visual repertoire of sports officials (he never spoke), and handed a card to one of the lieutenants. Play stopped. The lieutenant read the card out loud, and his words were repeated by each of the other three soldiers.

"Stonewall Jackson is dead," read one of the cards. The performer in black turned out the lights, and the four men in uniform moved slowly together through the spectators and the cardboard markers carrying lighted candles in glass cups. At the center of the board they softly harmonized on one verse of an old song:

> We shall meet, but we shall miss him.
> There will be one vacant chair
> As we gather in the twilight
> To recite our evening prayer.

The man in black touched one of them on the shoulder, and he said, "Let us cross over the river and rest under the shade of the trees." Abruptly, the lights were turned back on, the loudspeakers blared again, and the players returned to their positions.

The other card read, "The Wilderness is on fire." The lights were switched off, and the sound went silent. Lighting a propane torch, the man in black picked up one of the soldiers and began to burn it. Silhouetted by the roaring flame, the heavy fire-resistant cardboard struggled to stay erect. Finally it burned, charred, and crumbled. The man holding it stamped it out on the floor. During the burning, Civil War photographs taken by Matthew Brady – the awkward postures of the dead, soldiers staring blankly at the camera – were thrown from the rear on the hanging sheets at either end by opaque projectors. When the cardboard soldier was finally destroyed, the game resumed. These two interludes were repeated several times in the order and frequency the "referee" felt advisable.

After perhaps twenty or thirty minutes, an infantry marker of one side entered the opposing "capital." The game was over. The man in black walked quickly off. The music surged up. The losing general slowly walked forward to surrender his sword. The cheerleaders rushed out throwing paper flowers and crowned the victors with paper laurel wreaths.

The game was played five times that evening. Some spectators stayed for all of the performances; others came and went. Perhaps seventy-five people attended. When it was all over, the North had been victorious three times; the South twice.

8

FLUXUS

George Maciunas

FLUXUS HQ P.O.BOX 180 NEW YORK 10013
FLUXSHOPS AND FLUXFESTS IN NEW YORK
AMSTERDAM NICE ROME MONTREAL TOKYO
V TRE - FLUXMACHINES - FLUXMUSICBOXES
FLUXKITS - FLUXAUTOMOBILES - FLUXPOST
FLUXMEDICINES - FLUXFILMS - FLUXMENUS
FLUXRADIOS - FLUXCARDS - FLUXPUZZLES
FLUXCLOTHES - FLUXORGANS - FLUXSHIRTS
FLUXBOXES - FLUXORCHESTRA - FLUXJOKES
FLUXGAMES - FLUXHOLES - FLUXHARDWARE
FLUXSUITCASES - FLUXCHESS - FLUXFLAGS
FLUXTOURS - FLUXWATER - FLUXCONCERTS
FLUXMYSTERIES - FLUXBOOKS - FLUXSIGNS
FLUXCLOCKS - FLUXCIRCUS - FLUXANIMALS
FLUXQUIZZES - FLUXROCKS - FLUXMEDALS
FLUXDUST - FLUXCANS - FLUXTABLECLOTH
FLUXVAUDEVILLE - FLUXTAPE - FLUXSPORT
BY ERIC ANDERSEN - AYO - JEFF BERNER
GEORGE BRECHT - GIUSEPPE CHIARI - ANT-
HONY COX - CHRISTO - WALTER DE MARIA
WILLEM DE RIDDER - ROBERT FILLIOU
ALBERT FINE - HI RED CENTER - JOE JONES
H. KAPPLOW - ALISON KNOWLES - JIRI KOLAR
ARTHUR KØPCKE - TAKEHISA KOSUGI - SHIGE-
KO KUBOTA - FREDRIC LIEBERMAN - GYORGI
LIGETI - GEORGE MACIUNAS - YOKO ONO - BEN-
JAMIN PATTERSON - JAMES RIDDLE - DITER
ROT - TAKAKO SAITO - TOMAS SCHMIT - CHIEKO
SHIOMI - DANIEL SPOERRI - STAN VANDER-
BEEK - BEN VAUTIER - ROBERT M. WATTS
EMMETT O. WILLIAMS - LA MONTE YOUNG
FLUX - ART - NONART - AMUSEMENT FORGOES
DISTINCTION BETWEEN ART AND NONART,
FORGOES ARTIST'S INDISPENSABILITY,
EXCLUSIVENESS, INDIVIDUALITY, AMBITION,
FORGOES ALL PRETENSION TOWARDS SIG-
NIFICANCE, RARITY, INSPIRATION, SKILL,
COMPLEXITY, PROFUNDITY, GREATNESS,
INSTITUTIONAL AND COMMODITY VALUE.
IT STRIVES FOR MONOSTRUCTURAL, NON-
THEATRICAL, NONBAROQUE, IMPERSONAL
QUALITIES OF A SIMPLE NATURAL EVENT,
AN OBJECT, A GAME, A PUZZLE OR A GAG. IT
IS A FUSION OF SPIKES JONES, GAGS,
GAMES, VAUDEVILLE, CAGE AND DUCHAMP

GEORGE BRECHT:

3. A small object on
   the clock face.

2. A fingertip on
   black bulb.

1. A fingertip on
   child's right foot.

A score from George Brecht's *Water Yam* (1963). (Courtesy of the Gilbert and
Lila Silverman Fluxus Collection Foundation, Detroit.)

GEORGE BRECHT:

DRIP MUSIC (DRIP EVENT)

FOR SINGLE OR MULTIPLE PERFORMANCE

A SOURCE OF DRIPPING WATER AND
AN EMPTY VESSEL ARE ARRANGED SO
THAT THE WATER FALLS IN THE VESSEL.

SECOND VERSION: DRIPPING

(Photo by Peter Moore.)

JOE JONES:
PREDICTIONS 1963, TIME 3.5 MIN.
COMPOSED FOR YAM FESTIVAL, 1963
SCORE CONSISTED OF NOTATIONS
ON GRAPH PAPER FOR EACH
INSTRUMENT.

(Photo by
Peter Moore.)

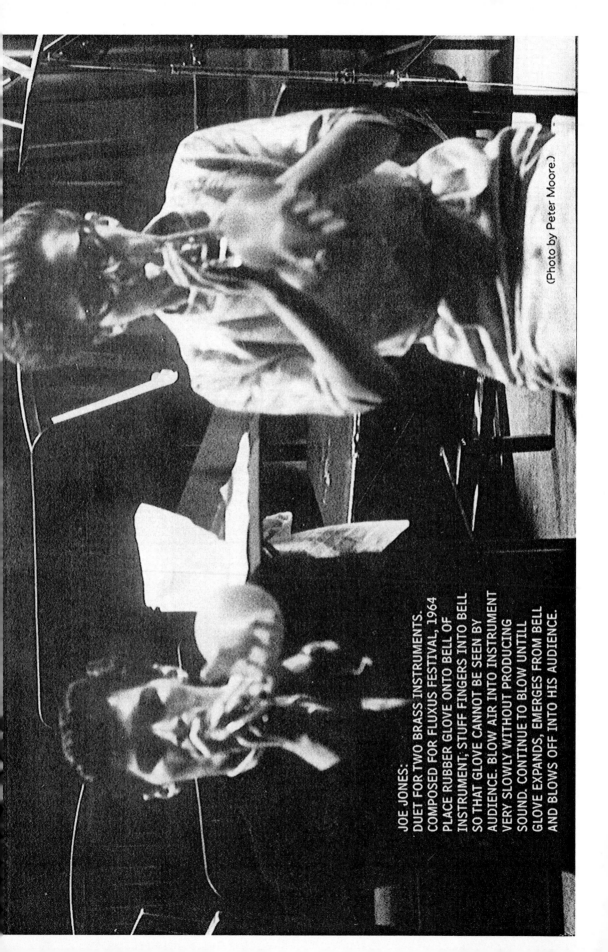

JOE JONES:
DUET FOR TWO BRASS INSTRUMENTS.
COMPOSED FOR FLUXUS FESTIVAL, 1964
PLACE RUBBER GLOVE ONTO BELL OF
INSTRUMENT; STUFF FINGERS INTO BELL
SO THAT GLOVE CANNOT BE SEEN BY
AUDIENCE. BLOW AIR INTO INSTRUMENT
VERY SLOWLY WITHOUT PRODUCING
SOUND. CONTINUE TO BLOW UNTILL
GLOVE EXPANDS, EMERGES FROM BELL
AND BLOWS OFF INTO HIS AUDIENCE.

(Photo by Peter Moore.)

ALISON KNOWLES: CHILD ART PIECE, 1962-4. PERFORMED IN STOCKHOLM
PRESENT A CHILD TO AN EMPTY STAGE. ONE PARENT MAY BE PRESENT WITH SOME
FAMILIAR OBJECTS. HE MAY, FOR EXAMPLE BE BATHED. HE IS ALLOWED TO PLAY
THERE. THE PERFORMANCE IS OVER WHEN THE CHILD LEAVES THE STAGE.

VARIATION: (WRITTEN SPECIFICALLY FOR THE CARNEGIE HALL FLUXUS CONCERT
BECAUSE OF THE CENSORSHIP OF VERSION NO.1 BY THE DEPT OF CRUELTY TO
CHILDREN OF NEW YORK CITY. THIS VERSION USED THE AISLES RATHER THAN THE
STAGE. IT WAS PERFORMED BY ENNIS PATTERSON AGE 3.)
EXIT, WEARING A NEW SUIT.

ALISON KNOWLES: PROPOSITION
MAKE A SALAD
VARIATION – MAKE A SOUP
1962

PERFORMED IN LONDON,
COPENHAGEN, NEW YORK.

(Photo by Peter Moore.)

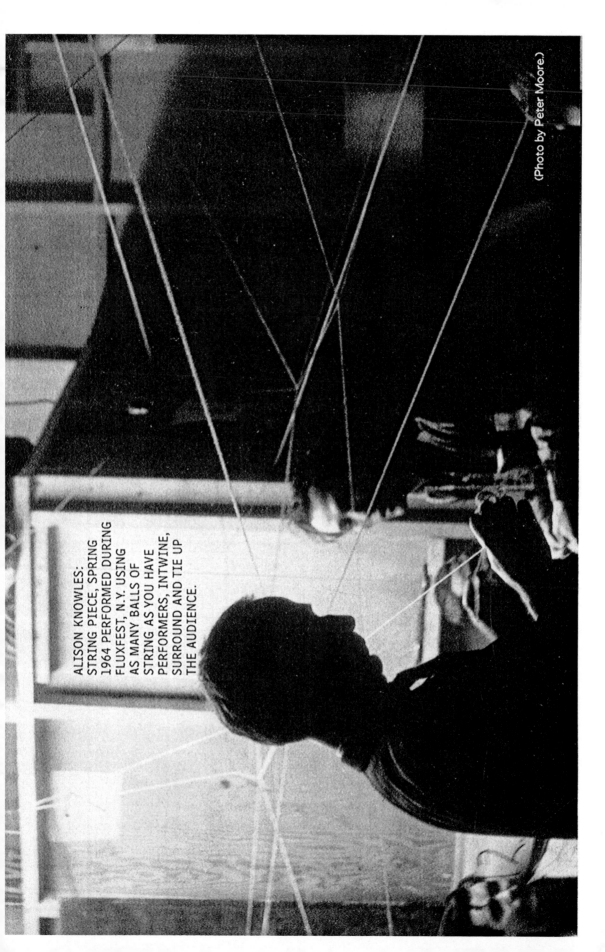

ALISON KNOWLES:
STRING PIECE, SPRING
1964 PERFORMED DURING
FLUXFEST, N.Y. USING
AS MANY BALLS OF
STRING AS YOU HAVE
PERFORMERS, INTWINE,
SURROUND AND TIE UP
THE AUDIENCE.

(Photo by Peter Moore.)

GEORGE MACIUNAS: IN MEMORIAM TO ADRIANO OLIVETTI, 1961
A USED OLIVETTI ADDING MACHINE PAPER ROLL IS USED AS A SCORE. EACH PERFORMER CHOOSES A NUMBER.
METRONOME BEAT INDICATES TIME OF EACH HORIZONTAL ROW OF NUMBERS. PERFORMER PERFORMS
SHARPLY AND EXACTLY ON BEAT WHENEVER HIS NUMBER APPEARS IN A ROW.
VERSION 2. PERFORMED BY FLUXORCHESTRA AT CARNEGIE RECITAL HALL, 1964
PERFORMER RAISES BOWLER HAT ON FIRST APPEARANCE OF HIS NUMBER AND LOWERS HAT OVER HEAD ON NEXT APPEARANCE
OF HIS NUMBER, RAISES ON 3RD, LOWERS ON 4TH, ETC. CONDUCTOR USES A TOP HAT.

(Photo by Peter Moore.)

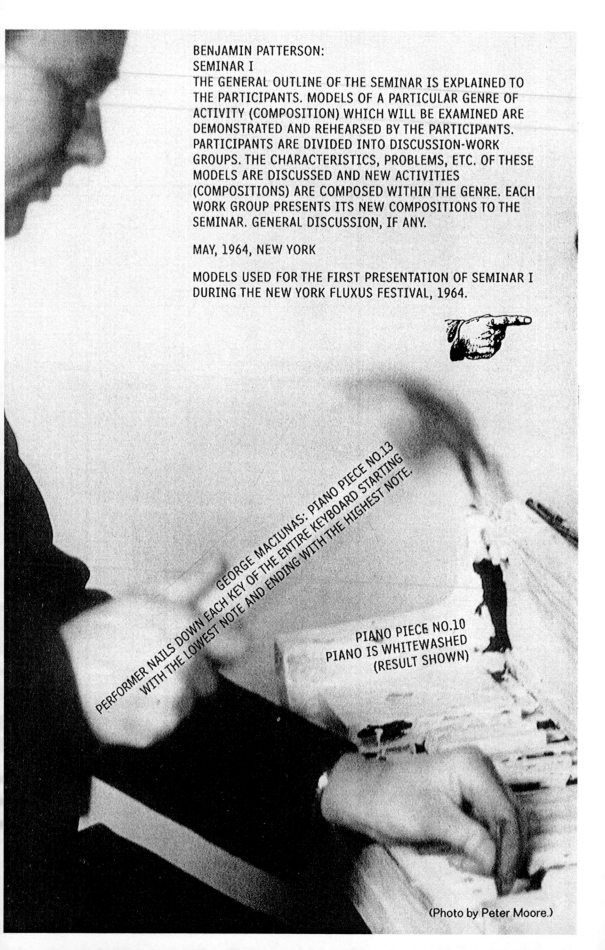

BENJAMIN PATTERSON:
SEMINAR I
THE GENERAL OUTLINE OF THE SEMINAR IS EXPLAINED TO
THE PARTICIPANTS. MODELS OF A PARTICULAR GENRE OF
ACTIVITY (COMPOSITION) WHICH WILL BE EXAMINED ARE
DEMONSTRATED AND REHEARSED BY THE PARTICIPANTS.
PARTICIPANTS ARE DIVIDED INTO DISCUSSION-WORK
GROUPS. THE CHARACTERISTICS, PROBLEMS, ETC. OF THESE
MODELS ARE DISCUSSED AND NEW ACTIVITIES
(COMPOSITIONS) ARE COMPOSED WITHIN THE GENRE. EACH
WORK GROUP PRESENTS ITS NEW COMPOSITIONS TO THE
SEMINAR. GENERAL DISCUSSION, IF ANY.

MAY, 1964, NEW YORK

MODELS USED FOR THE FIRST PRESENTATION OF SEMINAR I
DURING THE NEW YORK FLUXUS FESTIVAL, 1964.

GEORGE MACIUNAS: PIANO PIECE NO.13
PERFORMER NAILS DOWN EACH KEY OF THE ENTIRE KEYBOARD STARTING
WITH THE LOWEST NOTE AND ENDING WITH THE HIGHEST NOTE.

PIANO PIECE NO.10
PIANO IS WHITEWASHED
(RESULT SHOWN)

(Photo by Peter Moore.)

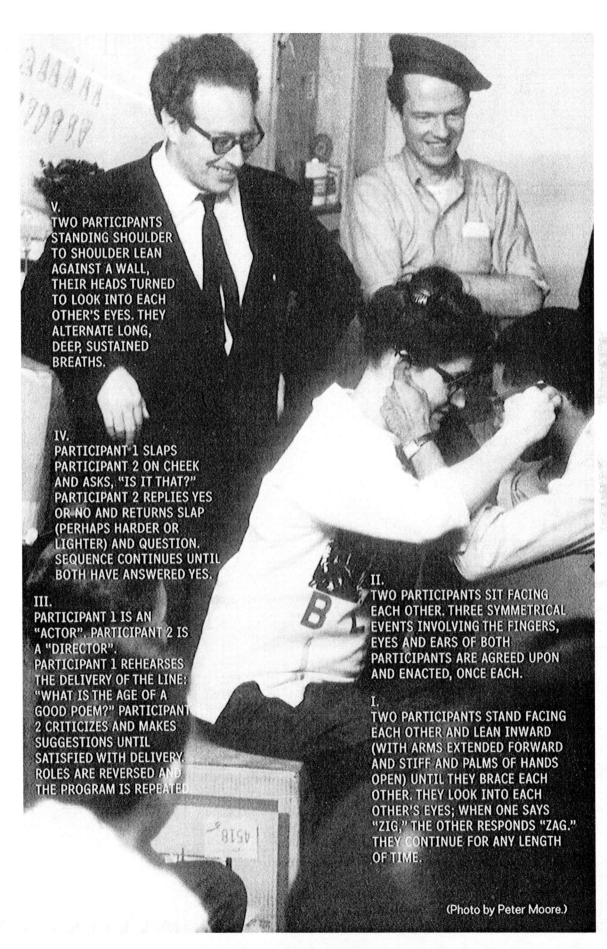

V.
TWO PARTICIPANTS
STANDING SHOULDER
TO SHOULDER LEAN
AGAINST A WALL,
THEIR HEADS TURNED
TO LOOK INTO EACH
OTHER'S EYES. THEY
ALTERNATE LONG,
DEEP, SUSTAINED
BREATHS.

IV.
PARTICIPANT 1 SLAPS
PARTICIPANT 2 ON CHEEK
AND ASKS, "IS IT THAT?"
PARTICIPANT 2 REPLIES YES
OR NO AND RETURNS SLAP
(PERHAPS HARDER OR
LIGHTER) AND QUESTION.
SEQUENCE CONTINUES UNTIL
BOTH HAVE ANSWERED YES.

III.
PARTICIPANT 1 IS AN
"ACTOR". PARTICIPANT 2 IS
A "DIRECTOR".
PARTICIPANT 1 REHEARSES
THE DELIVERY OF THE LINE:
"WHAT IS THE AGE OF A
GOOD POEM?" PARTICIPANT
2 CRITICIZES AND MAKES
SUGGESTIONS UNTIL
SATISFIED WITH DELIVERY.
ROLES ARE REVERSED AND
THE PROGRAM IS REPEATED.

II.
TWO PARTICIPANTS SIT FACING
EACH OTHER. THREE SYMMETRICAL
EVENTS INVOLVING THE FINGERS,
EYES AND EARS OF BOTH
PARTICIPANTS ARE AGREED UPON
AND ENACTED, ONCE EACH.

I.
TWO PARTICIPANTS STAND FACING
EACH OTHER AND LEAN INWARD
(WITH ARMS EXTENDED FORWARD
AND STIFF AND PALMS OF HANDS
OPEN) UNTIL THEY BRACE EACH
OTHER. THEY LOOK INTO EACH
OTHER'S EYES; WHEN ONE SAYS
"ZIG," THE OTHER RESPONDS "ZAG."
THEY CONTINUE FOR ANY LENGTH
OF TIME.

(Photo by Peter Moore.)

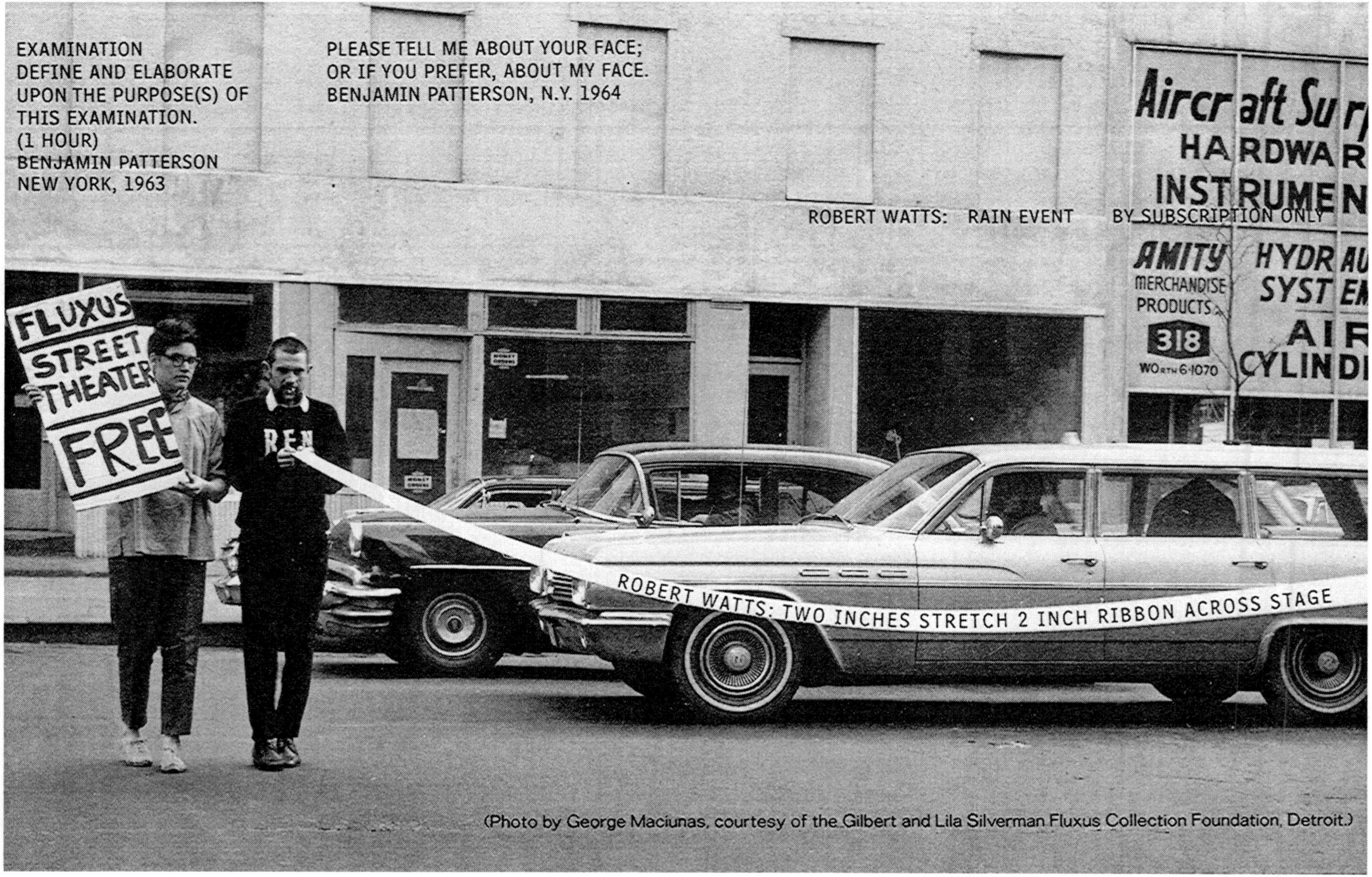

EXAMINATION
DEFINE AND ELABORATE
UPON THE PURPOSE(S) OF
THIS EXAMINATION.
(1 HOUR)
BENJAMIN PATTERSON
NEW YORK, 1963
PLEASE TELL ME ABOUT YOUR FACE;
OR IF YOU PREFER, ABOUT MY FACE.
BENJAMIN PATTERSON, N.Y. 1964
ROBERT WATTS: RAIN EVENT
BY SUBSCRIPTION ONLY
ROBERT WATTS: TWO INCHES STRETCH 2 INCH RIBBON ACROSS STAGE
FLUXUS
STREET
THEATER
FREE
AMITY
MERCHANDISE
PRODUCTS
318
WORTH 6-1070
(Photo by George Maciunas, courtesy of the Gilbert and Lila Silverman Fluxus Collection Foundation, Detroit.)

(Photo by George Maciunas, courtesy of the Gilbert and Lila Silverman Fluxus Collection Foundation. Detroit.)

ROBERT WATTS: NO EVENT

9

THE NIGHT TIME SKY

Robert Whitman

I began with an idea about a piece that had to do with the making of a theatre work, with itself as its own subject. It seemed to me that one of the first theatrical things is when the sun goes down, night falls, the stars come out, and people imagine what the constellations are.

Out of this came *The Night Time Sky*, performed in May 1965.

The audience arrive a few at a time and walk down a tunnel toward the place. They hear steel drum band music, crowd noises, and steamship whistles: boat-leaving sounds. At the end of the tunnel is a movie, projected on a white cloth, of passenger liners leaving. As an audience member approaches this, his shadow is cast on the screen. His shadow is momentarily in the movie, participating in the boat leaving. All this is seen on both sides of the screen.

One enters the space by pushing this cloth aside. Inside there are mats on the floor to sit on. The people walk around to find a place and then sit. Floor and mats are lighted so that they are green. This green light and the boat movie provide all the light. Other people's shadows join the movie as they come down the tunnel. If a person came right on time and went right into the place he might see seven or eight minutes of this. Then it is over and the green lights go out too.

The space into which the people have come is a billowy dome shape fifty feet in diameter and sixteen or seventeen feet high. The enclosure is of cloth and the billowy shapes are soft and cloudlike. In the center of the space is a cloth-covered thing about six feet high. It is rather squared off but was meant to be mound or haystack shaped. The set-up time didn't allow some things to be done as perfectly as one would have liked.

Very, very slowly the space is lit a red-orange sunset color, from lights on the outside. This holds for a while, then it goes out even more slowly and blue comes up; the interior space is now the night time sky.

Up in the dome, spaced fairly evenly around, are four holes. Three are

A man in a lab coat watches over the equipment in one of the raised openings of the cloth ➡ dome setting for Robert Whitman's *The Night Time Sky* (1965). (Photo by Peter Moore.)

about ten feet long, rounded at the corners and top, and about five feet high. The fourth is about five feet wide and a little more squared off. All of these holes are about ten feet off the floor.

There is quiet for a while, then one of the holes lights up slowly. There is a man in a white lab coat, a clipboard in hand, at an instrument panel. He reads the meters, adjusts dials with knobs, switches switches. He is at work running some kind of industrial process, and checking it.

Another film starts up, close to this stage. It is below and to the right. It is of a steel mill. The men move about in slow motion, there are glowing things and sparks flying. The image is about six feet high and rectangular. (It was meant to have been circular, about the same size.) At a certain time the man in the lab coat switches on the light behind a foot-square panel of translucent plastic which is on his control panel. For the rest of the performance the plastic panel glows with shifting colors and lights.

A light comes up in another hole. There is a pretty, thin, dark girl in black tights. The light in the other hole fades out very slowly. The girl takes dirt and marbles (which we can't see) and puts them into an opaque projector at one side of the platform. The projector projects them at an angle onto the ceiling, so that we see her fingers moving the three or four many-colored marbles about in the dirt on the roof of the space. They might be like stars in the sky. Then the girl sits and smokes a cigarette. Her light slowly goes out.

The haystack thing in the middle begins to glow a red-orange. This comes up so slowly that it is not noticed until it is really glowing. As this is happening the sound of wind is coming up too. The wind shrieks and the haystack glows, then both suddenly subside and there is silence and darkness.

The light on the man in the lab coat comes up again. He is still at the same kind of business. Sometimes only sitting there. A light on the smaller hole comes up slowly. It is a blue light. There is a girl in a raincoat behind a cheesecloth curtain that is hanging in front of the hole. The girl walks to a chair, sits down, and puts a record on a record player which is on a table next to the chair. The record is of rainfall. The girl listens to the record and when it is over she takes it off as the light slowly dims and goes out. The light on the man in the lab coat has slowly gone out during the beginning of this.

Now the light on the girl in black comes up. She is suspended and flying. She flies slowly across her little area and the lights go slowly out again.

The lights come up on the second girl again. Now the light is red and her coat is off. She is dressed in a dress of aluminium foil and plastic pieces, the average size of which is about six by eight inches. These parts shine and reflect the light. The curtain is gone now. This time she plays and listens to a sound-effects record of fire. When the record is over her light goes out slowly and comes up on the man in the lab coat. He is at the same business, it never changes. Marking down figures, sitting at a table, walking around, reading dials, turning knobs, switching switches.

The light on the flying girl comes up and she makes another slow flight. This time a different kind. The light fades out again.

There is darkness and three lights come on, spotting three areas on the floor in which six people appear in three groups. They are grouped together as: a man and a man, a woman and a woman, and a man and a woman. They are standing. The three groups are spaced out in the area so that each part of the audience can see two of the groups, or if some in the audience are standing they'll be able to see at least one of the couples. Each performer has a razor blade with which he cuts down the middle of his partner's chest. Then, with the other hand, he smears black or white pasty paint around on the shirt. The paint has bled from the wound. Half the people have black or dark shirts or blouses, the other half have white. The white-shirted people bleed black, the dark-shirted people bleed white. During the smearing part all the lights go out at once. In the darkness the performers leave the area.

The light on the girl in aluminium foil comes up and this time it is green. The record that the girl plays now is of waterfront sounds. When the record is over the girl gets up, turns off the record player, and goes about doing things that we can't identify. She may reach out of the area that we can see and do something with her hands, or to one side or the other, or above or below out of our sight. She does a few different things this way. Then she begins to take her costume apart one piece at a time. As she takes off these pieces she piles them on top of one another, making a wall between herself and the audience.

Then the light comes up in the fourth hole. This is an amber spotlight on a girl who looks as though she has nothing on. Very slowly she peels off her skin and she becomes a blue person. The light on the other hole has dimmed and gone out now and this is all that is visible. The girl continues and peels off the blue skin, to become a yellow person with silver hair. This whole series of actions takes a lot longer to do than to describe.

As the girl is finishing, a film appears projected on the top of the space. We also begin to hear a watery sound with rattling, bubbling, and drips. The film starts out as a vague kind of abstract film of watery patterns with something happening that is hard to see or identify. The movie goes on and it becomes impossible not to understand what its subject matter is. It is a movie of what the toilet sees. The sounds are also clear now. They are the toilet flushing, and bubbling sounds. The toilet sees a cigarette being tossed into it, then the reverse with the rushing water bringing the cigarette back, then throwing it out of the toilet. Then a man urinates into the toilet. Then more reverse vague stuff until at the end of the shot a lady gets off the toilet. Then the reverse of a man urinating. Then the reverse of a man defecating. It is possible to avoid the subject of the film until about halfway through this shot. People begin to react now and there's a lot of giggling and comment from the audience. The last shot is a straight shot of a man defecating and the toilet being flushed. The movie ends, the sound ends, and lights come on coloring the floor blue. Then a light is on in the entrance/exit tunnel and the cheering crowd, steel drum band, steamship boat leaving sound comes on loud and it is clear that the piece is over. The sound continues until all the people are gone.

Now I will just mention some of the things that I was concerned with when I made certain images, to make as obvious as possible one context in which the images are presented. I have already mentioned that in a way it is about itself. This was a night shadow voyage. The self-cast shadows of entering the movies-fantasy. Projections of fantasy in the dark sky. Making them from constellations. The shape and nature of the tent suggest all kinds of things and among them I thought especially of a few. In the circus the acts are spaced out and presented so as to accent their fantastic and superhuman qualities, attributes, and functions. It is another entrance into fantasy land, the land of make-believe, the land of death. We also see living images. Exaggerations and celebrations of life and weird dreams. Entrance and exit to and from the worlds of real and strange. The people appearing and cutting each other are real people on the same level as the audience. Something violent and surprising like the wound of finding something out or understanding. I also thought of people thinking things, digesting them, defecating them, a work fertilizing something. The audience, fertilized by the experience, leaving. People-boat-turds leaving the pier, shat out into the streets as they leave the performance. In spite of my ponderous description I also thought it was funny.

Anyway, these things are like the plot of a story, the framework. The real context is the time the piece takes and how it is composed. The images make real the experience of the time. Things like comment, acting, exposition, in the terms of conventional theatre are extraneous and lessen the depth of the experience of the real time of the piece. The direct presentation of the images and the character of the time are the most important things.

10

WASHES

Claes Oldenburg

Creation of *Washes* followed the procedure established in previous pieces:

1. A period of about two weeks, of priming myself with possibilities – practical and impractical – for a pool piece, recording these in a book, and writing a number of script drafts.
2. Familiarizing myself with the particular place. In this case by signing up for massage, etc., at Al Roon's. Noticing the importance of sound in the hall, the impossibility of any rapid action. Details of the normal activity of the Health Club.
3. Recruiting the cast from volunteers, some new and some familiar from past performances. Setting up schedule of rehearsals. First meeting.
4. Purchase of objects and costumes. In this case mostly from Canal Street stores, Avenue C used clothing stores, several "thrift" shops, swimming pool suppliers, and sporting goods stores.
5. First three rehearsals, combining prepared ideas, actual place, individuals in cast, and objects and costumes. Confusion and numerous trials and errors.
6. Final rehearsal: simplification of results of first rehearsals to strongest incidents, discarding of the rest. Imposition of simple time scheme of cues.
7. Four performances before audience in May 1965, with changes continuing to final performance.

Washes depended as usual very much on place. The involvement of the audience was mostly through place conditions: humidity, difficult placement (they had to stand on the narrow edges of the pool), tension of wet and dry. A mass audience swim which had been planned was called off at the last minute because of the management's objections. Audience was asked to wear bathing suits.

The final script of *Washes* contained ten untitled parts. The timing of the parts was done by me and light signals were used to cue beginning and end. White lights were placed over the water and over the shallow and deep ends; turning these on cued action. The intervals between parts were lit by dim blue lights. The length of each part varied for each performance according to my intuition of the pace. I watched the action with my back to the pool through a window reflection.

Al Roon's pool is in the basement of the Riverside Plaza Hotel on Manhattan's West 73rd St. The pool is seventy-five feet by twenty-five feet, and is surrounded by an edge about a foot wide. Back of this edge is a space around the pool on the two long sides and the shallow end varying from two to three feet wide. On one long side, doors open the length of the pool to a gymnasium (which relieved the crowding of audience on that side).

The water is mostly over the head. The shallow portion extends only about ten feet, beyond which one must swim. Numbers mark the edges of the pool every five feet. There are two ladders at both the long ends. At the deep end the space behind the pool edge widens, and this is the area referred to as the deep stage, where the audience was not permitted to stand. At the back of this area are doors leading to a Hot Room and Steam Bath and Solarium, overhung with yellow plastic awnings. To the left facing the deep stage is the locker room and offstage, where the players waited and dressed.

The audience waited in the adjoining gym until the pool was ready. The water was calm and a red light was set floating in the water. The light stayed in the water throughout the performance, as did all the objects that were placed in the water, so that the pool – a strong green color – changed from a perfectly still body of water to one in which clothing, furniture, people, pipes, and other debris bobbed as after a flood.

A figure called Lifeguard (so identified by his costume on which the title was printed) and I (wearing oversize overalls dyed a bright yellow) aided the ushers of Theater Rally in positioning the audience around three sides of the pool. I was friendly, shaking hands with people while telling them not to smoke, not to throw things in the pool, etc. – instructions from the management. When the audience was placed I took a position at my window. On the first three nights I asked the audience to be as quiet as possible so that the small sounds of the piece would not be missed. But at the cast's urging I did not make this announcement the fourth night, which permitted laughter and applause, and which, as it turned out, did not prevent the small sounds from being heard. I suppose I wanted to inhibit the audience.

The situation at the beginning of the piece was as follows: on the deep stage there were a massage table, a phonograph with a record of continuous thunder, two oil drums with a folded giant American flag on top, and a bridge (later to be placed across the center of the pool) on the floor. On the edge of the pool at the deep end, Pat, or a fat Humpty-

Dumpty-like figure holding a net at the end of a metal stick, fished for plastic bananas and pears which she threw in. At the edge of the shallow end were a woman, Letty, in a bathing suit, and a man, David, fully clad. These three players were in position as the audience entered.

I signaled the man stationed at the lights, D. Farbman, and the white lights turned blue. I signaled him again and the white lights returned, starting the piece.

Part One

Marjorie enters, in a white costume like a flier, with a white flier's cap and dark blue sunglasses. She puts on the phonograph record of thunder and commences exercising on the massage table. She counts, $\frac{1}{8}$, $1\frac{1}{8}$, $2\frac{1}{8}$, etc., or $\frac{1}{4}$, $1\frac{1}{4}$, $2\frac{1}{4}$, etc., while exercising.

Lucas enters in a suit and shirt and hat, all dyed blue, carrying a yellow chair. He crosses the deep stage, walks along the pool edge to a point near the center. He tries the chair on the water several times. Then tries sitting on it and sinks. He repeats the action. After several sittings/ sinkings he takes off his clothes and ties them on the chair, jacket over back, pants across, shoes on seat, as a man going to bed might place his clothes. From this point the chair becomes a free piece, floating with its load of clothes this way and that during the remaining composition. Lucas also, in a bathing suit and carrying a stainless steel disk, becomes a free piece, or "floater," with instructions to improvise action until his appearance in Part Eight. Through my glass I see him study himself from the edge in the disk like Narcissus. (Another time he floated on his back like a seal looking up into the disk.)

David, as soon as the part begins, starts walking fully dressed into the water down the shallow ladder, until only his head is above water. He walks out, waits a moment, and then walks in again. To the audience his figure under water appears compressed like a midget's. When the part ends, David becomes a "floater" or free piece, continuing to improvise around the action of cutting his clothes off with scissors until Part Nine, and also helping Letty tie red balloons to her body with string.

Letty begins putting on her balloons at the start of Part One and continues to do so until Part Nine.

Pat continues to fish, moving around the edges of the pool, intruding herself into other actions, and obscuring the view of the audience, until Part Eight.

Approximate time: four minutes.

Part Two

After a blue interval (about $\frac{1}{4}$ minute), white lights again.

Rudy dives into pool immediately on entering deep stage.

Anina enters, walking along the pool edge, carrying a small silver cup and wearing a leopard skin fur, like water wings. Tied on her ankle is a cow bell which hangs over the pool edge and sounds as she walks. She struts, walks jerkily, stops, runs, and in this variety of gaits makes her way all around the pool. Meanwhile Rudy throws himself against the pool sides trying to grab at her ankles, following her in an irregular pattern through the water, sometimes crossing the pool to return violently. When she reaches the point from which she started, Rudy pulls her into the pool. The part ends and they swim out in blue light; exit.

Approximate time: two minutes.

Part Three

Gloria enters carrying a styrofoam and plastic floating chair (white and green with blue trim and plastic drinking glasses sunk in the arms). Also magazine, banana, safety razor, and folding measuring stick (and other objects of her own choosing). Wearing a net cap and one-piece black bathing suit. Launches chair and climbs in. Thereafter she moves freely around the edges of the pool, measuring them, sometimes using the stick as a fishing rod, reading the magazine, shaving her legs, eating banana, and saying at intervals: "I lost seventy-eight pounds" or variations thereof, while looking up at the audience or tugging at their ankles. Gloria continues as a "floater" through as many parts as she wishes.

Dorothea and Max enter. Max launches the two oil drums, throwing them in the water with a great splash. Dorothea takes the folded giant American flag, walks to the center edge and there slips into the water with the flag. She wears gold gloves. Max composes a percussion piece slamming the barrels together with a variety of resonant sounds. Dorothea spreads the giant flag in water. After a while the wet flag is draped over both barrels in a funeral effect. When the part ends, Max and Dorothea remove the flag and let it sink to the pool bottom.

Approximate time: four minutes.

Part Four

Marjorie re-enters in same white costume, puts on record of thunder. Exercises as before.

Yvonne walks around the pool in a white costume, to the shallow end. Walks into water, costume floating around her body.

Walter enters with ladder, walks down opposite side, puts ladder into water, and composes it in relation to the pool edge, also extending it to Yvonne who swims away from it (as if avoiding an attempt at rescue).

Walter slips into pool, continues to manipulate ladder towards Yvonne, raising ladder in water, turning it around. After about a minute and a half, Yvonne leaves the water and strips off the white dress to a black net bathing suit. She returns along the pool edge and Walter, leaving ladder to float in the water, follows her. She waits for him but walks away just as he reaches her. This is repeated until she returns to the point where she entered. As he nears this time, she jumps in the pool. Walter leaves stage. Yvonne swims out. Marjorie turns off record of thunder and leaves deep stage.

Approximate time: three minutes.

Part Five

Barbara and Debby enter carrying a parachute dyed red. Each taking one end they walk the length of the pool on opposite edges. The parachute unfurls as they walk and drags in the water. Reaching the shallow end, they let go the parachute, which spreads in the pool. They are wearing summer dresses which they strip off to white underwear and slide into the water. They wrestle in the water entangling themselves in the parachute. As they wrestle, they laugh, pausing from time to time to spread the chute in the green water.

Henry enters on deep stage, carrying a yellow rubber boat with a blue bottom, a "soft" paddle (pipe painted ivory with a red rubber paddle flapping), a newspaper, a folded white plastic sheet and smoking a cigar. He wears sunglasses and a robe. With the aid of the Lifeguard, he climbs into the boat and paddles out with some difficulty to about the center of the pool. He reads his paper and smokes. After a time, he puts down the paper and covers himself entirely with the white plastic sheet.

Barbara appears on the deep stage after Henry has "slept" a while. She wears a bathing suit, harsh red lipstick, and has kept her hair dry. She enters the pool by the ladder and stealthily and slowly swims to Henry's boat, carrying a rope which she attaches to the boat. She swims back pulling the boat and Henry. On reaching the deep end ladder, she ties the boat, leaves the pool and stage.

After a moment, Henry wakes up, takes off the sheet, gathers his possessions, climbs out, leaving the rubber boat tied to the ladder.

The white lights go out and the wrestling girls leave the water and walk out along the edge in blue. The parachute remains in the pool.

Appoximate time: six minutes.

Part Six

Ellen and Sarah appear on deep stage. Sarah climbs into the water, being careful not to wet her hair. Ellen takes a position at the end of the long edge of the pool. Slowly they proceed the length of the pool, Ellen walking, Sarah swimming in a straight line. Their eyes are fixed on each other. Each anticipates the other's action. If one moves slightly forward, the other immediately makes up the distance, so that they remain perfectly parallel. When they reach the shallow end, Ellen joins Sarah in the water. They stand facing one another absolutely still just to the side of the shallow ladder.

Al and Geoffrey enter with the girls but remain in the background pacing the deep stage until the girls reach the center of the pool. Then they begin to wrestle, slapping one another's flesh so that it resounds in the hall. When the girls reach the shallow end and face each other, Al and Geoffrey pick up short lengths of dry two-by-fours and smack them together. They move down opposite sides the length of the pool, as if their battle continued despite the interposition of the water. They wear aprons of rubber and bathing suits. The sounds are sharp and earsplitting. When the two reach the shallow end, they put the sticks down on the edge and leap in the water, continuing to wrestle. Sarah and Ellen leave the pool at this point and both walk slowly the length of the pool and offstage. Al and Geoffrey swim the pool length vigorously and climb out.

Approximate time: four minutes.

Part Seven/Part Eight/Part Nine

Part Seven, Part Eight, and Part Nine are not separated by blue intervals. But the blue light does go on during film projection in Part Eight.

When the wrestlers exit, a bridge which fits over the pool, of reinforced wood, about two feet wide, is lifted from the floor of the deep stage and carried by the Lifeguard and me to a spot about center of pool under a light. The bridge is tested.

Pat, who as a "floater" has moved fishing around the edges, mounts the bridge and begins removing her fat costume of many garments, laying them as if to dry along the bridge.

Four men, Raymond, Michael, Richard, Jon, in bathing suits enter deep stage with a set of stovepipes joined in different ways through which a clothesline dyed red has been threaded. Two of them enter the pool and tie the end of the line to the bridge. The other two remain onstage pushing the stovepipes down the line into the water. At the same time, four women, Elaine, Martha, Nancy, and Jackie, enter through the audience at the shallow end. They are fully dressed. They walk into the water by the shallow ladder. One of them carries a length of the red clothesline, swims out to the bridge, and attaches it. The other end is attached to the shallow ladder. The women remove their clothes, including shoes, and hang them on the red line with clothespins.

The four men interrupt their threading of pipe to grunt and to lie on the edges of the pool breathing very hard. The four women from time to time wash each other with a long brush and sponges and whistle one note.

Performers on the bridge spanning the pool in the basement of the Riverside Plaza Hotel for *Washes* (1965) by Claes Oldenburg. In the background, men string flue pipes on a clothesline. (Photo by Peter Moore.)

The action of the four men and four women (Part Seven) continues through the dance of Lucas and Pat (Part Eight) and the balloon sequence of Letty and David (Part Nine).

Pat, having removed her fat clothes and laid them out, makes herself up, sitting on the bridge, and puts on white kneesocks and a white short sailor blouse.

Lucas gives up his role as "floater," mounts the bridge, dries himself, and puts on a pair of oversized ivory-colored nylon pajama pants. He "walks" in different ways, putting different parts of his body in the pajamas. At one point, his hand wearing a shoe "walks" one pajama leg while he holds one of his legs up inside. He attaches small plungers to his body which stick out under the nylon. He stuffs the pajama bottoms with a rubber green alligator. When he has finished his pajama-bottom dance and Pat has finished making up and redressing, they join in a dance with a sheet. The sheet is first held out horizontally, then shaken, then turned vertically. It catches the white light of a film projector running without film, which projects the silhouettes of the sheet and dancers on the audience and wall at the shallow end. The blue light is on during projection. Pat and Lucas come together, kiss for a moment, fold the sheet once, repeat the horizontal-shake-vertical action. Come together again, kiss, fold twice and so on until the sheet, having been folded several times, is just a bundle and hard to shake. The sheet is loosened, the projector goes off. Lucas covers himself and Pat with the sheet, holds her upside down, and the dance continues with limbs protruding. After a while, Lucas removes the sheet, places it carefully on the surface of the pool, picks Pat up under the arms and drops her toes-first into the sheet. She plummets into the water, the sheet closing around her.

Near the climax of this dance, Letty, who is now completely covered with blown-up red balloons, rises from her position seated at the shallow edge and enters the water with the aid of David on the shallow ladder. She floats. She floats out into the water bounded by the bridge and the women's clothesline, perfectly rigid. David, who during the performance has cut his clothes off, walks into the water in his bathing suit and swims up to and around Letty. After a moment of letting her float, he begins biting the balloons, holding them so that they pop with a loud sound that resounds in the hall. He bites one balloon after another until all are bitten and broken and Letty sinks. Then he swims away.

Approximate time of Parts Seven, Eight, Nine: ten minutes.

Part Ten

A blue interval, brief. When the white lights come on, all players except Marjorie and Lifeguard enter water and float as if drowned.

Marjorie puts on record of thunder and exercises. After about a minute, the Lifeguard (Alex) blows his whistle. Marjorie leaves the deep stage. The drowned come to life and swim toward deep end.

A record is put on of Brahms Symphony No. 1, Finale, played by David Rose in syncopation.

Approximate time: two minutes.

The piece is over.

11

VERDUROUS SANGUINARIA

Act I

Jackson Mac Low

This play was composed in January–February 1961 by chance operations upon a gamut of twenty-six dictionary entries, including single words, two-word phrases, and proper names – all selected by chance. The words of the title and the names of the four characters were among these twenty-six words and phrases.

The play was first produced in April, and again in June, 1961, in New York. It was broadcast by station WBAI on 10 November 1962.

Some elements of the play, such as silences and nonverbal sounds, are completely indeterminate, that is, they must be different in every performance. In two whole acts, and in a few speeches elsewhere, both the words and all other elements are, in this sense, indeterminate.

Actions, including the production of musical sounds and noises, are improvised throughout, except for two actions explicitly directed in Act III, scene i.

Pauses are free except for Act II, scene i, where the speeches should follow each other on cue as repartee, and Act V, where no long silences should occur except for those happening in the simultaneous speeches from asymmetries.

If a performer is uncertain whether his cue word has been given he should (usually in a whisper) ask the performer who should have said the cue word whether he has said the word or completed his last speech. If widely separated from the other performer, the uncertain one may inquire out loud in forms such as "Did you say your last 'butter knife'?" or "Did you say 'ropy'?"

Seven speeches out of thirteen should each be addressed to a particular person.

VERDUROUS SANGUINARIA

a play for 4 people

CHARACTERS

The Holy Grail (man or woman)
The Isle of Wight (woman)
Edward Eggleston (man)
Catherine (woman)

Act I

EE: Shortage (phototaxis) running knot! Sash: ropy; butter knife; Catherine "hindbrain" obeisance.

HG: Shortage? Prima donna . . . inhabitancy? Edward Eggleston second fiddle.

IW: Holy Grail! Scutch . . . verdurous! Sicken, sanguinaria. Hindbrain, jail delivery; hemathermal: phototaxis, leitmotiv obeisance – sicken sash, extemporize "Holy Grail" – prima donna, Isle of Wight . . . Isle of Wight?

HG: Verdurous thralldom! Catherine. Scutch? Thralldom – ropy hemathermal (extemporize) . . . resurrectionism? Arrestor "leitmotiv"? Sanguinaria resurrectionism: second fiddle – butter knife!

EE: Running knot "jail delivery" inhabitancy "Isle of Wight" leitmotiv obeisance?

HG: Inhabitancy jail delivery; thralldom! Verdurous? Edward Eggleston. Second fiddle, Isle of Wight, prima donna. Holy Grail running knot, resurrectionism butter knife! Sanguinaria! Hindbrain; shortage (scutch): ropy – butter knife sash? Running knot.

IW: Phototaxis? Second fiddle "thralldom" arrestor, sicken! Ropy (inhabitancy)? Sanguinaria? Resurrectionism hindbrain sash, shortage? Holy Grail?

HG: Sicken . . . prima donna. Verdurous! Extemporize 'scutch' (jail delivery), Edward Eggleston: Catherine – leitmotiv hemathermal?

CATH: Hemathermal phototaxis, obeisance Catherine extemporize, shortage Edward Eggleston: thralldom "Isle of Wight" sanguinaria – leitmotiv leitmotiv! Inhabitancy; verdurous: resurrectionism! Ropy shortage (extemporize) "obeisance"?

HG: Sash "sash," arrestor "phototaxis" thralldom! Second fiddle butter knife – sanguinaria: extemporize; Holy Grail? Jail delivery – hema-thermal ... prima donna 'hindbrain' arrestor (Catherine): verdurous "obeisance"!

CATH: Scutch; running knot, Isle of Wight.

HG: Edward Eggleston, Holy Grail!

EE: Second fiddle! Sicken (phototaxis). Ropy ... inhabitancy jail delivery, sicken. Butter knife, Catherine. Hemathermal, prima donna! Running knot; scutch resurrectionism hindbrain; Isle of Wight, running knot: sash ... resurrectionism?

IW: Sanguinaria hindbrain. Inhabitancy. Running knot Edward Eggles-ton ... second fiddle! Leitmotiv hemathermal? Holy Grail 'photo-taxis': scutch, prima donna: hemathermal – obeisance (jail delivery) 'jail delivery' arrestor, sicken!

HG: Scutch! Sicken – verdurous inhabitancy – Edward Eggleston ... verdurous "obeisance": arrestor 'sanguinaria': prima donna? Ropy – hindbrain – shortage. Thralldom, thralldom "butter knife" ... extem-porize. Catherine. Butter knife Holy Grail extemporize!

EE: Catherine (shortage). Isle of Wight sash (second fiddle) ... resurrec-tionism: phototaxis; ropy, jail delivery, sash. Resurrectionism, scutch! Extemporize obeisance inhabitancy? Hemathermal, thralldom sicken ... phototaxis, shortage, sicken?

End of Act I

Note: If the players feel very strongly about the matter, they may change the order of the speeches in Act I. If this is done, each player still says only the speeches assigned to him, without making changes within them, but says the speeches at points in the act different from those where they now occur. This should be done purely: the speeches are to be said either *in the order here given, with no changes whatsoever,* or *in an entirely different order, never the same in any two performances.*

The most interesting thing about *Verdurous Sanguinaria* – and the reason Michael Kirby took it for this issue of *TDR* – is the variety of ways in which the small gamut of twenty-six words is used in the different acts and scenes. The first act alone gives an entirely erroneous impression of the play. It would seem to the casual reader that the entire play is composed of punctuated but only partially syntactical speeches (in the sense of the usual English syntax). But the fact is, of course, that the twenty-six words are also used as neuclei upon which ordinarily syntactical speeches are built, as well as in a number of other ways, in the course of the play. One of the main effects of the play is that produced by the passage from one way of using the gamut of words to another. The effect of the breakthrough into ordinary English syntax, especially the first time, is quite startling, I have been told. It is therefore an editorial mistake to print just one act of this play.

Editor's note: Because of space limitations we have printed only Act I of Verdurous Sanguinaria. *If readers would like to see the entire script we shall be glad to supply it. Those interested in production must write directly to Jackson Mac Low, 42 North Moore Street, New York, NY 10013–2441.*

12

GRAPHIS

Dick Higgins and Letty Eisenhauer

The Graphis series is the result of a feeling that conventional theatre notation in which one action follows another leaves untried an enormous variety of techniques that could enrich our experience. This feeling was of course one of the causes of my "milieu play" form of which *The Tart* is an example. With the Graphises, I was trying to set up a form that was unsemantic, even choreographic, in conception if not in execution.

Experimental music has frequently used extraordinary notations. Stockhausen, Graettinger, and Cage have found notations which expand musical vocabularies. So I started out with drawn notations such as, "The higher up on this page this line goes, reading from left to right, the louder you speak. Where there are two lines to be read vertically, you choose." What I did not specify was what was to be said. I thought people would quote the newspapers. These notations had a graphic look and so I called them *Graphis*. That was in the autumn of 1958. By winter I was doing notations for music and theatre together and I was asking myself, "Is there any visual material which cannot be used as a notation?" I began to use ready-made notations, like things I found in the street. I used the actors' bodies (I called them "athletes" at the time because the concept of "acting" turned me off) and they "read" each other.

In 1959 I concentrated on sharing stock material as a way of doing performances. I stopped the more anarchistic *Graphis* where each person performed a range of possibilities so wide that only a nervous confusion prevailed, and I began to give people lists of things which were placed in relationships to other things. If I heard you say "Why" that would be my cue to say "Why not" and so on. These pieces became too literary. Then I decided that these activities had to happen in space and I started to draw notations again: very large and on the stage so that the performers could follow the lines and share these as well as materials. These pieces were the high point of the series which includes *Graphis 82*. Notice that the location of material is arbitrary. You cannot walk from "Locks" to "Locksmith" without "Macaroni" there in between. The implications of this delighted me.

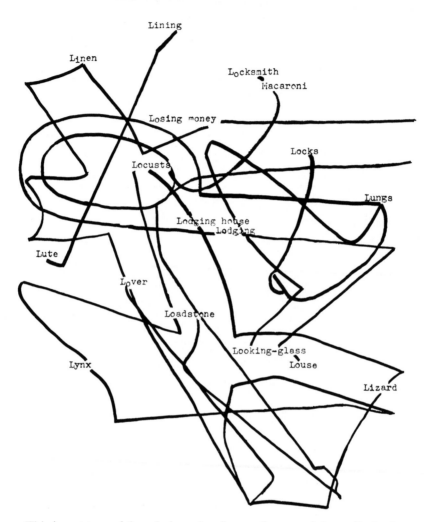

This is not true of the whole series. In one the materials are limited to stuff associated with a good breakfast. One can perform it and make breakfast at the same time.

At the performance of *Graphis 82* we established several conventions that were not implied by the form but were necessary if we were to begin. We started everyone at "Lungs" because one must start somewhere; we asked everyone to develop, in his own way, his concept of "Lungs." From "Lining" anyone could go offstage – this was because it was near the wings and one couldn't get off at the two blank lines that seemed the logical place. We needed an exit place because the performance was the length of a half-hour tape of circus music which would weary a performer if there were no chance to rest. And when the music stopped at the end everyone left. What these conventions had in common was that they made it possible to do the piece. Everything else came from the notation; everything, in other words, but the stage business.

Presently there are over 130 pieces in the *Graphis* series, and I expect there will be more. Many of the recent ones are simple geometric structures which one either follows or interprets. And some include vertical space: one is a large number of arrows converging on a point in the air. I'd like to be around when that one happens.

Dick Higgins

The small group of people stand knotted together. With great gulps, sighs, whistles, and snorts they stir the air. Whum pa pa, whum pa pa, ta de da da da the circus sound blares forth. The knot breaks, scattering performers in all directions scuttling along white line paths. "The Renaissance influence reveals itself more clearly in such a house as Longleat with ..." Marilyn Monroe steps forward and throws kisses, pouts and wiggles her ass. She somersaults forward and stands on her head. A lover grabs any loved one in a hysterical embrace, the passion of which knocks the desired to the ground. The lute starts playing and it is instantly joined by the musician who adds his skillful technique to the action, plucking the round body deftly, causing it to vibrate and tremble delicately. A plague of locusts descends buzzing the gambler who rolls dice with a loser's frenzy. The dice are continually getting caught in the macaroni which is being jostled and sloshed through a machine. The lizard suns himself and the lynx screams and claws in frustrated fertility.

This chaotic scene is not a passage from *The Snake Pit*. It represents the kind of complexity, confusion, and visual richness that should result during a performance of *Graphis 82*. This chance theatre piece was performed 1 and 2 May 1962, at The Living Theatre in New York City. It was part of a rather lengthy program including the work of La Monte Young, Carolee Schneemann, and Phil Corner. Variations on the piece were eventually done in Wiesbaden, Paris, and Cologne.

Graphis 82 is just what its title suggests: "[something] drawn or written." In this particular case it is both drawn and written. At first glance it appears to be a series of half-connected lines and curves recalling the automatic writing used in some paintings (Mathieu, Tobey). Actually, the original form of *Graphis 82*, as published in *One Hundred Plays by Dick Higgins*, came about by making incomplete and over-lapping outlines from a pair of tin snips lying on a piece of paper. The "something written" part of the definition – the words which are randomly superimposed on the diagram – were culled from a Puerto Rican dream book, *King Tut's Dream Book*.

The plan of *Graphis 82* was enlarged onto a piece of black polyethylene, twenty feet by twenty-four feet, which could be folded up and easily carried to the theatre, where it was stretched out on the stage floor. In this way it served as both set and script (or score) for the performance.

At the first rehearsal the scoring and rules of the piece were explained to the performers. In *Graphis 82* each player had to make up an action for each word on the graphis and a method of moving from one word to another. Usually the actions would have something in common with the words; for example, the actor may devise actions deriving from his own feelings about the word, or attempt to describe the word in pantomime, or use a dictionary definition. In some cases he may put nonsense activities with the word. Some typical actions: at the word "linen" someone sewed up a giant imaginary sheet with great physically executed stitches, at "lodging" someone actually lay down and slept. "Lizard" inspired various interpretations of reptiles slithering around in the sun, spitting out forked tongues. One actor struggled with a huge weighty imaginary stone at "loadstone." A leftist political harangue was pantomimed at the word "lynx," construed as the German "links" meaning "the left." "Lodging house" inspired research into the construction and appearance of lodging houses and produced the only spoken material in the performance: "The Renaissance influence reveals itself more clearly in such a house as Longleat with its balance and symmetry, fundamental to the Renaissance. The exterior with its flat roof superimposing order, regularity, and proportions reflects the Italian influence; the large number of openings, bay and mullioned windows are due to the medieval English tradition." When the piece was performed in Paris, an artist, Daniel Spoerri, contributed an action which I think should be mentioned here because of its originality. He mapped a course which would not ever touch on a word and followed this path very slowly, with very small measured steps. It provided a beautiful contrast to the frantic activity of the other performers.

Once the actions were determined we had to link them. The performers used the graphis like a map – following each line and arriving at a word where the appropriate activity was performed. Usually there was no preconceived route. Decisions to advance, retreat, go right or left on a branched path of the diagram, were made by the actor on the spot. In order to move from word to word each actor had to devise a cueing situation or situations. Methods of cueing could be simple, such as counting to ten (or twenty, or five) while performing an action, and then moving to the next word and activity. For example, the performance started at the word "lungs" and each performer used his own cueing situation to move from "lungs" to the next word. I counted slowly to fifty before leaving "lung" for my next action. Whenever performer A moves, that may be a cue for performer B also to move. The audience's involuntary and voluntary reactions can be used as cues (coughing, laughter, heckling). A move could be made whenever a spectator – picked from the crowd at the start of the performance – laughed, coughed, or crossed his legs. Or the audience could be treated as a whole, giving cue whenever it laughed, etc.

In one case, a performer cued himself. He did not move until his activity had been performed to his satisfaction. Sometimes when a particularly enjoyable action came up the actor would continue doing it for some time. The speech given at "lodging house" was one of these activities. First the speech was given at a regular speed, then in slow motion, then with the player's back toward the audience, and again facing the audience. Having finally completed this action to his satisfaction the performer moved on to the next word. Combinations of any and all of these methods of cueing can also be used, or any others which the performer finds compatible.

The more keen the imagination and industry of the performer the richer the piece. The cueing situations vary widely from one performance to another, since chance governs how often an actor might arrive on a certain word, or how much he relies on audience reaction for cueing. Some performers devised activities or actions to use as bridges between words. "Lynx" may inspire a catlike activity to be performed while stationed at the word "lynx." When cued to move, the actor may continue the cat activity until he has reached the next word. However haphazard this may seem, all actions, words, and cueing situations are individually examined ahead of time by the director. Changes may be suggested to give the performance more variety.

During rehearsals we were encouraged either to spread out widely or bunch up. After several rehearsals certain words were suggested as being good places for bunching up because of the actions involved. This is one way the director can control the performance. In some cases it was pointed out that certain actions had more impact when performed together. A good example of this from *Graphis 82* is the word "lute." There was someone who pretended to be a plucked lute; there was also a lute player. The director encouraged these two to perform together if possible. Thus, if one arrived at the word "lute" the other would try to work his way to "lute" as quickly as possible, so that the musician could play the instrument. This type of direction must be answered with flexible cueing.

In reality the business of rehearsals is different to deal with in this kind of performance. There comes a point at which continued rehearsal would negate spontaneity. However, it is entirely untrue that such theatre pieces are unrehearsed. Many hours are spent working together to perfect a sense of timing and sensitivity to each other, as in any legitimate theatre production. Since *Graphis 82* is a continuous performance during which no performer leaves the stage, props to help delineate the action are not encouraged unless they can be easily concealed and carried on the performer. With the exception of the Graphis design on the floor, no stage sets are used and costumes are frowned on. While it is not absolutely necessary, the piece is usually accompanied by music of the director's choice.

To help you visualize the possibilities, I will describe a portion of my performance in *Graphis 82*. The action starts at "lungs" with everyone breathing, and then as the actors receive various cues, they begin their trips along the branched routes of the diagram. I stayed at lungs until I had counted to fifty slowly. The background music was taken from *The Greatest Show on Earth* (Cecil B. De Mille). This music inspired me to do a "cakewalk" from one word to another. In other words, I added actions to bridge the gap from one word to another; these additional actions were not always the same. I "cakewalked" from "lungs" to "losing money." At this point I had no action I really felt was good enough to do, so I decided that on certain words, where I had failed to think up a really good action, I would just stand on my head. I stood on my head at "losing money" and counted to ten. At ten (my cue) I moved to the next word by doing somersaults (a bridge action) to "lining." There I stood like an old empty coat on a hanger. Some of my cues were geared to another actor's actions; when Actor A moved I would move. In this way I had a very erratic and seemingly uncontrolled performance. I left "lining" and "cakewalked" to "lute." "Lute" became "loot" and I looted the nearest person to me. As soon as I had succeeded in picking a pocket I could move to the next word. Here I followed through on the action of "loot" and advanced in mock secretive manner (bridge action), on tippy toes to "lover." At "lover" I stood on my head, counted to ten, and somersaulted to "lynx," where I posed as the sphinx. When the proper cue came up I left "lynx" as a cat and crawled along the path to "loadstone." Here, according to dictionary definition "something that attracts," I became Marilyn Monroe, throwing kisses, giggling, wiggling my ass. When I was cued, I swung into a saunter to the next word. Arriving at "macaroni," I skipped around in a circle, blowing on an imaginary flute and whistling "Yankee Doodle." On cue I moved from "macaroni" to "lodging house" where I opened an invisible door and put down my suitcases, over and over again until cued on, etc. . . .

The length of the accompanying circus music determined the duration of the performance. This is just one solution to the problem of performance time. The director can use chance methods to end the performance, such as setting an alarm clock or deciding (with the actors) on some event which would probably occur during the performance as a signal to end; or he may want to leave it open, and have the actors themselves decide to stop the piece by walking off the stage when they feel they have performed long enough. As is generally the case in Dick Higgins' theatre pieces, the performance duration is usually pushed to the limit – the audience begins to get restless, they talk and squirm in their seats, some suspect that this will go on all night, and after twenty to twenty-five minutes they begin to leave. When the music ends (thirty minutes) the actors simply leave the stage.

Letty Eisenhauer

13

THE TART, OR MISS AMERICA

Dick Higgins

THE THING ABOUT *THE TART*

The thing about *The Tart* is that I wanted to be specific and unabstract. Most experimental theatre has been done by painters who think abstractly. But I was a musician in rebellion against my medium; I didn't come to Happenings from the visual arts. I felt that the painters were too elegant and iconoclastic. What was missing was danger. So I wrote *The Tart* to express a sociological concept through choreography. It was not successful; neither was it intended to be. As it has no psychological empathy, *The Tart* does not permit the audience to view it as a play or ballet. But my hope was that audiences would sympathize with the performers (not the characters) in their social contexts and that the lines would be more tragic than funny.

We performed *The Tart* in the Sunnyside Gardens boxing ring in New York. Here people come expecting combat between two men. If we have developed an aesthetic expectation in theatre, there is little of that in boxing. Style is theatre's mark while catharsis rules prize fighting. Furthermore there is something marvelous about the ring: a pedestal onto which one mounts, enacts a ritual act of (implied) violence, and goes away. The light, heavy with smoke, is broken up by the movements of the fighters, like "atmosphere" in an impressionist painting. The setting is free from the traditional trappings of theatre and the mind is free to wander among the pillars, lights, and hot dog stands.

Formally, *The Tart* is not a conventional play. I worked out its form seven years ago when I was looking for ways to apply collage to theatre. Most of my work since then has followed this form, though only recently have I gone through with its implications. I call my pieces "Event Theatre," but Allan Kaprow called them Happenings and I'm not interested enough in semantics to quarrel.

Each performer is given material to work with. In *The Tart* they have the same lines but different actions (invented by the performer). Both lines and actions are cued by lighting, other performers' events, sounds, and so on. No narrative sequence is possible. Consequently the aesthetic

impact of the play depends upon the clarity of the lines (and their ability
to withstand repetition), the skill of the performers in picking up their
cues, and the overall lucidity of the piece. This last factor – my
responsibility – is the most important. It means that the effect depends
upon the simplicity of the message. The form is therefore best suited for
dialectical and socially oriented stuff. Anything else has a nightmare
effect.

The Tart is about women although only the title role is played by a
woman. Each performer identifies with a stock urban character, but each
line is attributed to a persona, such as: "Light and Electricity, say the
electricians." Each performer becomes a persona or reacts directly to a
persona. Through collage principles I try to suggest a cross-section of
society. Chance techniques emphasize the subject matter by eliminating
narrative. To keep the performance clear and exciting I made the cueing
the responsibility of the "special performer(s)." These people produced
cues and thereby started or stopped things from happening. At first I
thought of them as merely means, but now I think they say something
about power. In *The Tart* the special performers were dressed as
Salvation Army workers.

We only had about forty-four hours of rehearsal and we needed eighty-
eight. The performers lacked security, though most of them were
veterans. We did the play on Easter Saturday and Sunday 1965, and we
had small audiences; the performers were conscious of this.

On the other hand, the Tart, Letty Eisenhauer, to whom the piece is
dedicated, played perfectly. I view the persona as part of the *nouveau*
middle class, complete with eye makeup and an Alpine, New Jersey,
address (a discreet Levittown). Letty played her as an urban-minority
trollop who was "going places." Ay-o, the wild man from Japan, led the
special performers, threw gigantic (three-foot cube) dice, projected slides
over everyone, set bonfires with carnival fire (which burns at 120°), and
so on. Sunday's show was much better than Saturday's and I wish there
had been one on Monday. Also I wish the production wasn't called a
Happening, because it wasn't.

THE TART
– for Letty –

Between three and eleven regular performers and one special performer
are required for performance. The special performer does not perform
according to the general procedure of this piece and so will be discussed
later. Each regular performer centers his part around one persona. The
personae which must be included are the young man, Mr. Miller, and the
tart. Other possible personae are the old man, the prophet, the butchers,

the doctors, the drinking man, the chemist, the yogi, the steelworkers, and the electricians.

Each performer considers the possibilities for objective characterizations for each persona. They then independently of each other select personae around whom to center their performances. Next they compare notes to make certain that there is as least one each of the young man, Mr. Miller, and the tart. It is assumed that there can be any number of each persona.

Each performer now lists twenty-two stage actions of his own devising such that no action requires the use of a particular prop or the presence of a particular person on the stage. To this list he adds "exit" ten times and "entrance" four times. This list of actions is now assigned to the thirty-six situations given below at random, with any number of actions assigned to any of the situations. In the case where there is more than one action for a given situation, the performer now determines whether he will perform all the actions or choose among them. Exit and entrance actions are always followed.

Next the performer assigns all the thirty speeches given below to situations, with the option of assigning a speech to more than one situation but never of assigning more than one speech to a given situation. The performers now may begin to rehearse together.

The special performer examines the list of situations and determines how he can produce any of them which the regular performers cannot produce themselves. He now makes possible any number of ways of producing each situation. Next he amasses a collection of relevant Americana, the relevance to be determined by the social intent of the performance. At random during each performance he produces or withdraws any particular specimen of Americana. Finally he determines methods of beginning or ending any performance. He familiarizes the performers with these, and both begins and, at a time of his own devising, ends the performance.

The director, if any, gives the performance direction and makes any necessary alterations and supervises rehearsals. Rehearsals continue till there is no longer any technical obstacle to performance, and no longer.

When the line is spoken the performer becomes to some extent the persona to whom the line is attributed, but he never entirely abandons the persona whom he has developed for himself. He devises means of making each persona very specific, especially his own. When any action is performed, it is performed in a manner that is in some way consistent with the persona to whom any accompanying line is attributed. If there is no line, then the persona used is the base persona which the performer has selected.

A minimum of lines and actions is used in such a way as to include other performers. All performers stay six or more feet apart from each other or less than a foot close to each other as much of the time as possible. Some efforts are made to encourage the bunching up of the performers on each side of the performance area, particularly on one side. Performers offstage should frequently laugh softly and comment and whisper together, in such a way as to stress the moral values involved. All action except for this last provision should be confined to the performance area.

Situations

1. Someone dressed as a Salvation Army worker slowly crosses the stage diagonally.
2. Someone dressed as a Salvation Army worker shoots craps.
3. Someone dressed as a Salvation Army worker kisses somebody.
4. A very large object is brought in or removed.
5. A postage stamp is attached to something or somebody.
6. A key is dropped or milk is spilled.
7. A huge collage transparency is projected over the performers for about three seconds.
8. Red light falls on a performer.
9. Amber light falls on the performer.
10. Yellow light falls on the performer.
11. Green light falls on the performer.
12. Blue-green light falls on the performer.
13. Blue light falls on a performer.
14. Violet light falls on the performer.
15. Magenta light falls on a performer.
16. A shadow falls on the performer.
17. White light falls on the performer.
18. The performer is hidden by smoke, gauze, wrapped tissue paper or cloth, or some similar material.
19. Some other performer is hidden by smoke, gauze, wrapped tissue paper or cloth, or some similar material.
20. An empty paint bucket is given to some performer, then taken away.
21. Ten seconds pass after performance has begun or after the special performer has again signaled the beginning of the performance.
22. A very loud, clanging piece of music ends.
23. A very loud noise is heard.

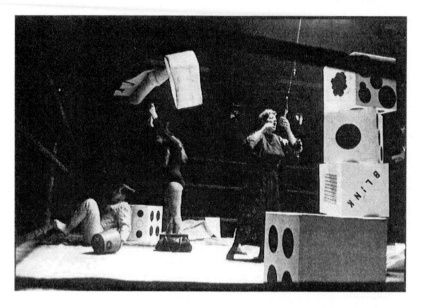

The yogi, the young man, and the prophet in Dick Higgins' *The Tart* (1965) at the Sunnyside Garden boxing ring in New York. (Photo by Peter Moore.)

24. A soft, tinny piece of music has been going on for nearly a minute.
25. A dull thump has been occurring regularly for over a minute.
26. Somebody is eating something or somebody in the audience is acting up.
27. Suddenly it is very hot.
28. The performance has been going on for a very long time, or nearly all the performers are onstage.
29. A performer is touched by another performer.
30. A performer collides with another performer.
31. A performer asks another performer a question.
32. A performer makes a statement in somebody else's persona.
33. Somebody shakes a performer.
34. Somebody criticizes a performer or his base persona.
35. Almost all the performers have been led offstage or the stage is darkened or there is nobody visible.
36. Colors fall on the performer in extremely rapid succession.

Speeches
1. Thank God it was nothing, says the tart. I know nothing about that, says the tart.
2. Your plumbing is all screwed up, say the doctors, I don't know if it's worth fixing it up. Can you afford it, ask the doctors.
3. That is unspeakable, says the young man, but what can you do?

4. There are no goats on this cliff, says the old man.

5. Behold the sea, saith the Lord.

6. Should I wear a skirt, asks the tart. Is there anything I can do, seriously, asks the tart. What do you want to give me, asks the tart. Do I really want to love them all, asks the tart.

7. Everything that ever happened is my fault and my responsibility, says the drinking man.

8. What do I want from Mr. Miller, asks the tart.

9. What is a good fuck, asks the young man, is it only me that's supposed to be involved?

10. How anonymous can you get, asks Mr. Miller.

11. I wonder what it's like to love me, says the tart.

12. One of my lambs fell off the cliff last week, says the old man, but it landed on a ledge. I hauled it in in the morning, says the old man, and it was none the worse for wear.

13. The steelworkers say no. No, say the steelworkers. (No. No.)

14. Thy word be my word, saith the prophet. Thy highways and byways be my skyways and my ways, saith the prophet.

15. In my country, loving a woman is a homosexual experience, says the drinking man.

16. But what can I do about it, ask the electricians.

17. I know all about that, says the tart.

18. Is there any woman who gives a damn, asks Mr. Miller.

19. If you are not willing to commit yourself to loving, you are dead, says the drinking man, because you are not willing to be alive.

20. I have nothing for you, baby, says the tart, you have given me too much and I have nothing to give you.

21. Light and electricity, say the electricians.

22. Does he want a raise from me, asks Mr. Miller, and if I give him a raise, am I investing too much in his future with me and too little in updating my operation here.

23. In Alpine nobody has anything to think about except himself and his spanking new life in the suburbs, says Mr. Miller. Know thyself is the credo of Alpine, says Mr. Miller, and lots of gups just know too much.

24. Why do I have to wait till I'm forty for the union to let me do the work I was trained for, asks the young man. And why did they let me get trained for it, asks the young man.

25. We have lots of people in Alpine, says the yogi.

26. If it's been five men, says the chemist, it might as well have been five hundred. Roll them bones, says the chemist.

27. Just what is my fault, asks Mr. Miller.

28. Why am I the wrong one if I love her, asks the young man.

29. In Alpine what is there to do, asks Mr. Miller. In Alpine you are not master of your fate, says Mr. Miller, and you are not responsible for what you do.
30. What would loving him be like, asks the tart.

17 June 1962
revised version

14

YVONNE RAINER INTERVIEWS
ANN HALPRIN

HALPRIN: I was trained as a traditional modern dancer. The big break came for me about fifteen years ago when I left the scene. I didn't know what I wanted to do except to leave that scene – that's when we built our outdoor platform.

RAINER: Had you been doing solo work before that or collaborating?

HALPRIN: Solo work. I also had a group.

RAINER: And you choreographed for the group?

HALPRIN: Yes. I had a studio together with Welland Lathrop, and was part of that tradition of modern dance. But then I felt a break. I was in a New York Dance Festival, an ANTA thing. I wasn't very stimulated, as I had gone to New York as the only dancer from the West Coast, but hadn't seen what was really going on in dance. When I came back I wasn't excited about anything. That's when the big break came. The workshop idea started when I left San Francisco and came out to Kentfield. Some of the students who had been working with me in San Francisco followed me. Because I didn't know what I wanted to do, or what I wanted to teach, we set up a workshop situation in which I gave myself permission to explore. Even though I was the catalyst of the group and somehow or other the teacher, I still made it very clear that I wasn't teaching in the usual sense. I didn't feel that I had to know an answer and teach it to somebody.

RAINER: What was the role of the people you brought?

HALPRIN: They simply wanted to have the opportunity to stay in contact with the kinds of activities I was interested in. They also wanted to explore and work together.

I wanted to explore in a particular way, breaking down any preconceived notions I had about what dance was, or what movement was, or what composition was. I began setting up situations where we could rely only on our improvisational skills. Everything was done, for quite a few years, with improvisation. The purpose of the improvisation was not self-expression. I was trying to get at subconscious areas, so things would happen in an unpredictable way. I was trying to eliminate stereotyped ways of reacting. Improvisation was used to release things that were blocked off because we were traditional modern dancers.

RAINER: Was the focus physical? Did you start out with the body?

HALPRIN: Sometimes it would be purely physical; we worked on technique this way. My training is in anatomy so it was easy for me to go into the bone structure and the muscle structure and to work like a kinesiologist. We would isolate in an anatomical and objective way the body as an instrument. We would improvise with rotation or flexion or other anatomical structures. We would say, we're going to begin to work with how you can articulate this part of the body, isolate it from another part of the body – what is the efficient way to do that movement, do we really need to do this or is it just habit? When we improvised we were finding out what *our* bodies could do, not learning somebody's else's pattern or technique.

As the teacher or director of the group, I never told anybody why a movement should be or how it should look. In that sense, too, they had to build their own technique. Even now in our company there is no unified look; there's a unified approach but everybody is different in movement. And we used improvisation to explore space and certain kinds of dynamics. We would set up a situation where two people had a focus that concerned the amount of space between them. They would improvise to get a feeling of what could happen, and what one person did would elicit a reaction from the other. We got involved in cause and effect. After a while we noticed that this was restrictive. But that period gave us a certain technique which is still one of our resources. All of us began to feel the need for another step.

RAINER: How long after was this?

HALPRIN: I think we worked together for four years using improvisation and starting really from the beginning. Out of that period we evolved compositions which were completely improvised with particular focuses. We began to allow the voice to become an integral part of movement, where breathing became sound or some heightened feeling stimulated certain associative responses and a word came, or a sound, or a shout. Free-association became an important part of the work. This would very often manifest itself in dialog. We began to deal with ourselves as people, not dancers. We incorporated actions that had never been used in dance before. Works that came out of this period included the *Trunk Dance* [1959] and *Four-Square* [1959].

RAINER: Were the dances improvised for performance?

HALPRIN: No. They were improvised in order to get at the result; once that result was there it was fixed. You can see how that would wear itself out. The next step was a system whereby we would be forced to adapt ourselves to some outside direction.

RAINER: In performance?

HALPRIN: No – now we go back to work. Each performance represents several years' investigation. Each new work represents a new concept, a new system of composition. We have never been a repertory company; we may repeat a piece within the year that we're doing it, but once we have felt the need to explore another area, we drop what we're doing.

We began to explore systems that would knock out cause and effect . . .

RAINER: You mean between people?

HALPRIN: Between everything. Anything that had to do with cause and effect got you back into your own resources again. I wanted to find out things that I'd never thought of, that would never come out of my personal responses.

RAINER: Did you find that you moved in patterns?

HALPRIN: Yes. It wasn't so much repeating patterns, it was a repetition of similar attitudes that didn't lead to any further growth. Improvisation is still a basic part of our technique. Everything we do keeps growing; it's not that we don't do something any more, it's just that the skill is there but it's not used in the same way.

The next step was to find a way to separate the elements that we were using. We had gotten enormously involved in a lot of complex and diverse materials. We were using vocal materials and words, musicians were improvising with us: La Monte Young, Terry Riley, Warner Jepson, Bill Spencer. We were using objects, and props – we were using space in a determinist way. I wanted to isolate these elements. I began to work with a system where all these things became independent of cause and effect. In order to get the music to do *this* you didn't have to do *that*.

RAINER: The musicians worked out their things in a different place, or what?

HALPRIN: We separated from the musicians for a while. I began to chart movement; I put everything on charts; everything became arbitrary.

RAINER: Movement patterns, space patterns?

HALPRIN: Anything I was dealing with. I could do it with a movement. I have a great pamphlet in which I've taken every possible anatomical combination of movement and put them all on sheets of paper and given them numbers. One sheet had to do with flexion, different joints, another sheet had to do with extension. I would pick off these things and I'd make a pattern. These were movements I hadn't evolved myself. And then I tried to do it. I got into the wildest combinations of movement, things I never could have conceived of. All of a sudden my body began to experience new ways of moving. We applied this in bigger compositional ways. We would experiment with all the elements we worked with, even combinations of people. In *Birds of America* [1960] I used a pie shape and I made pies with a different interval for each one; I put different elements into each pie, and then I'd have another transparent wheel on top of that to mix them up so that each one could be rotated for a different combination. I'd say: "We'll try this combination and we'll make a composition based on these particular elements coming together, now let's see what'll happen."

Even though I got the composition system formalized, we still worked it out with improvisation.

RAINER: So you invented new movement.

HALPRIN: We invented new movement possibilities, new ways of combining the elements. But when the dance was finished it was fixed.

RAINER: In arriving at the final product you improvised with those things you had found through manipulating the wheels?

HALPRIN: That's right. I could have manipulated the wheels several times and gotten any number of versions, and this is what I intended to do, but we got too involved in our next problem so we took another jump before we explored any further. *Birds of America* was about fifty minutes, our first long work. We spent two years doing exercises, exploring things that led to this system; then it took us about three months to compose the work. We performed it once. By that time we had gotten into doing something else. With that system we could have composed other works, but I wasn't interested. Something else was happening.

By chance I happened to become very aware of the space in the theatre, the stage. I just didn't like it, it bothered me, I didn't know what to do. I got this flash: just before performance I put a bamboo pole in everybody's hands including mine, and we had to do the dance that we'd always done, holding bamboo poles.

RAINER: Throughout the fifty minutes?

HALPRIN: Yes. The poles were very long and they created their own spatial environment. This was the beginning of our next jump. I became preoccupied with movement in relation to environment. I began to feel that we had paid such strict attention to self-awareness, kinesthetic responses, and each other, that we developed a stifling introspection. So we began to extend our focus to adaptive responses in the environment. We had worked with musicians, painters, all kinds of artists . . .

RAINER: Could you go into some detail about that?

HALPRIN: In *Birds of America* they came into a situation we had already established as dancers. Their influence was not a real cross-fertilization yet. But the music wasn't accompaniment, we'd gotten away from that when we began to work with separate elements.

RAINER: Background?

HALPRIN: Not even background. The dance was always first. It was a matter of finding sound, finding costumes – whatever it is that would be suitable to the dance. In that sense the dance was still the focus, but I felt that breaking up the categories would be much more exciting. The people we were working with had many resources and they weren't really using them. We were by that time interested in finding out about what there was on the outside that could affect our ideas for movement.

The next big thing was *Five-Legged Stool* [1962]. This was a full-length evening, in two acts. This work further developed the cross-fertilization idea. Up until then we had been content with using the space that we had. But I got discouraged with having to be up there in that relationship to an audience. I began to look at the lobby, the aisles, the ceilings, the floor. Suddenly I thought: "Who says we have to stay on that stage, this is a whole building." In *Five-Legged Stool* what happened was that all these independent elements were developed: the use of sound, vocal material, the word and its content, the painter and the way in which a painter became, very often, the choreographer. For example, in Act II, I wanted to keep bringing objects out and putting them down and going back, taking objects out and putting them down. The painter we were working with, Jo Landor, kept watching this going on and one day she came in with forty wine bottles and said, "Here, I want you to bring these in." She almost set the kind of movement I did. It's pretty hard for me to know who choreographed that work, Jo Landor or me.

RAINER: Supposing you had not wanted to do what you had to do with those wine bottles?

HALPRIN: It worked out fine, because I had also gotten attached to the idea that I wanted people to have tasks to do. Doing a task created an attitude that would bring the movement quality into another kind of reality. It was devoid of a certain kind of introspection.

RAINER: I remember that summer I was here with you and you assigned tasks. But as I understood it, the tasks were to make you become aware of your body. It wasn't necessary to retain the task but to do the movement or the kinesthetic thing that the task brought about.

HALPRIN: Afterwards we became much more concerned with doing the task itself. Then we set up tasks that would be so challenging that the choice of a task would be the idea of the movement.

RAINER: Rather than it being transformed?

HALPRIN: That's right. Jo was in on all this. The wine bottle task that she gave me was so challenging and so difficult that I was quite content to do it. I couldn't get up and down; I had to stay in a stooped-over position or I'd break my back. Then I had the task of taking these wine bottles, putting them overhead, getting them to disappear in the ceiling. I had to balance on a stool. The task was sufficiently compelling in itself that I was able to turn my full attention to it. It took me forty minutes.

RAINER: Did all the movements in *Five-Legged Stool* have to do with tasks?

HALPRIN: Yes, and all the tasks were chosen for different reasons. For example: John Graham had a plank that was on a diagonal resting on a ceiling beam. He crawled up to the ceiling and his task was to slide down that beam head first. It was a complete fantasy; it had nothing to do with anything functional; it wasn't the kind of task that had to do with something as recognizable as carrying out a bottle and placing it.

RAINER: Did he do it?

HALPRIN: Yes. By achieving the impossible he arrived at an incredible bit of fantasy.

RAINER: In that particular piece did being yourselves, not having a character, carry through?

HALPRIN: Yes, quite automatically. Actually I was very pleased by it. In doing these tasks we were not playing roles or creating moods; we simply did something. By the choice of the objects and tasks we could determine the over-all quality. For example, in the first act of *Five-Legged Stool* each person had several gambits that could be done in any combination, even though each time they had to be done the same way. Things like pouring water. I had a big box of colorful material and tin cans, and other things that I had chosen, and just throwing them as high as I could would be another task. There would be a task like changing clothes. There would be another task that had to do with falling, a movement task. Even though these things were repeated exactly the same way in every performance, their sequence changed so that the composition would be different for the audience and the performer. This was the first composition where we had a different performance every night.

RAINER: In looking at the photographs, a lot of the visual impact has to do with the decor and costumes, which were not essential to the carrying out of the tasks.

HALPRIN: True. There was an enormous amount of juxtaposition in *Five-Legged Stool* and it was done deliberately. There was an attempt to really break down cause and effect. I wanted everything to have such a sensory impact that an audience would not question why. I didn't want anything to look as if it had meaning, or continuity. What we wore had nothing to do with the tasks. We went down to McAllister Street and everybody was asked to collect things that interested them for costumes. I had a jag for dresses from the 1920s, those spangly things, beautiful colors and very luminous. I had a thing about those dresses and I'd go down and collect as many as I could. Other times we used everyday clothing. It was a big thing for us – the first time we hadn't used tights and leotards. They were taboo. We danced with shoes on. I felt like a naughty little girl the first day, because a modern dancer used bare feet, and suddenly I was wearing high-heeled shoes. Leath was wearing tennis shoes.

This was for us a very important breakthrough, and helped us have completely new images of who we were. It was the last time that we ever really thought of ourselves as dancers. The other thing about *Five-Legged Stool* was that we began to use the space; we explored the entire theatre – it was a small theatre – the outside, the corridors, the ceilings, the basement, the aisles, everything. What happened was that the audience was in the center, and the performance went all around them. Above them and below them and in front of them, and outside, sometimes they would hear things out on the street.

RAINER: In that theatre the sidewalk is right outside.

HALPRIN: Something happened in that performance that we'd never experienced before, and began to establish a next step. We got a violent audience reaction. That's when people started throwing things at us. That was the first time. People would throw shoes onstage. The dance ended with five minutes of just feathers falling from the ceiling; all you saw was five minutes of feathers falling. The windows in the theatre were open so that the street sounds came in, and the wind came in, and just these feathers dropping.

RAINER: Were the performers on the stage?

HALPRIN: No. Everything was cleared away. This got people quite involved for some reason. I remember one woman said, "Isn't this the silliest thing? I'm just sitting here in this theatre spending my time just looking at those feathers drop." The people would talk, they wouldn't just whisper to each other, they would talk loudly so that everybody could hear.

RAINER: What happened during the performance?

HALPRIN: They talked all during the performance, they talked to the person next to them as if that person were ten miles away, as if everything they said to each other was a public announcement. There was a definite kind of involvement that we had never experienced before, nor did we know what to do with it, or why it was there.

RAINER: They didn't actually interfere?

HALPRIN: Often they did. People would come up onto the stage and start to grab the feathers. One time during the bottle dance, when Leath and I balance on a stool and shout at each other, people in the audience started shouting and throwing shoes at us. We were completely naïve about what we were doing. We didn't know this would affect anyone else. Everything made complete sense to us because, after all, we spent two years investigating these techniques. We'd worked with juxtaposition, this kind of unrelatedness. We couldn't figure out what was wrong, why everybody was getting so excited. People would walk out in a rage. We gave sixteen performances of this and always got this kind of a reaction. When we did it in Rome it was ten times worse. Just absolutely violent. When we came back we were concerned about what we were doing to an audience.

RAINER: This was after Rome. What else did you bring to Europe?

HALPRIN: *Esposizione*, a commission. Luciano Berio saw *Five-Legged Stool* and felt that he wanted to work with us. He had been asked to write a small opera for the Venice Biennale. He asked us to work with him. We started out with the architecture of the Venice Opera House. The first thing that occurred to me was that the stage looked like a fireplace in somebody's living room – if we tried to dance on the floor we'd look like little ants. There were only six of us in the company, we'd be drowned by that space. It's built like a horseshoe; there are five tiers of seats and only 200 people on the bottom floor. The first problem was how to integrate ourselves into that space. I felt that we needed something vertical, and we evolved the idea of suspending a cargo net across the proscenium, forty feet in the air. The bottoms were stretched out like wings over the orchestra pit and way back into the stage. This is the way in which we were able to alter that proscenium and allow the dancers to be able to move vertically.

RAINER: Was one cargo net enough?

HALPRIN: Yes, it was a very big one. We built a big ramp, too, on the floor, so that we really had no floor. The floor itself was a slant.

RAINER: You built the ramp out of boards?

HALPRIN: Out of fiberglass. We cut down eucalyptus trees from Marin County and we shipped them all the way over to Italy because we had worked with this cargo net on those trees and it was real scary forty feet in the air. We weren't about to take any chances, so we shipped our own trees there. That dance evolved out of a spatial idea, an environmental idea. We said the theatre was our environment and we were going to move through the theatre. And we took a single task: burdening ourselves with enormous amounts of luggage. The whole group had this one task, to be burdened with things.

We chose objects for their texture and form; they were all everyday objects: automobile tires, gunnysacks filled with things – at one point we had a big hassock filled with tennis balls – bundles of rags, parachutes that were stuck into containers, newspapers rolled up that were stuck into things, things that could come out and explode. Each person had to carry these things and to allow his movements to be conditioned to speeds that had been set up for him. Some started in the plaza, some started in the prompter's pit; they started all over the place, so that it was like an invasion. The music started at a different time, dancers started at different times. You just didn't have any idea when anything started. The cargo net started going up during intermission, and people couldn't tell if things were starting or if this was preparation. The whole dance – it took forty minutes – was a series of false beginnings. Nothing ever got anywhere. As soon as something got started, something else would be introduced. The dancers' task was to carry things and to penetrate the entire auditorium. This meant they had to go through that stage area which included the cargo net. One of the most compelling parts of the dance was the effort of carrying those things up that cargo net, because the stuff would fall.

RAINER: It actually did fall?

HALPRIN: Yes. We had a hassock filled with 200 tennis balls and one dancer's task was to take that hassock up there and when she got it up there to overturn it, so that the tennis balls came flying down. When we reached the high point – there was an enormous amount of objects there by that time – automobile tires were rolling down, tennis balls were falling, it was just a great crash of things. The tennis balls bounced all over so that the whole space exploded. People's bodies dropped down through the net and were caught by ropes, they would hang on; we turned into acrobats. We worked on that cargo net for a year. We got so that we could fall from one point to another, catch ourselves on a rope, hang upside down. We developed a whole technique to operate on that cargo net. The nine-year-old child who was in it, started off at the top of the cargo net, jumped into a perpendicular rope, and swung; she got a big momentum going and she swung clear across the heads of the audience in the first few rows and all the way back into the stage. *Esposizione* was a very bold use of the architectonic concept of space. It also was just a continual repetition and variation of one task.

RAINER: Did people have set speeds that were constant throughout?

HALPRIN: Yes. We had time scores. Everything was done according to seconds. We never heard the music until the night of the performance and the time score helped us correlate with the music. We had so much time to get from here to here. This is what determined the effort of our movements. Sometimes it was almost impossible to cover a certain terrain in a certain length of time, because of the burdens we carried. We would stumble, it was like a life and death situation.

Objects are carried up a cargo net in *Esposizione*, performed at the Venice Opera House ➡ as part of the 1963 Venice Biennale. (Photo courtesy of Anna Halprin.)

RAINER: You had cues in the music

HALPRIN: No. We never heard the music.

RAINER: How did you keep time?

HALPRIN: We had five people stationed all over the place who were giving us cues.

RAINER: Vocally?

HALPRIN: We would keep track of them, we would look and they would give us hand signals. Each person in the dance had his own conductor who managed to get to various spots, and just like musicians we looked at our conductor from time to time and found out where we were. We just jolly well had to be where we had to be when the time came.

RAINER: The conductor would be where you were supposed to be?

HALPRIN: No. He would be in a place where we could see him. We had worked it out.

RAINER: So they moved around?

HALPRIN: Yes. It was so important for us to do that task that if necessary we had to drop one of our bundles in order to get somewhere. We left a trail of litter everywhere. Litter in the balconies, in the aisles.

RAINER: Did you take all this stuff over with you?

HALPRIN: Yes, we did, which was really stupid. We got very possessive about the things we collected. And our costumes were designed in such a way that we could only wear them for the night of the one performance. The cargo net ripped the costumes to shreds. The task, the effort of doing it, the amount of stumbling, and having to get through certain environments would just rip us to shreds. We would start out absolutely beautifully attired.

RAINER: What kind of costumes?

HALPRIN: The costumes were designed as extensions of our props. Each person was very different. John Graham had a tuxedo and a gold helmet, and it was all black and white. Daria was just full of different transparent, thin things; she was very bulky but very soft and transparent. Each person was really designed as an object. We never wore our costumes until the night of performance. By the end everybody was in shreds. John Graham only had his trousers left. His coat had been ripped off, he was completely bare from his waist up. We had a vocal score in three different languages. We had to sing and speak in Italian, English, and Greek.

RAINER: How was this established?

HALPRIN: Berio simply gave us the score. At certain times, according to its elements, we said the score, or sang it.

RAINER: You learned it?

HALPRIN: Yes. The parts were sent to us. John Graham did an amazing thing on the cargo net. I was giving him one task and Berio was giving him another. They were both very difficult. He had to be going as fast as he could up that cargo net carrying this tire and other baggage, and at the same time Berio gave him a score which took seven minutes to read in which he was constantly talking and shouting. He had to alternate speaking Italian and English. He didn't understand a word of the Italian, so he memorized it. It was just this continual bla-bla-bla-bla of words coming out and every word had to be memorized, it had a particular sound value to Berio. It was considered a small opera because we had that much vocal activity. Then he had vocal people – two young boys and a woman who sang. The only trouble with the vocal material was that we never heard it in performance because the audience shouted so much and responded so excitedly to all the vocal material that you couldn't hear ours as being any different than theirs.

RAINER: Do you know what the vocal material was, I mean in Italian?

HALPRIN: Yes, we knew. Rona had a passage in which she was sitting out in one of the tiers, blowing soap bubbles and wearing a yellow raincoat, telling a biblical story in Latin. We were trying to get up to the top of that cargo net with all of our baggage falling. We were scrambling and being torn apart. And she was, at that time, sitting out there and telling this biblical story in Latin. These are things that Berio had planned and that became very interesting juxtapositions.

RAINER: You never did *Esposizione* here?

HALPRIN: We've never done it anywhere else. It was a difficult work because of the musical score and an eighteen-piece orchestra. It was a very complicated thing.

RAINER: What are you doing now?

HALPRIN: When we came back we took a long rest. Then we began to explore the audience. We wanted to find out what an audience was, to understand a little bit more what we were doing to an audience.

RAINER: I'd like to know. Was it mostly outrage that you experienced in Europe?

HALPRIN: Not with the cargo dance. They were very excited; they'd never seen anything like that. They had never been so overwhelmed with performers all around them, and so forth. I felt hostility only one time: when the music became very repetitive and monotonous, they started yelling "Basta! Basta!" The press was interested in it as a new form and there was no hostility. They responded to it for what it was, not because it was or wasn't dance. They were appreciating the fact that it was a new form; what Stuchenschmitt called a "sur-naturalism," a new use for dance and movement, that had gone into new areas. There was hostility to *Five-Legged Stool*. It was very controversial in Zagreb. It was almost canceled after the first performance.

RAINER: Why?

HALPRIN: "Decadent Western art." That audience didn't say a word. They just sat absolutely still. Apparently there was enormous hostility. In Italy they threw things at us, but asked us to come back. They said they'd never had such a gorgeous scandal. That's apparently what they enjoyed. They didn't care whether they liked the dance, they had permission to misbehave.

RAINER: The response affected you?

HALPRIN: I was concerned not that it offended me, but that we had this kind of power to stir people up. If we have this kind of power, how should we use it? I was concerned with our own naïveté. In Rome the audience was very hostile; they really knew how to be effective with their hostility. When they threw a shoe, it hit. There was no pussyfooting.

Did you hear the famous story about the guy who came twice and waited for the special time when everything was quiet? He marched down and stood in the spotlights and turned and announced to the audience: "It's all Christopher Columbus's fault." And he marched out and everybody applauded. That really was clever. These are people who really know how to use their power. For the first time I realized there was a real encounter going on between audience and performers. This is what we were interested in exploring next. We invited fifty people to join a series. It was announced as *A Series of Compositions for an Audience*. We explored this power: where is it, who has it, and how can we use it? We set up situations where the audience could investigate its role as an audience and learn how to use its power and then we could measure what it did to us.

RAINER: Do you feel that it's a moral issue? Can this power be misused, do people have to be educated?

HALPRIN: No, it's not a moral issue. It's throwing something away. I never realized that we were stirring people so deeply. I know now why. It gets at their preconscious and kinesthetic responses. It's very sensory and primitive. The more we know about this power the stronger we can be in using it. The audience has a power too, and if they can be given an opportunity to use it, we could have an encounter that would really send sparks. At Cal when a girl got up and smashed a lantern, she was using her power as an audience, but because we didn't appreciate the fact that she was using her power we threw it away. Had we responded and allowed the audience to realize that her act was a spontaneous, unplanned, vicious attack – WOW would they have had an experience! Instead, we just threw it away, by pretending that we didn't really react to it.

RAINER: Describe what happened to you.

HALPRIN: Let's go back a little. In three works this year, incidents happened. Chuck Ross, a sculptor, brought some big-scale things down the aisles – it was just overwhelming: they're over your head and they're all around you. He blew up great big weather balloons that started flying all over the place. The whole place was full of sound, action, and props. When we did it outdoors in Fresno, it was like a gigantic three-ring circus. People laughed; they had a wonderful time. But when we did it in a closed area, it was always terrifying. These big things were moving around, crashing, flying, and exploding, and the dancers were moving in such risky ways.

RAINER: Was this at Cal?

HALPRIN: Yes.

RAINER: Did it happen over the heads of the audience?

HALPRIN: Well, the big weather balloon was over their heads, the stuff that was carried in the aisles was going right past them. They could put their hands out and feel the metal. They could see the dancers, they could feel the tension of their movement right at their feet, or balancing on something over their heads – they were that close. It really did get them enormously involved. We knew that it was going to do this; we knew it would stimulate this kind of response in our audience. So it happened. About three-quarters of the way through some girl just couldn't stand it and she got up from her seat, rushed onto the stage, took this lit lantern – it was the only light – everything else was black at that moment – and smashed it against a metal frame. Glass went flying all over the place and kerosene. The plastic – there was a lot of it around – could easily have caught fire. The dancers were shocked; they just gathered together and took a bow as if nothing had really happened. The audience thought that this thing was planned. They didn't appreciate their power and we didn't use ours.

RAINER: Stalemate.

HALPRIN: We learned from that summer that we and the audience had power. What we didn't have was the experience to deal with it when the encounter happened.

RAINER: Can you really prepare for this kind of thing?

HALPRIN: We did. We had a week of thorough therapy on this. We became completely brainwashed; we analyzed that thing from beginning to end. Now we're just waiting for the opportunity to see how we'll use their power, not throw it away, and not throw ours away.

RAINER: Are you going to deliberately provoke an audience?

HALPRIN: No. Never. Now we know that because of the things we do and the way we do them, we will stir people up. We've accepted that, we're not naïve about it any more. Now also we have to take the consequences when we stir up an audience, and we have to have an attitude for dealing with it.

RAINER: What was the name of that piece?

HALPRIN: *Parades and Changes*. It is compositionally one of the most satisfying fulfillments of an idea that was started in *Birds of America*. A very complicated score was worked out by the musician Mort Subotnik and me. It permitted us complete and total flexibility. When we take this to Stockholm in August [1965], we will take absolutely nothing but the score. We will use only the materials that we have in the theatre and collect when we get there. *Parades and Changes* has a set like cell blocks. Each person is in his own medium: the lighting person, the musician, the dancers – everybody has his own series of blocks.

RAINER: Which are not coordinated?

HALPRIN: They're not coordinated at all. They can last five to twenty minutes. The selection of the blocks was made on the basis of their contrast – there are eight completely different uses of sound. One might be magnetic tape, one might be lute, one might be live sounds, one might be vocal sounds, another might be a Bach cantata, for example. Each block has been chosen on the basis of the differences.

RAINER: Different lengths?

HALPRIN: Yes, they're completely flexible.

RAINER: The Bach cantata can go on and on?

HALPRIN: No, that is the one thing that can't. That's "a set piece." It's exactly four minutes. That's the only one, and it can be coordinated with any number of things. Sometimes the dancers work as musicians, and sometimes the musicians use our material. We are conducted by a conductor. The dancers become musicians and sometimes they are also environmentalists: we work as crew.

RAINER: What determines when things take place?

HALPRIN: All these little cell blocks – it's like you arrive with a trunk full of different clothes, and then, depending upon the weather, you decide what you're going to wear that day. This is exactly what we do. We come into that theatre and look at it and study it. What is it? What will work here? So we say: "I'm going to pick out five of my blocks, I'm not going to do two of them because they just won't work here." The musician picks out what he wants, and so forth.

RAINER: No one depends on anybody else?

HALPRIN: That's right. Then we get together and decide which ones will work in sequence, which things will work together, based on practical matters. Very often a whole new section is invented during the performance in order to make a link between one block and another. Sometimes blocks overlap in a way that they never have before, in order to fill the space or contract the space.

This has been a delightful composition to work with because so far we have given three performances of it and they are so completely different that people that have seen them all don't even know that they are the same dance. It's been a culminating point for us in developing a system of collaboration that we started five years ago.

This is completely different from another work, *Apartment 6* [1965], that we're not taking to Europe because of the language barrier. It's done with a lot of dialog. It's more of a play than *Parades and Changes*.

RAINER: How long is *Parades and Changes*?

HALPRIN: It can be anywhere from five minutes to five hours – completely fluid in its duration.

RAINER: And *Apartment 6*?

HALPRIN: We've done it as a full-length work, a two-hour piece in three acts. This is new for us and it's very hard for me to talk about it because I don't quite know what it came from except that [A.A.] Leath and John and I – there are only three people in it – have been working together for fourteen years. We know each other so well that our relationships are terribly complicated. What happened was that we set up a problem for ourselves: let's use each other as material, let's see what will happen if we don't use any props, music, or anything. Let's just use each other. Let's explore who you really are in terms of me.

RAINER: Are you talking about feelings?

HALPRIN: Yes – what we really feel about each other. We were in therapy together, the three of us, to explore what our feelings were about each other. We worked on the piece for about two years. We had outside supervision, a psychologist to help us expose our feelings.

RAINER: Why did you think this was important? Artists can work without knowing their feelings, or analyzing them.

HALPRIN: Partly by chance, and partly by intuition. We felt that unless we began to work this way we wouldn't be able to work together any more. We wouldn't be able to get any feedback from each other any more. We had to go further, otherwise we were finished with each other. Everything that we evolved, we evolved together with Patrick Hickey, Jo Landor, Morton Subotnik, Terry Riley, and La Monte Young. But the three of us, John, Leath, and I, were the nucleus.

Also it was something that we were beginning to feel about everybody. The person who is the performer is working with his body as an instrument, he's making sounds, and he's doing everything as if he were an object, when he's more than an object; he's full of the most fantastic psychological phenomena, but he's completely cutting these off and blocking them. But these are the most unique parts of the performer. The musician can't do this because he's got an instrument between him and the thing he's doing; and the painter has his material. But the dancer and the actor are their own instruments. They can find out why they are different from chairs or flutes or tape recorders.

There was also a desire to find out more about the human interior. To tell you the truth I was scared to death about this whole thing. I

With a score composed of individual and variable "cell blocks" for the lighting technicians, ➡ musicians, and dancers, each performance of *Parades and Changes* was completely different. Shown here is the version from the Five Arts Festival Arena Theatre in Fresno, California, on 9 May 1965. (Photo courtesy of Anna Halprin.)

don't know if I'm the only one, I don't know how you feel about it, but when you start exposing your unconscious behavior – perhaps that's the wrong word – but when you start exposing your feelings about other people or yourself, you're opening up a lot of areas which are very uncomfortable, and it would be much easier if you just left them alone. It was uncomfortable and torturous. I approached it as a technical problem. I said, "OK, this is just new material that's been buried for a long time. I'm going to expose it, and try to find the skill to use it." There were times when I was upset and depressed because I was beginning to find out things about myself that I'd just as soon not know. I kept working on it from the point of view of: "How can I use it as an artist?" That's how *Apartment 6* grew. We set it up as a domestic scene, so that the audience would have definite things to deal with. We cooked. I fixed a breakfast for John onstage, we read newspapers, we played the radio, we talked.

RAINER: Your roles in relation to each other, were they what they really are, so you were not acting?

HALPRIN: I was myself. John was himself. I pretty much knew by then what some of our relationships were all about. We spent three years developing the skill to deal with this. We would set up focuses. I would set a task for myself to do. John would set a task for himself. Each person had something to do, so that we had a very formalized structure. The process of trying to do this task would always be encountered and interfered with by the other person; this is what we couldn't help. We were so aware of how we were using each other.

RAINER: Was it always interference?

HALPRIN: It was either interference or reinforcement. Both altered the work. Also we developed a technique that we called "three realities." When those three realities went on at different times there would be a fourth reality. One was the simple act of doing something, which could be cooking – I made my pancake mix and I just made it. I followed the directions on the box. People would come to the theatre and they would see John reading the newspaper, really reading what was in the newspaper that day. It was absolute, complete realism. Then there would be another kind of realism – say that Leath is reading the newspaper, John is playing the radio. The radio is beginning to annoy Leath, so he wants to turn it off. He's dealing with another reality at this point. He's beginning to get feelings about that radio which put him in contact with John. All Leath's hostility against John is stirred up by the blasted radio. So he puts the newspaper down and does the most violent movement you've ever seen. He might explode in midair. That's how he's feeling about John at that particular moment.

RAINER: It's not what he would do in reality necessarily.

HALPRIN: No. That's it. We had great limitations. John was allowed to express these kinds of feelings in words, Leath was not, Leath had to express them in movement.

RAINER: Why did you restrict them?

HALPRIN: It's very complicated. We wanted to guarantee that Leath would be able to make very sudden shifts. If he talked out his feelings, the audience would lose direct touch with what he was feeling because his verbal material came out so sarcastically. But when he used movement he was direct. John uses words, and they come out in a way that transfers.

RAINER: You're making aesthetic judgments on the basis of . . .

HALPRIN: On the basis of our particular skills and development at that moment. We were able to bring certain formalized controls to these things.

RAINER: It had to do with effectiveness?

HALPRIN: It had to do with our skills at that particular moment. At that time Leath couldn't handle words in that situation so he used movement. In certain areas of fantasy he would start using words which would come through fine.

We got strange juxtapositions of realities going on at the same time. I might be in an absolute tizzy about my pancakes and go into a terrific fantasy about those pancakes and Leath would be just sitting at the table eating his grapefruit and reading his paper, while John was listening to the radio. Do you see what I mean?

RAINER: Yes. Sometimes people were using different realities at different times. What was the third one?

HALPRIN: The fantasy. Leath would simply turn into a dog, or a dart board, and John would throw darts at him. But he really fantasized these things, like daydreaming. So he could do it in action.

The fourth reality is when the other three [realities] come together in their peculiar ways. We had it divided up: Leath and John first, then John and me, then Leath and me. There were three completely different relationships, which became the three acts. The performances were completely different each night. It was the here and now, you couldn't do any pretending. Everything was completely real at that moment. What came out of the radio, what you read in the papers, your feelings about the other person might change a little bit from one day to another. It was very, very exhausting to use your skill at a consistent level all that time. It wasn't until the last, the sixteenth, performance that I felt we had captured what we wanted to do, which was to simply have two hours on that stage of a real-life situation, in which you as performer and you as a person were completely the same thing. That finally happened. It worked for us and it worked for the audience.

RAINER: The Stanislavsky Method, as it's taught in New York acting schools, seems close to what you were doing.

HALPRIN: I don't know anything about it. I tried to read Stanislavsky but I don't understand it. It doesn't appeal to me.

RAINER: You don't see any connection?

HALPRIN: None at all. In our situation there's absolutely nothing pretended. We don't play any roles. We just are who we are. I don't know where it's going to lead to. We use our skills as artists to respond to the material. We use certain structures to guarantee a possibility for the audience to be in on it. We avoid personalizing.

RAINER: Do you feel a necessity to relate what you're doing to dance any more?

HALPRIN: No. I don't even identify with dance.

RAINER: Do you have another name for what you are doing?

HALPRIN: No. It's as much dance as anything – if you can think of dance as the rhythmic phenomena of the human being reacting to his environment. Essentially this is what dance is. If the audience accepted this definition, then I'd say yes, it's dance.

RAINER: What was the response of the audience? How did the power thing relate to this situation?

HALPRIN: There was not any of that. It affected them very differently than *Parades and Changes*. They laughed a lot and they cried a lot. Some people were crying and some people were laughing at the same time. I don't know why. Nobody really cried and felt sorry for anybody. And we cried and our thing onstage was the material we used for our crying. It was a very curious thing. I don't ever remember feeling sorry that so-and-so was crying: "He's crying, that's my material, I really feel it, I'm crying." You may not know why you cry; something hits you and you cry. The audience does the same thing. I never experienced anybody crying before in an audience. I don't really know very much about this yet. There was none of that power bit.

What I heard from people is that they identified with us closely. There were people who walked out, too – who thought they came to see a dance concert. One person had an interesting reaction, she said: "I enjoyed myself thoroughly while I was there but I'll never come again." Patrick asked why. And she said, "It just isn't art."

15

SOME RETROSPECTIVE NOTES ON
A DANCE FOR 10 PEOPLE AND 12
MATTRESSES CALLED *PARTS OF
SOME SEXTETS*, PERFORMED AT
THE WADSWORTH ATHENEUM,
HARTFORD, CONNECTICUT, AND
JUDSON MEMORIAL CHURCH, NEW
YORK, IN MARCH 1965.

Yvonne Rainer

1. Origins of piece. Earliest recollections go back to April '64 concert in Philadelphia where I did *Room Service*, a big sprawling piece with three teams of people playing follow-the-leader thru an assortment of paraphernalia which is arranged and rearranged by a guy and his two assistants. At this performance it spilled off the stage into the aisles, into the seats – displacing audience – and out the exits. I was excited by a particular piece of business: two of us carrying a mattress up an aisle, out the rear exit, around and in again thru a side exit. Something ludicrous and satisfying about lugging that bulky object around, removing it from scene and reintroducing it. No stylization needed. It seemed to be so self-contained an act as to require no artistic tampering or justification.

Later – May or June – at a Judson Church concert in which half the evening was devoted to individual improvisations, I invited Bob Morris to help me do some "moving." We moved all the furniture in the lounge into the sanctuary (which was the playing area), including the filthy dusty carpet. Thoroughly irritated everybody by interfering with their activities, broke a leg off the couch, spilled ashes and sand inadvertently all over my black dress. This situation was definitely not satisfying. Was the difficulty in the nature of the materials? Could it be that a living room couch is not as "plastic" as a mattress? Hard materials versus soft – or more flexible – materials? (An absurd area of speculation? – like comparing the virtues of plastic or wood toilet seats?) Having completed the job I found myself with no ideas. In exasperation Bob left and in desperation I fell back on some of my more eccentric improvisatory techniques. (At that time I had not yet made the decision to abandon the loony bin and the NY subways as sources of inspiration.)

Decided to stick to mattresses. Began thinking about a sextet, six people plus a stack of single mattresses the height of a man. Meanwhile, was working on a duet with Bob Morris. Material for a man and woman, mildly gymnastic, explicitly sexual, that when condensed could be a duet (there was a performance opportunity coming up at which I wanted to present something new) or when broken up could go into a pot for six people. Duet was called *Part of a Sextet*. (By the time it was finished, the larger projected piece had expanded to ten people, but I liked the corny pun on sex.)

August – Went to Stockholm with Bob. Shared a concert at the Moderna Museet in which I did solos and the duet; he did – among other things – *Check*, a piece for forty Swedes. I was very excited by that piece, never having experienced those exact circumstances before: A huge room 300 feet long by about 100 feet across – the center filled with chairs, most of them empty; on the periphery and also in the sea of chairs standing and sitting, the audience – about 800 strong; simple activities alternating in different parts of the room; Bob and I getting in and out of a box with a dozen faces looming over us; twelve people out of 800 knew what we were doing; the forty performers assembling at a signal into two groups marching determinedly thru the audience; darkness: a man running back and forth on a wooden platform at one end while I moved slowly in front of an image with vertical lines thrown by a slide projector at the opposite end of the space from where the man was running. Simple, undistinctive activities made momentous thru their inaccessibility. A "cheap trick" to play on an audience in excluding them from the action? Or rather another device designed to counter the venerable convention of serving it all up on a platter?

2. The work. We next spent six weeks in Düsseldorf. Bob prepared sculpture for a show. I went every day to a tiny sixth-floor walk-up ballet studio in the Altstadt; I could see the Rhine beyond the old rooftops. One day there was a fire in the next block. Much smoke and scurrying around. I felt like a cuckoo in a Swiss clock observing an intricate mechanized toy go thru its paces. All those little firemen and townsfolk seemed wound up. And in the distance that flat river and green-washed Rhinemeadow. The whole scene was decidedly depressing.

Since there was nothing else to do, I worked. Worked mechanically and at times despairingly on movement. It was necessary to find a different way to move. I felt I could no longer call on the energy and hard-attack impulses that had characterized my work previously, nor did I want to explore any further the "imitations-from-life" kind of eccentric movement that someone once described as "goofy glamour." So I started

The "Corridor Solo" and "Crawling Through" were two of the thirty-one choices of movement material charted for *Parts of Some Sextets*, seen here at the Wadsworth Atheneum in Hartford, Connecticut, on 7 March 1965. (Photo by Peter Moore.)

at another place – wiggled my elbows, shifted from one foot to the other, looked at the ceiling, shifted eye focus within a tiny radius, watched a flattened, raised hand moving and stopping, moving and stopping. Slowly the things I made began to go together, along with sudden sharp, hard changes in dynamics. But basically I wanted it to remain undynamic movement, no rhythm, no emphasis, no tension, no relaxation. You just *do* it, with the coordination of a pro and the nondefinition of an amateur. It's an ideal, still to be worked on.

I was also doing a lot of thinking about my group piece. The impact of *Check* had become a strong reference point. I wanted to make a piece that had the same effect, but I wanted the whole situation to take place directly in front of the audience. In other words, something completely visible at all times, but also very difficult to follow and get involved with. How I decided upon the system that I ultimately used is now not too clear to me, especially since in retrospect it seems there were many possibilities that might have more successfully achieved what I had in mind. However, it *was* clear that there must not be a flowing or developmental type of progression in the action, but rather whatever changes were to take place must be as abrupt and jagged as possible, perhaps occurring at regular brief intervals. So I resorted to two devices that I have used consistently since my earliest dances: repetition and interruption. In the context of this new piece, both factors were to produce a "chunky" continuity, repetition making the eye jump back and forth in time and possibly establishing more strongly the differences in the movement material – especially the "dancey" stuff – that some of the movement episodes were simply small fragments used randomly and some were elaborate sequences made from consecutive phrases. Interruption would also function to disrupt the continuity and prevent prolonged involvement with any one image. So it began to take shape in my head: dance movement of various kinds; activities with mattresses; static activities (sitting, standing, lying); continuous simultaneous actions changing abruptly at perhaps thirty-second intervals, sometimes the whole field changing at the same time, sometimes only a portion of it, but every thirty seconds something changing. Thirty seconds began to seem like the right interval length. I did not realize until much later that a given duration can *seem* long or short according to what is put into it. So my scheme, when applied to the diversity of materials that finally filled it out, did not really produce the insistent regularity I had thought it might. However, by the time I made this basic discovery I had begun to like the irregularities of the piece.

Returned to New York beginning of November 1964. Had already decided on the sound track for the piece. Spent the next five weeks in the N.Y. Public Library perusing the index of and copying excerpts from the *Diary of William Bentley, D.D.*, a late eighteenth-century Episcopal minister who lived in Salem, Mass., and kept careful stock of the local goings-on during his forty-year tenure. Continued to work on movement material. Began to assemble the chart that would dictate the final arrangement of materials and people.

The chart, reading down, lists thirty-one choices of material; reading across, numbers consecutively thirty-second intervals, one thru eighty-four. The piece is as long as two sheets of 22" × 17" graph paper allow, with one-half inch of ruled space equivalent to thirty seconds. The chart is divided into squares, each indicating the juncture of a given piece of material with a given interval in time. The physical space of the dance – where the material would take place – was to be decided by necessity and whim as rehearsals progressed.

The thirty-one possibilities as briefly described on the chart are: 1. Duet: Corridor solo; 2. Duet: Bob's entrance thru Y's squeals; 3. Duet: Leaning away thru first embraces; 4. Duet: Diagonal run to end; 5. Bird run; 6. Running thru; 7. Racing walk; 8. Solo beginning with shifting of weight; 9. Standing figure; 10. Bent-over walk; 11. Quartet; 12. Rope duet (with rope); 13. Rope movements one thru four; 14. Rope movements five thru eight; 15. Rope movements nine thru thirteen; 16. One vertical mattress moving back and forth on single layer; 17. "Swedish werewolf" (always offstage); 18. Human flies on mattress pile;

19. Formation #1 (fling); 20. Formation #2 (with "bug squash"); 21. Move pile to other side; 22. Peel one at a time; 23. Crawl thru below top mattress; 24. Standing figure on top of pile; 25. House lights; 26. One person running another into pile; 27. Bob's diagonal; 28. Sitting figure; 29. Sleeping figure; 30. Vague movements; 31. Formation #3 (pile-up).

In December began asking people to perform in the piece. The cast materialized as Lucinda Childs, Judith Dunn, Sally Gross, Deborah Hay, Tony Holder, Robert Morris, Steve Paxton, Me, Robert Rauschenberg, Joseph Schlichter. Joe's wife, Trisha Brown, considered being involved for awhile, even though she was pregnant, and even came to a few of the early rehearsals. I had very much wanted her to participate, especially in the very pregnant condition we thought she would have been in by the time of the performance. The idea was that there were no stars in this dance – just people – and if one of them was pregnant, well – that would be a pregnant one. Thinking about it now, I feel that a "pregnant one" would have stood out as the only one whose activities were restricted to the less strenuous material. (Trisha's decision to withdraw was fortunate: she gave birth to a boy less than a week before the concert.)

Began teaching the dance material. (The nontrained people, Morris and Rauschenberg, learned everything except "Quartet.") Had been putting off the actual filling in of the chart, but now with the mattresses bought and rehearsals proper ready to start, there could be no more delay. So one night I took the plunge and with a pencil made random marks all over the chart paper. Mostly in isolated squares, but sometimes in two, three, or even four consecutive ones.[1] Then the work began: in column #1 (the first thirty seconds) marks fell in the squares indicating Duet: Corridor solo, Bird run, Bent-over walk, Quartet, Peel one at a time, House lights, Sitting figure. The remaining decisions to make were who – and how many – were to do these and where were they to do them. Column by column I filled in initials of the cast. The decisions were based both on expediency (e.g., "do the rope movements wherever you happen to be" or "J. can't continue doing that because she has to do Corridor solo here," etc.) and my feelings about the constantly shifting churned-up quality I was after. So when one activity went on for more than two columns (one minute), I usually added to or reduced the number of people doing it or even replaced them halfway thru.

The final problem was that of cues. Eventually we would take word cues from the taped reading of the diary, but I hadn't yet made the tape because I thought it would be too difficult to learn movement sequences and cues at the same time. So I made a work tape with my voice saying

Yvonne Rainer and Robert Morris in *Part of a Sextet*. (Photo by Peter Moore.)

➡

"change" every thirty seconds. Now I feel that using the double learning process from the very beginning would have meant a considerable saving in time and work. As things stood, after we had learned the dance with the work tape, we had to plod thru it innumerable times for the extra familiarizing process involving the cues in the reading.

The dance took eight weeks to learn. For the first four weeks we rehearsed four times a week; after that two or three times a week. It proved to be dry, plodding work, partly due to the length and repetitiousness. Also, since there was no "organic" or kinesthetic continuity, some of us found it extraordinarily difficult to learn and ended up memorizing it by rote, like multiplication tables or dates in history.

For a while I couldn't decide whether to keep the same consistency of texture from beginning to end, thru forty-three minutes of activity, or introduce changes midway. It might be said that I "chickened out" of the first alternative, but only slightly. What actually happened was that on the second half of the chart I made more deliberate choices, with an eye to larger and simpler configurations, one of which was two groups alternating Racing walk, Human fly, Werewolf, and Solo shifting weight. In the last thirteen minutes I had "YJPJo" (chart abbreviation for "Yvonne, Judy, Paxton, Joe") do Quartet and Solo shifting weight in staggered unison from beginning to end while "CB" (Cindy, Bob) did Rope duet. The Quartet, etc., lasted half that time, permitting the Rope duet to be the next-to-last image. The dance ended with all of us perched on the single stack of mattresses.

3. Postscript. All I am inclined to indicate here are various feelings about *Parts of Some Sextets* and its effort in a certain direction – an area of concern as yet not fully clarified for me in relation to dance, but existing as a very large NO to many facts in the theatre today. (This is not to say that I personally do not enjoy many forms of theatre. It is only to define more stringently the rules and boundaries of my own artistic game of the moment.)

NO to spectacle no to virtuosity no to transformations and magic and make-believe no to the glamour and transcendency of the star image no to the heroic no to the antiheroic no to trash imagery no to involvement of performer or spectator no to style no to camp no to seduction of spectator by the wiles of the performer no to eccentricity no to moving or being moved.

The challenge might be defined as how to move in the spaces between theatrical bloat with its burden of dramatic psychological "meaning" – and – the imagery and atmospheric effects of the nondramatic, nonverbal theatre (i.e., dancing and some "Happenings") – and – theatre of spectator participation and/or assault. I like to think that *Parts of Some*

Sextets worked somewhere in these spaces, at the risk of losing the audience before it was half over (but that is yet another matter of concern, not to be investigated here). Its repetition of actions, its length, its relentless recitation, its inconsequential ebb and flow all combined to produce an effect of nothing happening. The dance "went nowhere," did not develop, progressed as though on a treadmill or like a ten-ton truck stuck on a hill: it shifts gears, groans, sweats, farts, but doesn't move an inch.

Perhaps next time my truck will make some headway; perhaps it will inch forward – imperceptibly – or fall backward – headlong.

NOTE

1. It is apparent that the placement of the marks was not truly "random," as my choices were intuitive and subliminally aesthetic. "Randomness" precludes motivation and the exercise of taste.

16

NOTES ON DANCE

Robert Morris

My involvement in theatre has been with the body in motion. However changed or reduced the motion might have been or however elaborate the means used might have been, the focus was this movement. In retrospect this seems a constant value which was preserved. From the beginning I wanted to avoid the pulled-up, turned-out, antigravitational qualities that not only give a body definition and role as "dancer" but qualify and delimit the movement available to it. The challenge was to find alternative movement.

I was not the first to attempt such alternatives. Simone Whitman, together with others, had already explored the possibilities inherent in a situation of "rules" or gamelike structures which required the performer to respond to cues which might, for example, indicate changes in height or spatial position. A fair degree of complexity of these rules and cues effectively blocked the dancer's performing "set" and reduced him to frantically attempting to respond to cues – reduced him from performance to action. In 1961 Simone Whitman held a concert in a loft in New York. This concert involved the use of such devices as a 45° inclined plane about eight feet square with several ropes coming from the top of it. Performers were allowed to climb up the plane, pass between each other and rest when tired – all by means of the ropes. Here the rules were simple and did not constitute a game situation but rather indicated a task while the device, the inclined plane, structured the actions. (This single example does not do justice to the implications this seemingly simple concert held.) Here focused clearly for the first time were two distinct means by which new actions could be implemented: rules or tasks and devices (she termed them "constructions") or objects.

While possibilities for generating movement by task situations or devices had become clearly established, it was essentially an indirect method in both cases. Movement had not been approached directly but had resulted, willy-nilly, from going about getting this or that task accomplished – moving over a dominating eccentric surface, etc.

By the uses of objects which could be manipulated I found a situation

Performers circle behind the two leaders carrying flags, in *Check* at the Judson Memorial Church on 24 March 1965. (Photo by Peter Moore.)

An element of the work as persistent as the use of objects is the coexistence of the static and the mobile – e.g., a sequence of ten Muybridge slides of a nude man lifting a stone followed by a similar movement by a nude male performer executed in the same space and illuminated by the beam of the slide projector (*Waterman Switch*, 1965);

Site was performed at a TV studio as part of the First New York Theatre Rally, 5–7 May 1965.
(Photo by Peter Moore.)

which did not dominate my actions nor subvert my performance. In fact the decision to employ objects came out of considerations of specific problems involving space and time. For me, the focus of a set of specific problems involving time, space, alternate forms of a unit, etc., provided the necessary structure.[1] While dance technique and chance methods were both irrelevant to me I would never have denied the value, necessity even, of perpetuating structural systems. But for my purposes the need for such systems was for syntactical rather than methodological bases. My efforts were bound up with the didactic and demonstrative and were not concerned with the establishment of a set of tools by which works could be generated.

The objects I used held no inherent interest for me but were means for dealing with specific problems. For example, the establishment of an inverse ratio between movement, space, and duration was implemented by the use of a T-like form which I could adjust and move away from, adjust again and move away from, and so on until the sequence of movements according to the ratio had been completed. Or again, the establishment of a focus shifting between the egocentric and the exocentric could be accomplished by swinging overhead in a fully lighted room a small light at the end of a cord. The lights in the room fade as the cord is slowly let out until finally in total darkness only the moving point of light is visible as it revolves in the large space above the heads of the audience. Both of the above instances occurred in *Arizona* (1963), the first dance I made.

or the rotation of the upper torso through 90° over a five minute period – the movement itself being imperceptible – accompanied by a taped description of strenuous movements (*Arizona*); or a taped verbal description of actions which occur at a remove in time (*Waterman Switch*); or the illumination of a runner with stroboscopic-type light which, because of the briefness of the illumination, gives a static image (*Check*, 1964). In one form or another the static coexisting with the mobile occurs in every work.

Time, insofar as considerations of length are concerned, has seemed irrelevant. Since the movement situations were primarily those of either demonstration or exposition, time was not an element of usage but a necessary condition; less a focus than a context. Only at those points where there was no movement did time function as an isolated, observable focus – i.e., durations of stillness were not used as punctuations for the movement but in the attempt to make duration itself palpable.

Space, like time, was reduced to context, necessity; at most a way of anchoring the work, riveting it to a maximum frontality. In *Site* (1964) a triangular spatial situation occurs with an immobile female nude reclining against a white rectangle upstage, right of center, a white box downstage right (a visible source for a sound which varies hardly more than the nude), and a performer downstage left manipulating a white rectangular board and moving within an area of a few square feet. The extreme slow-motion element in *Arizona* came from experiencing the dancer's movements being soaked up, dissipated, in a concert given in an enormous skating rink in Washington, DC. It was apparent that only the smallest movements kept their weight or mass in such a large, nonrectangular space. A consideration in *Arizona* was to make movements which would keep their focus in any space – a case of spatial opposition rather than cooperation or exploration. In *Check* space was used centrifugally, the movement occurring largely at the periphery of the audience. For all its apparent scale, *Check* made use primarily of the factors of distance and interruption; the space remained relatively unpunctured.

Check bears further elaboration for in several ways, other than the inside-out spatial situation, it was purposely antithetical to my previous works. It had no central focus, climax, dramatic intensity, continuity of action; it did not involve skill in performance, nor did it even demand continuous attention from an audience. In a room some 100 by 300 feet (the central gallery at the Moderna Museet, Stockholm) 700 to 800 chairs were placed at random in the center area, leaving aisles around the perimeter. Various actions by individual performers occurred in these aisles. Forty other performers, men, women, and children, "wandered" through the entire space; totally at random and as individuals. Upon a signal the forty assembled into two respective groups for simple, simultaneous actions. They again dispersed upon a signal to resume wandering, talking, observing as a kind of proto-audience: i.e., they occupied a zone somewhere between performers and audience. The 700 in the audience were free to sit or stand as they chose. Due to the space and numbers of people no performed action was visible to the entire audience. (This work was later performed in a space approximately one-third of the size of the Moderna Museet and failed totally as the actions did not have a chance to "disappear.") The actions occurred cyclically with the exception of one which endured throughout.

I have made a total of five dances: *Arizona*, a solo of twenty-minutes; *21.3*, a solo of ten minutes; *Site*, a duet of seventeen minutes; *Waterman Switch*, a trio of twenty minutes; and *Check* for over forty performers which lasted thirty minutes. Each work attempted to solve what was at the time seen as a problem or set of problems. To qualify and clarify "problem solving" as a process of thought appropriate to making dances would require elaborations beyond the scope of this article. Rather an attempt has been made to indicate how the problematic has served as syntax. It seems irrelevant that what was seen as a particular problem often remains a distant and unimmediate element in a performance; the structure of some musical scores is unapparent in performance. Much about the work has not been dealt with: the quality of performers' actions, uses of sound, certain persistent imagery. These considerations also lie beyond the scope of this article. I have only attempted to touch on what seemed the foremost concerns that underlay whatever imagery, objects, etc., were employed.

NOTE

1. Quite a lot has been written lately about the so-called "new dance." Some of it is good, most is bad. But there is undeniably a need for a criticism devoted to focusing the problematic and the viable in the recent dance activity. Such writing would require the development of a vocabulary which could articulate the constructs of a functioning group. It might be possible to proceed by locating what a given group regards as its necessary questions together with its replies: its concrete actions. Only by the articulation of this dialog can any coherent tradition be traced; even a recent tradition. And it would be revealed, I am sure, just as it has been revealed in the other arts when carefully observed, that dance like the other disciplines is no less involved in a dialog of self-criticism.

17

CITY SCALE

Ken Dewey, Anthony Martin, and Ramon Sender

City Scale was the culminating event of a season devoted to exploring performer-audience relationships. We decided to use the city environment as totally as possible, to create a trip out of which more or less controlled elements would emerge. Many of the events were purposely ambiguous so that audience members would not have the certainty of knowing whether a given incident had been planned or was happening anyway.

The most meaningful events of the evening were those which impinged upon the life of the city, interacted with it, transformed it, or absorbed it into the structure of the work. The arrival of the audience in two trucks at a small park perched high on a hill overlooking the Mission coincided with a collision between two teenage gangs in the park. I had arrived early to inflate four seventeen-foot weather balloons, and noticed the kids collecting. Just as the two groups started toward each other, our trucks full of excited participants roared up. Sixty people started running across the park toward the balloons, and the teenagers scattered to the periphery. I don't know what went through their minds in the minutes that followed, as adults chased balloons and each other through the park.

City Scale was a natural extension of sound experiments with which the Tape Music Center members were involved – group improvisation, or tape pieces unfolding on many simultaneous levels of control. Out of it developed our present interest in environmental works – sound and light events controlling as much of a given space as possible.

Ramon Sender

My intention was to externalize visually the world in ourselves by providing a maze of the manmade, a sequence of events in the city.

Anthony Martin

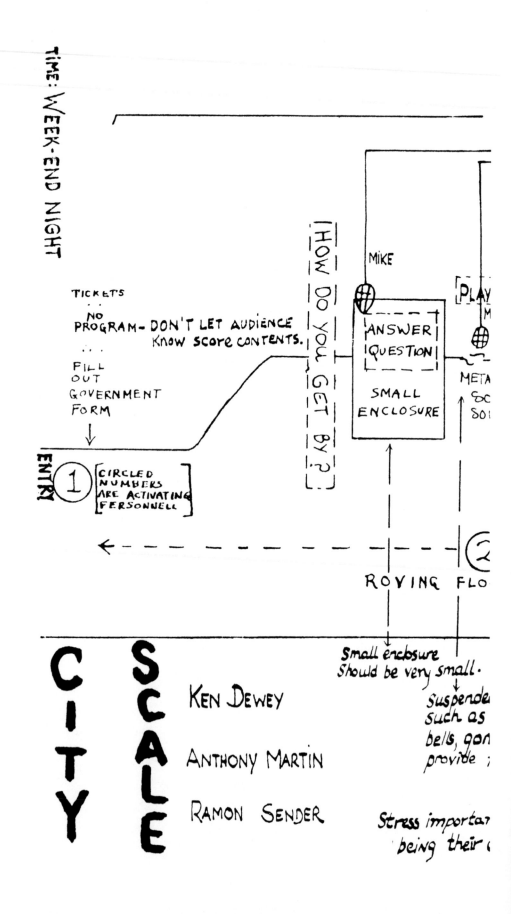

I

Recorder 1

Recorder 2

④ COMPOSER PREPARES
SOUND SCORE TO BE
PLAYED BACK AT III

SOMETHING
KE

LLIC
UND
RCES

```
┌─────────────────────────────┐
│  ┌ ─ ─ ─ ─ ─ ─ ─ ─ ─ ─ ┐   │
│  │ FILL IN SOME        │   │
│  │ BLANK  SPACE        │   │
│  └ ─ ─ ─ ─ ─ ─ ─ ─ ─ ─ ┘   │
│                             │
│  AUDIENCE COMES             │
│  TOGETHER  IN               │
│  LARGE   ROOM               │
│                             │
│      PAPER ON WALLS         │
│  ③  PAINT, BRUSHES,        │
│      CRAYONS, ECT.          │
└─────────────────────────────┘
```

MIRROR
TEAR
YOUR
SHAPE

HOLD ON
TO YOUR
SHAPE

THERE WILL BE A TAKER OF THE SHAPES

) ─ ─ ─ ─ ─ ─ ─ ─ ─ ─ ─ ─ →

3R MANAGER

Each person should be
encouraged to get thru
part I as fast as he
can. As soon as he has
finished making his shape
he should be ushered out
and be given written
directions for either Rte 1
or Rte 2.

d metal objects
  car bumpers,
gs, cymbals, etc.
mallets + hammers

ce of shape
own.

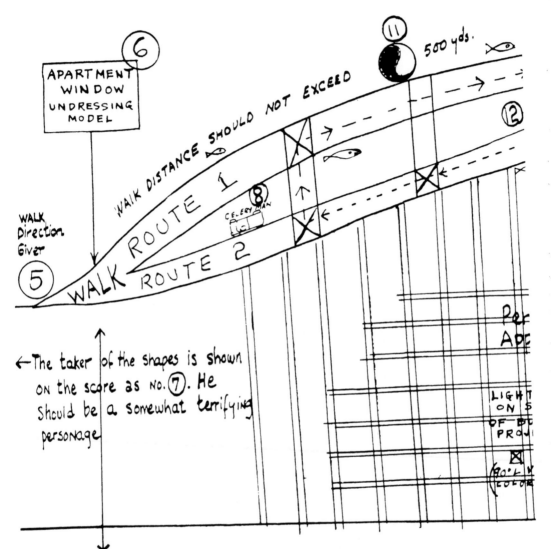

⑥ APARTMENT WINDOW UNDRESSING MODEL

WALK DISTANCE SHOULD NOT EXCEED

WALK ROUTE 1

ROUTE 2

WALK Direction Giver ⑤

CELERY MAN ⑧

⑪ 500 yds.

⑫

←The taker of the shapes is shown on the score as No. ⑦. He should be a somewhat terrifying personage

All the 'en route' occurances should appear quite natural and unprepared. The model at the window should not be too obvious. The audience should feel that she lives there and just forgot to draw her shades

∞ · fish should be placed along the routes to act as cat attracters.

⑪
⑫ 2 pairs of lovers should be placed at 2 points

CELERY MAN: A parked car, radio
⑧ on, man eating celery.

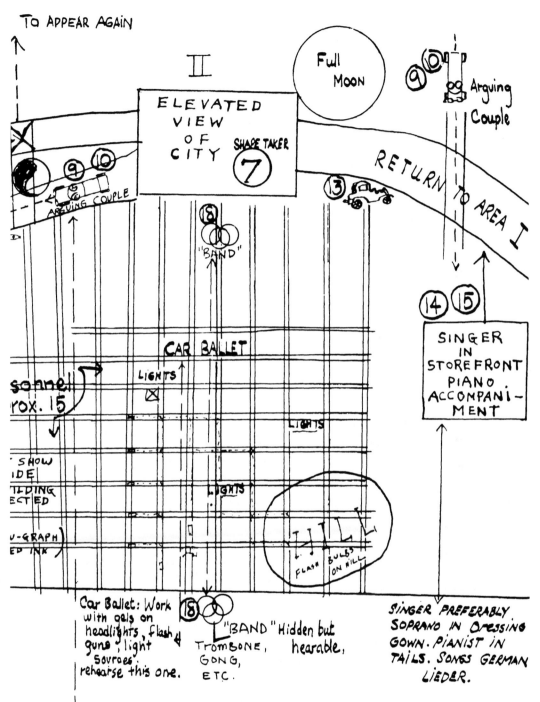

TO APPEAR AGAIN

II

Full Moon

ELEVATED VIEW OF CITY

SHAPE TAKER ⑦

⑨ ⑩ Arguing Couple

RETURN TO AREA I

Ⓧ ⑨ ⑩

ARGUING COUPLE

⑧ "BAND"

⑬

⑭ ⑮

SINGER IN STOREFRONT PIANO. ACCOMPANI-MENT

CAR BALLET

LIGHTS

Ⓧ

sonnel rox. 15

LIGHTS

SHOW IDE ILDING ECTED

LIGHTS

U-GRAPH) ED INK

J J L L

FLASH BULBS ON HILL

Car Ballet: Work with gels on headlights, flash guns, light sources. rehearse this one.

⑧ "BAND" Hidden but hearable, Trombone, Gong, ETC.

SINGER PREFERABLY SOPRANO IN DRESSING GOWN. PIANIST IN TAILS. SONGS GERMAN LIEDER.

Arguing Couple: MAN IS GIVING WIFE DRIVING LESSON IN CONVERTIBLE. SHE STALLS IN INTERSECTIONS MARKED X. MAN AT WIT'S END - LOUD QUARREL. CONTINUES THROUGHOUT THEIR SCENE.

⑬ — TRANSPORTABLE DEFUNCT VEHICLE MAN, tools laid out, working

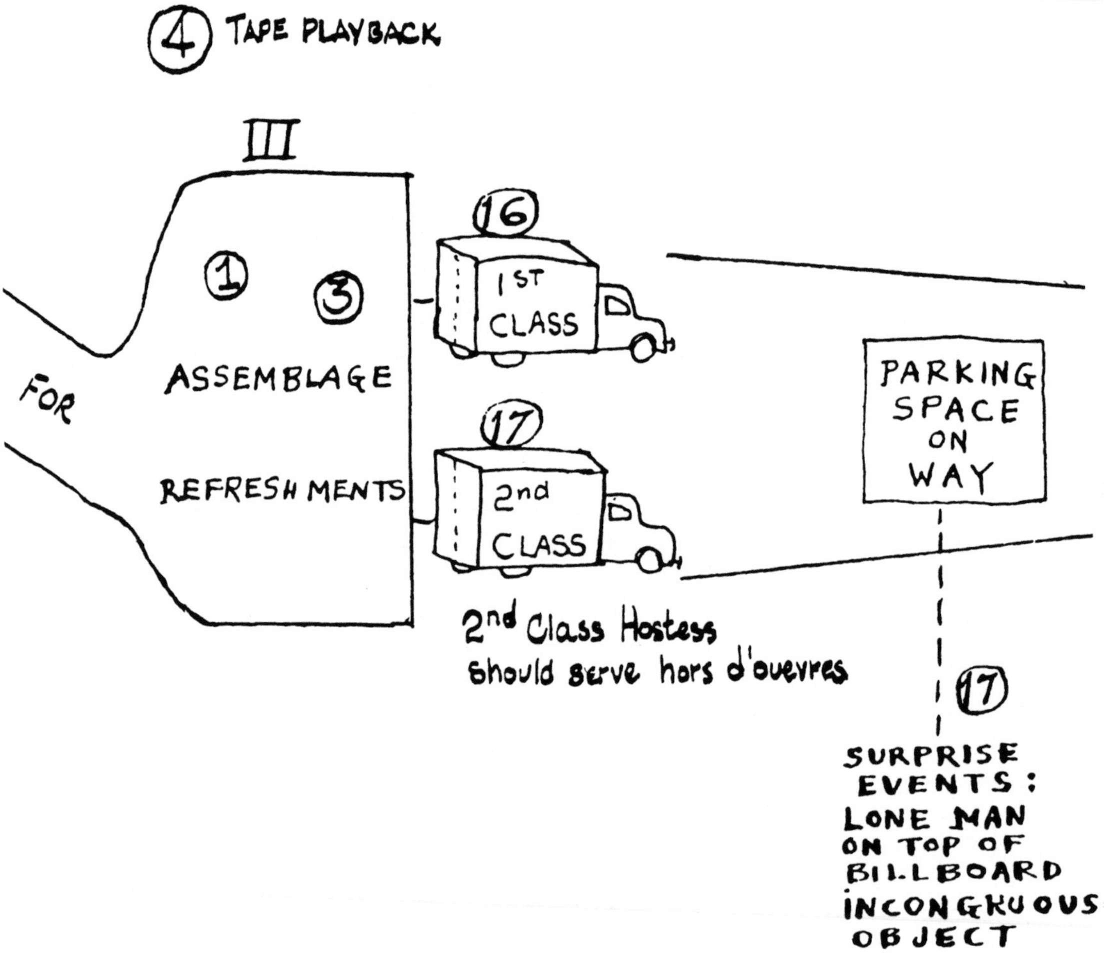

④ TAPE PLAYBACK

III

⑯ 1ST CLASS

① ③

ASSEMBLAGE

FOR

REFRESHMENTS

⑰ 2nd CLASS

PARKING SPACE ON WAY

2nd Class Hostess should serve hors d'ouevres

⑰

SURPRISE EVENTS: LONE MAN ON TOP OF BILLBOARD INCONGRUOUS OBJECT

OBJECTS ARE PROVIDED FOR ASSEMBLAGE BY GROUP IN LARGE ROOM. PLAYBACK OF TAPE (I.). GROUP USHERED INTO TRUCKS (CLOSED VAN TYPE) EACH TRUCK HAS HOSTESS. DARK IN CLOSED VAN, HOSTESS WITH LANTERN.

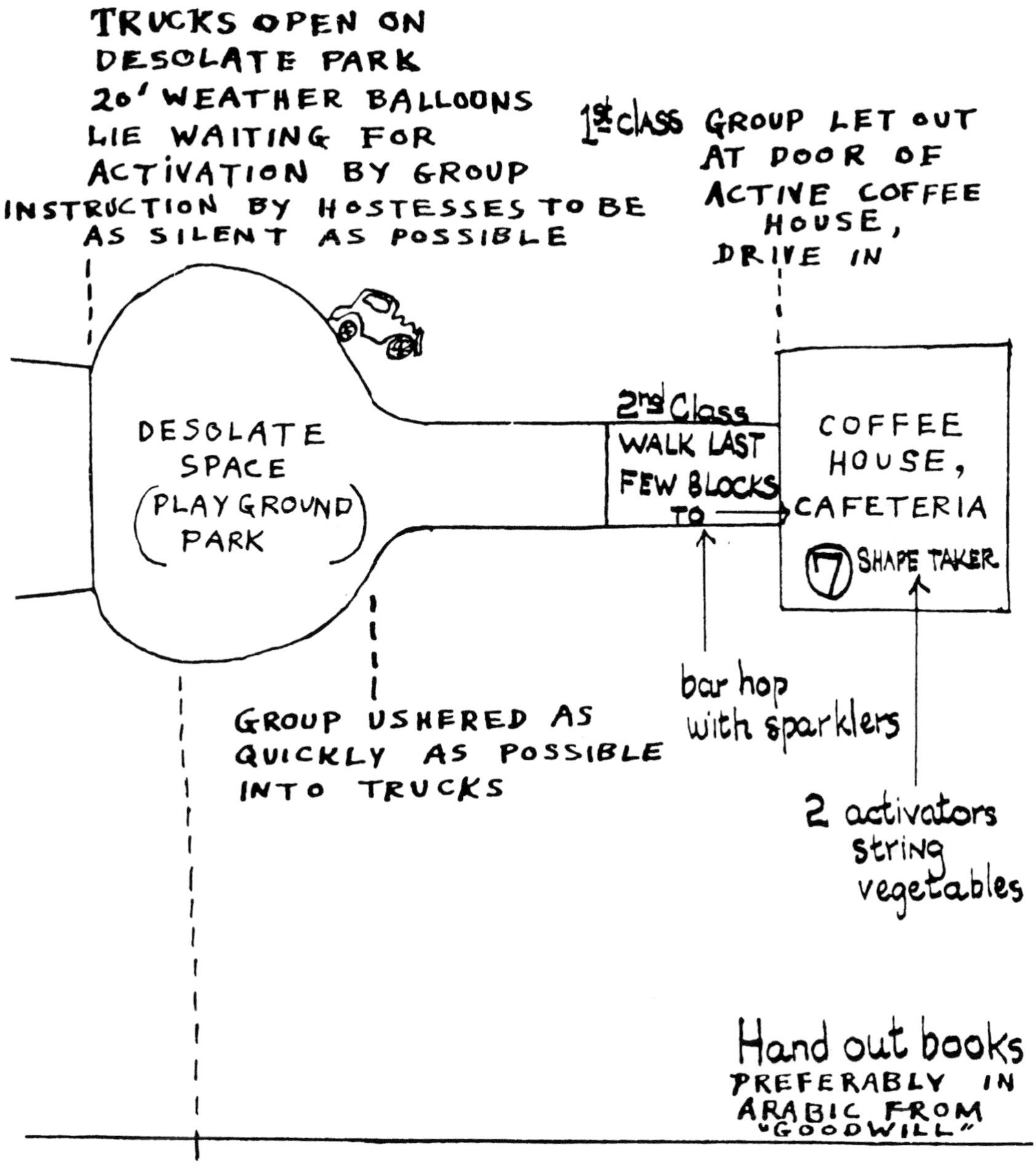

TRUCKS OPEN ON
DESOLATE PARK
20' WEATHER BALLOONS
LIE WAITING FOR
ACTIVATION BY GROUP
INSTRUCTION BY HOSTESSES TO BE
AS SILENT AS POSSIBLE

1st CLASS GROUP LET OUT
AT DOOR OF
ACTIVE COFFEE
HOUSE,
DRIVE IN

DESOLATE
SPACE
(PLAY GROUND)
PARK

2nd Class
WALK LAST
FEW BLOCKS
TO

COFFEE
HOUSE,
CAFETERIA

17 SHAPE TAKER

GROUP USHERED AS
QUICKLY AS POSSIBLE
INTO TRUCKS

bar hop
with sparklers

2 activators
string
vegetables

Hand out books
PREFERABLY IN
ARABIC FROM
"GOODWILL"

Balloons 2⁵⁰ each Army Surplus,
blown up by reversible vacuum cleaners.

8 min. each to inflate

THE EVENING SHOULD

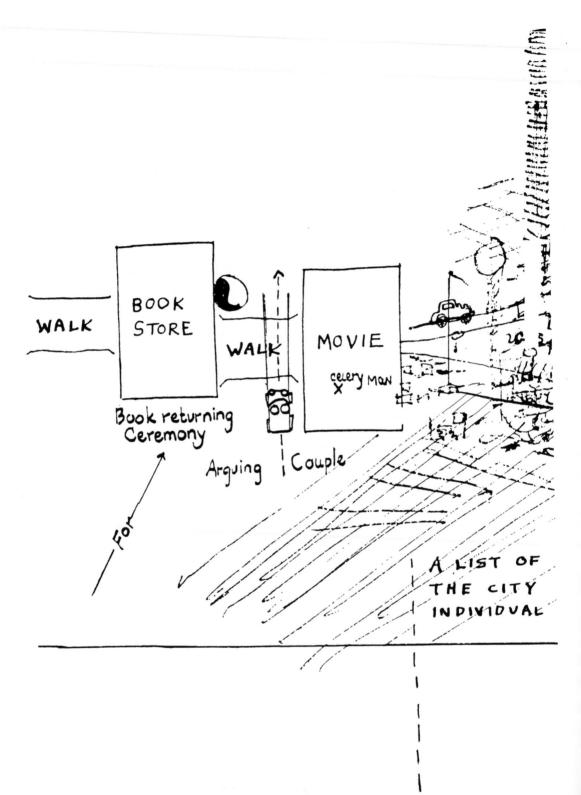

GET MORE AND MORE EXPLORATIVE

SPOTS, PLACES THROUGHOUT
IS PROVIDED FOR EITHER
OR SMALL GROUP JOURNEYS

A.M.

18

THREE PIECES

The ONCE Group

EVENING
Robert Ashley
From *in memoriam Kit Carson* (opera),
stage version as performed in December 1963

Eight men sit in armchairs arranged in a circle at a comfortable distance
for speaking. Each man's wife sits on the right arm of his chair in a
casual, intimate way. Within the circle, on small, separate tables are: 1. a
large, portable transistor radio; 2. a small, portable television set; and
3. a portable record player with a popular record. The radio and
television set are pretuned to broadcast immediately when they are
turned on. One of the men has a small transistor radio in his pocket. Each
of the women carries a small, white paper bag full of grains of rice.

Each performer's part is a list of eighty-one consecutive "moments."
There is no time schedule for these moments; they follow one another at
any pace the performers as a group establish, and this pace can change
continuously throughout the performance. At every moment at least one
of the performers has an action that he must perform. Thus, the piece is
no more than a play for sixteen actors, except that the actions have no
dramatic continuity and are valuable only as sound or gesture events; and
when more than one action occurs on the same moment, these actions
must be performed simultaneously. There is no conductor, and each
player privately keeps count of the moments as they pass, in order to fit
his actions into the sequence of events.

The set of eighty-one moments is performed three times consecutively
and without pause. At each repetition of the set the main actions (cues),
while remaining essentially the same and given in the same order, are
simplified in their structure. This simplification is accomplished by
reducing or eliminating elements of a compound sound-gesture action;
otherwise, the implication of the action and the relationship between

One page from the score for Robert Ashley's *Evening.* ➡

	I man-wife	II man-wife	III man-wife	IV man-wife	V man-wife	VI man-wife	VII man-wife	VIII man-wife
73			[OFF t-v T-V lw					
74	STOP great		T'CH				"THANKS" lm	
75	STORY IIIm	"YES" VIIIw	"YES" lm					C/L STOP story
76			L/S	C/L				
77	STOP story							
78		"NO" IVw		RETURN IVm	T'CH			
79	OH!	"NO" VIw				RETURN IVm / OH!		
80	OFF t-v							STOP "THANKS" great VIIIm
81	OH!						[-OH! [-RIGHT	

Underlined signs indicate an action that continues between and through subsequent moments until the performer is directed to stop (or, in the case of men listening to a program or record, until the machine is turned off). These actions must be interrupted to perform momentary actions when they occur. In some cases two continuous actions will be in effect simultaneously. Roman numerals and initials below signs designate the addressee. All persons should be addressed by first names. These should be performed consecutively without pause, in either order, or simultaneously when possible. Pairs of events joined by a dotted bracket are double events for a single person.

roles (performers) is constant throughout the performance.

Definitions of the *signs* that are used on the score are given below. Men performers use one set of signs, women performers another set. The modification of the action that a sign calls for – on the second and third times through the sequence of events – is described in the instructions, while the sign, of course, remains constant on the score. In addition to the actions that are modified in the course of the performance, both men's and women's parts involve other simple actions (responses to actions by other performers) which remain the same through all three sequences.

All specified spoken phrases should be *literal* repetitions of the phrases given in the instructions. At the same time, these phrases should sound as natural as possible. No performer is to "project" his speech or actions to the audience. However, all phrases – including the quasi-intimate ones – are to be spoken in the "theatrical" way that people often adopt in a large group, i.e., the phrases are spoken for the benefit of the whole group.

Men Performers

(sign)	(sequence)	(action) ... speech italicized
STORY	1st	"[addressee], *did I ever tell you that story about* [*name all of the characters in the story*]? *Well....*" Tell any anecdote at a natural pace until the adddressee answers, "*Yes.*"
	2nd	No address. Name all of the characters in the story above slowly and continually until the addressee answers, "*Yes.*"
	3rd	"*Well,*" [only] to the addressee as though to begin the story.
GREAT	1st	"*That's great,* [addressee]*!*" Clap softly in mock acclaim until the addressee answers, "*Thanks.*"
	2nd	No address. Clap, as above, until the addressee answers, "*Thanks.*"
	3rd	"*That's great!*" No clapping.

RADIO T-V PKT.RADIO RECORD	1st	*"Listen to this [program/record], [addressee]. It's terrific."* Place the assigned machine in front of you, pointed at the addressee, and turn it on.
	2nd	No address. Turn on the machine, as above.
	3rd	No address. Turn on the machine, as above.
LATER	1st	*"I've got some things to say to you later, [addressee's name or an affectionate name]!"* Smile and shake your finger playfully at the addressee.
	2nd	*"I've got some things to say to you later."* Do not point.
	3rd	No address. Smile and shake your finger at the addressee.
T'CH	1st	*"T'ch, my God!"* Make the chucking sound with the exclamation and shake your head slowly.
	2nd	Make the chucking sound only and shake your head, as above.
	3rd	No sound. Shake your head, as above.
C/L	1st	Cough *or* laugh in a natural manner.
	2nd	Cough, only.
	3rd	Laugh, only.
"YES"	(all)	*"Yes,"* said to a man to terminate a story addressed to you.
"NO"	(all)	*"No,"* said to a woman to terminate her sitting on the arm of your chair.
OFF	(all)	Rise and turn off the assigned machine.

Women Performers

(sign)	(sequence)	(action ... speech italicized)
STORY	1st	"[addressee], did I ever tell you that story about [name all of the characters in the story]? Well, ..." Tell any anecdote at a natural pace until the addressee answers, "Yes."
	2nd	No address. Name all of the characters in the story above slowly and continually until the addressee answers, "Yes."
	3rd	"Well," [only] to the addressee as though to begin the story.
SIT	1st	"Will it be too crowded for you, if I sit here, [addressee]?" Go to the assigned chair and sit on the left arm until the addressee answers, "No."
	2nd	No address. Sit on the arm of the chair until addressee answers, "No."
	3rd	No address. Rise in place – as though to move – then, sit down again.
RICE	1st	Throw grains of rice playfully until the addressee's partner brushes his shoulders.
	2nd	Throw rice, as above.
	3rd	Throw rice, as above.
RIGHT	1st	"I think that's absolutely right, don't you, [addressee's name or an affectionate name]?" Nod and smile at the addressee.
	2nd	"I think that's absolutely right, don't you, [addressee's name or an affectionate name]?" Do not face or smile at the addressee.
	3rd	No address. Nod and smile at the addressee.

OH!	1st	*"Oh! that's wonderful!"* Clap hands once, in exclamation.
	2nd	Clap hands, as above, but do not speak.
	3rd	*"Oh!"* [only], in exclamation. Do not clap hands.

L/S	1st	Laugh *or* sigh in a natural manner.
	2nd	Laugh, only.
	3rd	Sigh, only.

"YES"	(all)	*"Yes,"* said to a woman to terminate a story addressed to you.
"THANKS"	(all)	*"Thanks!"* said to a man to terminate his clapping to you.
BRUSH	(all)	Brush your partner's shoulders lightly, as though to brush off rice.
RETURN	(all)	Return to the right arm of your partner's chair.

KITTYHAWK

(An Anti-gravity Piece)
10 May 1965, New York City

Kittyhawk is composed of any number of developing episodes concerned with flight, elevation, levitation, or exploration of the three-dimensional performance space. Each episode has as its subject a woman – a single performer-object – who is in some manner raised above the performance area surface through the actions of a man or men. Each episode states that the woman could not achieve the elevated position by herself. Any mechanical or "magical" device for raising the woman-object can become the basis of an episode, but no mechanical principle or magical illusion should be used more than once.

Episodes can have any duration, and all episodes are performed simultaneously. (In some instances, the conditions for the appearance and manipulation of the woman-object will have to be prepared in performance prior to her appearance.)

Each episode should have a quasi-culminated or quasi-consummated nature. That is, the episode should end while the woman-object is elevated or in motion, or before the consequences of a sequence of actions are fully explicit. The quasi-culminative points in various episodes can be coordinated or left indeterminate in performance.

Six Episodes for *Kittyhawk*:

1. Prior to the performance each member of the audience is given a sheet of paper, on two sides of which is a mechanical drawing whose function is not obvious. A girl appears riding on a hydraulic hoist dolly pushed into the performance space by a man; she is holding a piece of paper like those the audience has. A voice from a loudspeaker begins reading instructions for folding the paper. She follows the instructions, and at the same time she is lifted very gradually (in short, aperiodic, abrupt bursts) by the hoist. Sudden darkness (and the noise of airplanes from the loudspeaker): girl and hoist disappear. Voice re-enters reading instructions for flying a paper airplane. Countdown: to popular music.

2. A girl walking through the performance space is attacked and slammed against a wall by two men. Another man appears with suitcase, from which he takes (first) masking tape. The girl is taped to the wall (completely covered). The two men attackers leave and the man with the suitcase ravages the wall fixture, cutting away tape, pulling out articles of clothing, exposing parts of the girl's body. Sudden darkness: the man disappears. A dim light comes on, exposing the girl-fixture to the audience. Sudden darkness: the girl disappears.

3. A girl appears following instructions (a man's voice) from a walkie-talkie radio. She triangulates the performance area according to instructions, fixing the position of various properties obtained from a trunk brought into the space by two men. These include a number of bowling balls, a block and tackle fixture, and a huge bag. She receives the bowling balls into the bag according to instructions and climbs into the bag with the balls. The two men appear again and hoist the bag, using the block and tackle, as high into the performance space as possible. Sudden darkness: the bag (with its contents) disappears.

4. A girl enters the performance area walking blindfolded along narrow planks arranged on the floor by a man. In the course of the walk the man introduces ladders under the ends of the planks, successively raising units of the walking surface to as high on the ladders as he can reach and leading the route over and through sections of the audience. Finally, he lays the route under an archway exit so that the girl must walk into the overhanging wall. Sudden darkness: the girl disappears.

5. A girl appears carrying a rope, goes directly to a plank resting on two

stools (prepared), and ties herself prone to the plank. Two men appear with a six-foot (one-inch) pipe fixed to a tripod. The men lift the plank above their heads and balance it on the end of the pipe. The girl balanced on the plank is left unattended. Sudden darkness: the girl disappears.

6. A girl appears and sits in a chair in the performance area. Four men step from the audience and surround the chair. They thrust their index fingers into her armpits and kneepits and lift her above their heads. Sudden darkness: the girl and the men disappear.

• • •

The six episodes described above have been used in all of the performances of *Kittyhawk* by the ONCE group in the spring of 1965. They were designed to be suitable to the typical theatre situation, in which lighting is the most thoroughly controllable element of production. In each episode the quasi-culminative point is a sudden, total darkness of the performance area. When all of the episodes take place in the same performance space (within view of the audience) these points are coordinated. When the episodes are dispersed to different areas, the darknesses are reached indeterminately. The possibility of special performance situations (open-air places, elaborate sound facilities, etc.) has suggested other kinds of episodes, involving balloon ascents, intricate sound-plots, smoke-screens, and so forth, but so far these opportunities have not been available to us.

COMBINATION WEDDING AND FUNERAL
Robert Ashley
10 May 1965, New York City

Notes
All members of the cast dress conventionally, and with the dignity and style that is appropriate to a wedding ceremony.

The Bride wears a bridal gown, etc., but her face and hands are made up with thickly matted hair so that she appears to be some sort of animal. She is shackled with white ribbons to the frontside of an open box (6' long, 2' wide, 1' deep, with carrying handles on either side) which rides upright on, but not attached to, a small, caster-wheel dolly. The open side of the box (facing toward the audience) is curtained with an opaque veil that can be lifted aside. The nude girl (the "cake") rides inside the box, hidden from the audience. At the entrance of the Bride in the wedding ceremony the Father of the Bride pushes the rolling structure with the two girls into position in front of the minister.

The minister uses conventional liturgies for the wedding and funeral

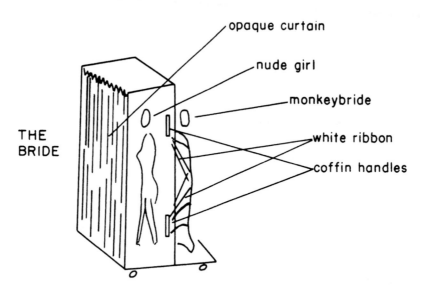

THE
BRIDE

opaque curtain

nude girl

monkeybride

white ribbon

coffin handles

ceremonies. He refers to the Bride as "Monkey," as though by name.

In preparation for the performance a plaster cast of the nude girl (pelvis to chest) lying on the serving table is made. This cast serves as the foundation for a wedding cake large enough to serve the entire audience. Thus, at the unveiling of the Bride, when the nude girl steps out and is lifted onto the serving table, the wedding cake will be fitted to her. During the funeral service, while the cake is being served to the audience, she should remain as though asleep.

Organ: vamp background music

Ushers show families to their seats: #2 takes Bride's mother to front row left; #3 takes Groom's mother to front row right (Groom's father follows); nonperformers can be ushered in as members of the families.

Singer: "I Love You Truly" (Carrie Jacobs-Bond)

Organ: vamp march preludes

Minister enters from stage right.

Groom enters, accompanied by Best Man; file out from stage right, and stand in place facing the audience.

Ushers enter, down the aisle: #3 and #4 together, #2 behind and alone; file into places and stand facing the audience.

Bridesmaids enter (#4-3-2-1 order) down the aisle: widely spaced (four rows apart at all times) and walking very slowly (step with the left foot, *wait three seconds*, step with the right foot, *wait three*

POSITIONS FOR THE CEREMONY

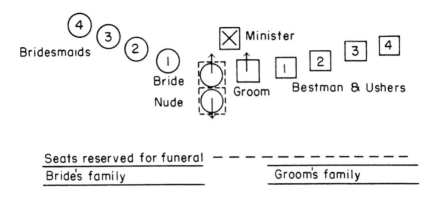

seconds, etc.) They should try to move at the same time. Each turns at the altar, goes left, and when she reaches her place, turns and stands facing the audience.

Organ: "Bridal Chorus" from *Lohengrin* (Wagner)

Entrance of the Bride: the Father of the Bride pushes the structure to which the Bride is shackled down the aisle to its place in front of the minister.

The Groom takes his place beside the Bride, facing the minister, and as he does this the men and the bridesmaids also turn and face the minister. When the Groom has taken his place by the Bride, the Bride's father goes to sit with the Bride's mother.

Singer: "The Lord's Prayer" (Albert Hay Malotte)

(no music) *At this point the minister performs the Wedding Ceremony:* The Groom, the Bride, and the other participants are directed in their actions by the minister according to the instructions in the ceremony; *except* (1) the Bride will be exempted from any physical responses because of her shackles, and (2) her vocal responses should be muffled and, perhaps, slightly distorted. The wedding ceremony leads directly to the presentation of the Bride and the next music cue.

Organ: "The Wedding March" from *A Midsummer Night's Dream* (Mendelssohn)

The men and women parties prepare for the presentation of the Bride. These actions are taken simultaneously and lead to the lifting of the veils.

POSITIONS FOR THE PRESENTATION OF THE BRIDE

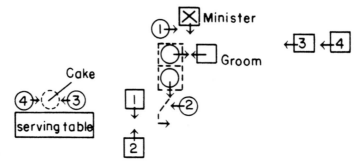

Women

Maid #1 unshackles the Bride and turns her toward the Groom.

Maid #2 goes to the Groom's side of the box, faces stage left, and waits to lift aside the curtain.

Maids #3 and #4 bring in the serving table with the cake from stage left, lift off the cake, and wait, holding it.

Men

Men #1 and #2 go to the Bride's side of the box.

Men #3 and #4 wait in place.

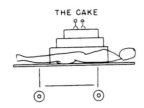

THE CAKE

Maids #1 and #2 simultaneously lift aside the Bride's veil and the curtain on the box.

(The emergence of the nude girl and the nuptial kiss occur simultaneously.)

The Groom steps forward and embraces the Bride. The nude girl steps out of the box, faces stage right, and is lifted onto the serving table by Men #1 and #2; Maids #3 and #4 place the cake upon her. Meanwhile, Men #3 and #4 are bringing in the bier from offstage right.

During the nuptial kiss the minister steps backward a few feet (to his position for the funeral ceremony); *Men #3 and #4* place the bier in front of the minister and place the box (that held the nude girl) on the bier. (One of the men should remove the caster-dolly to offstage right.)

The Groom goes to the Bride's right, and he and the Bride face the audience (to receive congratulations). The men and bridesmaids pass behind the minister to a position at stage right where they pair off

POSITIONS FOR THE WEDDING RECEPTION

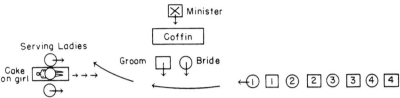

(1&1, 2&2, etc.) to be received by the Bride and Groom.

The wedding party couples go through the reception line (comprising the Bride and Groom) to offer congratulations (shake hands, kiss, smile, mimed talk, etc.); the couples group informally at stage left.

Organist: when the "Wedding March" is concluded (at some point during the reception sequence), begin immediately the hymnlike background to the funeral service.

Serving ladies roll the table with the cake to the Bride and Groom. The Bride and Groom cut the first piece together and feed each other ceremoniously. Photographers appear and begin taking pictures.

The couples of the wedding party file past the cake (stage left to stage right) and are served by the serving ladies; they regroup at stage right to eat the cake (with muted conversation, gestures, etc.) (At stage right there should be an inconspicuous table to put their empty plates on.) Photographers leave.

The Groom embraces the Bride again, and in a continuous movement from this embrace he lifts her in his arms and places her in the coffin. (This action should follow naturally upon the eating of the cake and will probably occur as the wedding party is being served.) He arranges the Bride's flowers upon her breast and places the flower that he is wearing in the coffin. He should pause only a moment in reflection at the coffin and then take a seat in the first row of the audience at stage left.

The serving ladies serve the remainder of the cake to the audience. They move down the center aisle, slicing and passing the cake to the audience seated on both sides; their actions and talk should be muted, but happy and oblivious to the funeral ceremony. The serving of the cake should be paced, if possible, to continue throughout the funeral ceremony, and they should exit (at the back) only slightly ahead of the men bearing the coffin.

The men and bridesmaids file by once more (stage right to stage left) to view the body and place their flowers in the coffin. They should be irregularly spaced (e.g., 1&1 together, 2's separately, maid #3 alone, man #3 and maid #4 together, man #4 alone). They take seats in the front row (stage left) next to the Groom.

Singer: "Standing in the Shadows" (Ashley), or any appropriate hymn.

(no music) *At this point the minister performs the funeral service.* It should, if possible, include a brief and original eulogy, and it may include a sermon on some topic related to the mystery of death. The form of the service should lead directly to the removal of the coffin.

Organ: "Funeral March" (Chopin)

The men file forward on either side of the coffin (#1 left, #2 right, #3 left, #4 right) *and bear it out the center aisle and exit.* They are followed by the bridesmaids, the family, and then the minister.

Organ: when the "Funeral March" ends, vamp hymnlike background until the audience has left.

END

19

CALLING

Allan Kaprow

A Happening for performers only. Performed Saturday 21 August and Sunday 22 August 1965.

In the city, people stand at street corners and wait.

FOR EACH OF THEM:

A car pulls up, someone calls out a name, the person gets in, they drive off.

During the trip, the person is wrapped in aluminium foil. The car is parked at a meter somewhere, is left there, locked; the silver person sitting motionless in the back seat.

Someone unlocks the car, drives off. The foil is removed from the person; he or she is wrapped in cloth or tied into a laundry bag. The car stops, the person is dumped at a public garage and the car goes away.

At the garage, a waiting auto starts up, the person is picked up from the concrete pavement, is hauled into the car, is taken to the information booth at Grand Central Station. The person is propped up against it and left.

The person calls out names, and hears the others brought there also call. They call out for some time. Then they work loose from their wrappings and leave the train station.

They telephone certain numbers. The phone rings and rings. Finally, it is answered, a name is asked for, and immediately the other end clicks off.

• • •

In the woods, the persons call out names and hear hidden answers. Here and there, they come upon people dangling upside down from ropes. They rip the people's clothes off and go away.

The naked figures call to each other in the woods for a long time until they are tired. Silence.

NOTES TO *CALLING*:

1. Places (other than train station) and times are to be decided just prior to performance.

2. Performance should preferably take place over two days, the first in the city, and the second in the country.

3. At least twenty-one persons are necessary to perform this Happening properly. For this number, six cars are required. Thus there would be three persons waiting at street corners, a car containing three people including the driver, to pick each one up; and a matching number of second-stage cars, also manned by three people, to carry the wrapped persons to the railroad station. But this basic number of participants can be multiplied proportionately for as large a group as is desired.

4. Names used throughout are to be the names of those involved.

5. Wrappings of foil and cloth should be as thoroughly applied as possible, the face covered except for breathing gap.

6. Second-stage cars should be parked at pre-chosen self-service garages, widely separated from each other. Drivers then proceed to part of city where first-stage cars are parked at meters. There the two drivers exchange car keys, the first-stage trio hurrying to garage positions, where they enter the autos and await the arrival of the human packages. The latter, of course, are brought by the second-stage trio. Timing for this, and all other stages of the event, must be worked out exactly.

7. The cars depositing packages at garages next proceed to the homes of their drivers, where phone calls will be received.

8. After the human packages unwrap themselves at the information booth, calls should be made from a public booth to the drivers of the last-mentioned cars. Phone is allowed to ring fifty times before it is picked up. Answerer says only "Yes?" Caller asks if it is X, (stating the right name), and X quietly hangs up.

9. The people hanging from ropes in the woods are those who drove and accompanied the cars the day before. An exchange of positions takes place here (underscored by the inverted positions on the ropes), with the former package people taking the active role. There should be no less than five bodies suspended, although all car people may choose to hang this way. If less than the total (of, say, eighteen), the others should sit

A passerby on 14th Street in New York examines a foil-covered performer seated in a station wagon on the first of a two-day performance of *Calling* (21–22 August 1965). (Photo by Peter Moore.)

motionless beneath each rope and join in the answering and the calling of names. When called from afar by the package people, the answer is simply "here!", "here!" until each body is found and violated.

10. The package people, arriving at the woods, call out the names of the car people hidden over a wide area among the trees. Moving as a group, they follow the sounds of the voices and reach each dangling figure. Its clothes are rapidly cut off, and after all have been so treated, the group leaves. Each suspended person (and those sitting beneath him) should cease answering to his name when found. Gradually the answering will diminish to silence, and at that point they start to call out each other's names, like children lost.

CALLING IN AUGUST

Although there were two preliminary meetings at which the people involved received instructions and worked out procedural details, the piece titled *Calling* by Allan Kaprow "officially" began at 4:00 PM on Saturday 21 August 1965. At that time, on three different street corners in New York, a participant was waiting: a girl stood on the southwest corner of 5th Avenue and 14th Street, another girl was on the northeast corner of Hudson and Christopher Streets, and a man waited at 10th Avenue and 42nd Street. Each carried a paper bag which contained

Two muslin-covered performers, one standing and one seated at lower left, unwrap themselves at Grand Central Station in New York in *Calling*. (Photo by Peter Moore.)

aluminium foil, muslin, and a ball of cord.

The people had been waiting for at least half an hour when, at 4:30, cars stopped near each of them, and their names were called. They got into the cars. As they were driven randomly about the city (the schedule allowed ample time before they had to be at the next required locations), the three people were completely covered with aluminium foil.

At 4:50 each car parked, all occupants except the foil-wrapped figure got out, the car was locked and a coin placed in the meter. During their rides the foil-covered participants had occasionally caused mild surprise and curiosity (as they would continue to do), and the interest of passersby was somewhat greater now that the cars were parked. The girl who had waited at 5th Avenue and 14th Street was now in the parking area above Union Square at 18th Street and Park Avenue South; the second girl had been taken from Hudson and Christopher Streets to the north side of 14th Street between 5th and 6th Avenues; and the man picked up at 10th Avenue and 42nd Street was sitting in a parked car on the South Side of 23rd Street between 8th and 9th Avenues.

Other participants were waiting at these points. While the first three cars had been making their pick-ups, these second groups had parked three more cars at various public parking garages. (The six cars were of different makes and models, ranging from a large station wagon to a small Volkswagen. The public nature of the garages used was important because the people could park their own cars rather than having an attendant do it.) Now the driver of each of the first three cars traded keys with the driver in the waiting group, received a parking stub, and was informed of the exact location (by floor, aisle, row, etc.) in which the "second stage" cars had been parked. The group from each of the first three cars proceeded by taxi or subway to the parking garages, leaving their silver "packages" in the locked cars.

The "second stage" crews drove off with the wrapped people. Their destination was the same parking garage at which they had each left a "second stage" car less than an hour earlier, but there was no need to hurry, and as the cars drove about the silver wrappings of their special passengers were removed and the people were rewrapped in muslin and tied with cord.

At 5:20 the "first stage" cars with their new drivers and crews arrived at the parking garages. The girl who had started at 5th Avenue and 14th Street was now at the Municipal Parking Garage on 8th Avenue between 53rd and 54th Streets; the second girl was taken to the Coliseum Parking Garage at 59th Street and Broadway; and the man was driven to the Lincoln Center garage on 65th Street near Broadway. The wrapped people were taken out of their cars and left on the concrete. The cars drove off. The other participants – who had originally picked up and wrapped the three "packages" and left them in the locked cars – picked up the muslin-wrapped figures and loaded them into the "second stage" cars.

Leaving their respective garages soon after 5:20, the three cars drove about the city until 5:45, when they were scheduled to deposit their wrapped passengers at Grand Central Station. Because of the heavy traffic, however, all three cars did not arrive at exactly the same moment, and it was more than five minutes before all three wrapped people were carried into the station and propped against the information booth. When the third "package" arrived, a large crowd had already gathered, and the other two participants had begun calling out each other's names. For some time each of the three people called out the names of the other two. Then they removed their wrappings and went directly to telephone booths.

Each of the three dialed the number of one of the participants who had helped to wrap or drive them during the second stage. (The "second stage" people had dispersed and gone home after leaving the parking garages, as the others had done immediately after leaving the wrapped people at Grand Central.) For five minutes the three people in Grand Central and the people in the three apartments throughout the city listened to the ringing. After each telephone had rung fifty times, it was picked up. "Hello." The correct name was quizzically asked, but the recipient hung up without saying anything more. Saturday's part of *Calling* was complete.

The next day – a Sunday of overcast skies and very light scattered rain – the participants all met at a farm in New Jersey. Because of trouble with one of the cars, some of them were delayed on the one-hour drive, and the second part of the piece did not begin until late afternoon.

After receiving brief instructions, all of the people except the three who had been wrapped in foil and muslin on the preceding day filed into a wooded area to the rear of the farm house. No paths were visible among the trees. The ground was soft and wet, and water fell from the foliage when it was pushed out of the way. Four or five of the people were asked to wait at each of five previously selected locations until all had been assigned a spot. At each of the locations a piece of heavy sailcloth with a hole in the center dangled from ropes attached to the branch of a tree, and Kaprow demonstrated how, when the signal was given, the volunteer in each group was to climb into the canvas sling and hang head downward.

Each group was isolated in the damp woods. None of the people in one group could see any of the participants in any of the other groups. It was quiet. After a time Kaprow's voice was heard calling "Come on" to the two girls and the man who had been left behind when the others entered the woods. At each location one person climbed into the apparatus and hung upside down. His head, thrust through the hole in the sailcloth, was perhaps a foot above the ground, and the arms and legs were supported by ropes on either side.

When the three "searchers" reached the edge of the woods, they called out the names of the five people – the three men and two women – who, somewhere out of their sight, were hanging inverted among the trees. When a hanging person's name was called, he and the three or four participants who were sitting or squatting silently nearby answered, "Here." By following the sounds, the trio located each hanging person and quickly cut and ripped away all his or her clothing before moving on to find the next group. The calling and responses continued until the last hanging person was found and stripped of clothing. Again the woods were silent.

The people in the first group, when they became aware of the final departure of the three searchers, began to call out the names of the four people who hung at the other locations. The others began to call, too. For perhaps ten minutes the names of the five hanging people were the material for a random vocal symphony sounding from various locations and with various volumes and qualities. Finally the pauses in the calling grew longer, and the voices stopped. The five people who had been stripped of their clothing still hung in their uncomfortable positions.

After a moment, a sound was heard among the trees indicating that someone had begun to leave. The hanging people swung down, and everyone moved slowly and quietly out of the woods.

20

THE GREAT GAMING HOUSE

A Précis

Kelly Yeaton

A DREAM/IMAGE

Strangers had come to town to construct and operate a new kind of recreation: a great fun house for adults. A sinister Disneyland with overtones of the World's Fair, carnival, gambling house, brothel, sideshow, circus, and *The Balcony*. Here one could buy adult adventure. The strangers leased a great, empty warehouse near the docks and in it they built a labyrinth of rooms and passages. There were gates, obstacles, puzzles, games, and other people. What choices one had no one knew, and these choices would often be changed. It was all synthetic and symbolic, safe and legitimate.

But rumors alerted the town that concealed within the Great Gaming House were *real* games: gamblers could find high stakes, hostesses would sleep with patrons, etc. There was no way to distinguish the real from the synthetic, nor could the player sort the shills from the guests. And, of course, the House could rid itself of unwanted clients – through the next gate the piker or cop would find himself in the alley.

The combined promise and threat of an underlying reality excited the town. But whether the rumors were true – that was another question. The strangers could have started them. And the Great Gaming House was obviously the front for con games ranging from the small deals associated with carnivals to the "big stores" of Chicago and Miami. The greedy mark would be sorted from the entertainment seekers and fleeced. But this was no threat to most people – a mark wants to be made. In any case one could refuse to play.

Even the knowledge that the House was loaded with shills had a double edge. If I met a neighbor, would her familiar face guarantee my safety? Thus the insecurity and ambivalence of illusion and reality extended itself into the life of the town.

THE FORM

A journey through a sequence of choices, situations, puzzles, obstacles, and games. All of these maintain a fixed but unknown relationship to each other. One moves from choice to choice; unlike a walk-through World's Fair there is more than one sequence. Indeed, each player undergoes a unique experience, depending upon his choices. The Gaming House differs from theatre in that the end is unknown; also the "audience" in the House are the players. In the Gaming House we are offered our own personal adventure which fits our mood, personality, skills, and potential. The total experience reflects our personalities as clearly as do our reactions to projective tests like the Rorschach.

Yet this freedom is illusory, for the alternatives are set by the structure of the House. Only certain choices are possible. Charles Morgan says that illusion is form in suspense and that dramatic illusion means that "while the drama moves *a* form is being fulfilled." He defines suspension of form as "the incompleteness of a known completion." Susanne Langer adds that this form is "the illusion of Destiny itself." Does the player's set of choices have this suggestion of Destiny? I think so.

The Gaming House is, in fact, a model for the "games of life" in which every choice leads only to other choices. This pattern of unstable progress marks the rites of passage and secret societies (from the early Christians to the KKK), and it is the pattern of *Everyman*, *Pilgrim's Progress*, *Mother Courage*, and dozens of others. It is the shape of subjective experience. The Gaming House differs from the older maps because it is not interested in the One True Path, the Right Way, and so forth. If there *is* a True Path among the others we do not know about it.

THEMES

A mixture of illusion and reality: the theatre is the natural place for such confusion because the very employment of actors opens itself to such speculations. In the Gaming House every effort is made to blur these distinctions. There is neither stage nor script nor program. The second theme is that of the game. The O.S.S. used games for spy training, primarily as an assessment of technique. In these schools the real and the artificial were gradually mixed so that agents were never sure when supervision was relinquished. They were carefully trained in a symbolic mode and then reality was gradually substituted for the symbols, until agents responded to real events precisely as they had been trained.

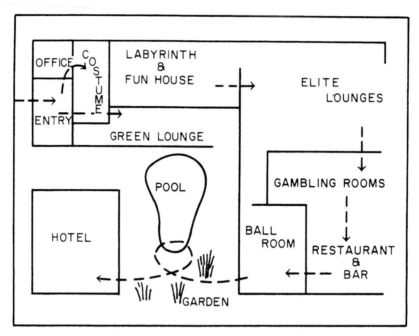

THE PROJECT

It can be built, large or small. Bits of it have been done here and there. Joan Littlewood's Funhouse is an equivalent structure. But this Great Gaming House has never been attempted.

It is impossible to solve such a world metaphor and impossible to leave it alone. The mind clings to it, returns, and won't shut off at night. This Great Gaming House would take about a city block. It could expand to fill a small island or contract to several floors of a small hotel.

A POSSIBLE SEQUENCE

Entrance: interviews and fortune-telling (Tarot and I Ching).

Admission to the House. Rules given, contracts agreed upon, counters issued.

Masking, costuming, etc. A player may return here to change often. A player may pass this by.

Lounge where new identities are tested. Secret games, duels, party games.

The hundred gates where many choices are offered. These are changed every few days.

The labyrinth, mirror maze, and fun house: these choices are emotional, physical, and "mysterious." Some players may panic.

Obstacle course: physical tests, puzzles. There are several ways past the guards, including bribing. But even here the House may decide to pass a player through free, or send someone back for no reason.

Elite lounges where "special" people are admitted either by chance or through testing.

Gambling rooms, restaurants, bars.

Ballroom and theatre for dances, shows.

Garden, patio, swimming pool. One must cross this area to get from the Hotel to the ballroom. A maze of hedges and trees enable the breaking-off of relationships, etc.

A "secret level" contained *within* the others (hidden rooms, special arrangements, etc.). These "secret games" don't show on any ground plan, nor is the player certain when he has entered one of these places. Here illusion becomes reality, or "special" illusions are offered.

RULES AND PRINCIPLES

"There is no guarantee and not much justice. One must accept chance as an operative factor."

All play is voluntary.

If the House is caught cheating a bonus is paid. No cheating in gambling rooms.

Problems of perception are continually offered, ranging from simple changes in perspective, mazes, and mirrors to more complex identity games.

House personnel are unidentified for the most part. A player may choose to wear the House uniform as a costume.

21

X-INGS

Ken Dewey

It should be easy to get off a few words about one's work – exchange useful debris and so forth. It isn't. It's hard to know where to start, but even more one senses so-called Theatre at the edge of provoking an explosive degree of consciousness. I mean, once you get away from what Paul Sills has aptly called the GOD'S WORD way of doing things –

Creative Artist	Playwright
Creative Coordinator	Director
Supportive Artists	Design: Set, Costumes, Lights, Music
Support Coordinators	Stage Manager & Technicians
Interpretive Artists	Performers
Interpretation Coordinators	Audience

– once a form begins through participation or outright collaboration to deliberately engage the individual imaginations of audience and performer alike, across the board as it were, then you're into a fairly serious realm. What form? What realm?

Let me start with a reference point. With all the cover terms around (Happenings, Events, Pieces, etc.) it's hard to use any of them and know what one is talking about. This is further complicated because Happenings themselves often include the everyday, so, to many, anything is a Happening. And because new terms are meant to indicate new forms we seem to have a variation on Jimmy Durante's old horror of moving to Hackensack to forget Hoboken and then going to Weehawken to forget Hackensack, and so on . . .

"It should have been made clear that Happenings came about when painters and sculptors crossed into theatre taking with them their way of looking and doing things." Taking with them, that is, their *aesthetics*. Claes Oldenburg said that this summer and it's worth passing on as a sort of key. Someone with an aesthetic sought techniques outside his field in order to articulate experiences. The results were hybrids, with characteristics of their own, the products of some kind of fusion. This is a pretty good reference point. In one direction you've got the *how*, a kind of working definition based on process. In the other direction, a broad spectrum of similarly based activities has opened up.

FORM	ORIGIN
Montage, Collage, Construction, Assemblage, Mobile, Environment, Happening	Painting, Sculpture
Pieces, Events	Music
Improvisational, Psychedelic, and Action Theatre	Theatre
Psychodrama	Psychology
Marches, Sit-ins, Demonstrations, Vigils, Rallies	Religion, Politics
Picket Lines, Strikes	Labor
Fairs, Exhibitions	Industry
Simulators	Science

Jet simulators, trade fairs, sit-ins, psychedelic theatre, have all come from "crossing over." If one wanted to get academic about it and still ask a valid question, one could identify new forms, indicate sources (as above) and then inquire what the other elements of fusion were. The following is a series of crossings one knows are taking place and which have either been identified within a larger form or have not been considered independent activities.

Dancers ——————————— > Painting, Sculpture
Designers, Commercial Artists ——— > Painting (Pop)
Painters ——————————— > Science (Op)
Poets ——————————— > Theatre, Music
Architects ——————————— > Theatre (Programmed
 Environments)
Composers ——————————— > Mathematics, Science
 2nd Cousin Department
Ad-Men < ——————————— > Happenings

In seeking roots one can go back to Bauhaus or the Dadaists, to numerous individual artists like Dali, Duchamp, Schwitters, and even to all the obscure projects undertaken over the years in the name of Art by those absorbed with vengeance, simple curiosity, or complex boredom. Obviously, the causes of Happenings have been "in the air" for at least fifty years, probably longer. All the casual, instinctive, and scattershot contacts – which play a large part in that continuity of experimentation which comprises a form's "birth" – had to wait for development of the awareness that here was something of independent interest. Someone had to make it stick as a separate form. That, of course, is exactly what Allan Kaprow did for Happenings.

What we have now are "forms" coming almost at the rate of synthetic chemicals. Personally, I think that's great. We need new methods and new techniques of articulation: ways in which people can express themselves. But there's a problem. Dada's big failing was that when it broke through the hierarchy of objects it didn't go all the way and change the relationship of the artist to the viewer. And artists are still greedily homesteading on techniques that should have simply been put into the public domain as useful processes. This problem is likely to be resolved when people (as a whole) get themselves to stop worshipping and to start doing.

Vogues are a good example of how curbs get set on the realms of individual imagination. Perhaps they *are* urban worship. For instance when hippies got onto the techniques for a little harmless jacking off at "in" parties, and toilet paper rolls, signs, and bras got rejuvenated as "happeners" gear on the college circuit, the lazy of the world's editors who'd been confused on how to bag Happenings finally got them nailed down as *that*. Happenings and related crossings have had the potential of being neutral terrains where anyone could come, check his luggage, and make it. At his own best depth. When the mass media set shallow response as the standard, they slowed things down, for a short while.

Concerning realm, my own lot's been to work from pretty much the same assumptions about emotional scale and physical scale that Artaud projected. The crossings have been into music, reporting, and sports. With the exception of one piece in New York last spring the work has been in other countries (nine of them) during the better part of 1963–1964. Before that I worked on the West Coast, mostly in San Francisco. In 1961, when the prevailing cross-over was into the theatre (having been there myself, for seven years, as student, technician, and playwright), I was trying to get out. I mean that literally: out of the text, out of the building, and, most earnestly, out of theatre's way of doing things. Looking back, the actions seem methodical; but at the time they were anything but. It's interesting how closely they parallel what Kaprow has described as his progression: out of the frame, off the wall, into the room, into other spaces – gradually adding objects and people.

The frames for theatre are text, building, and rehearsal. My early efforts were to decrease dependency on all three. I had written, by then, two full-length plays and ten short ones. Some of the short plays had been produced. Texts were so important to me that I couldn't bear to fuss with my own. Instead I took Camus' *The Misunderstanding* and, for a lab project at the Actor's Workshop, replaced the play's set and all but one character with the music of Edgard Varèse ("Poem Electronique," "Hyperprism," and one other). Yvette Nachmias – an actress with mime and dance training – played the character who was left. Alternately she talked to the music, allowed it to reflect her thoughts, and treated it as part of the environment. That was 1961. By then, Happenings had already been going on in New York for some time.

If it was cowardly to choose Camus, the next time I paid full dues when we turned one of my own texts over to the process. Two dancers from Ann Halprin's company – Lynne Palmer and John Graham – treated a short play, *The Gift*, kinesthetically. As director I went along, forcing weak smiles of approval as the text became progressively less intelligible. We worked for two months and the play kept coming in and out of focus like James Lord reports Giacometti's paintings do. I never knew how it would end and I squashed recurrent urges to get protective. At a certain point rehearsals ended. The words had come back but by now the thing was something so complex that one couldn't have notated it. It conformed to what Braque said a finished painting was: when nothing remains of the original idea.

The Gift's greatest achievement was to get us into the streets; because the performers carried everything they used on their backs, we could set up anywhere, indoors or out. And we were taken by the idea of being out and around. A fixed text is unwieldy in a street but the accidental audience was fantastic and I dreamed up scroungy little manifestoes calling for a break with theatre buildings. At about the same time, at the end of 1961, I saw Bob Whitman's *American Moon* in New York. Later, when Whitman came west, I was in one of his Happenings. I was very impressed. At the same time we were working with John Cage's *Theatre Piece* at Ann Halprin's workshop. Through these exposures I encountered the possibility of composing with events. However, it wasn't until early 1963, when the Tape Music Center produced *City Scale*, that I got a chance to actually try the style. This audience-journey piece was worked out with the composer Ramon Sender and the painter Anthony Martin (TDR 10, 2 (T30) 1965 [and in this volume]). It was also my first try at collaborative scoring.

Of the three frames, essentially text was freed at Edinburgh two years back. It's necessary to say "nude" Happening I suppose since that's what all the newspapers talked about. Anyway, having been asked to show the Drama Conference a Happenings demonstration, three of us (Charles Lewsen, an English playwright, Mark Boyle, an English assemblagist, and myself) studied the Conference itself through four days. On the fifth day an eight-minute piece comprised of some fifteen events dealing with

Conference themes was introduced back into the Conference. This reportage-type Happening is an alternative to writing a play or essay about the whole thing later.

Space was freed by composing with it. Enclosures like the Modern Museum in Stockholm became the source. All ideas were generated by working with the spaces and considering the city of which they are part. On various projects with which he was involved, sculptor Jerry Walter drew attention to plastic qualities. More recently an architect, Robert Mitchell, drew attention to static aspects by doing an anthropomorphic study of a performance enclosure. He asked in effect what the building itself wanted. In an era which can produce a major concert hall with poor acoustics and a stadium in which players can't see the ball this isn't an idle question.

Where text obviously controlled *time*, and stage defined *space*, the real surprise was to notice that the rehearsal process – the terms on which people met – automatically set *motion* and emotion within limits even before anybody did anything. *The Misunderstanding*, *The Gift*, and *City Scale* clarified issues. Successive projects focused on elements much as painters focused on just color, or just texture, etc. Projects with the Swedish composers tended to solve problems of form. At the Pistol Theatre in Stockholm and particularly in Helsinki at the Finnish Student Theatre, Lilla Teatern, and with Henrik Otto Donner, new ways of dealing with content or realm came about.

The further out one moves, the simpler one's understanding becomes of what theatre is. I now would accept only that theatre is a situation in which people gather to articulate something of mutual concern. This is why my work has moved toward an exploration of the problems related to group articulation while, on the other hand, those artists who've come into theatre from fields of individual expression are concerned with communicating an individual image. There isn't time here to discuss the problems of replacing controls with rapport as the binding agent within such a performance. However, a piece is at its best when two agons are working at once: the first between people and themselves and the second between the whole group and something beyond itself. And when a group allows the content of its working together to generate its own form (and I include the audience as part of the group), it's like the difference between dynamite and, you know, the next one. And that to my mind is the potential *motion* of these crossings.

22

A MONSTER MODEL FUN HOUSE

Paul Sills

Here is the GOK, the monster, a model for a popular theatre, something for every taste, a trip through your own personality in a direction towards your person, a fun house with a belief in meaning; in other words, a "literary" piece in which the players, who are also the audience, are given the free choice to discover themselves as they are that day, and, just as important, the intensity of participation they allow themselves in their own life; all leading to the final free choice which is destined for all who will escape from fantasy (and in the GOK everybody wins!), towards relation, becoming whole, play, and revealed meaning.

It is at the same time a personal record of our life in the theatre, starting with the Previews of Coming Attractions of Saturday matinees through the written, classical theatre, to improvisation, and finally to Theatre Games with side journeys into films, TV, Artaud, and the Absurd. An audience-player, therefore, will participate not only in his own life's experience, but also in ours. It is for this reason a literary piece, this fun house, and thus its meaning, no matter how hard-won in our life, can be held in question, which is as it should be.

It can be done with six actor-guides in a gymnasium, say, with cooperation of the art, theatre, literature, and music departments of a college. We almost did it professionally in Chicago. The money was raised but the producer got cold feet when he asked some psychoanalysts if it would work and they said "no," that "art is a vicarious experience" for most, and that overcoming distance, etc., would frighten people off.

| THREE ENTRANCES | These are pure carnival, or like marquees on 42nd Street. Barkers can spiel and entice. Entrances are a Giant Mouth, say, or are through gauze and fog. |

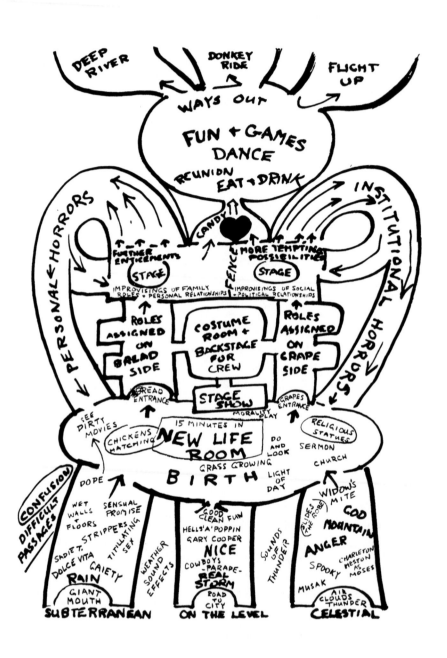

PASSAGE THROUGH THREE CHAOTIC PASSAGES FULL OF ALLUREMENT	These three rooms allow for the audience to sit or stand along the walls which should be slotted, made of canvas, with visible openings for mysterious occurrences of all sorts. The actors can be directed to supply suspense, titillation, a kind of preview of coming attractions happening for ten minutes, if desired, or long enough to build expectation of the fantasy pleasures to come. Sound effects as of stormy weather, wind, water dripping, appropriate music should be used. Lantern sides, film, projections. Dramatic light changes.
IN NEW LIFE ROOM EXHIBITS AND STAGE SHOW	Bright lights. A bring-down. Pitiful movies seen through peepholes. Plaster church statues. The three groups are reunited. They mill about with a feeling of having been cheated. There is an incubator and chickens are hatching. Grass grows in small pots. After an unbearable delay, actors appear on the stage and perform a written show, preferably homemade verse drama. They stand for it like groundlings. They are then offered a choice of two ways onward: Bread or Grapes.
INTO BREAD OR GRAPE SIDES: ROLES ASSIGNED	As they file through their chosen door they see three more doors. These are faced with images denoting, perhaps, a) The Little Old Winemaker ad; b) Receiving the Sacrament; c) A celebrity-padded liquor ad. Bread is also a sacrament, staff of life, cake, white bread, etc. They make this choice and enter a small room, where after being treated to pertinent exhibits, special effects, lectures, or what you will, after being involved by discussion techniques or left to languish in boredom, as desired, they are asked by their guides to cast each other in roles. The Grape side for society's institutional roles, the Bread for family and community. They are chosen by their peers to be the Boss, the General, the Bum (among the Hard Drinkers, for

instance). The Staff-of-Lifers can choose Mom and Big Sister. The Cop, the Boy Friend, the Judge, and on and on as desired. Costume pieces given.

IMPROVISINGS OF LIFE ROLES	They enter a large room divided down the center by a fence they can see through but not pass. They sit or stand around central stages. Here the actors go through satirical, structured improvisations which call for Mom and the Judge to perform their actions and make their responses. They participate as much or as little as they can and wish to. The Bishop, the Virgin, the Radical, the Successful Man, all are possible roles, as are Reverend Vanity, Miss Style Conscious, Joe Doaks, the Wise Man, the Fool. The actors call for the cast ones when readying the bit.
TO REUNION OR INTO HORRORS	To leave the improvising stockade they must choose among four exits; one on each side clearly labeled "This way joins the other side and leads to the Fun and Games Room." The other three exits on each side tempt and entice with sex, wealth, fame, evil, salvation, and general American or local fantasies. The doors leading to the Games Room open on a small room where candy is passed out in a valentine heart box. The doors to enticement lead to long corridors in which players follow a Pilgrim's Progress to disillusionment since they are after all in the theatre, where all back alleys of sin are made of canvas. An attempt here to set up fun house where they are rolled, watered, chased, scourged, and ridiculed back to the only ways out. No moralizing mayhem.
FUN AND GAMES ROOM	Here is dancing, reunion, games, fishing for trinkets, bobbing for apples, and whatever all can join to celebrate their common escape from

fantasy, again insofar as they are able to participate. Theatres Games are played. By this time
many have come gladly from out of the early
passivity of the previews, passed through their
spectatorship, accepted a role, participated in the
self-comprehension of satire, been scourged for
their illusions, and are ready to join the games as
players.

WAYS OUT	There are three ways out, corresponding to the entrances. One is a tunnel-of-love, deep-river ride. The middle, a donkey ride on real donkeys. Third, a flight up, even if only a basket hoisted above the crowd. It should be arranged that all can see and wave to each other from boat to air to donkey path.

23

HAPPENINGS

Richard Schechner

In a large part the new art is already with us. But it is forbidden. Attention is diverted by the vested interests' promotion of pornography, and by brutal exclusion from the pages of leading reviews such as *Evergreen* of anything that tends to be concrete in favor of the [LeRoi] Jones school of compradors.

Dick Higgins, *Postface*

One thing alone will not delight the bourgeoisie: a decrease in income, a loss in social power, a threat to its property.

Irving Howe, *Dissent*

Art and politics have long been bad bedfellows. Politicians have converted art into propaganda and artists have welcomed alienation from bureaucratic societies. It very well may be that the modern nation is inimical to art, knowing at best how to "tolerate" it and at worst how to "suppress" it. In which case, my discussion is ended. But if art and politics are not oil and water; if, indeed, *perception* is basic to "social action," we may develop a rapport whose possibilities should make both artist and politician stop and think.

The same may be said about art and science, where perception is at the heart of verification.

Science, art, and politics are less simple now because our tools no longer permit us a naïve understanding of perception. Bishop Berkeley, though certainly extreme, was not altogether wrong when he attributed an event to those who witness it. The reaction against his views located perception in the thing-itself. Today we think in terms of "messages sent and received" and understand that perception is a *relationship* between the sender, the message, and the receiver. These vary so greatly that abstractions, of whatever kind and in whatever field, remain useful but recognizably "untrue." In the midst of this complexity we know that politics and science have become more "artful" in their representations of their abstractions just as artists have sought more frequently the specificity of the streets.

Happenings (and I use the word to mean all the things compiled in this issue of *TDR*) are rooted in two seemingly unrelated interests: (1) an attempt to bring into a celebratory space the full "message-complexity" of a downtown street and (2) a playing with modes of perception. John Cage wants to hear a fly buzz; Allan Kaprow exhibits in Grand Central Station human figures wrapped up in muslin; Claes Oldenburg offers floating and sinking variations on the theme of water in a midtown pool. Performances are paced by "chance" techniques, relieving everyone of the burden of choosing when to do something. (One should note that scientific experiment is often carried on with the same methodology: a controlled environment in which the "natural object" under study is allowed to choose its own way of doing things.) Shows are sometimes unrepeated, never have a run, or the creator always insists that things go differently from night to night. Other techniques anathematic to conventional theatre also abound: multifocus, no plot, noncharacterized performances (what Kirby calls nonmatrixed performing), a shifting, nondefinitive relationship between piece and audience. In some activities, such as Kaprow's *Calling*, parts of the performance took place simultaneously out of sight and ear-shot of some of the performers – obviously no usual audience can attend such a show. Frequently human beings become automatons and things take on surprising life. Happenings, however, are different from their historical and theoretical predecessors: the Absurd theatre, Artaud, Surrealism, and Dada. These concentrated on the message received; that's why shock, cruelty, and the *insolite* were so important. Happenings deal with all three terms of the perception triad. It is this that has jolted our aesthetics. We can no longer "locate" aesthetics' subject matter as the center term – the message – of the triad. The thing-done is no longer any more important than those who do it and those who witness it. Works can no longer be evaluated abstractly; that is, on paper. And the aesthetician (or critic) must know a lot more than before about psychology and sociology.

But these consequences are nothing compared to those for the artist who now finds himself in an entirely new (for our time) relationship to both his material and his spectator. Artists who not long ago could pride themselves on their isolation are now confronted by a group on either side of their message, and each group profoundly shapes the message. In some cases audience and performer have merged – who is what in a Theatre Game or an Activity? Through their own maneuvering, then, artists find themselves in the world to a degree undreamed of even ten years ago. Not all artists, of course; traditionalists in every field are resisting the changes, and the traditional forms are in no danger of dying. In some cases there is little danger of them learning.

Being in the world, the artist reciprocates and tries to make his

Happening an image of that world, particularly of its busy-ness. The multifocus complexity of these pieces is astounding, and offensive to those schooled in theatre's single-focus. Recognizing that structuring is that part of perception which belongs to the receiver, Happenings leave to the audience (or the doers, if the two groups have merged) the job of "putting something together" or "making something out of." The result, generally, has not been the Absurdist cry against a complex world, but a celebration of the world's complexity. Those few who have seen or participated in a Happening have undergone the beginning of a perceptual re-education. Accustomed to "packages" of every kind in every walk of life (from A&P commodities to political theories), the receiver now confronts a freedom which is difficult to avoid once presented, and equally risky to accept.

The profoundest political implications of Happenings are their rejection of packaging, not by parody, which is the Absurdist technique, but by forcing on the receiver the job of doing the work usually done by the artist/educator/propagandist. Thesis play and figurative painting give way to a set of messages which the receiver must decipher; indeed the "messages" are often random impulses which the receiver may construct into messages or leave alone, depending upon his attitude. The single-focus stage and the framed picture are identified with the billboard and the press, and rejected. Performances range over an entire city and take several days. The paradox here is that propagandists have long recognized this useful "universality," and saturation is the mark of mass persuasion. But just as Pop Art has made us somewhat immune to certain kinds of advertising, so, perhaps, we become somewhat immune to other forms of mass persuasion after participating in a Happening.

Aesthetically, Happenings are different from Abstract Expressionism, which ran the hubbub of the world through an internalizing process producing on the canvas a cogent reaction to something. Graphic in the way that a sheet of brain waves might be graphic, Abstract Expressionism represented feelings, not things. Happenings, on the other hand, choose everyday objects and people for material and destroy the figurative by confronting it, not by distorting or ignoring it. The theatre could never benefit from abstract Expressionism (a show really does need people and things), but it can learn much from Happenings. Happenings challenge theatre people to re-examine the stage (should there be a stage?), focus, and the relationship to the audience (should there be an audience?). Only two theatres are mentioned in this issue of *TDR*: The Living Theatre and the San Francisco Actor's Workshop; these two alone gave their facilities and personnel over to those who were experimenting with Happenings. Surely it is not accidental that these were our two most adventurous and productive theatres during the past ten years.

24

IN RESPONSE

A Letter from Allan Kaprow

To the Editor:

I believe that the emphasis you have given [T30] to Cage and McLuhan as germinal influences on Happenings may be oversimplified and, as a result, really unfair to these men. As quite a few of us see the Happenings, what is astonishing is that they are pan-artistic phenomena, in which energies originally developing within the separate fields of painting, dance, music, poetry, etc., began to cross each other's paths at various and unexpected places. This was what mutually affected all of them, and in turn produced new hybrid arts and new ideas as well. Mike Kirby has observed this, certainly, but in dealing with only the American (and largely the New York) group, he has tended to localize the whole business around Cage. Cage's indirect stimulation should not be underestimated, but to place upon him the burden of sponsorship for a range of activities which in part he had nothing to do with, and which in part he is not comfortable with, is to do him a disservice. I do not know how McLuhan feels about this, but Cage is apparently uncomfortable with his assigned role; his interview in T30 made that perfectly clear.

With respect to the first Happenings group in New York, consisting of painters, the direct line of historical stimulation (usually conscious) seems to have been the Futurist manifestoes and noise concerts, Dada's chance experiments and occasional cabaret performances, Surrealism's interest in automatic drawing and poetry, and the extension of these into action painting. All focused in one way or another on the primacy of the irrational and/or the unconscious, on their effect upon undirected body responses, and on the elimination of pictorial and other professional skills as criteria of art. Thus the idea of art as "act" rather than aesthetics was implicit by 1909 and explicit by 1946. Between this background and Cage, there was Bob Rauschenberg, who, as costume and set designer for Merce Cunningham's dance group, not only kept the painters aware of Cage's thought, but also suggested how the plastic arts can become part of a performance situation. In other words, our prime sources were visual, whatever nonvisual outcome these led to.

Now, speaking personally, my studies with Cage followed a direction I had begun to take a few years before when I was concerned with the implication that action painting – Pollock's in particular – led not to more painting, but to *more action*. I perceived that Cage could help, especially in the area of noisemaking which I was using in my Assemblages and Environments then. Needless to say, he did not discourage me, and I did my first Happenings in his classroom. Yet I possibly learned things which Cage was not inclined to teach, although I was quite satisfied. This is reason enough to relieve him of any responsibility for my different interests. Moreover, to complicate matters, some of the other painters who may have gotten ideas from my example, not only didn't study with him – they misunderstood what *I* was doing. Is Cage to be held responsible for them, too? Am I? Isn't this what's great about it all?

As far as McLuhan is concerned, his name never came up in any conversations before a year or so ago. And now that it has, his basic insight, the famous "the medium is the message," is hardly unusual, when you come down to it. French formalist art from Manet to at least Cubism offered precisely this recipe for our understanding, and it became a staple of academic modernism by 1940. McLuhan's present interest lies in his application of the theory to the mass media (such as TV). So far as I know, he has had no effect upon the Happenings at all.

Marshall McLuhan aside, we still must take into account more than thirty Happeners outside the United States, living in at least twelve countries, including Japan, Argentina, Spain and Czechoslovakia. They have their own ideas, even if they are aware of us here. It might be a thought for some future issue of *TDR*.

25

EXTENSIONS IN TIME AND SPACE
An Interview with Allan Kaprow

Richard Schechner

KAPROW: Many of the events of *Self-Service* had a fragile, not-quite-invented, not-quite-prank quality. Some of them concerned just one person – such as standing on an overpass and counting 200 red cars or calling up somebody and letting the phone ring, and then he calls you back and you let the phone ring. Things like that have a somewhat hallucinating quality.

SCHECHNER: Was there any attempt to achieve a coherent situation?

KAPROW: Not consciously. There are of course submerged intentions. Everything had a casual, sometimes frightening atmosphere. Casual in the sense that it was summertime, all of the events were "self-service" – a person could choose to participate in as many as he wished down to one; if anything came up – as it will during the summer – a person had the right to cancel out and substitute something else later on. There was cohesion and casualness, an in-and-out-of-your-daily-lifeness. Other of my Happenings have had far more dramatic and deliberate imagery.

The majority of events involved doing something and leaving it. For example, we set up a banquet in the Jersey marshes on the side of a busy highway – a complete banquet with food, wine, fruit, flowers, and place-settings, crystal glasses and silver coins in the glasses. And we simply left it, never went back. It was an offering to the world: whoever wants this, take it. So many of the things had just that quality of dropping things in the world and then going on about your business. The whole thing teetered on the edge of not-quite-art, not-quite-life.

SCHECHNER: Why did you extend the space from Boston to New York to Los Angeles?

KAPROW: I used the maximum amount of space within every city without specifying exact sites – leaving those choices up to the "subcontractors," people who took charge of particular events. And it seemed to me that because the events were already extended in time and place, why not extend them further? Isn't there something inclusive about this awareness in each of the participants that some of the things in his own city or in a city across the continent will not be taking place for him nor will he be involved in them – but he is aware of them? Everyone has the program. (The "program" is what I now choose to call a scenario; I'm looking for terms that are less and less related to the arts.) The thing was programmed so that everyone participating knew exactly what else was going on.

SCHECHNER: It reminds me of nonliterate ritual theatre. The Orokolo in New Guinea have a ritual cycle play that has many, many parts and takes between six and twenty years to complete. The whole village knows the "program" but few will survive to see it all enacted in order. And it doesn't make any difference whether event A is done in year one or year three. The cycle is organic and flexible, it depends upon the climate, the economy of the society, the local social organization – sometimes one event is done and sometimes another. By the end of the cycle everything is completed; and some pivotal events are done in relentless order. But there is a kind of haphazard quality that is quite unknown to Western aesthetics. Time is treated differently; it takes its shape from the events and not vice versa. When the masks are finished, when the dancers are ready, when the weather is right, when the medicine man is in fine strength – then "the time is right." There is an impressive combination of seriousness – almost the entire material surplus of the community is devoted to the ritual theatre – and casualness. It's got to be done, the village leaders say, but we don't know exactly when. *Self-Service* seems to have this same kind of feeling. The artwork is embedded in everyday activity, inseparable from it, sometimes identical with it.

KAPROW: Yes, and the very materials, the environment, the activity of the people in that environment are the primary images, not secondary ones. The environment is not a setting for a play (if you want to use that theatrical allusion) which is more important than the people; the accented or oblique activity within the environment is the event. There is an absolute flow between event and environment.

SCHECHNER: Would you describe some other extended events you've done?

KAPROW: One is about to take place [November 1967]. *Fluids* will center within the fifty-mile circumference of Los Angeles and I am trying to get people in other parts of the country to participate too.

Instead of a variety of events, as in *Self-Service*, *Fluids* is a single event done in many places over a three-day period. It consists simply in building huge, blank, rectangular ice structures thirty feet long, ten feet wide, and eight feet high. The structures are built by people who decide to meet a truck carrying 650 ice blocks per structure. They set this thing up using rock salt as a binder – which hastens melting and fuses the blocks together.

The structures are to be built in about twenty places throughout Los Angeles. If you were crossing the city you might suddenly be confronted by these mute and meaningless blank structures which have been left to melt. Obviously, what's taking place is a mystery of sorts; using common material (at considerable expense) to make quasi-architectural structures which seem out of place amid a semitropical city setting. The structures indicate no significance. In fact, their very blankness and their rapid deterioration proclaims the opposite of significance.

SCHECHNER: But it does have a significance, and you can't be ignorant of it. It's almost a parody. Here we are, a country that builds monuments at great expense helter-skelter; a terribly property-conscious country with people who want to own everything. But plainly ice in sunlight is something that can neither be possessed nor preserved. And if you build a monument that immediately deteriorates, you are running against the American grain. It's not the disintegration of the self-destroying machine, but the ineluctable natural process of sunlight and warmth. It's mysterious because it is a suggestive metaphor for all kinds of monumental things which really do disintegrate slowly the moment we've created them. And also the human body, which is constantly deteriorating.

KAPROW: I was aware of these things, and many more – if you're looking for allusions after the fact. I called it *Fluids* after the fact. I usually name things after I've thought of them and planned them. *Fluids* is in a state of continuous fluidity and there's literally nothing left but a puddle of water – and that evaporates.

If you want to pursue the metaphor further, it is a comment on urban planning and planned obsolescence.

SCHECHNER: I suppose you wouldn't be happy with just one ice structure?

KAPROW: Well, after all, in this country we're brought up on multiplicity; it's the very stuff of our spiritual and economic life. The sense of seriality, of continuousness – within which everything quickly grinds down only to be replaced by something else. These things make me aware of time and space in a way that traditional approaches to aesthetics never could.

SCHECHNER: Isn't there an ambivalence: parody and celebration at the same time?

KAPROW: Absolutely. I think *Fluids* is funny as hell, and absurd. On the other hand it's fabulous in the best sense of that word because at heart it's mysterious. The same consciousness that plans obsolescence plans continuous renewal. It's not that everything stops, but that everything is replaced.

It's this double aspect – the celebration – that the prophets of gloom, the old *Partisan Review* boys, have missed – from Ruskin on down (I know he was before the *PR*): the real implications of industrial and technological processes are regenerative.

SCHECHNER: In working on this issue of *TDR* [T39], I have been struck by the fixed thinking of theatre people. When they talk of space they assume a limited space of inflexible organization. The most fluid space they can conceive is a theatre in which the walls can move – or the floors or ceiling. There is always a frame around the space, a container to which the event is fitted. But in speaking to you I sense a different approach to space – an indeterminate notion of space in which events make the space, or create isolated nodes of spatial meaning.

KAPROW: Well, the reason I stopped painting was because it was like the theatre, framed. I was an action painter, and I thought of the large canvas as an arena (Harold Rosenberg's term) – a damned fine metaphor for thinking of yourself as thrashing around in there with the lions. The painting was really a floor plan of a gladiatorial combat where you fought with your demons.

But, after all, that still is a theatrical space – even if it's as big as a football field. It doesn't make any difference that it's very large, it's still a stage. It's pretty comfortable working in the middle, but as soon as you get to the edges you have to stop; and I didn't feel like stopping. So I simply gave up the whole idea of making pictures as figurative metaphors for extensions in time and space. (Incidentally, I always thought of my painting in temporal as well as spatial terms.)

It was a tremendous relief to become attuned to the world around me, and to participate directly in it – really as an action artist and not merely metaphorically as one. Once that became possible for me I saw a way out of the canvas, the gallery, the stage.

SCHECHNER: How much is this related to McLuhan's thing? Is it the flexibility of electronic media, an extension of environment, that prompted this? What McLuhan is saying is that the duplication of the industrial process is being superseded by the simultaneity of the electronic situation: a change of mode.

KAPROW: Although I've only known of McLuhan for the last two years, there's a very strong relation between his ideas and mine. If you simply think about TV – that 17 million people (or however many millions there are) are watching the same thing at the same time – that can create a terrific sense of community, or at least provide the underpinning for that sense to build on. But the rub is that the TV community is passive and I am interested in a variety of modes including contemplation, observation, and participation.

Also I think there is one attitude in McLuhan that is not so much wrong as limited. And that is his contention that every man is immersed in an informational deluge; that everyone is in touch with everything instantly and that the individual's job is to dig this and not run away from it. This may present itself as informational overload; or it may be kicks. You dig the whole noise or you may go crazy because you can't sort it out. But the limiting factor here is that we aren't always sitting down receiving this deluge of information. Many times we've got lots of things to do. We travel, we work. I'm interested in what happens after a person pays attention to the informational deluge. Does he go to the supermarket in the same way? What happens when his eye becomes a wide-angle lens that takes in the whole scene and not just the box of cornflakes? What happens when he flips the TV dial from station to station? I've let the vertical control on my set go out of wack and just played with it going faster and slower, watching the frames slide by. And sometimes I'll buy five different brands of cornflakes.

SCHECHNER: What you're doing is disrupting and analyzing a conceptual experience. You don't accept TV programming or cornflakes advertising; you convert your "education" into an ability to play with and modify your environment. You break it down into its perceptual components and enjoy these rather than submitting to the conceptual tyranny of what you "should" do. But that's the function of abstract art.

KAPROW: It's the function of analysis in general. But what it leads to are new concepts. You play around and then you put your feet back on the ground.

SCHECHNER: New concepts? American society is in a mess. Our "social arrangements" are dysfunctional. And I feel that art should have its roots in the social life and social structure. That leads me to doubts, because I think that lots of artists have copped out: they just say, "Dig it, baby, and don't worry." And in concentrating on the boxes of cornflakes or on the TV set spinning they say, "We can't control the world, so fuck it." On the other hand, I see a tendency to reconstruct perceptions, to make, as you put it, new conceptions. I guess what I'm trying to ask is what social significance is there in all this?

KAPROW: I'm not so ambivalent as you are; but I do feel helpless.

Like you I am concerned about the state of our society. And when I said just jump in and dig it and later you can find the new concepts I didn't mean to suggest that there was a specific time gap, that you could wait five or six years and in the meanwhile act irresponsibly. I was only suggesting that coming armed with concepts and making an artwork to illustrate those is not a worthwhile activity. Art should be discovery – including the discovery of useful social tools. The discovery that *Fluids* was a comment on city planning didn't come to me months after planning the event; it came as I worked.

Work such as I do has latent social values. I am in a quandary because during times of crisis I sometimes feel that the work is useless. But art cannot be simply topical. I am not able to be indifferent to what's going on in America and so sometimes my work is embarrassing to me because I can't use it immediately. But then I suppose that most shopkeepers and lawyers who think about it are in the same quandary. And the majority of us aren't politicians.

SCHECHNER: Luckily.

KAPROW: Luckily.

SCHECHNER: I want to move into another area. Historically, at least since the Renaissance, art has been made by professionals. But you don't use professionals. You mastermind a work, but you can't supervise what little rehearsal there may be and you cannot possibly see the finished work, extended as it is over time and space. There may not even be a finished work in the traditional sense. That raises the question of "artistic control." You know the charges that have been thrown at Happenings.

KAPROW: I have not so much given up professionalism as an evil as I have questioned its meaning. No one knows what good craftsmanship is anymore. It is difficult to pinpoint – and need it be pinpointed? The arts have been mixing it up with each other for at least the last fifteen years; and many artists are willing to give up the trade they have been trained in, I as a painter, maybe you as a writer, someone else as a film-maker. Each of us is finding that the professional side of our background is not bad but limiting. It's not totally useless and it is pleasant to reminisce about one's professional past. But it's a wry kind of pleasure because you know that past no longer has a purpose.

Playing mastermind, as you call it, is a professionalism of a kind. I don't play a starring role in my Happenings because there are no starring roles; and I usually take what the other people leave behind. This is no more than courtesy. And it is not for the purpose of demonstrating that the inept are better than the carefully trained that I eliminate rehearsals; it's because rehearsals are useless for the kind of thing I do.

SCHECHNER: Where does this leave the professional performer – the kid who's training at Carnegie Tech, Yale, or NYU?

KAPROW: I can only use them – or you – as I would a physicist or a lawyer: as a human being. And your training would be as useless to you at that moment as when you go on a picnic.

SCHECHNER: What if I want to become a "professional Happener"?

KAPROW: If you have been trained as an artist you are in a better position than most. But only because you are ripe for a crisis. And you can give up your training the way saints gave up their worldly lives. If you hang around Happenings long enough you begin making your own. In that sense you become a professional. But no one is going to put you in the paper: "The great actor Richard Schechner was seen performing in a banquet setting in Allan Kaprow's *Self-Service*." There will be no reporter there on the highway.

Claes Oldenburg, when in New York in 1962, did Happenings that were much more theatrical than mine. And he was able to develop a performance truth as honest as any actor's. That could be profession-alized. And I suppose that people who work on my kind of thing as "subcontractors" could develop a skill in this kind of organization and then they could travel around – like medieval wandering poets – and set up Happenings. These people wouldn't be performers but dissem-inators of ideas. But we must guard against the limiting nature of professionalism; the huckster attitude.

SCHECHNER: As a tangent to that, in New York and I assume in other parts of the country as well, places like the Electric Circus or Cheetah have sprung up: pseudo-psychedelic turn-on, packaged Happenings. I have ambivalent reactions to these places because most of the people who come there are so passive and are so obviously manipulated. It's the Broadway of intermedia.

KAPROW: Unless you're sympathetic to the underlying philosophy of this stuff, these extremely slick presentations are fascistic because not only do they expect people to be as passive as any nightclub crowd, but they tune up the information to such a density and intensity that everyone's cowed. Some people like to be beaten. Looking at these things more kindly you could say that they are rites of passage from a more inattentive being to a more attentive one – so it's worth the pain. However, I find them more a masochistic exercise than a pathway to rebirth.

SCHECHNER: The next question I have relates to artistic control and professionalism. People beat Happenings with two sticks: control and "what use is it all?"

KAPROW: People are referring to isolatable situations in which certain goals are predetermined. In that case of course you control what you're doing. If you play a Bach fugue you've got to know how to do it. On the other hand, if you understand control in a broader sense – that the mind is incapable of more than a limited number of perceptions at once – then there is a different, and nonconscious, control. From this point of view, you can't make a mess; you can't be uncontrolled, even if you wanted to be. It is easy for us to say, "Look at that mess on the floor which the cat made. The cat had no control." But we say that only because we don't like the cat to make a mess in that place. The cat was responding to body needs – the gut reacted to the brain and the cat shat on the floor. But it is a very orderly situation; one which displeases us. I prefer a more flexible approach to order and purpose.

SCHECHNER: In other words, your Happenings have an implicit control built into the organisms of the people carrying out the operations. And when you relinquish the chance to see the "whole thing" you are not abandoning control but redefining it.

KAPROW: That's it exactly.

SCHECHNER: You don't think of yourself as being in the theatre. But your work obviously has implications that concern the theatre. What would you have to say to the directors of the Tyrone Guthrie Theatre in Minneapolis, for example?

KAPROW: There may be ties between my work and traditional theatre. Certainly there can be exchanges. The only advice I would have is to say, relax. The definition of theatre need not be limited to the stage, scripts, actors. The theatre can include rodeos, TV commercials, excursions – and 101 other things that have a performance function.

Some sports are not arena sports – such as Grand Prix racing, cross-country racing, surfing. These have an indeterminate locale. I think of theatre in broader terms than most theatre people. This doesn't mean that the traditional theatre of the last few hundred years has to be moved out. Let's just add to it.

There is a range of techniques now available in every art adapted from all the other arts. It is possible to think of single performances that comprise a very wide range – from unconsciously structured portions to highly consciously organized ones. I don't want to put anyone out of business.

SCHECHNER: You couldn't do it anyway. An art goes out of business when it no longer fills a social need. The process is impersonal.

KAPROW: Right.

SCHECHNER: Any final words on space?

KAPROW: Our space nowadays is no space. It used to be that space was those places that you couldn't get to, that were too far away. Now we can get anywhere. In the past we had a closed, relatively focused space. Today we feel a lot freer and we can celebrate extended space. I think this new feeling needs to be recognized by the traditional theatre, which still treats space in the old way. Why not move the locales of plays around, do each scene on location and have the audience follow?

SCHECHNER: Franklin Adams of the New Orleans Group had the same idea. We were going to do *A Streetcar Named Desire* on location around New Orleans. Each night we'd do a different scene in an appropriate place. Combine the theatrical reality of performance with the given reality of an environment. So that maybe the neighbors would say (and really think), "Oh, them! They're having a fight again."

26

SELF-SERVICE

A Happening

Allan Kaprow

Self-Service, a piece without spectators, was performed in the summer of 1967 in Boston, New York, and Los Angeles. It spanned four months, June through September. Thirty-one activities were selected from a much larger number. Their time and locality distribution were determined by chance methods. Participants selected events from those offered for their city; each had to pick at least one, although doing many or all was preferable. Details of time and place were flexible within each month; choices made from month to month overlapped, some actions recurring.

Activities took place among those of the participants' normal lives. These were not necessarily coordinated; it was by chance that some actions turned out to be similar in two or all of the cities. Just as fortuitous were parallels between the Happening and daily events.

The time pattern and the number of events for each city:

	June	July	August	September
Boston	8	6	3	7
New York	9	1	5	3
Los Angeles	24	12	18	21

Note – The printed format below has been condensed from my original spatial arrangement; my conception was to surround all activities with large amounts of emptiness, emphasizing their independent functions. Ideally, each activity should be printed on a separate, loose page; this would reduce the sense of hierarchies implicit in our book structure.

A.K.

NEW YORK (AVAILABLE ACTIVITIES)

On the shoulder of a stretch of highway, a fancy banquet table is laid out, food on the plates, money in the saucers. Everything left there.

People stand on bridges, on street corners, watch cars pass. After 200 red ones, they leave.

> An empty house. Nails are hammered halfway into all surfaces of rooms, house is locked, hammerers go away.

Couples make love in hotel rooms. Before they check out, they cover everything with large sheets of black plastic film.

Rockets, spread over several miles, go up in red smoke, explode, scatter thousands of scraps of paper with messages.

> On the street, kids give paper flowers to people with pleasant faces.

Couples kiss in the midst of the world, go on.

> People shout in subway just before getting off, leave immediately.

Warehouse or dump of used refrigerators. People bring packages of ice, transistor radios, and put them into the boxes. Radios are turned on, refrigerator doors are shut, people leave. On another day they return, sit inside with radios for a while, and quietly listen.

Everyone watches for either:
    a signal from someone.
    a light to go on in a window.
    a plane to pass directly overhead.
    an insect to land nearby.
    three motorcycles to barrel past.
Immediately afterwards, they write a careful description of the occurrence, and mail copies to each other.

BOSTON (AVAILABLE ACTIVITIES)

> Many shoppers begin to whistle in aisles of supermarket. After a few minutes they go back to their shopping.

> Two people telephone each other. Phone rings once, is answered "hello." Caller hangs up. After a few minutes, other person does same. Same answer. Phone clicks off. Repeated with two rings, three rings, four rings, five rings, six rings, seven, eight, nine, etc. . . . until a line is busy.

At a supermarket (on another day) transistor radios playing rock are put into shelves of cereals, soaps, freezers, bananas, napkins, etc. Left there. On still another day, bouquets are tucked in with products.

3:00 AM emptiness at a 24-hour washerette. Piles of clothes washed. Turning cylinders, blue-white fluorescents. Regularly on the half-hour, loud bunch of photogs burst in, flash pix, leave. Home at five.

In a neighborhood, people inflate by mouth a twenty-foot weather balloon. It is pushed through the streets and buried in a hole at the beach. The people leave it.

For a few moments at night, shouts, words, calls, all through bullhorns. Voices moving on the streets, from windows, around corners, in hall-ways, alleys.

Cars drive into filling station, erupt with white foam pouring from windows.

People tie tar paper around many cars in supermarket lot.

On another day, twenty or more flash-gun cameras shoot off at same time all over supermarket; shopping resumed.

LOS ANGELES (AVAILABLE ACTIVITIES)

Cars drive into filling station, erupt with white foam pouring from windows.

Many shoppers begin to whistle in aisles of supermarket. After a few minutes they go back to their shopping.

Photos of supermarket and washerette projected onto clouds, into air.

Night in the country. Many cars, mixing on different roads about a mile from a certain point, lights blinking, horns beeping sporadically, converge and disperse.

Photos of supermarket and washerette sent to everyone.

Two people telephone each other. Phone rings once, is answered "hello." Caller hangs up. After a few minutes, other person does same. Same answer. Phone clicks off. Repeated with two rings, three rings, four rings, five rings, six rings, seven, eight, nine, etc. . . . until a line is busy.

> Warehouse or dump of used refrigerators. People bring packages of ice, transistor radios, and put them into the boxes. Radios are turned on, refrigerator doors are shut, people leave. On another day they return, sit inside with radios for a while, and quietly listen.

3:00 AM emptiness at a 24-hour washerette. Piles of clothes washed. Turning cylinders, blue-white fluorescents. Regularly on the half-hour, loud bunch of photogs burst in, flash pix, leave. Home at five.

Everyone watches for either:
> a signal from someone.
> a light to go on in a window.
> a plane to pass directly overhead.
> an insect to land nearby.
> three motorcycles to barrel past.

Immediately afterwards, they write a careful description of the occurrence, and mail copies to each other.

> In glass booths, people listen to records. They look at each other and dance.

> On the streets, kids give paper flowers to people with pleasant faces.

People tie tar paper around many cars in supermarket lot.

> Some people whistle a tune in the crowded elevator of an office building.

> A car is built on an isolated mountain
> top from junk parts. Is left.

> People shout in subway just before getting off, leave immediately.

A daytime procession of cars on a highway, brights on. At random,

and momentarily, fifteen feet of thin plastic film streams from cars'
windows, is drawn back inside. Half-hour later, cars disperse.

People enter public phone booths, eat sandwiches and drink
sodas, look out at the world.

A long parade. Children and adults carry blank posters
and banners. Quiet rhythm on pots and pans.

Someone, waiting for a person with a sad face, rides on a bus.
The person is tailed until no longer possible. Then a person
with a really funny face is looked for. Time to go home.

An empty house. Nails are hammered halfway into all
surfaces of rooms, house is locked, hammerers go away.

People stand on bridges, on street corners, watch cars
pass. After 200 red ones, they leave.

A path of slices of bread and jam is made for a great distance
in the woods.

Rockets, spread over several miles, go up in red smoke, explode,
scatter thousands of scraps of paper with messages.

In a neighborhood, people inflate by mouth a twenty-foot
weather balloon. It is pushed through the streets and buried
in a hole at the beach. The people leave it.

Some torn paper is released from a high window, piece by piece,
and slowly watched.

27

EXCERPTS FROM "Assemblages, Environments & Happenings"

Allan Kaprow

Editor's note: In his seminal essay tracking the experiments of twentieth century avant-garde art, Kaprow detailed the materials and properties of Assemblages and Environments and traced the "extension" of Environments to Happenings. These two forms were the "passive and active sides of a single coin." But most of the early Happenings, warned Kaprow, were falling into traps that stifled experimentation and change. He argued that "the use of standard performance conventions from the very start tended to truncate the implications of the art." Contained by rooms, with audience separate from show, the Happenings set up "cultural expectations attached to theatrical productions." They were seen as "charming diversions" that "smacked of nightclub acts, sideshows, cockfights, and bunkhouse skits." But, wrote Kaprow:

> [F]or those who sensed what was at stake, the issues began to appear. It would take a number of years to work them out by trial and error, for there is sometimes, though not always, a great gap between theory and production. But gradually a number of rules-of-thumb could be listed.

The objective, as Kaprow stated in his list of rules (excerpted below) was to "allow for breaking the barrier between art and life."

[...]

(A) *The line between art and life should be kept as fluid, and perhaps indistinct, as possible.* The reciprocity between the man-made and the ready-made will be at its maximum potential this way. Something will always happen at this juncture, which, if it is not revelatory, will not be merely bad art – for no one can easily compare it with this or that accepted masterpiece. I would judge this a foundation upon which may be built the specific criteria of the Happenings, as well as the other styles treated in this book.

(B) *Therefore, the source of themes, materials, actions, and the relationships between them are to be derived from any place or period* except *from the arts, their derivatives, and their milieu.* When innovations are taking place it often becomes necessary for those involved to treat their tasks with considerable severity. In order to keep their eyes fixed solely upon the essential problem, they will decide that there are certain "don'ts" which, as self-imposed rules, they will obey unswervingly. Arnold Schoenberg felt he had to abolish tonality in music composition and, for him at least, this was made possible by his evolving the twelve-tone series technique. Later on his more academic followers showed that it was very easy to write traditional harmonies with that technique. But still later, John Cage could permit a C major triad to exist next to the sound of a buzz saw, because by then the triad was thought of differently – not as a musical necessity but as a sound as interesting as any other sound. This sort of freedom to accept all kinds of subject matter will probably be possible in the Happenings of the future, but I think not for now. Artistic attachments are still so many window dressings, unconsciously held onto to legitimize an art that otherwise might go unrecognized.

Thus it is not that the known arts are "bad" that causes me to say "Don't get near them"; it is that they contain highly sophisticated habits. By avoiding the artistic modes there is the good chance that a new language will develop that has its own standards. The Happening is conceived as an art, certainly, but this is for lack of a better word, or one that would not cause endless discussion. I, personally, would not care if it were called a sport. But if it is going to be thought of in the context of art and artists, then let it be a distinct art which finds its way into the art category by realizing its species outside of "culture." A United States Marine Corps manual on jungle-fighting tactics, a tour of a laboratory where polyethylene kidneys are made, the daily traffic jams on the Long Island Expressway, are more useful than Beethoven, Racine, or Michelangelo.

(C) *The performance of a Happening should take place over several widely spaced, sometimes moving and changing, locales.* A single performance space tends toward the static and, more significantly, resembles conventional theatre practice. It is also like painting, for safety's sake, only in the center of a canvas. Later on, when we are used to a fluid space as painting has been for almost a century, we can return to concentrated areas, because then they will not be considered exclusive. It is presently advantageous to experiment by gradually widening the distances between the events within a Happening. First along several points on a heavily trafficked avenue; then in several rooms and floors of an apartment house where some of the activities are out of touch with each other; then on more than one street; then in different but proximate cities; finally all around the globe. On the one hand, this will increase the tension between the parts, as a poet might by stretching the rhyme from two lines to ten. On the other, it permits the parts to exist more on their own, without the necessity of intensive coordination. Relationships cannot help being made and perceived in any human action, and here they may be of a new kind if tried-and-true methods are given up.

Even greater flexibility can be gotten by moving the locale itself. A Happening could be composed for a jetliner going from New York to Luxembourg with stopovers at Gander, Newfoundland, and Reykjavik, Iceland. Another Happening would take place up and down the elevators of five tall buildings in midtown Chicago.

The images in each situation can be quite disparate: a kitchen in Hoboken, a *pissoir* in Paris, a taxi garage in Leopoldville, and a bed in some small town in Turkey. Isolated points of contact may be maintained by telephone and letters, by a meeting on a highway, or by watching a certain television program at an appointed hour. Other parts of the work need only be related by theme, as when all locales perform an identical action which is disjoined in timing and space. But none of these planned ties are absolutely required, for preknowledge of the Happening's cluster of events by all participants will allow each one to make his own connections. This, however, is more the topic of form, and I shall speak further of this shortly.

(D) *Time, which follows closely on space considerations, should be variable and discontinuous.* It is only natural that if there are multiple spaces in which occurrences are scheduled, in sequence or even at random, time or "pacing" will acquire an order that is determined more by the character of movements within environments than by a fixed concept of regular development and conclusion. There need be no rhythmic coordination between the several parts of a Happening unless it is suggested by the event itself: such as when two persons must meet at a train departing at 5:47 PM.

Above all, this is "real" or "experienced" time, as distinct from conceptual time. If it conforms to the clock used in the Happening, as above, that is legitimate, but if it does not because a clock is not needed, that is equally legitimate. All of us know how, when we are busy, time accelerates, and how, conversely, when we are bored it can drag almost to a standstill. Real time is always connected with doing something, with an event of some kind, and so is bound up, with things and spaces.

Imagine some evening when one has sat talking with friends, how as the conversation became reflective the pace slowed, pauses became longer, and the speakers "felt" not only heavier but their distances from one another increased proportionately, as though each were surrounded by great areas commensurate with the voyaging of his mind. Time retarded as space extended. Suddenly, from out on the street, through the open window a police car, siren whining, was heard speeding by, *its* space moving as the source of sound moved from somewhere to the right of the window to somewhere farther to the left. Yet it also came spilling into the slowly spreading vastness of the talkers' space, invading the transformed room, partly shattering it, sliding shockingly in and about its envelope, nearly displacing it. And as in those cases where sirens are only sounded at crowded street corners to warn pedestrians, the police car and its noise at once ceased and the capsule of time and space it had become vanished as abruptly as it made itself felt. Once more the protracted picking of one's way through the extended reaches of mind resumed as the group of friends continued speaking.

Feeling this, why shouldn't an artist program a Happening over the course of several days, months, or years, slipping it in and out of the performers' daily lives. There is nothing esoteric in such a proposition, and it may have the distinct advantage of bringing into focus those things one ordinarily does every day without paying attention – like brushing one's teeth.

On the other hand, leaving taste and preference aside and relying solely on chance operations, a completely unforeseen schedule of events could result, not merely in the preparation but in the actual performance; or a simultaneously performed single moment; or none at all. (As for the last, the act of finding this out would become, by default, the "Happening.")

But an endless activity could also be decided upon, which would apparently transcend palpable time – such as the slow decomposition of a mountain of sandstone ... In this spirit some artists are earnestly proposing a lifetime Happening equivalent to Clarence Schmidt's lifetime Environment.

The common function of these alternatives is to release an artist from conventional notions of a detached, closed arrangement of time-space. A picture, a piece of music, a poem, a drama, each confined within its respective frame, fixed number of measures, stanzas, and stages, however great they may be in their own right, simply will not allow for breaking the barrier between art and life. And this is what the objective is.

(E) *Happenings should be performed once only.* At least for the time being, this restriction hardly needs emphasis, since it is in most cases the only course possible. Whether due to chance, or to the lifespan of the materials (especially the perishable ones), or to the changeableness of the events, it is highly unlikely that a Happening of the type I am outlining could ever be repeated. Yet many of the Happenings have, in fact, been given four or five times, ostensibly to accommodate larger attendances, but this, I believe, was only a rationalization of the wish to hold onto theatrical customs. In my experience, I found the practice inadequate because I was always forced to do that which *could be repeated*, and had to discard countless situations which I felt were marvelous but performable only once. Aside from the fact that repetition is boring to a generation brought up on ideas of spontaneity and originality, to repeat a Happening at this time is to accede to a far more serious matter: compromise of the whole concept of Change. When the practical requirements of a situation serve only to kill what an artist has set out to do, then this is not a practical problem at all; one would be very practical to leave it for something else more liberating.

Nevertheless, there is a special instance of where more than one performance is entirely justified. This is the score or scenario which is designed to make every performance significantly different from the previous one. Superficially this has been true for the Happenings all along. Parts have been so roughly scored that there was bound to be some margin of imprecision from performance to performance. And, occasionally, sections of a work were left open for accidentals or improvisations. But since people are creatures of habit, performers always tended to fall into set patterns and stick to these no matter what leeway was given them in the original plan.

In the near future, plans may be developed which take their cue from games and athletics, where the regulations provide for a variety of moves that make the outcome always uncertain. A score might be written, so general in its instructions that it could be adapted to basic types of terrain such as oceans, woods, cities, farms; and to basic kinds of performers such as teenagers, old people, children, matrons, and so on, including insects, animals, and the weather. This could be printed and mail-ordered for use by anyone who wanted it. George Brecht has been interested in such possibilities for some time now. His sparse scores read like this:

DIRECTION

Arrange to observe a sign
indicating direction of travel.

- travel in the indicated direction

- travel in another direction

But so far they have been distributed to friends, who perform them at their discretion and without ceremony. Certainly they are aware of the philosophic allusions to Zen Buddhism, of the subtle wit and childlike simplicity of the activities indicated. Most of all, they are aware of the responsibility it places on the performer to make something of the situation or not. As we mentioned before in connection with another of Brecht's pieces, this implication is the most radical potential in all of the work discussed in this book. Beyond a small group of initiates, there are few who could appreciate the moral dignity of such scores and fewer still who could derive pleasure from going ahead and doing them without self-consciousness. In the case of those Happenings with more detailed instructions or more expanded action, the artist must be present at every moment, directing and participating, for the tradition is too young for the complete stranger to know what to do with such plans if he got them.

(F) *It follows that audiences should be eliminated entirely.* All the elements – people, space, the particular materials and character of the environment, time – can in this way be integrated. And the last shred of theatrical convention disappears. For anyone once involved in the painter's problem of unifying a field of divergent phenomena, a group of inactive people in the space of a Happening is just dead space. It is no different from a dead area of red paint on a canvas. Movements call up movements in response, whether on a canvas or in a Happening. A Happening with only an empathic response on the part of a seated audience is not a Happening but stage theatre.

Then, on a human plane, to assemble people unprepared for an event and say that they are "participating" if apples are thrown at them or they are herded about is to ask very little of the whole notion of participation. Most of the time the response of such an audience is halfhearted or even reluctant, and sometimes the reaction is vicious and therefore destructive to the work (though I suspect that in numerous instances of violent reaction to such treatment it was caused by the latent sadism in the action, which they quite rightly resented). After a few years, in any case, "audience response" proves to be so predictably pure cliché that anyone serious about the problem should not tolerate it, any more than the painter should continue the use of dripped paint as a stamp of modernity when it has been adopted by every lampshade and Formica manufacturer in the country.

I think that it is a mark of mutual respect that all persons involved in a Happening be willing and committed participants who have a clear idea what they are to do. This is simply accomplished by writing out the scenario or score for all and discussing it thoroughly with them beforehand. In this respect it is not different from the preparations for a parade, a football match, a wedding, or religious service. It is not even different from a play. The one big difference is that while knowledge of the scheme is necessary, professional talent is not; the situations in a Happening are lifelike or, if they are unusual, are so rudimentary that professionalism is actually uncalled for. Actors are stage-trained and bring over habits from their art that are hard to shake off; the same is true of any other kind of showman or trained athlete. The best participants have been persons not normally engaged in art or performance, but who are moved to take part in an activity that is at once meaningful to them in its ideas yet natural in its methods.

There is an exception, however, to restricting the Happening to participants only. When a work is performed on a busy avenue, passersby will ordinarily stop and watch, just as they might watch the demolition of a building. These are not theatre-goers and their attention is only temporarily caught in the course of their normal affairs. They might stay, perhaps become involved in some unexpected way, or they will more likely move on after a few minutes. Such persons are authentic parts of the environment.

A variant of this is the person who is engaged unwittingly with a performer in some planned action: a butcher will sell certain meats to a customer-performer without realizing that he is a part of a piece having to do with purchasing, cooking, and eating meat.

Finally, there is this additional exception to the rule. A Happening may be scored for *just watching*. Persons will do nothing else. They will watch things, each other, possibly actions not performed by themselves, such as a bus stopping to pick up commuters. This would not take place in a theatre or arena, but anywhere else. It could be an extremely meditative occupation when done devotedly; just "cute" when done indifferently. In a more physical mood, the idea of called-for watching could be contrasted with periods of action. Both normal tendencies to observe and act would now be engaged in a responsible way. At those moments of relative quiet the observer would hardly be a passive member of an audience; he would be closer to the role of a Greek chorus, without its specific meaning necessarily, but with its required place in the overall scheme. At other moments the active and observing roles would be exchanged, so that by reciprocation the whole meaning of watching would be altered, away from something like spoon-feeding, toward something purposive, possibly intense.

(G) *The composition of a Happening proceeds exactly as in Assemblages and Environments, that is, it is evolved as a collage of events in certain spans of time and in certain spaces.* When we think of "composition," it is important not to think of it as self-sufficient "form," as an arrangement as such, as an organizing activity in which the materials are taken for granted as a means toward an end that is greater than they are.

This is much too Christian in the sense of the body being inferior to the soul. Rather, composition is understood as an operation dependent upon the materials (including people and nature) and phenomenally indistinct from them. Such materials and their associations and meanings, as I have pointed out, generate the relationships and the movements of the Happening, instead of the reverse. The adage that "form follows function" is still useful advice.

Otherwise, a sort of artistic schizophrenia can result if *any* subject matter and material is subjected to *any* interesting formal technique. It may be that some subjects, because of our familiarity with and wide use of them, allow for more alternatives of transformation and grouping than other subjects. An apple can be painted in the Neo-Classic, Realist, Impressionist, Expressionist, and Cubist styles and still be recognized as an apple, but an electron microscope cannot. The Impressionist mode, for instance, would blur it beyond recognition – and at that point the real subjects become light, optical sensation, and paint, and *not* the microscope.

Because the Happenings are occupied with relatively new (at least new for art) subject matter and materials, the stylistic conventions used by the other arts, or by such philosophical disciplines as logic, are best left alone. To illustrate why, several years ago I used serial methods related to Schoenberg's twelve-tone technique. A root-molecule of events was written down: "a jam sandwich being eaten in a dining room, a person laughing outside a window, and an alarm clock going off periodically in the bedroom." This was the basic cluster of situations that was to grow into the Happening. [...] I had in mind the very thorough way that the composer Karlheinz Stockhausen developed serialism, whereby all the elements of sound could be made mathematically consistent. But while this was possible in music, particularly electronic music, whose rudiments are relatively nonassociative, this was not possible with the materials of a Happening, with their high degree of everyday usage. And I did not want to lose all the advantages these provided by deliberately choosing more neutral events (about which I shall say more shortly). The worst difficulty to arise out of these procedures, however, was that as they became more exacting, performance became nearly impossible.

The results on paper were interesting enough, but in action (as far as any action was capable of being derived from the complicated scores) the effect was static and mechanical. The events were simply not eventful. A regimen unrelated to their natural qualities seemed to have been superimposed upon them. The scheme was self-evidently "formal" but the subject matter was not; or it had some as yet unrevealed form that was hidden because it was not respected. I concluded that to do this at all, limits had to be observed in choosing the initial stuff of the Happening.

And these limits were contrary to the principal direction the art was taking.

We generally mean by "formal" art (the fugues of Bach, the sonnets of Shakespeare, Cubist paintings) an art that is primarily manipulative. As in a chess game, the manipulation is intellectual, whereby elements of the work are moved according to strict, sometimes self-imposed, regulations. The weaving of these elements into groupings, regroupings; the losing and finding of themes, subthemes, and counterthemes, seemingly disparate yet always dominated by the relentless inevitability that they shall resolve at the end, is the peculiar fascination of such an art.

Formal art must be made of a substance that is at once stable and general in meanings. A formalist cannot easily use the horrifying records of Nazi torture chambers, but he can use a simple statement like "the sky is blue," abstract shapes such as circles and squares, the raising and lowering of an arm that does nothing else. The impact of the imagery, the "what," is not as important as the intricacy and subtlety of the moves the imagery is put through.

A formalist who wishes to make a Happening must choose with discretion situations that can be freely manipulated without jarring the overtones of the imagery within them. A group of men all in white doing calisthenics, a ticking metronome, a sheet of paper being moved variously across the floor are obviously easily formalized. But for this to become truly great, I think that some time must elapse. The media are still too undigested for us to feel at home with them. This is essential: to be profitably involved in an activity of arrangements, the materials arranged must not command attention. At present, the media are all rather unstable because their meanings in their new context tend to arise more quickly than anything else. Kleenex may be a commonplace, but collected in quantity in a Happening they would immediately push into relief all that we have only half-consciously thought about Kleenex and its intimate uses.

Therefore, in making a Happening, it is better to approach composition without borrowed form theories, and instead to let the form emerge from what the materials can do. If a horse is part of a work, whatever a horse does gives the "form" to what he does in the Happening: trotting, standing, pulling a cart, eating, defecating, and so forth. If a factory of heavy machinery is chosen, then the clanging of motorized repetition might easily cause the form to be steadily repetitive. In this way a whole body of nonintellectualized, nonculturized experience is opened to the artist and he is free to use his mind anew in connecting things he did not consider before.

Think of the following items: tires, doughnuts, Cheerios cereal, Life

Savers candy, life preservers, wedding rings, men's and women's belts, band saws, plastic pools, barrel hoops, curtain rings, Mason jar gaskets, hangman's nooses – one could go on almost indefinitely. They are all obviously united by a common circular shape (an observation that could be made by a botanist or a standard auto parts salesman as well as by any painter; for the recognition and use of physical resemblances is not the special talent of artists alone, even if the tradition of form analysis would seem to tell us so). By juxtaposing any half dozen of these items, an idea for a Happening could emerge. And from this combination, meanings not normally associated with such things could be derived by minds sensitive to symbols. [...]

Shifting things around can be an excellent mode of *performance* as much as of composition. Just as an Environment or an Assemblage can be maintained in prolonged transformation by allowing its parts to be rearranged in numbers of ways, the same can apply to a Happening. This would simply continue the compositional process into the performance process and the two usually distinct phases would begin to merge as the caesura between them is pulled out. Suppose, for example, that three environments and five actions are selected, partly by taste and partly by chance methods. [...] Each action may be performed once or twice, and at one or two prescribed environments and at their respective times, as desired.

At no time is it known if actions will be performed at all of the three environments, since the choice is left to the performers, nor what the number and kind of actions will be at the environments chosen. [...] The ninety-six possible combinations are numerous and dramatic enough to make this small list of events both unexpected and sufficiently different in every case.

There are related ways of setting off rearrangements of fixed numbers of actions such as by *cueing*, in which performers are given a set of actions that are signaled, knowingly or unknowingly, by one another or by natural occurrences such as the sound of a car horn or a cloud formation. These cues also may be responded to in any one of a number of alternative ways in each instance, so here again the combinations are quite varied.

Finally, chance may determine nearly everything, and personal preference and the rumblings of the imagination will be put aside. I say chance operations may "nearly" determine everything, for any sensitive mind will tend to make connections between the actions which he finds occurring and those in which he is taking part, even if he had no way of knowing them beforehand. [...] The advantage of chance methods, in my view, is that they free one from *customary* relationships rather than from any relationships. New ones will be noticed by the observant artist, whether he professes to like this or not. Most of the time he seems to like it.

The preceding discussion of composition has been a summary of all the rules-of-thumb raised respecting Happenings, rather than being merely technical. Problems of materials and content enter into the question at every stage and so I should like to re-emphasize the importance of a pervasive process which is manifestly organic and not divided into categories. Analytic writing, because of the very nature and history of the words we use, tends towards the broken-apart and divided and is necessary for the sake of convenience. But the only art that is so fractured is academic art, and thus I made it clear throughout the listing of the conditions I believe to be crucial to the Happening as an art, that they are not iron-clad rules but fruitful limits within which to work. As soon as they are found to be useless they will be broken, and other limits will take their place.

28

FROM *MORE THAN MEAT JOY*

Carolee Schneemann

FROM *THE NOTEBOOKS*

1958–1963

I assume the senses crave sources of maximum information; that the eye benefits by exercise, stretch, and expansion towards materials of complexity and substance; that conditions which alert the total sensibility – cast it almost in stress – extend insight and response, the basic responsive range of empathetic-kinesthetic vitality.

If a performance work is an extension of the formal-metaphorical activity possible within a painting or construction, the viewers' sorting of responses and interpretation of the forms of performance will still be equilibrated with all their past visual experiences. The various forms of my works – collage, assemblage, concretion – present equal potentialities for sensate involvement.

I have the sense that in learning, our best developments grow from works which initially strike us as "too much"; those which are intriguing, demanding, that lead us to experiences which we feel we cannot encompass, but which simultaneously provoke and encourage our efforts. Such works have the effect of containing more than we can assimilate; they maintain attraction and stimulation for our continuing attention. We persevere with that strange joy and agitation by which we sense unpredictable rewards from our relationship to them. These "rewards" put to question – as they enlarge and enrich – correspondences we have already discovered between what we deeply feel and how our expressive life finds structure.

Anything I perceive is active to my eye. The energy implicit in an area of paint (or cloth, paper, wood, glass …) is defined in terms of the time which it takes for the eye to journey through the implicit motion and direction of this area. The eye follows the building of forms … no matter what materials are used to establish the forms. Such "reading" of a two-dimensional or three-dimensional area implies *duration* and this duration is determined by the force of total visual parameters in action. Instance:

the smallest unit variation from stroke to stroke in a painting by Velasquez or Monet; by extension the larger scale of rhythms directing the eye in a painting by Pollock – this which is shaped by a mesh of individualized strokes, streaks, smudges, and marks. The tactile activity of paint itself prepares us for the increased dimensionality of collage and construction: the literal dimensionality of paint seen close-on as raised surface ... as a geology of lumps, ridges, lines, and seams. Ambiguous by-plays of dimension-in-action open our eyes to the metaphorical life of materials themselves. Such ambiguity joins in the free paradox of our pleasure with "traditional subject matter" where we might see "abstract" fields of paint activity before we discover the image of King Philip II astride his horse (Velasquez) ... or a rush of dark arcade concavities from which we learn, by his flying robes, that a saint is in ascension (El Greco).

The fundamental life of any material I use is concretized in that material's gesture: gesticulation, gestation – source of compression (measure of tension and expansion), resistance – developing force of visual action. Manifest in space, any particular gesture acts on the eye as a unit of time. Performers or glass, fabric, wood ... all are potent as variable gesture units: color, light, and sound will contrast or enforce the quality of a particular gesture's area of action and its emotional texture.

Environments, Happenings – concretions – are an extension of my painting-constructions which often have moving (motorized) sections. The essential difference between concretions and painting-constructions involves the materials used and their function as "scale," both physical and psychological. The force of a performance is necessarily more aggressive and immediate in its effect – *it* is projective. The steady exploration and repeated viewing which the eye is required to make with my painting-constructions is reversed in the performance situation where the spectator is overwhelmed with changing recognitions, carried emotionally by a flux of evocative actions, and led or held by the specified time sequence which marks the duration of a performance.

In this way the audience is actually, *visually* more *passive* than when confronting a work which requires *projective vision*, i.e., the internalized adaptation to a variable time process by which a "still" work is perceived – the reading from surface to depth, from shape to form, from static to gestural action, and from unit gesture to larger overall structures of rhythms and masses. With paintings, constructions, and sculptures the viewers are able to carry out repeated examinations of the work, to select and vary viewing positions (to walk with the eye), to touch surfaces and to freely indulge responses to areas of color and texture at their chosen speed.

During a theatre piece the audience may become more active

physically than when viewing a painting or assemblage; their physical reactions will tend to manifest *actual* scale – relating to motions, mobilities the body does make in a *specific* environment. They may have to act, to do things, to assist some activity, to get out of the way, to dodge or catch falling objects. They enlarge their kinesthetic field of participation; their attention is required by a varied span of actions, some of which may threaten to encroach on the integrity of their positions in space. Before they can "reason" they may find their bodies performing on the basis of immediate visual circumstances: the eye will be receiving information at unpredictable and changing rates of density and duration. At the same time their senses are heightened by the presence of human forms in action and by the temporality of the actions themselves.

My shaping of the action of visual elements is centered on their parametric capacities in space. In performance the structural functions of light, for instance, take form by its multiple alterations as color – diffuse, centralized, (spot and spill) mixture, intensity, duration in time, thresholds of visible/invisible. The movements of performers are explored through gesture, position and grouping in space (density, mass), color, and their own physical proportion.

The body itself is considered as potential units of movement: face, fingers, hands, toes, feet, arms, legs – the entire articulating range of the overall form and its parts.

The performers' voices are instruments of articulation: noises, sounds, singing, crying, commentary on or against their movements may be spoken; word-sound formations are carried forth which relate to, grow from the effect on the vocal cords of a particular physical effort they experience. The voice expresses pressures of the total musculature so that we may discover unique sounds possible only during specific physical actions and which provide an implicit extension and intensification of the actions themselves.

The distribution of the performers in space evolves the phrasing of a time sequence: levels of horizontal, vertical, and diagonal or the need for larger rhythms carried visually by an independent figure which moves in relationship to the overall environment – shifting dimensions, layers, levels. Every element contributes to the image. The active qualities of any one element (body, light, sound, paper, cloth, glass) find their necessary relation to all other elements and, through conjunction and juxtaposition, the kinetic energy is released.

My exploration of an image-in-movement means only that its realization supersedes (or coincides with) my evocation of it. This is *not* a predictable, predetermined process: in the pressure to externalize a particular sensation or quality of form other circumstances or "attributes" may be discovered which are so clear and exact that the function of the original impulse is understood as touchstone and guide to the unexpected. "Chance" becomes one aspect of a process in which I come to recognize a necessity – the way to unpredictable, incalculable advances within my own conscious intent.

1962/63

Vertical table legs pound into horizontal tops; supporting planes, stable leverage – or search out their pressure on the floor – definition of ground and grounding always a beginning again, against. How a strip of wood plays recession and a plane-of-advance to its adjacent surface, being active with minute variations ... light, marks, smudge, streak. The body moves through eyes recall, claim and disposition of its own measure (journey) in space.

GESTURE IS BOTH IMPLICIT AND EXPLICIT ACTION:
STRUCTURAL FORM AND ACTUAL ACTIVITY.
Gesture is the envelope of unity; contains the impulse uniting various parts of an object or scene; assumes the dominant rhythmic forces. Gesture is three-dimensional in quality; it is neuromuscular: remembrance and recognition are linked to basic kinesthetic identification. Gesture is in the spine; it is intangible and cannot be grasped without feeling it. First we feel the gesture of an object, then we may describe it.

1963

1963–1966

Our lives themselves as material, stuff for our art or our lives as art containers/or life the way we shape or discover it being a form of art, the Happening an intensification of our actions in life. The distinctions here swinging between intellection/perception/action.

It is not a part-time, compartmentalized (studio) activity: it is as if we are launched in some wondrous banal boat whose very motion transforms the landscape it moves through.

Notice this insistence on Motion. We cannot capture, hold a moment (Impressionism), repeat the moment's verbal content (theatre), capture the action itself (Futurism): we intensify the perceptions of change, flux, and release them in juxtapositions which grind in on the senses.

It is intimate and intense. Happenings: raw, direct, no intermediate crafting, fabricating. Kaprow's works stream mythic, socially edged by ritual process; Oldenburg's are netted in private memory as environment through which we refocus, discover strands of our own past time-relations; strong cultural and nostalgic roughness. Whitman's performances the most interiorized, tactile, plastic-poetic, evolving a less specific time-space than Oldenburg's. Whitman leaves the audience as discrete, perceiving agents; Kaprow physically engages them, moves them in a mass of linear participation. While Oldenburg uses the audience as physical material, packed in around, surrounding, holding the frame on an irregular rectangular performance-environment. Hansen's Happenings are loose, rangy, arbitrary, open to impulse; the audience hangs raggedly to anticipations, shifting conjunctions. (And Dine the first man to use explicitly personal material – his psychoanalytic tape, uncensored self-exposure ... just the voice in the dark. The audience didn't approve of that much actuality! A turning point for me. He had stripped it all down to bare desire, anger, the lived life. Audience didn't get it or couldn't stand it.)

Image – Whitman
Atmosphere – Oldenburg
Concordance – Kaprow (audience/participant must agree to his procedures)
Restraint, slowed durations, collectivity – Dewey
Social action, aggression, attack – Lebel
Comic strip, populist Americana – Grooms, Gross
Guilt and transfiguration – Vostell
Sensation and memory is tactile, plastic, palpable for painters – not verbal, musical, or conceptual. Sensation and memory evade the grasp of traditional media.

Note for *Fuses*: cut Greek white seduction into turning backside. . . .

"The trouble with Yoko Ono's pieces is that she wants to make you feel what she felt, to feel like her, and I don't think I want to do that," said Higgins tonight.

December 1965

from Diary 1965: Memoranda

Lively irony that I developed theatre to do for me in moments, what I wanted words to do infinitely: to provide compression, springboard to senses. . . . Very complicated ... evades statement ... being surprising to me, but I know the experience I sought to *hold* with words I now use gesture-action to release ... where vision can move most freely.

A despair with language re-enforced by its social-sexual action. When I am saying what I see, men find it difficult to hear that *I* say it – they take it away, use my words as their own because a female source of illumination registers negatively ... (not so with Jim, of course), but very often *they need what I say* but not from me – a peculiar withdrawal, (absence) or aggressive twisting to what is most possibly fine and fat as interchange – two people speaking *to* (not "at" or away from) one another. To some extent this also occurs in regard to my Happenings, Kinetic Theatre pieces. So – definitely – in its brief new life here – a man's enterprise, that I get a sort of wavery regard, as if my work is a vagary, dismissable, *because* my aggressions, anxieties are not those the male community recognizes, prizes.

1965

BE PREPARED:
to have your brain picked
to have the pickings misunderstood
to be mistreated whether your success increases or decreases
to have detraction move with admiration – in step
to have your time wasted
your intentions distorted
the simplest relationships in your thoughts twisted
to be USED and MISUSED
to be "copy" to be copied to want to cope out cop out pull in and away
if you are a woman (and things are not utterly changed)
they will almost never believe you really did it
(what you did do)
they will worship you they will ignore you they will malign
you they will pamper you
they will try to take what you did as their own
(a woman doesn't understand her best discoveries after all)
they will patronize you humor you
try to sleep with you want you to transform them with your energy
they will berate your energy they will try to be part of your
sexuality they will deny your sexuality/or your work they
will depend on you for information for generosity they will
forget whatever help you give they will try to be heroic for
you they will not help you when they might they will bring
problems they will ignore your problems a few will appreciate
deeply they will be loving you as what you do as what you
are loving how you are being they will of course be strong in
themselves and clear they will NOT be married to quiet

tame drones they will not say what a great mother you would
be or do you like to cook and where you might expect understanding and appreciation you must expect NOTHING then
enjoy whatever gives-to-you as long as it does and however and
NEVER justify yourself just do what you feel carry it strongly
yourself

1966

MEAT JOY

Excerpt from *Meat Joy* notes on prolog
[…]
MEAT & PAINT
painting of sex of each other by couple (interlude section
        myself bandaged head   cut up the chicken
        stand over it   on my lap   between my
legs   matter of factly)   build to amore-paint inundation   close focus inward / mirror behind

this feels better
for my right hand now
it may be alright from   from
or this is better is this better I get more turn or pace
why it is better I don't know but it is better than this is
try this
a fine point is dreadful
a gold point is rigid
after a couple hours

cela est certaine   *Lisa est-elle belle*   *cela n'est pas certain*
from certain sequences marked new york march **1964**
couple painting exchange   mixture   figures charg-
ing thru alley aisles   slipping
    1. woman hacking plucking throwing the bird
    2. tearing hair / painting self / falling running rocking
    poissons policier polisson pollen
group 3   the fish banging smashing follow a body's flight
    wild pig meat   slapping caressing rising falling
between heaps of debris   naked bodies all wash in bowls
drying each other   closely packed dull light banging on

jai mon idée de beauté   *se moucher*   *il a son idée de*
garbage lids   hammock   painted figures painted

beauté   *nos idée de beauté ne sont pas sûres*   *miroir mouchoir*
at   **water guns**   **begin clothing stapling to floor**

mouvement   *Lisa est-elle belle*   *il n'a pas de mesure pour*
la beauté   *sourire de femme*   *mouvement*   *est-ce que la*
femme est belle   *cela n'est pas certain*   *les plaisirs et la*

NAKED MATERIALS   TEARING INSTRUMENTS – POWER TOOLS   CONSTRUCTION – BUILT IN PERFORMANCE: GLUE PAPERS DOWN INTO STANDING PANELS: RUB ON THEM RUBBINGS   GLUING PAPERS & RUBBING: BLOOD / SEX CONCRETELY: THE CITY / THE BODY   SUCKING PULLING IN GRAB HOLD

douleur sont des sensations   *voilà des plaisirs*   *voici des*
plaisirs ensuite   *la balle*   *il est au bord de la mer*   *il est*
couché sur le sable   *il entend le bruit de la vague et il regarde*
la mer   *voilà des plaisirs*   *il prend un bain*   *simple*
simplement   *impresse*   *nager*   *plaisir*

MEAT JOY (certain instructions)
The images are realized by a process which unites visual obses-
et un concombre   *sans encombrement encombrer concombre cul*
sions and spontaneous physical action.
encombrer
The sequence developed by my partner and me will be counter-thrust in their relation to actions of the other performers. We should provide a focus which brings to *extremes* the qualities of the other performers – extremes of intensity, in the range of speeds and actions – from dream frame slow motion for virtual frenzy, and in concentrated presence.
essai étable étalon   *le plaisir et la douleur sont des sensations*
        étaler   *le plaisir*   *le plaisir et la douleur*
The focus is never on the self, but on the materials, gestures & actions which involve us. Sense that we become what we see, what we touch. A certain tenderness (or empathy) is pervasive – even to the most violent actions: say, cutting, chopping, throwing chickens.

apprendes   *on pose le doigt sur un objet*   *on a des sensations*
        on a une sensation de toucher de chaleur et de froid   *cet*
homme touche un morceau de bois avec ses doigts   *attirer*

Series

upper torso evolutionary naked covered with dark paint

ce bois est sec   ce bois est dur

smeared lower torso work pants rolled up shave legs

      FEET FOCUS under curtain or plastic

        3. debris pile on which I perform eye/body

les objects ne font pas plaisir

        4. spreading of clothing

        5. meat/running/slapping against self & objects

        6. kissing rolling couples to exhaustion

        7. sewing & being costumed

        8. leg choreography in débris

fleuves   nous font plaisir   un attrait   cet attrait nous

        9. sponge drench

attire   cet attrait nous plaît   nous ne cherchons pas plus

    10. running tray of objects falling involvement slow

motion   random   juggling

loin   nos désirs peuvent nous changer

    11. painting wrapping then the painted ones roll together

    12. blowing bubbles

    13. bouncing balls

    14. from the balcony lowering cloths & materials plastic

    15. the love paint exchange

    16. the chickens / hacking / plucking / tearing hair /

painting self / rooms / falls

    17. naked bodies all washed in bowls drying each other

    18. banging on garbage-can lids

    19. crawling

    20. hammock bed figures / jumping / painting at /

water guns

    21. the fish dance on the self / or / the nude follow-

ing contours

    22. performers behind plastic staccato touching

    23. group under within plastic rising falling angular

musculature

24. figures wrapped in plastic like presents rolling &

effréné effrénées ce regard égarer égayer égide églantier   silence

jumping running

    silencée   à demain   église   mais nos désirs peuvent

    25. reclining lovers   the independent space

nous changer   il y a certains désirs qui sont plus forts que d'autres

    26. women on boards

[. . .]

**From a letter to Jean-Jacques Lebel, February 1964,
responding to an invitation to create a "Happening" for Lebel's
Festival of Free Expression:**

There are now several works moving in mindseye ... tentatively identified as *Meat Joy*, and *Divisions and Rubble*; ... *Meat Joy* shifting now, relating to Artaud, McClure, and French butcher shops – carcass as paint (it dripped right through Soutine's floor) ... flesh jubilation ... extremes of this sense ... may involve quantities of dark fabric and paint drawn from performance area outward into audience to become inundation of all available space – action and viewing space interchanged, broken through. Smell, feel of meat ... chickens, fish, sausages? I see several women whose gestures develop from tactile, bodily relationships to individual men and a mass of meat slices. Specific sequence of collision and embrace ... a rising, falling counterpoint to bodies ... very dark (very bright). Hand-held lights spotting color cover movements.

My work can take substance from the materials I find ... this means that any particular space, any debris unique to Paris and any "found" performers ... would be potential structural elements for the piece. I've been working a great deal with the Judson dancers for love of their nondance movement and their aggressive, expansive interest in changing the very physical traditions which have given their bodies extraordinary scope and strength; and my pieces impose space relations for them, provoke personal responses which will work inclusively with any chosen or found environment. I do not require or want any specially predetermined "set-up." What I find will be what I need.

Editor's note: *Meat Joy* was first performed at Lebel's First Festival of Free Expression, 25–30 May 1964, at the American Center in Paris. The first U.S. production was at the Judson Church in New York, 16–18 November 1964.

Cast
CENTRAL MAN and CENTRAL WOMAN: hold the focus, are the main energy source.

TWO LATERAL MEN and TWO LATERAL WOMEN: perform as complements/doubles.

INDEPENDENT WOMAN: sets up a private world on her mattress at perimeter of action; she joins the others during "men lighting women under plastic."

INDEPENDENT MAN: joins Independent Woman from audience.

SERVING MAID: functions throughout as a stage-manager-in-the-open, wandering in and out of the performance area to care for practical details (gathering discarded clothing, spreading plastic sheeting, distributing props, allocating fish and chickens, etc.). Her matter-of-fact actions are deceptive, since cues and coordination of material and sequences often depend upon her.

Clothing color is coordinated with lighting. Independent Man arrives dressed in street clothes over bikini pants. Other men wear work clothes over bikini pants. The women wear bikini pants and bras covered with stringy, colored feathers. Central Woman enters dressed in blouse and skirt. Independent Woman wears a kimono over a bikini covered with scrappy tiger fur.

Score

As the audience is seated, the performers enter carrying a long table, chairs, trays with makeup, cups, brandy, water, etc. The table is set facing the audience, close to the entrance–exit area. They wear old shirts and robes over their costumes; they face the makeup mirror, their backs to the audience. The "Notes as Prolog" tape recording continues for twenty minutes during which the performers sit casually at the table, completing their makeup, sewing last feathers on, smoking, drinking. *The tape ends.* The audience is restless. The table is carried away. **BLACK OUT.**

Lateral Men climb to balcony. Lateral Women lie down in audience area.

Narrow spot from balcony to floor below. *Rock'n'roll Rue de Seine tape at full volume. "Blue Suede Shoes."*

From the balcony Lateral Men drop crumpled lengths of paper into central spotlight. Slow fall of paper mounts to crescendo making the central pyre five feet high. *Music begins when first paper has fallen.*

Low light fans into center. *"Tutti Frutti." Street Sounds.*

Lateral Men slide down rope from balcony, cross floor to find their partners (lying in audience area). They pull them out by their feet, lift and carry them to positions in front and to sides of central paper pile.

Central Man and Woman enter from under balcony, begin Undressing Walk – slow motion. **Soft spot, following.** She walks backward: no more than a few paces apart, their eyes on one another. Undressing occurs as a series of rhythmic exchange motions, one after the other, a pause in between. Only one hand at a time is used in a clear, sustained, slow reaching to the clothing of the other. If the action of undoing a button or pulling a skirt free takes more than a few moments, the action is left uncompleted; the other takes a turn. As they walk each article of clothing removed is dropped slowly, clearly.

Side lights to Lateral Men beginning Body Packages. The women rest on their backs where they have been carried; their arms remain free as the men slowly walk into the paper pile, select a few large sheets, and place them on the torsos of the women. *Street Sounds.* They pile up a fat mound of paper and tuck it around the hips, some vertically up over their shoulders. *"From Me to You."* When the Body Package is sufficient each calls to the Serving Maid: "Rope!" A length is brought for each, and they tie the papers at the women's waists. Each man walks away, breaks into long, circling runs of approaches/feints to his Body Package.

Dull amber-gold light.
Independent Woman walks in from the audience several times, bringing her mattress, tea set, pillows, books, cakes, and oranges, and sets up her space at the edge of the audience (their feet nearly in her bed).

After several feints. Lateral Men skid at top speed by Body Packages (like skidding into first base), gather the women in their arms and in unbroken motion begin Body Roll. *"Baby Love."* Their actions are not precisely coordinated; each pair has a particular speed and direction to their rolls (one cutting space laterally, fast; the other with short, slower rolls in eddying circles). *Street Sounds.* If they roll into each other or the Undressing Walk or the audience, they stop, rest, shift directions.

"Where Did Our Love Go." (Cue.) When they wish, each man stops, raises his partner to her feet. Papers flutter and spread; he adjusts the papers attentively, goes down and takes her on top of himself, begins the rolls again. *Street Sounds.* Or he may rise onto his knees and lift her to hers: they stretch arms out slowly and exchange slow pushes, bending back as far as the push propels them. They embrace and roll.

Central Man and Woman, now undressed, exit. **Brief BLACKOUT.**

Enter Central Woman, who hides in center paper pile completely covered. *Street Sounds.* Serving Maid with flashlight walks about gathering discarded clothing. Independent Woman continues to eat, pour tea, shift things about her space. *"That's the Way Boys Are."* Central Man sits in audience on the floor opposite the pyre. Lateral Couples lie where they were at BLACKOUT, resting.

Diffuse gold light.
Lateral Men carry women forward close to the pyre. (The women are acquiescent, relaxed.) The women are placed on their backs, their legs tucked up against their chests. **Brightening light.** The men then run to and from the central pyre carrying armfuls of papers, which they drop and spread over the women. They are brisk and conscientious (and do not expose the Central Woman).

Street Sounds. Independent Man comes from the audience; he walks slowly to the Independent Woman and speaks, asking if he may join her on the mattress. *"Baby Love."*

He carefully removes his jacket, shoes, and pants, and settles onto the mattress. She offers him tea and cake. They read something, talk, play a game of bouncing oranges on their stomachs and then exchanging them by bounces.

When the Lateral Women are completely covered with papers, the Lateral Men rush to the central pyre; rummaging, they find the Central Woman's feet, which they seize pulling her straight up into the air.

"From Me to You." Raised on her hips beneath the paper, she immediately begins Leg Choreography – legs moving as if dancing upright, walking, pedaling a bicycle, etc. *Street Sounds.* The Lateral Men quickly pack the loose papers down around her hips to expose the legs; they run around the pile punching and hitting loose papers into the center. They return to their own partners, repeating these actions, and then crouch down to watch the three pairs of legs they have set off.

Flickering amber beam follows Central Man. Central Man comes slowly, deliberately from the audience, across floor to central pyre. He seizes moving legs of Central Woman and drags her out of the pyre, papers streaming behind her. He lifts her into an Awkward Hold, moving across the floor.

Lateral Men slip off their outer pants and jump into the pile of papers; they lie flat on their backs, hips raised, buttocks touching the women's buttocks. They scoop and scatter papers over their heads and torsos until only their legs show: Leg Mixture.

Central man comes parallel to the paint table, suddenly drops Central Woman. *"Anyone Who Had a Heart." Street Sounds.* They freeze, look at each other. She raises her arms slightly. He grasps her hands and jerks her up as high in the air as he can, taking her weight against his chest. He shakes her long and violently until they fall over onto the paint table. He has fallen on his back, she on top of him. **Soft spotlight on paint**

table. Very slowly she slips off him, crouching to reach under the table with one hand, and pulls out brushes and paint bowls. She rises, moves toward his head, and begins Love-Paint-Exchange. Slowly painting his face, chest, arms, thighs, sex, feet, legs, she moves around in back of the table.

"Wishin' and Hopin'." Lateral Men stand up, begin running jumps across floor and back into the pile. They then leap over the women, between short circular bursts of running. *Street Sounds.* The women, still with their legs in the air slowly swiveling, complicate the hurdle they make.

As the Central Woman comes around the table painting his legs, the Central Man sits up, reaches for the paintbrush in her hand. He drops his legs over the side and begins gently painting her face; then, slowly standing, painting her body. *"My Guy."* She takes another brush and bowl to exchange body painting. *Street Sounds. "That's the Way Boys Are."* Gathering speed across the floor (where the Lateral Men still run), they drop brushes and bowls, mix wet paint on their bodies directly, surface against surface, twisting, turning, faster and faster. Exit. **BLACKOUT.**

(Lateral Couple exits. Serving Maid hands out plastic sheets to the women; flashlights attached to cords are given to the men. She then enters bringing one plastic sheet to the Independent Couple, and gathers up brushes, bowls, and clothing. Lateral Women and Central Woman enter performance area. There each covers herself with a sheet, arranging themselves into a roughly triangular formation. The Independent Couple cover themselves, remaining seated.)

Silence. **Flashlights only.** The men gradually release the flashlights into widening arcs. This proceeds into very large slow patterns of movement. The lights are red and blue. The men coordinate directions and rhythms as they stalk in wide circles: faster light arcs; variations of vertical, horizontal, diagonal patterns; as high as possible, over heads of audience, as low as possible, with sudden shifts of light shafts back toward the center. They come closer together – staccato light as they pull in the cords; drop quickly to their knees, fanning into Alarm (starfish) Positions. Wrist movement light. The Women begin slow, angular movements, shaping plastic with elbows, knees, feet. Independent Couple perform a variation of this together. Rustling in the dark – men move to crouch and light fragments or details of moving forms. Abruptly, back and forth. Movement subsiding as women slowly move under sheets into the center of the floor; men crawling on their stomachs, closing in, flickering lights on/off into the plastic. All figures are now

Meat Joy was first performed in Paris at the First Festival of Free Expression in May 1964. Shown here, a November 1964 performance at Judson Memorial Church. (Photo by Peter Moore.)

grouped closely together. They lie still.

"Non Ho L'Eta." **Slow central lights**. From this pile the performers call for "Rosette" – the Intractable Rosette: a sequence of attempts to form the women into sculptural shapes which can move as a unit. *Street Sounds*. Men gather the women into a circular formation, back to back. All improvise. *"Non Ho L'Eta."* *Street Sounds*. Women link arms and legs; the men may tie their legs with rope, arrange them lying down, sitting up, spread-eagled, rolled in a ball, and then try to move them as if one solid structure (star, wheel, flower, crystal). *"Maybe I Know."* *Street Sounds*. Each time the "unit" fails and falls apart: all shout instructions, suggestions, advice, complaints. *"My Guy."* *Street Sounds*. But each time the women are set and the men begin to move them, they roll apart, lose balance, fall over. The men may choose The Tree as the

final arrangement: here the men stand the women up, raise their arms and hands over their heads touching together in the center. Each man stands against the grouped women, encircling with his arms as many as he can. They all try to move as a free-wheeling circle (impossible). All fall over and lie motionless.

Full light. *"Non Ho L'Eta."* Serving Maid enters, carrying a huge tray of raw chickens, mackerel, strings of hot dogs. *Street Sounds.* Slowly, extravagantly she strews fish, chickens and hot dogs all over the bodies. *"My Boy Lollipop." Street Sounds.* Wet fish, heavy chickens, bouncing hot dogs – bodies respond sporadically; twitching, pulling back, hands reaching, touching, groans, giggles. *"Where Did Our Love Go."* They sit up to examine their situation. *"Baby Love." Street Sounds.* Individual rules are evolved: slips, flops, flips, jumps, throwing and catching, drawing, falling, running, slapping, exchanging, stroking. Tenderly, then wildly. All are finally inundated with fish, chickens, hot dogs.

"Bread and Butter." Street Sounds. A call goes out for "hats." Women again are propped in a circle, back to back. Serving Maid brings plastic scarves and hairpins. Each man makes a secure but wild hat for a woman. *"Any One Who Had a Heart." Street Sounds.* A call goes out for "paint." Serving Maid hurries back with large green and orange buckets full of colored paints, brushes, sponges – these she distributes among the men. *"That's the Way Boys Are." Street Sounds.* Deliberately, with care, each man paints a brilliant linear face on a woman (in the Egyptian style). Then each man thoughtfully paints a woman's body; faster and faster, through three thousand years of techniques, they continue to cover them with paint: stroked, streaked, thrown, hurled. The women may smile amused at first. *"I Only Want to Be with You."* They watch the movement of the paint until finally they are yelling, howling, twisting, turning, trying to rise slipping and falling on the splattered plastic flooring. They retaliate, throwing buckets of paint over the men. Each man grabs up a woman and carries her out over the littered floor into the paper pile where everyone buries everyone else as the Central Woman yells, "Enough, enough!" **BLACKOUT.**

Time: 60–80 minutes.

SNOWS

Editor's note: The technical elements of *Snows* are not detailed in the performance text that follows. Schneemann described the projections, sound, lighting, and electronic cuing system in the performance notes written for *More Than Meat Joy*. The film that began the performance (*The Red-Newsreel* in the text) is a five-minute silent newsreel from 1947 showing a series of catastrophes: a ship exploding, "red" Chinese being shot by nationalist guards, the Pope blessing crowds, a volcanic eruption in Bolivia, an American Legion parade in a snowstorm, car crashes, explosions, etc. Coincidentally, Schneemann had shot a still of one of the film's images from a book for *Viet-Flakes*. This film had been made by shooting newspaper and magazine photos of Vietnam, using a "close-up lens and magnifying glasses to 'travel' within the photographs, giving the effect of rough animation." *Viet-Flakes* appears near the end of the performance text. The accompanying sound collage by James Tenney combined fragments – so short they were only recognizable cumulatively – from both classical and top-forty popular music, as well as Vietnamese, Laotian, and Chinese folk songs. During early action sequences of the performance, *Snow Speed* and *Winter Sports* – both films of Bavarian winter sports shot during World War II – were projected on the ceiling and side walls. Later, the text describes a film of a snowstorm being projected on the torsos of three women; flashing overhead are "images from a winter diary": winter scenes shot by Schneemann in New York City and the upstate countryside.

According to Schneemann's notes: "Although sequences were fixed, durations were determined in performance: light cues for partnered actions and group convergences were always varied, made unpredictable by audience-activated electronic systems." The "electronic systems" were contact microphones, wired to spectators' seats, that fed into a switching system connected to the small motors that drove sculptor Larry Warshaw's revolving light machine as well as other sound and lighting mechanisms.

Snows was performed on 21, 22, 27–29 January and 3–5 February 1967 at the Martinique Theater, New York City.

SNOWS: to concretize and elucidate the genocidal compulsions of a vicious disjunctive technocracy gone berserk against an integral, essentially rural culture. The grotesque fulfillment of the Western split between matter and spirit, mind and body, individualized "man" against cosmic natural unities. Destruction so vast as to become randomized, constant as weather. Snowing ... purification, clarification, homogenization.

"The large arena stage of the Martinique Theater is covered in silver and plastic sheeting. Bare white branches hang down from overhead. The rear wall is flaked with large ragged sheets of white paper. Even the seats are festooned with white plastic scallopings; unoccupied, they look in the dark like receiving ranges of snowy mountains. The lighting is icy: chill greens, blues, lavenders, with sometimes a flash of fire or sunlight. Two movies of skaters, skiers and related scenery are projected here and there on the set. At the rear is a large double construction; up to eight or ten feet, white outlined squares of varicolored plastic and open space on top; and a revolving light sculpture by Laurence Warshaw – flickering, reflecting, moving, shading colors and intensities within striations of plastic. It is very beautiful and surprisingly not at all cold."

Michael Smith, *Village Voice*

Score

The audience has been led into the theatre through the backstage door. In the dark they squeeze through two floor-to-ceiling foam rubber "mouths" and crawl over and under two long planks which stretch from the stage to the rear wall (across aisles and over the seats). Technicians rest on these silver planks – assisting the audience or not. The performers, wearing gray shirts and work pants, are sitting in a basic Oriental rest position, (squatting).

The Red-Newsreel begins. "*Train & Orgasm sound-collage*. A woman sweeps snow debris along the stage. The performers watch the film; when it is over they disappear behind the water-lens.

The light machine flickers dimly. Silhouettes of the performers appear – shifting shadows – behind the water-lens construction. They crawl or fall through empty apertures, and begin a slow animal-intense crawl toward the audience, some partly onto the planks. Turning back, they meet in the center of the stage and form a knot, crawling in, through, and out of one another's bodies.

Blue floor lights. *Snow Speed* and *Winter Sports* are projected across the ceiling, then center on side walls at varying levels.

The performers move apart. Crouching, staring at one another, they begin *Grabs & Falls*. Bodies thunder onto the stage; instantaneous collisions, a giving over of weight and impulse upon impact.

After an unspecified series of alternating encounters, a man about to enact a *grab* with a woman instead lifts her. The two other men stand, leaving their partners where they have fallen in snow, foil, foam rubber debris. *Passing Woman*: in clumsy walks and holds, the men pass and

According to Schneemann: "*Snows* was built out of my anger, outrage, fury, and sorrow for the Vietnamese." The revolving light sculpture was designed by Laurence Warshaw, the environment for the Martinique Theater by Schneemann. (Photo by Peter Moore.)

carry the body until one of the men at last places it on the white horizontal disk.

After *passing* the remaining two women, all are seated on the disk and begin *Creation of Faces* **BLACKOUT. Strobe begins.** *T & O tape.*

In pairs determined by the preceding sequence, each partner begins to cover the other's face with clown-white, silently responding to the other in a series of exchanges. When both faces are covered, one partner begins to *shape* the other's face, which takes on whatever aspect is pushed and prodded into the musculature – a transformation inducing a correspond-ing but unpredictable emotion. The created face turns toward the audience until the muscles relax by themselves and the expression fades.

Simultaneous overlappings of faces among the six are caught in the **flashing strobe**.

After an unspecified series of face-creations, one person will begin to move another (not necessarily the face partner) into *Body Sculpture*.

As the audience shifts, settles, they trigger the **lights overhead which slowly brighten.** *T & O tape.* **Films.**

Initially the men shape the women, who accept and hold whatever position they are given. Suddenly one of the women being sculpted will grasp the hand shaping her: the shaper freezes his action and becomes the one to be sculpted.

After the series of *Body Sculptures* the men center the women on the white disk; they are gradually sculpted onto the floor. Here they hold the positions, immobile.

Having raised the white disk vertically the men carry the women and prop them against it. A **color film** of a snow storm outside the theatre is projected against their torsos. Lying on the stage, one of the men watches the film; the other two climb onto the water lens. On signal from the watcher, they slowly spill piles of "snow" over the women, who sink into a heap.

Audience motions are monitored and **the sculpture lights flicker sharply. Then flashing blue side lights.** Scrambling across the floor, two performers fall and roll, choose to be the "body balls"; two standing become the "pushers"; the two remaining are "watchers." The *Body Ball* is pushed, rolled, and shoved in an uncertain journey by the Pusher, who may not use hands.

Quickly, they begin *Crawl & Capture*: body balls become "victims," watchers become "pursuers," pushers become "interference."

Flat on the floor the Victim crawls to escape the Pursuer, while the Interference hangs onto the Pursuer's ankles. When the Pursuer catches the Victim, the Interference moves suddenly to grab from the other end: a tug of war. (Usually each victim can gather enough force to leap from the grips of both tormentors: the leap and cry stops any movement of the other two.) Audience reaction triggers **sudden flashes of blue floor lights.**

Victim now chooses between pursuer and interference, one of whom becomes the *Dragged Body* (to be dragged and then hung from the looped rope). Gathering foil, two persons completely cover the first body hung; two others cover the second Dragged Body.

These bodies will become the two *Silver Walkers*. The remaining four become two Cocoons and a Double Cocoon (the last two unwrapped performers cover each other as one form, falling together when wrapped).

The fallen cocoons slowly, slowly twist from their silver wrappings without using their hands. *Silence* but for the crackling foil. The silver walkers, nearly blind in their wrappings, walk out onto the planks into the audience area; projectionists with blue flashlights guide them. The planks are slippery and slope upward – the walkers precariously make

The Dragged Body is hung and then wrapped in foil in Snows (1967). (Photo by Charlotte Victoria.)

their way to the end, where they sink into the sitting position.

The first freed cocoons become *Rescuers*.
As **Viet-Flakes** begins against the white disk, a rescuer – sensing danger – crawls up the plank, and drags a walker down.

The walkers are corpselike, nearly unmoveable. The other freed cocoons wait prone at the end of the planks to assist the rescues. Together in desperate struggle and clumsy haste they gather in a pile, collapsing under the film projection. The snow machine begins – snow falling, filling eyes and ears, covering all.

29

ON THE NECESSITY OF VIOLATION

Jean-Jacques Lebel

We must also be capable of setting ourselves above morality; not with the uneasy rigidity
of the man who constantly fears to lose his footing and fall, but with the practised ease of
one who can float, disport himself above it! And how should we achieve this without art,
without the madman's aid? [. . .] And as long as you are in any way ashamed of yourself,
you cannot possibly be of our number.

Nietzsche, *Die Fröhliche Wissenschaft*

The middle-class hero, product of Western culture, still dreams of seeing
his moral sense triumphant over all rebellions. This mediocrity has a *bête
noire* – free art. He thinks that he, personally, is being attacked by the
transformations which young artists claim to be bringing into his life as
well as to their own. This tireless Philistine might perhaps be able to
consider avant-garde art sympathetically if only he did not feel that it
made him out to be guilty, or mentally deficient; he would not stand in
the way of any revolution, if only it left his *values* alone.

No one is prepared to admit that if there is still a chance of changing
life it resides in the transformation of the human being; humans cling to
their old ways of seeing, of feeling, of being. Art as it evolves, both
historically and spiritually, has to face a reaction similar to that which
neutralizes the reform of social structures. For painting and sculpture,
without having exhausted all their hypnotic power, foster to a considerable degree the misapprehension of private property and the commercial
value of images – a misunderstanding which, in the long run, has the
effect of making their psychical effect recede further and further into the
background.

The relationship which has grown up between art and the majority of
those who have to do with it is thoroughly defective – a voluntary
blindness and a refusal of communication. It was only to be expected that
certain artists should feel this alienation – legalized, generalized, and
imposed by culture itself – to be an inadmissible obstacle, a challenge
which could not go unanswered. But, to reply, a language and a new
long-range technique were necessary. This new language, by the frank

way in which it put the question of communication and perception, by its resolution to recognize and explore the forbidden territories which had hitherto halted modern art, had to force a complete re-examination of the cultural and historical situation of art. This language is the Happening.

Thus, about eight years ago and on three continents at once, authors of Happenings started to attack the problem at its very *foundations*. That is to say:

1   The free functioning of creative abilities, without regard for what pleases or what sells, or for the moral judgments pronounced against certain collective aspects of these activities.
2   The abolition of the right to speculate on an arbitrary and artificial commercial value attributed, no one knows why, to a work of art.
3   The abolition of the privilege of exploiting, of intellectually "bleeding" artists, which has been appropriated by vulgar middle-men and brokers who detest art.
4   The abolition of cultural "policing" by sterile watchdogs with set ideas, who think they are capable of deciding whether such and such an image, seen from a distance, is "good" or "bad."
5   The necessity of going beyond the aberrant subject-object relation-ship (looker/looked-at, exploiter/exploited, spectator/actor, colonialist/colonized, mad-doctor/madman, legalism/illegalism, etc.) which has until now dominated and conditioned modern art.

It is easy to see that the battle is joined around exactly those prohibitions whose violation is a matter of life and death for present-day art. This fight is concentrated around political and sexual themes – taboo above all others. We owe to Freud the elucidation of the displacement, substitution, and repression mechanisms which act on the human personality by means of laws and social restraints. "Prohibition," he wrote in *Totem and Taboo* (1927),[1] "must be thought of as the result of an affective ambivalence [. . .] whenever there is prohibition, it must have been motivated by an unconfessed, unconscious desire or longing." In the light of this pitiless theory, the function of art in relation to society becomes clear – it must express, at all costs, what is hidden behind the wall.

It was George Bataille in a 1957 lecture who defined the essential albeit imaginary nature of the wall: "Eroticism is born of prohibition and lives by it." Bataille added that in the absence of prohibition (or a feeling of prohibition), we could not be erotic in a sense implying violation, nor "have access to what is essential for us." Nor could we be filmmakers, artists, or poets, for all language turns on violation, and all art is founded on unveiling. The dialectical, supremely ambivalent nature of violation can never be sufficiently stressed. Violation is at once birth and unbirth, the going-beyond and the return, accomplishment and death.

All transmutation begins with a rape, with a reversal. We know that Kandinsky saw his own painting for the first time in a picture by Monet lying *upside down* on a table. Dialectical reversal is a constant in the history of art; it is one of the causes of the perpetual crisis of the spirit. The reversal of Hegel by Marx, of Vauvenargues by Lautréamont, show to what extent thought is contradictory in its development, in its very life.

No crisis of the mind can exist independently of the social predicament, and artists are far from being the only ones to have to bear the consequences, the horrifying anguish of the *sens perdu*. They are however almost the only people, together with criminals and revolutionaries, to react against this loss, to assume it and express it; which is, precisely, an infringement of the rules.

Adult civilizations – those which have brought to its highest point of blood-stained perfection the dictatorship of the death-wish – accuse art, indissolubly linked with childhood, of being degenerate. Brancusi's "When I am no longer a child I shall be dead" is the confession and the supreme riposte of the outlaw. Art is an illegal regression, in comparison with the "maturity" of industrial society. The emotive chord which the art of so-called primitive peoples still strikes in us, the electric shock which we feel at several centuries' distance, prove that the concept of progress has a different weight in art than in political economy. A sense of history has no validity on the prelogical, hallucinatory level occupied by true art. Surely this art, whose potency lies entirely in auto-examination or the reactive crisis which it touches off, must be a regressive process? Has it not been compared (though from the outside) to the games of children or madmen? As for genius, it is simply regression, since we commonly admit that it is a state of recovered childhood. In reality it is not a question of the inversion of values but of their transmutation.

Thus, the "progression" of modern art – from Impressionism to Cubism, for example – was directly caused by a return to the source: the art of savages and of madmen. *Les Desmoiselles d'Avignon* is not the only thing we owe to Negro art, to demential art; we are in their debt for an intense psychical necessity which white art, adapting itself to the civilization, has lost. Present-day art, too, continues and is accomplished thanks to a similar disdain for the aesthetic and moral values of the ruling class. In spite of appearances, the artist has everything to lose by concluding an alliance with Authority.

The artist of the second half of this century – whether in Europe or America – is a politically and spiritually decadent being in comparison with what various genial utopians would have liked him to be – but also in comparison with his own growing pains (1910–1930). Dispossessed of most of his intellectual resources, progressively depersonalized as he "succeeds" socially, the artist is nothing but the clown of the ruling classes. It is useless to interpret this downfall as a victory of apolitical feeling over that of revolt. To the watchdogs of tradition, upset by the generally sagging market, I say that not only will we not agree to limit or put a brake on this crisis, but we will take every opportunity to exasperate it to its highest pitch. For this is our only chance to have done with this exploiting society, with its slave-owning mentality and its irremediable culture. Art is in full and fundamental dissidence with all regimes and all forms of coercion, but especially with those regimes which use it for their own ends. To this mercantile, state-controlled conception of culture, we oppose a combative art, fully conscious of its prerogatives: an art which does not shrink from stating its position, from direct action, from transmutation.

The Happening interpolates actual experience directly into a mythical context. The Happening is not content merely with interpreting life; it takes part in its development within reality. This postulates a deep link between the actual and the hallucinatory, between real and imaginary. It is precisely the awareness of this link that the enemies of the Happening cannot tolerate, for it might threaten their defense mechanisms. When Merleau-Ponty decrees that "the phenomenon of hallucination is not part of the world, and is not accessible," he is saying that art, considered as a language of hallucination, has no place in that "normal life" we are expected to tolerate. The extremely limited space assigned to art in society in no way corresponds to its mythical volume. To pass from one to the other – at the risk of breaking the law – is the primordial function of the Happening.

It is avant-garde art that liberates latent myths; it transfigures us and changes our conception of life. If this is a crime, there is no reason why we should deny it – on the contrary, we should claim it for our own. The serious difficulties met with by the authors of Happenings (in London and Paris notably, with the police or culture-censors) at once put the struggle for liberty of expression on a political footing. This must not obscure the "mythical thought behavior" which Mircea Eliade has detected in avant-garde art. This "going into action," the poetical investigation and elucidation that make up the random element, the element of risk essential to any creative activity worthy of the name. If the concept of knowing each other, of knowing ourselves, has any meaning in the day of the Bomb, it is not only thanks to ethnologists, but to artists. Since Picabia, Duchamp, and their friends put culture on fire, the words *art* and *crisis* have designated one and the same phenomenon.

The Happening, like music or the cinema, is a language to which each person brings a different content; there is a distinction to be made between a Happening by Kaprow or Oldenburg, and a Happening by Ferrò, Pommereulle, or Kudo, for example. In Europe, the first of these "events" took place at the end of the Anti-Trial exhibition, and only artists associated with the Free Expression Workshop fully and directly tackled political and sexual themes in the course of their Happenings. This may have confused the misinformed as to the possible total and imaginary significance of this genre. Each Happening has a network of meanings linked to a precise psychological and social context; our position differs greatly from that of the Americans Kaprow and Oldenburg.

As far as we are concerned, we wish to delve more deeply into the very experience of painting. All that was left of "action painting" was action. We were determined to become one with our hallucinations. We had a feeling of apocalypse, an insuperable disgust with the "civilization of happiness" and its Hiroshimas. Everything which had not become irremediably meaningless revolved – and still revolves – round two poles: Eros and Thanatos. It is a question of giving form to the myths which are ours, while falling prey as little as possible to the alienating mechanisms of the image-making industry.

For a long time there has been in existence a method with which the Happening has unquestionable affinities. Hans Arp, when a soldier, blew his nose in the flag when his name was called; Jean-Pierre Duprey urinated on the "eternal flame" at the Arc de Triomphe and put it out: poetry is not a matter of words. And the demolition, during the Commune, of the Colonne Vendôme – the symbol of Empire – remains Gustave Courbet's best work. The authors of this kind of *chef-d'œuvre* have always had to pay for it dearly. In spite of everything, an art which does not face up to the principle of reality is one which has agreed to cheat, to compromise, to go down on its knees.

One of these days, an anti-racist and/or anti-war demonstration blocking the traffic in New York will end as a Happening. Note that the latter would not necessarily be synonymous with violence – that would be reducing it to the atavistic determinism of a civilization obsessed with auto-destruction; yet the breaking of bonds is the very essence of poetry. I have noticed how little it would have taken for several street demonstrations in which I have taken part to turn into riots. Is it only the threat of the bludgeon and the fear of murderous repression that prevent collective anger from bursting forth? Freedom of mind will have no chance of becoming freedom of action as long as the "special mechanism for coercion" (constituted on the cultural and social level by the State) has not been liquidated. It is less than ever possible to reform a limited segment of human life (even that known as the cultural sector) without reforming the whole, and its principle. It is true that even the Pythoness got paid, in the good old days of the golden century.

The domain known (for lack of a more precise definition) as that of magic is the only one in which art can exist. All art is magic, else it is not art. I mean that art is the means of transmission of certain psychic forces and that it has always, in all cultures, made it possible for man to express and satisfy a need for magic. Civilization regulates the transition, in man, from one state to another. Thanks to art, the multiple states of the human being must, in spite of everything, become livable possibilities. The only reality in art is furnished by the hallucinatory experience, around which crystallize (ephemeral) rites, and around which our mythical thoughts express themselves. The communication of this experience is essential to the life of the mind, yet it is clear that it has been interrupted. Every possible means must be used to re-establish it. The era of hallucinogenic drugs ushers in a new state of mind, breaks with industrial preoccupations, in order to devote itself to the revolution of being. Cubism, Dadaism, Surrealism, Expressionism, or Abstract Impressionism, and even "kinetic" or "op" paintings have (timidly) tried to approximate certain aspects of the hallucinatory experience. Now, it is no longer a matter of representing it, but of living it, and making it possible for others to live it.

It is unfortunate that the work of Lévi-Strauss and the recent developments in psycho-chemistry should not yet have provoked the upheaval so necessary to perception of the artistic deed and of its correlation with totemism. Of the hundreds of volumes of research and general nonsense directed against art, all that endure are several sentences which take its fundamental animism into account. Freud put forward an inspired supposition in *Totem and Taboo*:

> Art is the only domain in which the omnipotence of the Idea has persisted until our time. [. . .] It is correct to speak of the magic of art and to compare the artist with the magician. [. . .] Art, which certainly never began as "art for art's sake," at first found itself working for tendencies which are now, for the most part, extinct. It is permissible to suppose that among these tendencies were a good number of magical intentions.
>
> (Freud 1927)

Arts illustrated a pertinent article by Mircea Eliade with a photo of one of Claes Oldenburg's Happenings, accompanied by this caption: "Some of our contemporaries, in their yearning for 'initiation,' have gone as far as inventing new rites, if not new cults altogether." Eliade goes on: "We dream of being 'initiated,' of managing to decipher the occult meaning of all this destruction of artistic languages, of all these 'original' experiments which seem, at first sight, to have nothing left in common with art." And again: "[. . .] on one hand, we have an impression of

Election de Miss Festival disrupted a panel discussion at the 1967 Festival de Cinema at Knokke-Le-Aoute, Belgium. Performers included Tony Cox and Yoko Ono. The Happening was immediately followed by an anti-Vietnam War demonstration. Lebel was later arrested and charged with obscenity. (Photo by Francois Massal, courtesy of J.J. Lebel.)

'initiation' [...] on the other, we display clearly to those *others*, the crowd, our adherence to a secret minority; not, any more, to an 'aristocracy' (modern elites are leftward-looking) but to a gnosis, which has the merit of being both spiritual and secular, by being in opposition not only to official values but to the traditional Churches." Here the question is clearly defined by the terminology of an historian examining from a distance the history of art, initiation, and gnosis. It would seem that the Happening expresses "mythical thought"; it remains to be decided what is rational about it, and what eruptive.

Before deciding that the author of a Happening is a hierophant, an essential difference must be noted. The ceremony conducted by a medicine-man takes place according to a scheme which is the underlying principle of a complete rite; its progression strictly obeys a dogma, a cosmogonic theory. The artist taking part in a Happening is, on the contrary, looking for cosmogony in the action. He reinvents the world by coming into contact with it. He obeys no Rule. His action is undoubtedly conditioned by the collective subconscious which is its motor, but we may say that the man/world equation is an open one, to which each Happening brings a new and evolutive solution. The Happening tries to loosen the labyrinthine knot of the Real; it is, above all, a deliverance from the tangled thicket of the knots of culture. Each participant has a

À PROPOS DE L'EX-THÉÂTRE DE FRANCE

The Committee for Revolutionary Action (C.A.R.), together with the militants of the revolutionary student movement, has occupied the ex-theatre of France and transformed it into a permanent meeting place for all. During the night of 16 May, it transferred the responsibility for the unlimited occupation of places to a Committee of Occupation made up of actors, students, and workers whose political position is in line with their own. The goals of the occupation remain the same:

————The sabotage of all that is "cultural": theatre, art, literature, etc. (right-wing, left-wing, governmental, or "avant-garde") and the maintenance of the political struggle in highest priority.

————The systematic sabotage of the cultural industry, especially the industry of show business, in order to make room for true collective creation.

————The concentration of all energy on political objectives such as the expansion of the revolutionary movement, the struggle in the streets against State Power, and the reinforcement of the union of revolutionary workers, revolutionary students, and revolutionary artists.

————The extension of direct action: for example, by the occupation of the greatest possible number of places of work, of communications, of decisions.

The C.A.R. feels that it accomplished its goal in occupying the Odéon, ex-Theatre of France, when its political objective was clearly and publicly achieved: the government press (Paris-Presse) recognized, moreover, that the occupation of the ex-Theatre of France and certain workshops in the Renault factory at Cleon has provoked a drop in the Paris stock market. Today, this irreversible movement must be extended and reinforced. In regard to theatre, the slightest corporatist activity, the slightest intramural and organized entertainment, the slightest relaxation of revolutionary agitation, would be a betrayal of the *élan* which was revealed on the barricades and which must not diminish but increase and fortify at all costs. Never again must a single ticket be sold at the ex-Theatre of France; its free status must be maintained. The theatrical act of occupation was, under the circumstances, a political act:

————It laid siege to one of the bastions of Gaullist power.

————It revealed the collusion between certain counter-revolutionary trade-union elements and Management allied to the state (i.e., goons).

The C.A.R. has decided to move on to other things in other places. The C.A.R. expresses its solidarity and its sympathy with the Committee of Occupation of the ex-Theatre of France and remains at its disposal to aid in rejecting all attempts by the State to reoccupy these places, to prevent all reconversion of places back into theatres.

The only theatre is guerrilla theatre. REVOLUTIONARY ART IS MADE IN THE STREETS.

Comité d'Action Révolutionaire de l'ex-Théâtre de France
17 May 1968

different interior mandala, and thus communication takes place transconsciously. It would appear that there is a transition from inorganic to organic matter, and that, in the same way, the inorganic matter of thought – the pulsion – is transformed into an ideograph, a language, an action. Caught by and in the Happening in its rough pregrammatical state, the thought-process is free and undistilled. Seeking itself, it creates itself. During this intersubjective communication a certain phenomenon occurs – the manifestation of the "cosmic link."

Ornette Coleman has written about his record *Free Jazz*: "You can hear the others continue to build together so beautifully that the freedom even becomes impersonal." Such is the degree of direct interpersonal communication that the Happening aims for. This fundamental mediumism of thought must be maintained, in defiance of all rationalist conditioning. Recent experiences have shown that the ingestion of certain hallucinogenic substances creates a mood in which each person dreams the dreams of the others; the Happening is the concretization of a collective dream and a vehicle of intercommunication. At this level, expression escapes censure, sophistication, and trafficking.

The Tokyo Happenings, and those of Amsterdam or Paris, seem to have a point in common: the advent of sexuality. In this domain more than any other, spontaneity is forbidden by the coercive moralism of our society. Those offended should consider these words by Mircea Eliade in *Images and Symbols*:

> [... T]o interpret a psychical situation in sexual terms is most emphatically not to humiliate it for, except in the modern world, sexuality has always and everywhere been a hierophancy, and the sexual act a complete one (and thus, it follows, a means to knowledge *as well*).
>
> (Eliade 1961)

Absolutely the opposite of an act of profanation. To detractors, I further reply with a question: "Have you ever seen anything more obscene than two generals kissing each other?" That sort of people do it all the time at "investitures." As for us, we are not in favor of civil or military puppet shows – pretense games are not our forte.

Too often, Happenings are cited as attempts to *recover* "a lost world," a lost communion, a lost innocence. Without underestimating the importance of archetypes, we must nevertheless try to reply to the fundamental questions of *modernity*. At its highest point of tension, is not artistic activity the creation of a new world, never seen before, imperceptibly gaining on reality? Or is artistic activity a kind of subjective, sublimatory archaeology, focused on the interior distances of History?

Kaprow expounded (in *Art News*, May 1961): "In contrast with the art of the past, Happenings have structurally speaking no beginning, middle, or end. Their form is open and fluid, nothing obvious is pursued and consequently nothing is gained, save the certainty of a certain number of occurrences, events to which one is more than ordinarily attentive. They only happen once (or a very few times), then disappear forever, and others take their place." Let us continue an imaginary conversation with Kaprow.

> So, is the Happening a return to the "primitive," in reaction against the anaemic painting of the Paris or N.Y. schools?

> In a way, yes; but the word "return" is misleading. Let us say that what we find least tolerable is *de-signification* (Kosta Axelos' term), stagnation and censorship of the mind.

> Let us define the question. You have mentioned "collective exorcism" – does that mean you are bringing back magic, to combat the nonsignificant aestheticism of fashionable painting?

> Yes. Yet the Happening is not a language based on a specific pictorial, poetic, or hermetic tradition. There is always an imperceptible difference of method between magic and art; Marcel Mauss, moreover, anticipated this preoccupation of ours when he said: "Magical rites and magic as a whole are, first of all, facts of tradition. Actions which are not repeated are not magic. Actions in whose effectiveness an entire group does not believe, are not magic. The form of these rites is eminently transmissible and is sanctioned by opinion. Whence it follows that strictly individual actions [. . .] cannot be called magic" (Mauss 1959.)

> Therefore the Happening is not a magic ritual.

> For it to be so, the artist or artists taking part would have to be magicians. Whereas the artist can only be a magician if society, or a fragment of society, believes in him. Certainly, art and magic have always made common cause, and we have had the etymology of the word *technique* dinned into us sufficiently to be aware of its importance. Yet art as a vehicle for magic has not, for a long time in Europe, had the opportunity of being practiced or even tolerated. One hardly dares imagine what would happen if the general public were capable of seeing and understanding the way in which ritual images and objects should be used, for the secret region into which such art takes us is that of the revolution of the being – forbidden zone! Magic demands that those who aspire to practice it should hold themselves apart from society (refusal and challenge); the magician is indomitable.

Now, does the artist's spiritual opposition absolve him from all real

Lebel's Mode d'emploi du Pseudo-kini, les vrais faux seins, et Play-tex, le soutien-gorge qui tient was performed at the Restaurant La Tour d'Argent in Paris, 11 March 1965. (Photo by Monique Valentin, courtesy of the Dept. of Rare Books and Special Collections, Princeton University Libraries.)

opposition? This is the question that comes out of the *class collaboration* into which so many pure minds throw themselves. According to Allan Kaprow (*Art News*, October 1964), the artist is henceforth deprived of "his classical enemy, society." I completely disagree. Rebellion is, always will be, one of the main sources of artistic activity. I mean that industrial society has not yet succeeded in eliminating art as a form of social behavior. The network of alienations passing between the cultural and the social is so dense that it has become impossible to create anything at all without automatically calling into question the sociocultural *ensemble* in which we live. Thus authentic avant-garde art, contrasted with its civilization, is naturally revolutionary. Rimbaud's *Changer de Vie*, which has been the signal for nearly all the important artistic and scientific (one is tempted to add – political) creations of our time – is it not still, for most observers, the signal of a madman?

The Happening answers with actions. The marriage between theory and praxis is consummated – an extremely rare event. Transformation of thought, of the dream become Action in which Being in search of its sovereignty attains its greatest openness; the Happening, of all the languages at our disposition, is the least alienating. John Cage and Eric Dolphy play not only with notes but with sounds and noises; Picabia and Rauschenberg paint not only with colors but with everyday objects; Oldenburg or Ferrò will make a picture not only with images but with events. We no longer paint battles – we wage them.

A painting only exists when it is looked at, when its content is recognized and deciphered *qua* image. This subject–object relationship has the serious disadvantage of putting art at the mercy of the shortsighted or dishonest spectator or specialist, and to beat a one-way path, in the functioning of the image, leading to a checkpoint, to a form of censorship and a corruption of the senses. This could not be allowed to go on any longer.

The "going-beyond" postulated by the authors of Happenings has only just begun. Already, it has called into question not only painting, but also the habits of thought provoked by it, including the frustration of the spectator, the professional deformation of the looker-on, etc. The Happenings put into action (as opposed to merely representing) the varying relationships between individuals and their psychosocial environment. Contemporary art demands the active intervention of the spectator. In these conditions, the *voyeur*, by his very deficiency, has no part in the action. With the *art of participation*, the looker-on no longer makes the picture (as Duchamp remarked *à propos* the static picture); he plays dead outside the door.

The Happening is above all a means of plastic expression. By placing painting *in* (not, like Pollock, above) its veritable subconscious context, it carries out transmissions and introduces the witness directly into the event. A painter's solution for a painter's problem. We cannot expect critics or art-lovers to understand this urgent necessity of going beyond painting – they already have a terrible time trying to understand painting itself.

Whether it does in fact set off a chain of images, or dreams aloud, or tells a story, or is to be found in an objectified perspective, whether it is improvised or perfectly elaborated, a Happening never gives a stock answer to the question it asks. It imposes no restrictions on affective ambivalence. The Happening is neither an irrefutable theory nor an infallible system; its only criteria are subjective. In cases such as this, "success" cannot be gauged as if it were a boxing match, a corrida, or a play – according to "talent" and box-office receipts. Everything depends on the collective watchfulness, and on the occurrence of certain parapsychological phenomena. And these phenomena may have "delayed action"; they may also escape the obdurate or inattentive witness completely. The Happening is not an invariable ceremony – rather, a state of mind, an act of clairvoyance, a poem in action to which everyone adds a movement or a paralysis, a pulsion expressed or repressed, a feeling of rejoicing or despair. Art at last has some chance of being more than merely a screen on which each projects his own anguish – a looking-glass through which it will be possible to pass. No one can force the man who, fascinated or terrified by the reflection of his own image, prefers to stay on his side of the mirror. In spite of its dazzling powers, contemporary art has to some extent gone aground in mid-voyage. It has not managed to go beyond the "one-way street" of unilateral contemplation. In 1910 there did indeed begin a *révolution du regard*, from which time spectators have "done the painting." At last it was admitted that the origins and psychical content of art left no room for aestheticism, for propaganda and commercialism (those outward signs of the counterfeit). Without Picabia, Duchamp, Schwitters, and the Surrealists, we should still be at the level of Utrillo and the pot of flowers. But it is out of the question to be lost in admiration before anyone – idolatry is inadmissible. Once this is clear, a new mutation becomes imperative.

Thus, the Happening established a relation between subject and subject. No one is (exclusively) a spectator, but is looked at, considered, scrutinized. There is no monolog but dialog, exchange and circulation of images. No one can get away with flippant gibes, pulling faces in mirrors, or signing the visitors book. If someone does, he is playing dead.

The random element, the nonrespect of taboos, the broadening of awareness – these constitute an indictment of the falsehoods of civilization and of its rules for living. But this only partly explains the perpetual state of war which exists between art and society. There is a case for analyzing the nonavailability, the aggressivity, and the power-lessness (to perceive and to participate) in which some of those "responsible" for culture take refuge. Art and Society try to profane one another; at one moment demolishing, at another negotiating. It is time this duel became a dialog. Yet nothing arouses quite so much hostility and puerile negation as an invitation to dialog. The wish to attack, sabotage, and destroy is provoked as much, if not more, by the shameful desire to climb up on the stage in a forbidden zone, as by the action taking place there. In Milan in 1960, the police burst into the Anti-Trial manifestation and seized four paintings (the Collective Antifascist Picture among them). The London police, for their part, were content with purely and simply forbidding our second Happening in Dennison Hall (1964). There are many, many such examples.

In the midst of the generalized deliquescence of the cultural and political scene, the Happening appears like an intruder, an interrupter of the censorship exercised over art by economic authority. The Happening was the first artistic concretization in Europe of a new consciousness, sharpened by adversity. The structural transformation of human relation-ships is beginning to be methodically advocated. The following state-ment by Alexander Trocchi accurately corresponds with the steps which have brought us from the Anti-Trial to the Happening:

Sunlove with the Soft Machine was part of Lebel's 1967 Fourth Festival of Free Expression in Saint-Tropez. (Photo by Jacques Prayer, courtesy of J.J. Lebel.)

> *Artists will have control of their own means of expression.* When they achieve that control, their "relation to a community" will become a meaningful problem, that is, a problem amenable to formulation and solution at a creative and intelligent level. Thus we must concern ourselves forthwith with the question of how to seize and within the social fabric exercise that control. Our first move must be to *eliminate the brokers.*
>
> (Trocchi 1964)

This is a clear statement of the social aim of many an artist. Such a radical attitude, in relation to the power structure, comes as the only possible solution for the creative mind – striving towards an artistic *and* political revolution – faced with the industrial or commercial demands of contemporary society. On all sides, artistic action finds itself obliged to go beyond the pitiful limits of legality.

The political element of its combat, however determining it may be, must never replace the Happening's psychical intent. My opinions may not be shared by my American friends Kaprow and Oldenburg but it cannot be denied that our Happenings have something in common – they give back to artistic activity what has been torn away from it: the intensification of feeling, the play of instinct, a sense of festivity, social agitation. The Happening is above all a means of interior communication; then, and incidentally, a spectacle. From outside, its essential part is unintelligible.

The principle of stage–audience integration, the preeminence of artistic creation over rational examination, the importance given to mood and environment constitute the specificity of the Happening in comparison with the theatre and with the psychodrama as defined by Moreno. If the basic hallucinatory raw materials are the same, there is no question of reducing them to their simplest expression, even less of making them disappear, but of transforming them into a visible language. Theatre and psychodrama have not the same field of action, and the Happening has a third. I am of the opinion that the Happening must keep its distance from the commercial preoccupations of the theatre, and from the therapeutic ones of psychodrama. Already, in the U.S., Happenings are being turned out to order for universities or smart parties. Certain playwrights and filmmakers have begun to plagiarize the findings of Happenings – they completely distort the significance of what they use. It is well-known that the avant-garde theatre's greatest difficulty is to find a "market"; its promoters are trying to drum up an audience "even in the suburbs."

We are doing exactly the opposite. It will be remembered that during the Happenings which Kaprow did for the Théâtres des Nations in 1963, we met the spectators in the Théâtre Récamier and took them half a kilometer away, to the second floor of the Bon Marché. Environment is the essential element in any Happening. Art must literally "go down into the street," come out of the cultural zoo, to enrich itself with what Hegel (without humor) called "the contamination of the casual." Thus, the first European Happening (at the end of the second Anti-Trial, June 1960) took place partly in the streets and on the canal of the Giudecca in Venice. In 1963, Wolf Vostell organized *Cityrama*, moving across Cologne. We have used the spaces of the Boulogne cinema studios (*Manifestation for conjuring the spirit of Catastrophe*, 1963), the Musée d'Art Moderne in Paris (*Incidents*, 1963), and the American Artists Center (Festival of Free Expression, 1964 and 1965). We hope to do other things in a station, a stadium, an airplane. To be elsewhere. To be radar. To be there. The conventional theatre, the art shop or gallery, are no longer (and perhaps in themselves have never been) sacred places – so why shut ourselves up in them? Artistic activity is founded on high telepathy – a contact high – and everything which comes into its field becomes a *sign*, and is part of art. It is therefore evident that the primary problem of today's art has become *the renovation and intensification of perception*.

> *Editor's note*: Jean-Jacques Lebel's essay (in a longer form) was originally published in *New Writers 4* (London: Calder and Boyars, 1967)

and is reprinted by permission. The piece is somewhat dated: Happenings, politics, France, and Lebel have all moved and changed since it was written. Just before this issue went to press, we received the following note.

PARIS POSTSCRIPT, MAY/JUNE 1968

Something has changed. After the Sorbonne and the Sud Aviation factory in Nantes, the ex-Théâtre de France was taken and occupied by a Comité d'Action Révolutionnaire and transformed into a totally open forum, a day and night *agora* for political discussion and action. This ex-theatre ceased to be the toy of the power elite, became a place where everybody (not just the professional clowns) had the right to the most extreme expression, contestation, and communication. No more theatre or expensive spectacles for a passive audience of consumers – but a truly *collective* enterprise in political and artistic research. A new type of relationship between the "doers" and the "lookers" is being experimented with. Perhaps we will succeed in helping hundreds of thousands more to let go of their alienated social roles, to be free of mental Stalinism, to become the political and creative doers they dream of being.

Art has always been halfway between wishful thinking and wishful doing – isn't that why it has often been prophetic? Today more than ever the emphasis is on getting things done. This brings us to a specific type of collective effort which implies an out-front rejection of the present cultural system: guerrilla theatre, street Happenings, and similar activities. The important thing these various creative attempts have in common is that rather than seeking integration into the industry they seek to disrupt it. These experiments in liberation theatre are in open conflict with the capitalist environment, and they are related in their opposition: the Living Theatre, the San Francisco Mime Troupe, and the German revolutionary student theatre group, the Bread & Puppet Theatre, and European Happeners. We can no longer be satisfied with loopholes and cracks in the System; we can no longer accommodate ourselves with the pseudo-liberation of a profit-oriented economy which winds up controlling not only the distribution but the actual conception and materialization of the theatrical vision.

The Great Society is not the only one which is trying out its new weapons on rioting blacks, war-resisting demonstrators, or mind-dancing hippies. The streets of many large cities in Europe are similar testing grounds. But the Japanese Zenkaguren have developed a weapon of their own: shit in loosely sealed cellophane bags. Truth grenades: highly recommended when attacked by MACE-spraying rioting police. It's time for mass shit-ins. Hit the impeccably toilet-trained "adult" civilization where it hurts – in its heavenly cleanliness. The sooner everyone realizes that

ART IS $HIT

the better. From then on, it's pure spontaneity.

Jean-Jacques Lebel

NOTE

1. References have been added, where available, by the editor of this edition and are not necessarily the editions used by the author.

REFERENCES

Eliade, Mircea (1961) *Images and Symbols*. Kansas City: Andrew and McMeel.

Freud, Sigmund (1927) *Totem and Taboo*. Translated by A.A. Brill. New York: New Republic.

Mauss, Marcel (1959) *Sociology and Anthropology*. Paris: P.U.F.

Trocchi, Alexander (1964) "A Revolutionary Proposal". *City Lights Journal*.

30

REFLECTIONS ON HAPPENINGS

Darko Suvin

The great difference lies in man's knowing what he is; only then is he truly that.

Hegel ([1892] 1963)

1 TAXONOMY

There are at least four different types of Happenings: Events, Aleatoric scenes, Happenings proper, and Action Theatre (but see the reservation about the latter in 1.4, which reduces the number of types to three).

1.1 Events (or Pieces)

An Event is a scene containing one activity, either brief or repetitively drawn out; it is close to a children's game or an adult gag. An Event can range from an exercise in perception (John Cage's *Silent Piece* or *4'33"*) to the enactment of a basic metaphor which allegorizes the participants. A good example of the latter is Allan Kaprow's *Overtime*:

> Sundown. (flashlights) 200 straight feet of snow-fence erected in woods. Groundline drawn with powdered chalk. Posted with red flare and marked number 1.
> Fence moved next 200 feet, maintaining direction. Groundline drawn. Flare and marker number 2.
> Fence moved next 200 feet. Groundline. Flare. Marker 3. (portable radios, food deliveries.)
> Process repeated every 200 feet for a mile. Lighted flares maintained along entire line throughout night. Fence removed. Line and markers remaining. Flares out.
> Sunup. (in Schechner 1969: 150)[1]

Any interpretation of this Event would have to start from Kaprow's "grounding" of the age-old metaphor of the wild dark wood, present in art from *Gilgamesh* through Dante's *selva oscura* to our time. Its menace in the wintery season is being tamed; it turns into a humanly mapped grid, a surveyed space complete with food, light, and communication.

The enactment thus "de-charges" the metaphor, and, by collective labor which unites man and nature, translates it from a horror into a domesticated piece of environment. Its nonurban character is due to Kaprow's personal propensity for the bucolic – most authors of Happenings work in an urban environment, where metaphors are less easily identifiable in terms of the cultural tradition though no less present or powerful.

Events are related to music and dance – primarily modern – since they deal with the rhythmic use of a *delimited time-duration*. In *Overtime* this is sundown to sunup; its title is, I take it, a pun on "overtime" work which is also victorious "over" a structured time (as well as space). Cage's pieces indicate this relationship still more clearly, being largely unconcerned with space. Space, say a concert hall, is for Cage a neutral constant and not a dynamic variable – which is the aesthetic characteristic of music as the purest time art. Insofar as an Event is homologous to a basic "compartment" within Happenings proper, which ideally also enacts one basic metaphor, this Cage strain or orientation is significant for all Happenings.

1.2 Aleatoric Scenes

The provenance of aleatoric or chance scenes, such as Jackson Mac Low's *Marrying Maiden*,[2] is clearly musical. Their structure is based on a combination of authorial choice (Mac Low chose the text – the *I Ching* and a list of 500 adverbs indicating the manner of speaking fragments from it) and chance (in this case the order, duration, tempo, volume, and inflection of the verbal material). As Dick Higgins has pointed out, Cagean aleatoric technique in reality only places decisions at one remove from the composer, allowing the material to be determined by the artist-composer's system: "And the real innovation lies in the emphasis on the creation of a system" (Higgins 1969:55–7). Though permutations exist, any performance still will be a performance of Jackson Mac Low's *Marrying Maiden* – i.e., within a field of possibilities which, although larger than that of a univocal script, is in principle as closed a field as *Hamlet*. (Conversely, any theatre or concert performance is always one variation on an underlying score, libretto, or text.)

Unless aleatoric technique is used simply to modulate unit-Events (a rather primitive limit-case), its meaning lies basically in its commitment to a quantified view of the world as an assemblage of neutral molecular units, which obey the law of large numbers (the only way to escape utter boredom in permutations). I would imagine that aleatorics, as an exclusive principle of structuring, work only with fairly general texts which have low message significance and high entropy – texts of a general incantatory nature such as the *I Ching*, applicable to everything vaguely because (and therefore) applicable to no precise interpersonal situation at all, like a soothsayer's prediction or a horoscope. Aleatorics also would seem to work dramaturgically only with fairly neutral *dramatis personae*, which are neither individualistic characters nor allegorical in any clearly defined system.

1.3 Happenings Proper
Three examples are necessary to indicate the main outlines of this type.

1.31 In Kaprow's *Eat* (see Kirby 1965c [and in this volume]) there is a field of possibilities – physical materials and gestures – connected with food and the ritual situation of a communal meal-feast (the author calls it "a quasi-eucharistic ritual"). Its performance depends on the inter-action of the participants and a rehearsed troupe. This Happening is situated halfway between a religious Mass and the cold buffet at a modern Individualistic party, and its rehearsed actors halfway between acolytes and hosts at the party. The participating audience is supposed to be reawakened to a sense of communion and the miraculousness of food. Yet it remains unclear what type of communion is desired and why food is miraculous: the only value system implied is the basic biological solidarity of human beings.[3] In view of the real complexity of human relations, this approach is a convenient jumping-off point but little more. Let us take for the moment a grisly real-life Happening, such as the My Lai massacre: it is surely true to say that the massacred Vietnamese were human beings, and that this (as against a comparably gratuitous killing of 200 or 300 apes or boars) is the basis for our feeling of outrage. But the deeper, significant, operative truth about My Lai is not that both Vietnamese peasants and American soldiers are biologically human: it is that the latter are killers and the former are their victims, at which point a political, economic, and ideological analysis of the reasons for that situation would have to set in. To stop at the first approach is simply liberal sentimentality. Analogously, Kaprow's refusal to make further distinctions which could adequately deal with the complexities of our civilization is simply a Rousseauist persuasion that a return to supposed fundamentals outside civilization will illumine present-day life. Pseudo-biological values substituted for historical ones: a Eucharist without a Real Presence, a dumb Symposium.

Indeed, one whole aspect of Happenings reposes on what I have called the Rousseauist approach, either by escaping into nature (*Eat*'s cave being in this respect prototypic, indeed a touch of genius), or trying to convert the urban American environment into a new naïvety without physically changing it. This second wing is more original and sets itself a more difficult goal. Yet it too approaches its new environment in a very old way, by a yoga-type process of re-education from within. It supposes, or wants to achieve, a *"dérèglement systématique de tous les sens"* (as Rimbaud and the surrealists would have it) which would make out of the jungle of cities a wonder, and out of city-dwellers swains of an urbanized pastoral – "peasants of Paris," as Aragon once formulated it. Circuitously, we are back at a debased Rousseauism: Rousseau at least wanted *the whole society* to devolve back into natural nobility. (A tempting way to account for the debasement would be to note that Happenings are sociologically a product of the same class Rousseau hailed from – the petty-bourgeois artistic intelligentsia – but that this class in the meantime has been forced from the public into the private sphere.)

All these observations are, of course, not exorcisms, but merely attempts at understanding and judging. For any surer judgment, however, we would need far more sociological data. In the meantime we must make do with basically impressionistic hypotheses. It seems that nobody writing about Happenings has escaped such a proceeding.

1.32 Claes Oldenburg's *Fotodeath* (1965:85–93 [and in this volume]) is a developed urban Happening conventionally divided between actors and spectators. It can be compared to a commedia dell'arte *canovaccio* (scenario) without speech and the *lazzi* tradition, or to a multifocus mime without a plot. It consists of three sets of five Events (scenes) each, forming a spectrum of situations from a crowded urban environment. The unit-events are contiguous in space (as in medieval mysteries), but the space is not coordinated along the axis of a firm value system (e.g., from Heaven upstage left to Hell upstage right). Oldenburg himself, quite lucidly, calls his Happenings "Events" in an associational pseudo-plot and confesses to a preference for "a structure which is an object in itself," such as photographs or circus (in Kirby 1965a:201–02). Oldenburg's Events also have no temporal focus; they are done simultaneously on a neutral, geometrically divided stage. This results in a multifocus stage, with all five Events of the same set contiguous and simultaneous. They are coordinated like a family of parallel, coexisting time/space systems in a roughly synchronic cross-cut, i.e., like Einsteinian covariant island universes each of which is autonomous but all of which are deduced from the same basic formula by varying some parameter(s) in it.

Each of Oldenburg's three sets of five Events has a common theme; each set seems to have a "pilot-scene" explicating more clearly than the other scenes the common denominator of the set. The theme of the first set is the futile enacting of roles in a topsy-turvy world – by implication our world: (1) man posing before mirrors; (2) girl in jingoist poses; (3) man wrestling with a soft laundry bag; (4) transvestite confusion of sexes; (5) pilot-scene showing a family posing unsuccessfully for a photograph in front of landscape samples. There are marked similarities to the allegorizing painters from fourteenth-century Italy to sixteenth-century Flanders, say to Breughel's *Wedding* or *Proverbs*. The theme of the second set is futile search for partnership: (1) a narcissistic woman; (2) bygone times of a naïve adolescent friendship; (3) man leaving invalid woman for a party; (4a) two drunks unsuccessfully helping each other up; (4b) man picking up spilled cans but not the fallen partner. The third set tops the futility of social posing and the breakdown of human friendliness with a final bogging down of all situations in a mechanical, reified denial of vitality, as in a nightmare of arrested or viscous time. It features: (1) a mechanical majorette; (2) a wounded man (a soldier in the performance) unable to sit down, like Clov in *Endgame*; (3) the pilot-scene of the USA as a collage of objects in a viscid paste; (4) dinner with a dead woman; and (5) men degraded to movers of a huge assemblage of black boxes.[4] In the whole Happening (itself only one part of a tripartite Piece called *Circus*) there is a clear progression through the three sets from singular through dual (the girl in 2.1 is dual, faced with her own mirror-image; the family in 1.5 constitutes only one unit) to general, and from futility to death. This was effected by a series of brief snapshot situations (an idea developed in a more formalistic way by the Living Theatre's "snapshots" scene in *Mysteries and Smaller Pieces* [1964]), amounting to a kind of foreshortened, aerial survey of the American situation. *Fotodeath*'s title indicates the diagnosis.

1.33 In Dick Higgins' *The Tart, or Miss America* (1965:132–41 [and in this volume]), words acquire greater importance. There is an abundant use of chance techniques, but the material manipulated is, first of all, cliché phrases, written by the author, combined with physical action, optic or acoustic effects, and some scenery (this Happening was done in a boxing ring – an old dream of Brecht's). Secondly, these words and gestures are performed by "stock urban characters" (1965:133), what Diderot called "conditions." Their number is changeable, and the same stock character can be acted simultaneously by several actors, but at the very least a central triangle is always present, consisting of the Tart, the Young Man, and Mr. Miller, a suburban Babbitt-Everyman; further typical characters include a Prophet, a Steelworker, a Drinking Man, etc. Each performer had thirty-six different nonverbal situations in which he was assigned at random one sentence, one action, and one special (optic, acoustic, or kinetic) effect. Collage-scenes resulted, overlapping actions supplemented by the activity of a Special Performer, a coordinator responsible for cueing and flow, who had a collection of Americana – "the relevance to be determined by the social intent of the performance" (1965:135) – which he produced at random. There are only thirty-six lines in the whole play, and they were always explicitly quoted as said by one of the "roles" – regardless of who actually pronounced them. (I particularly liked sentence 13: "The steelworkers say no. No, say the steelworkers. [No. No.]") Higgins was clearly aiming at an estrangement-effect of the Brechtian type, which would prevent the audience from empathizing with the *persona*: "I wrote *The Tart* to express a sociological concept [about women. . . . M]y hope was that the audiences would sympathize with the performers (not the characters) in their social contexts and that the lines would be more tragic than funny" (1965:132).

This type of Happening explicates the specific allegorical quality of characters, and begins to utilize the suggestiveness of language. A similar approach is used in the first scene of *Mysteries* (a performance which is in a way an anthology of different types of Happenings). It featured a pantomime of militarism developed from a scene of *The Brig* and joined to fugal chanting of a poem by Jackson Mac Low consisting exclusively of the words found on the one-dollar bill ("One dollar. – In God we trust. – Douglas C. Dillon." – if memory serves). It ends with the gradual formation of a drilling platoon and a final incomprehensible harangue by the commander, saluted with a roar of "Yes, Sir!" Its effect is a powerful, foreshortened glimpse of the military-industrial complex operating in the flesh of men. Not much is needed to transform this type of Happening into Action Theatre – only to allegorize the performance space and thus conjure up the vague outline of a fable.

1.4 Action Theatre

When Happening techniques are elevated into a staged performance "matrixed" in space and plot – such as in Kenneth Brown's *The Brig* (1963) – one gets a play using repetitive and permutative techniques and a minimum of verbal information, yet clearly nearer to drama than to Happenings. Except in terms of influence and coexistence there seem to be no valid reasons for aesthetically grouping Action Theatre with Happenings.

1.5 Comment

This brief survey describes a *typological series* of ascending complexity, starting out from single nonverbal activities (Events) and longer aleatoric activities where text is treated mainly as sound and the allegorizing of participants is vague and very general. Kaprow seems to be the master of this approach, and he is out of his element as soon as he leaves it for what I have called Happenings proper, e.g., in *Eat* or *Courtyard*. It should be remembered that the Kaprow performance which gave a name to this genre was called *18 Happenings in 6 Parts*, i.e., that he thinks of Happenings in terms of Events. The culmination of this typological series (excluding Action Theatre) are Happenings proper, which range from a nonverbal symbolic field of activities with the nuclear performing troupe used as seeders only, through mime containing personae demanding well-rehearsed actors and a clear compositional progression, to aleatoric use of a purposefully composed text with stock characters like those in modern allegorizing plays (Expressionist, Surrealist, Brechtian, Absurdist, etc. – the conception of *The Tart* seems rather akin to a play such as Pirandello's *To Clothe the Naked*).

There seems to be little reason to treat Happenings with less scholarly attention than, say, *Gorboduc* or the plays of Noel Coward. Their significance can be looked at from two aspects (which are blended in any particular Happening in very different proportions): it may be defined as an exercise in unclogging the perceptiveness of participants, in which case it is properly speaking pre-theatrical or propedeutical; or it may lie in their use of a meaningful semiotic structure with some kind of role-playing and an organized rhythm – even if the figures and the organization of events are difficult to recognize because they are of an unfamiliar type.

Many Happenings were simply Events or Aleatoric scenes; often they seem to have resembled unclear and underrehearsed mimic psycho-dramas. This is, however, not the fault of the form as such, but of the social and ideological situation in which they were performed. This situation also accounts for the frequent indifference or hostility toward the audience. Though this is sociologically very significant it seems aesthetically more important to note that Happenings can assign the audience the same ontological status as the performers: both can provide performance-events by action and provoked reaction; both can be, and often are, treated as objects.

2 AESTHETIC LOCATION AND AN ATTEMPT AT DEFINITION

2.1 Location

Are Happenings theatre or not? The answer is an exercise in semantics. If we define theatre as the performance of an action organized in a plot, which has been the dominant trend since the fifteenth-century Aristotelians, then they obviously are not. If we define it, say with Cage, much more broadly, as a performance which engages simultaneously the two public senses of eye and ear, then they are. It might be more useful to start by identifying Happenings as a form of *spectacle*, a wider aesthetic category embracing dramatic theatre, mime, ballet, and opera as well as the nonplotted genres such as pageants, fairs, jugglers, and circus, and the intermediary genres of music-hall and cabaret, vaudeville, burlesque, etc. The common earmark of spectacles is the presence of *actions by human performers*; by the immediacy or reality of that presence theatrical spectacles are differentiated from movies, TV, etc. The nonplotted genres are sociologically, as a rule, lower-class forms.

In the 1920s, the Russian Formalists held a theory that literary and artistic genres evolve not in a straight but in a zigzag line.[5] The pioneering work of Viktor Shklovsky held that in each artistic period there are several schools in any one art; they exist simultaneously, with one school the most orthodox at any given time, and others coexisting with it, uncanonized and spurned by official aesthetics. In the early nineteenth century in Russia, for example, the courtly tradition in literature existed simultaneously with "low" vaudeville verse and adventure-novel prose which – on a despised, subliterary level – were creating new forms. This creativity brings forth a "junior line" which grows up to replace the old: "Chekhov introduces the low farce and *feuilleton* into Russian literature; Dostoyevsky raises to the dignity of a norm the devices of the dime story" (Shklovsky 1921). The eighteenth-century Western European novel stems from imaginary voyages and travelogs (Defoe), diaries and manuals of letter-writing (Richardson), etc., *not* in a straight line from the major epic form of the preceding epoch, the verse epic. Pushkin's lyrics come from album verses and folk songs, Blok's from gypsy ballads, Mayakovsky's from comic period-icals. The "junior line" or "low" genre (which is as a rule also a "small" form) is then canonized by an artistic revolution which transforms it into the accepted "senior line" or "high" genre (and as a rule into a "large" form) of the new period.

The Formalists recognized that artistic evolution is never as pure as a critical model, but is contaminated by many inner and outer factors. Nevertheless, they asserted that there is a law in the history of art by which "the legacy is transmitted not from father to son but from uncle to nephew" (Shklovsky 1923b). The admission of attitudes and genres of popular culture, existing on the periphery of official aesthetics, into the consecrated precincts of official art, runs parallel to social changes whereby the tastes of the "upper" classes are supplanted by "lower" popular tastes. Today, we might add to the Formalists' insights that artistic and social change are in certain complex ways causally con-nected. In France in the 1820s, for example, the assumption of devices from eighteenth-century bourgeois sentimental comedy into the ossified *ancien régime* tragedy resulted in the romantic tragedy of de Vigny, Dumas père, and Hugo. This was clearly related to the sharp conflict between the life-styles and worldviews of the feudal reaction and those of the young democrats, a conflict representing antagonistic class interest. A history of literature or theatre should seek to explain the rise of any new genre by focusing on the "lower" artistic levels and forms from which it sprang. "Each period of creative flowering is preceded by a slow process of accumulating means of renewal in the lower, often unrecognized strata" (Tomashevsky 1925). In spectacle too, the non-plotted genres which I am discussing are sociologically, as a rule, lower-class forms. In our century – just as in antiquity and in the Middle Ages – these forms are lifted into the realm of official aesthetics by the pressure of new social forces and tastes.

2.2 Elements for a Definition

As soon as there are human performers – implying a real or imaginary audience – it is inevitable that they adopt implied or explicated, shifting or stable *roles* of some kind, e.g., "young intellectual Everyman," "the artist as sufferer" (or more rarely "as celebrator"), etc. Robert Whitman, for example, wanted "clean-cut American teenagers" for two girl-performers in *Water*, and dressed them accordingly (in Kirby 1965a:180). As Donald M. Kaplan (1965:95–98) pointed out against Michael Kirby,[6] misunderstandings arise primarily from the fact that these roles are matrixed unclearly (usually in very vague allegorical frameworks) so that they do not amount to individualistic characters. I called them types of Diderotian "conditions"; Higgins called them stock characters, and possibly a better name may be found: but surely this *different* matrixing should not be taken as representing nonmatrixed acting. Whatever their seeming unorthodoxy to our conditioned eyes, they are aesthetically nearer to a Shakespearean or Sophoclean character than to a man walking down the street. Furthermore, it is clearly not necessary that Happenings be based on improvisation, or on aleatorics, or on the absence of a division of labor between troupe and audience; the testimony of *Fotodeath* could be multiplied. However, Kirby's identi-fication of Happenings as nonmatrixed in regard to *time and space* seems valid, fundamental, and never seriously transgressed. A forest/room/street/city, or whatever the space of a Happening may be, does not pretend to any other imaginary localization; the time duration likewise. Space and time revert to an empirical status identical to the epistemo-logical level of the audience's direct experience before and after the performance. Space becomes, in principle at least, the sum of all objects (including people) and the dimension of their displacement; time is not the space of causal sequences but the measure of qualitative change (very slow or – more rarely, alas – very fast). Both space and time are no longer conventions but problematic materials whose extent and character, structured through object-relations, largely *are* a Happening. The structuring will necessarily be compartmentalized, carrying to its ultimate conclusion the tendency of modern theatre toward episodic autonomy (cf. Chekhov, Brecht, Beckett).

If a theatre's time and space do not pretend to a different epistemological or even ontological status (which is what I take it matrixing means), its situations cannot be organized into an imaginary universe which impinges on our universe only on the privileged "holy circle" of the stage. This imaginary scenic universe with its own laws and constellations of forces is formed by a causal *plot*. Borrowing a term from film theoreticians and aestheticians like Etienne Souriau,[7] one can call this universe of the theatrical plot a *diegetic* one (from the Greek *diegesis*, a story told) (Souriau 1962:11). The unfolding of a Happening does not give rise to another imaginary but vivid and coherent space/time universe overlapping with our own: *a Happening is nondiegetic*. Paradoxically, any diegetic theatre genre, such as mime or indeed drama, can thus be seen aesthetically as a limit-case of a nondiegetic genre (such as the Happening) whose time and space had become fixed into a constant. In mathematical notation, if a Happening is a function of time, space, dramaturgic figures, and dramaturgic situation:

$$(1)\ H = f\ (t, s, fig, sit)$$

then for $(2)\ t/s = k$, which is the situation for drama:

$$(3)\ Dr = k \cdot f\ (fig, sit)$$

The constant k is then the time/space relation or form characteristic for each major epoch of drama (and diegetic theatre).

Historically, Happenings have used various materials grouped around stylized human activities, as dramatic and diegetic theatre also does (dance and mime, music and noises, light and scenery, film, literature, etc.). But Happenings have used these materials in new and sometimes startling ways. Persons are treated as objects, enclosed in shrouds or sacks, wrapped in paper or tin foil, painted, or used as surfaces for movie projection, etc.; indeed, many Happeners seem uncomfortable with normally clad or normally nude figures. Only the best escape this syndrome, an aspect of the Happenings style which Susan Sontag explains by the experience and pressures of New York painters, preoccupied with urban junk and highly aggressive not only against the audience but above all against their medium and materials – a style based on the artifacts and human relations of the modern American city: "the brutal disharmony of buildings in size and style, the wild juxtaposition of store signs, the clamorous layout of the modern newspaper" ([1966] 1969: 271–72).

2.3 A Tentative Definition

Happenings are a genre of theatre spectacle, using various types of signs and media organized around the action of human performers in a homogeneous and thematically unified way, and a nondiegetic structuring of time and space.

Happenings are differentiated from dramatic (opera, ballet, mime) theatre by the absence of a coherent diegetic universe. They are differentiated from fairs, pageants, and other similar nondiegetic spectacle genres by their dramaturgic homogeneity, and from circus (a genre to which they appear to be aesthetically closest) by their more unified themes or fields.

A definition of drama adapted from Aristotle's *Poetics* (part 6) by updating the language – leaving out the parts specific for the Greek conception of theatre and for tragedy, as well as the dubious, contested and structurally unnecessary reference to catharsis – might be: Drama is the presentation – *mimesis* (see Savin 1967:58–59) – (1) of a complete action; (2) which is of a determined magnitude; (3) in differentiated and heightened language; (4) in the form of events, not of narrative. Compared to the above definition of Happenings – and leaving aside for the moment the moot factor of language – we note the universal hallmark of spectacle common to both in (4) and the differentiating factor of plot in time in (2), which latter is a hallmark of diegetic genres only. We are then left with an open question about factor (1) – are Happenings simply "free form" or are they thematically unified, possessing a complete action (*praxis*) or indeed fable (*mythos*)? I would argue that there is no free form in art: a form called free is either inoperative or new. In that sense, any successful Happening has a limited thematic field, and its action, though oscillating, is complete unto itself. Further, I would argue that – as different from plot, which is based on univocal causality – Aristotle's notion of *fable* could and should be salvaged for any modern theory of theatre and spectacles: The fable (mythos) is the presentation of action; for by fable I mean the arrangement (composition) of incidents. This is elastic enough to encompass both univocally causal relations and any number of transformational or associational arrangements of incidents, just as in contemporary poetry and other arts: e.g., isomorphic, isogenic, isothematic (by formal, proveniential, or thematic resonances).

2.4 Genetics
This is not to deny that Happenings evolved by theatricalization and spectacularization of music and the plastic arts, and only secondarily from older scenic genres such as dance. Historically, plastic arts evolved into temporality through mobiles, collages, and kindred developments; Calder, Duchamp, Gabo, Rauschenberg, Tinguely, and many other experimental artists and groups attempted to make an art form out of the environment. At a later stage, human beings used as objects were brought

into the environment (see Kaprow 1966b:165–66) – which then immediately tended toward theatre. Traces of that procedure are frequent in
painters' Happenings, e.g., in Kaprow's *Eat* or Oldenburg's *Washes*, and
have infiltrated the style of the whole genre. Simultaneously, concert
music evolved into spatiality, directly from performance (Cage) or still
more easily through scenic dances to music (Cunningham, Halprin).

3 SOME HISTORICAL ANALOGIES

Happenings have some curious and instructive analogies with a number
of other nondramatic scenic genres, which should be discussed within a
proper theory of theatre based on a sociology of spectacle forms. I shall
mention a few, centering on the English Masque, in an attempt to bring
out some features of Happenings' unique sociological profile.

3.1 The Masque

The Masque has been defined as "an evening entertainment in which the
chief performers were masked courtiers, accompanied by torchbearers,
all in costumes appropriate to the device presented: the elements of song
and dialog were developed later, the original nucleus being dances and
conversations with spectators selected by the masquers" (Cunliffe
1907:146). It developed when a variety of medieval folk customs –
chiefly the "mumming," a procession of disguised people, but also the
"king-game," election of a mock Saturnalian ruler, and the sword-dance,
a mimic combat – were appropriated by the upper class for an evening
entertainment leading up to a banquet. The entertainment absorbed, in
the sixteenth century, influences from Italy (directly or by way of
France), where Renaissance revels had reached unprecedented splendor
in theatricalizing public living and translating it into a scene in which all
the known arts were used to express a world of ideal loveliness. This led
to many modifications of the original simple procession with dance, chief
of which is the introduction, first, of conversations and set speeches, and,
at the apogee of the Jacobean Masque, of elaborate singing and plotted,
diegetic dialog. The nucleus of the Masque is thus nondiegetic, simply
a potlatch-type procession-cum-dance organized within a certain field of
possibilities (the "device," e.g., of the Green Men or similar) to which
costumes, masks, and dances were related. Its primal character as
communal fertility rite was modified into aristocratic convivial conventions promoting Tudor upper-class unity and, increasingly, the splendor
and magical position of the court itself.

3.2 Parallels and Oppositions

Some obvious parallels include the one-shot or two-shot nature of any particular Masque performance and its division into open-air and "palace" forms. Further, it was based on a close-knit, numerically small social group, which resulted in the use of allegorized themes and figures played by members of the audience (also using a few resource persons such as the author and the choreographer). Though disguised as symbolic stage figures for the duration of the performance, they returned into the audience for the final celebratory dance (as is often the case in Action Theatre today, e.g., *Mysteries and Smaller Pieces* [Living Theatre] and *Dionysus in 69* [The Performance Group]). The Masque took over from Italian public entertainments a new method of combining all known types of semiotic signs on the scene. Happenings, though more hesitant (perhaps because they have not – not yet? – had the evolutionary span of the Masque), and more suspicious of the celebratory media of speaking and singing, similarly pillage new music, plastic arts, and, in some indirect and incomplete ways, even drama and poetry. The Masques' fascination with theatrical machinery has no full parallel in Happenings, but it has cropped up in projects such as E.A.T. and Joan Littlewood's planned electronic fun palace – not to mention the modern gadgetry often present in Happenings themselves. Most important perhaps, the Masque also attempted to allegorize the audience, and its appeal, as that of any coterie "myth-play," was "a curious mixture of the popular and the esoteric; it is popular for its immediate audience, but those outside its circle have to make a conscious effort to appreciate it" (Frye 1966:282). Finally, the Masque "even at its best was an attempt rather than an achievement, but although it never quite gained in intrinsic and permanent value, it had a deep, fruitful, and lasting influence" (Welsford [1927] 1962:243–44) – not only on poetry but also on theatre, which enriched itself by incorporating many of its elements and ways of using space, music (i.e., time), and actors.

On the other hand, the late Jonsonian Masque added a danced scene which showed disruptive powers at work against the advocated harmony and which was often more striking than the celebratory scene. The basic aim of this "anti-Masque" was to enact a deadly threat to or sickness of the contemporary way of life, identified with the monarchist state, and its final triumphant recovery in the symbolic harmony of banquet and dance. The Masque often relied in both its general form and its dance patterns on a quasi-Pythagorean or Neoplatonic numerology, representing an arithmetical, geometrical, and musical harmony of spheres which symbolized the political microcosm and guaranteed its harmony. "The masque writers were bound to represent both marriage and monarchy, not as faulty human institutions, but as joyful mysteries. [...] This enforced orthodoxy led, as it was bound to do, to a stiff insincerity, very alien from the true spirit of romance" (Welsford [1927] 1962: 290–91). Unlike the more sophisticated and mediated medieval approach from which it ultimately derived, the late Masque idealized the pragmatic values held by its audience, the ruling social class. Compared to medieval dramaturgy – which was based on an Augustinian theory of salvational history – the Masque had no institutionally or mythically intrinsic *telos*. The Elizabethan history play still had the ideologically powerful, though secularized, "Tudor myth" to inform its structure, which therefore emphasized the deadly threat of civil war with only a perfunctory final communion (e.g., at the end of *Richard III*): but the Masque had to fall back on a stock morality plot and a narrow cast of types, usually from classical mythology. "The dramatist might depict life as sorrowful or ridiculous or contemptible, but in the masque absurd or malevolent beings appeared only to be put to flight by the entry of the noble, joyous and joy-bringing masquers" (Welsford [1927] 1962:366).

Reacting against new Individualist myths which celebrated a false civil community, late nineteenth-century drama began to search for more mature allegorical forms. Much of modern drama from Jarry on is an anti-Masque-like recognition of the "absurd and malevolent" as the new normality, or indeed – with Wagner's *Ring of the Nibelungs*, Ibsen's *Ghosts*, or Strindberg – of bourgeois reality as a horrifying and haunted space and time. For example, Mallarmé envisaged the future work of dramatic art as a sacramental participation in mystery, presenting the mise-en-scène of state religion.[8]

As opposed to all attempts at sacramental yea-saying comedies, the nay-saying Happenings want either to escape from capitalist society or to pull it down; they emphasize either the necessity of a nonexisting communion or the alienation of life without it (sides of the same coin, in fact). For the authors of most Happenings there is both a crying need for and a total absence of any supraindividualistic social entity in which one could believe sufficiently to celebrate its order. That is why – unlike the Masque or the early French *mascarade* and ballet – Happenings have steadfastly refused to take their cue and devices from the prevalent dramatic form, even to the point of being somewhat hysterically suspicious of its dominant medium, words, regardless of its uses. Again, numerology is very evident in Happenings, but it is based on nineteenth-century thermodynamics, implying that humanity and its affairs exist as aggregates in a mechanical, valueless universe subject to the laws of chance and large numbers (that "Welfare State of the mind" [Kaplan 1966:96]). Though Happenings often revert to ritual attitudes, their ritual is subjective and almost mythless. The "anti-Masque" stage has completely taken over. If one looked at them from a world of clear and constant values it would not be too difficult to see the world presented in the Happenings as a demonic chaos rampant with secularized monsters of ultimate neo-capitalist alienation.

4 HAPPENINGS AND THEIR TIMES – COGNITIVE AND NIHILIST ESTRANGEMENT

4.1 Effect

Most Happenings seem to have been rather unsatisfactory in their own terms – primitive or muddled, often through lack of time and money, but also through lack of clear aims. One has to insist that in Happenings, as in all spectacles, the effect depends on clarity of gestural and verbal actions, on their social meaning (different fields of possibility are not aesthetically equivalent), on the skillful performance of a coordinated series of situations, and on the overall consistency of purpose embodied in the material's selection and space/time spread: i.e., on the author's artistic point of view. The audience's possible reactions often have to be included as a margin of co-authorship in the author's point of view; this will be touched on later.

However, theoretically, if and when the above demands are met, a Happening should have a specific effect on participants. By getting drawn into a "real" event – i.e., one not taking place in a diegetic universe – the participants should experience a shock of poetic cognition directed at the performance's thematic field, and beginning with themselves and their environment. A Happening "is designed to stir the modern audience from its cozy emotional anesthesia" (Sontag 1969:275); "some specific frustrations, caused by cybernated life, required accordingly cybernated shock and catharsis" (Nam June Paik in Ay-o *et al.* 1966:24); "the highest priority must be given to the re-education of its perceptions" (Baxandall 1966:29). A Happening is, according to Richard Schechner, "(1) an attempt to bring into celebratory focus the full message-complexity of a downtown street and (2) a playing with modes of perception" (1969:148); it isolates events or images in order to revitalize them: "Deadened habits, routine images, unused sensibilities, and even places (Kaprow's highways and supermarkets) are reinfused with meaning," he concludes optimistically (1969:154). Fossilized views of reality should, when juxtaposed to "unpackaged" events, reveal them-selves "as grotesque, inadequate and dangerous."

> In a performance by the Once Theatre, bureaucratic dossiers on young people were monotonously read, while technicians encased the individ-uals, upright and nearly nude, in a box one by one between layers of plastic sheeting. They looked like frozen fish on ice, bugs in an ice tray, people

in an apartment house. The banal, aggressive or grotesque may also be aestheticized before one's eyes. In *Meat Joy* by Carolee Schneemann, the lovers, having undressed one another, paint the flesh of the other. In Ken Dewey's *Without and Within* a rough tug-of-war with audience participation is transformed into a deliberate ritual, then into dancing which ends with rock-and-roll. Hostility into beauty into joy.

(Baxandall 1966:32–3).

4.2 Baxandall's "Alienation Antidote" Hypothesis

Even if one does not share the millenarism of Dick Higgins, who programmatically states that we are "approaching the dawn of a classless society, to which separation into rigid categories is absolutely irrelevant" (1969:11–13), Happenings at their best may prefigure possible new modes of human relations and living. Hopefully, these can be construed as fragments or elements of a new aesthetics (and ethics), "the outlines of everyday life for the post-compulsive, post-manipulated man" (Baxandall 1966:33). Upon such elements, some left-wing or radical critics such as Baxandall and Schechner have based their defense of Happenings, claiming for them the hypothetical status of an antidote to existing forms of alienation (reification, desensualization) in the mass society of corporate capitalism. They argue that Happenings use special devices to overcome communication barriers in a manipulated consumer society, in an age of TV addiction, public-relations credibility gap, mass propaganda techniques marketing everything from pollutants to genocidal imperialist wars such as in Vietnam. In such a context, a re-education of audience perceptions, a depollution of senses, is most urgent; mimetic recognition (*anagnorisis*) in Happenings functions as therapy counteracting the brainwashing effects of profit-oriented life and demystifying ruling relationships both in life and on stage. They envisage Happenings exclaiming with Yvonne Rainer:

> NO to spectacle no to virtuosity no to transformations and magic and make believe no to glamor and transcendency of the star image no to the heroic no to the anti-heroic no to trash imagery no to involvement of performer or spectator no to style no to camp no to seduction of spectators by the wiles of the performer no to eccentricity no to moving or being moved.
>
> (Rainer 1965:178 [and this volume])

This leads to a fundamental question. Are Happenings really all that demystifying, or do they bear in themselves a new mystification? Do they shock for therapeutic or terroristic ends? Do they celebrate a forward-looking defiance of the ruling myth or a black mass of their own? Have they, in Schechner's terms, the cruelty of childish gratification or of adult perception? This may be a variant on the general question facing critics of the establishment or state power machines – namely, how much destruction is necessary for a reconstruction – but the answer has to be found in each separate instance. Artaud's and Camus' ambiguous plague imagery is clearly unable to help us here. It seems therefore most useful to approach an answer in terms of the other main figure and tradition in modern theatre, Brecht.

4.3 Brecht, and Happenings, and Their Times
Brecht's work is the major example in this century of assimilating a plebeian spectacle tradition into drama. Logically, its substratum of popular fairs, cabaret, burlesque, and other spectacles – what I have called the Azdak-Schweik "look from underneath" of lower-class demystification (1967)[9] – has some affinities with Happenings. He also passed through a phase of writing for a closed and homogeneous group, during which his aim, in the "plays for learning," was to make the participants more active and critical, with the audience being secondary or unnecessary. More generally, he felt that routine actions and situations representing the anthropological commonplaces of our way of life should be estranged in order to expose their alienated quality. Happenings estrange basic conventions of spectacle such as entering by an aisle or sitting in front of the performance area. They also lift everyday commonplaces – "the visit to the supermarket, eating TV dinner, TV, the preliminaries of sex" (Baxandall 1966:32) – out of the "ordinary" aura and into the focus of attentive scrutiny. They very rarely – and this is a clear weakness – focus their attention on political or economic relation-ships of any kind: Happenings are more than a little socially inbred. Nonetheless, they theatricalize the audience and its relationships: the audience becomes to a certain extent its own spectacle. This may be in a way a logical extension of Brecht's approach; yet the methodology of Brechtian dramaturgy and of Happenings differs considerably, and for good reason.

The comparison is crucial because Brecht started out (1916–1928) as a Villonesque or Rimbaudesque nihilist. The post-World War I upheavals in Europe, the exemplary experience of the Leninist phase of the Bolshevik revolution, proved to him that human relations – i.e., man's "nature" – could be changed by intelligent and organized, though painful, intervention. After *The Threepenny Opera* he ceased writing for bourgeois audiences, however liberal or dissident they might be, and turned to an audience of workers and schoolchildren (1929–1934). At that point, he began functioning as a partisan or guerrilla in the Lukácsian sense of a creator, who coordinates his actions with a disciplined revolutionary "main body," but proceeds on his own responsibility, autonomous yet not independent. (This epicyclic way of operating makes nonsense out of the division between inner-directed and outer-directed action, which has befuddled so many liberal critics of Brecht before and after Esslin.) These experiences fused the nihilist clean sweep of the artists – the familiar which is systematically rendered incomprehensible to the senses – with Marx's gnoseology and dialectics which used the resulting view of alienation not as an object of subjective empathy but of cognition. Even after 1933, Brecht never forsook this synthesis. Indeed, his path through the "didactic" phase, and, in particular, the critically much undervalued impact of his new audiences, made it possible for Brecht to return in his mature phase to a new concreteness enriched by insight into the inner model of empirical existence, the "events behind the events."

The Happenings' authors' critical dates were not 1917 and 1933 but 1945–1947 and the period from the mid-1950s to the mid-1960s. The first period is the time when many of them had their first conscious experiences of social relations. They grew up in a U.S. turning from contradiction-filled Rooseveltian antifascism to the cold war outside, and McCarthyite repressions and stagnation inside. The second period is the breakdown of that stagnation in an inconclusive flurry of shocked recognitions of America's papered-over contradictions. Happenings were created in this period and shared its inconclusiveness. The New York *bohéme* lacked available or persuasive foreign models, lacked strong native workers' or Socialist movements, and was subjected to new and more pervasive methods of mass persuasion based on the lure of prosperity. For these and other reasons the Happenings' authors did not emerge out of nihilism into a universe of man enmeshed into political economy and into a theatre interested in civic responsibility. Instead, they emerged as an isolated little group catering mainly to each other: their lack of interest in audience was formally analogous but sociologically poles apart from Brecht's second phase. Rejecting American capitalism but not believing in the possibility of a humanizing social change, their Happenings were as a rule more pessimistic than Brecht's plays. Together with much contemporary European drama, they postulated an absurd, meaningless reality:

> there is the traffic jam, the construction job, the bus that gets four flat tires all at once for no readily explainable reason, the train that stops mysteriously in the middle of the tunnel under the East River. To the average person, these might be minor tragedies; a happening person would exult that the normal, mundane order of things had been suspended or changed vividly.
>
> (Hansen 1965:34).

Faced with such attitudes, one recalls the witty definition of the absurd as "a dialectical situation seen by a masochist" (Eco 1967:237).

4.4 Cognitive and Nihilist Estrangement

Comparing the above quote from Al Hansen to, say, Brecht's stance toward a traffic accident in his essay "The Street Scene", it becomes evident what Happenings assume: that the techniques of mass persuasion have badly weakened the normative powers of reason, and the only approach left is to subject people to a nonexplicit, more primitive and aggressive kind of experience, which will reorient them through "direct perception." The premises of such a proceeding are strictly magical: Professor Schechner calls it the infantile celebratory myth of "social reconstruction through sensory awakening" (1969:155). In other words, the Happenings' authors expanded their magic nihilism in the only other direction available when one rejects the Brechtian horizon: toward a religious, noncognitive estrangement. Taking a ritual and mystical rather than a cognitive approach, Happenings therefore opposed *nihilist estrangement* to Brecht's cognitive dialectics. Of course, it might sometimes be useful to think of these oppositions as polar possibilities present in each significant Happening, and reduced to the nihilist pole only in the less significant ones. It would then be the task of a sensitive critic to characterize each particular performance on its own merits, differentiating anew for each singular case (certainly *Fotodeath*, for example, is not predominantly absurd or nihilist: it shows absurdity up).[10]

Brecht himself did the spade work in defining a noncognitive estrangement by pointing to Asian and generally pre-Individualistic theatre techniques. Such estrangement "from the right" is nihilist in a religious rather than a political sense – a very American form of nativistic movement (see Schechner 1969:155). The most sophisticated nihilist religion is, of course, Zen Buddhism, and a quote from the Zen precept of Gautama Buddha in his fundamental text on contemplation and meditation, *Satti-patthana-sutti*, immediately calls to mind the technique of primitive Happenings:

> How does the anachorete carry out the exercise of contemplating the body in the body? Having gone into a wood, at the foot of a tree [...] the anchorete sits with feet crossed, holding his body in a vertical position, with fixed attention. He breathes in with full attention, and breathes out with full attention. Drawing in a long breath, he knows: "I am drawing in a long breath," drawing in a short breath, he knows: "I am drawing in a short breath." Drawing out a long breath, he knows: "I am drawing out a long breath," drawing out a short breath, he knows: "I am drawing out a short breath"; that is the way to exercise. "I will breathe conscious of my whole body"; that is the way to exercise.

(Compare Kaprow's *Calling* [1965:203–10; and in this volume].)
Buddhist contemplation paradoxically uses estrangement and a perverted
form of cognition to advance to Nirvana; the beatific vision of the
discontinuous flux of things is related to a consciousness of the limits of
philosophical humanism and of the positive meaning of alienation. As
such it is the horizon of all consistent nihilist estrangement – it may be
unnecessary to mention how strong an attraction Zen Buddhism
has provided for the social group from which Happenings too have
sprung.

Even if one assumes that Happenings are not predominantly a new
mystification of the Zen type but a necessary forerunner of cognitive
estrangement, "a greater art emerges from the dramatization of historical
reason, than from theatre historically condemned to prepare the ground
for reason's resurgence" (Baxandall 1966:35).

5 SOME WORDS AT THE END, BUT NOT IN CONCLUSION

Happenings have forced us to rethink a number of basic spectacle
concepts. Their nondiegetic organization leads us to reexamine a concept
of dramaturgic fable as an integrated use of nonverbal materials and
nonnarrative relationships. The very concept of theatre has to be
redefined in order to include a number of genres hitherto neglected as too
vulgar (*vulgus* meaning "people") for official aesthetics. This can only
lead to a more precise definition and delimitation of drama and other
canonic genres, and have a quite salutary effect. However, when the
impact of Happenings works toward a simple-minded denial of the
relevance of drama, fable, etc., in our times, sterility ensues. The struggle
between cognitive and nihilist attitudes is at its clearest in the theoretical
domain, which by nature does not tolerate much vagueness. Nevertheless, such sterility is not a consequence of the rise of Happenings, but
of their context. Happenings are in part a sociocultural document: but
above all they show the potentiality of new forms and materials for
theatrical communication and challenge our aesthetic.

Yet the uncertain status of Happenings in theatrical theory and practice
is to a large extent due to intrinsic problems of their development. As I
tried to point out in this essay, their point of view or principle of
allegorical stylization is unclear. In the allegorical mode an antecedent
situation is juxtaposed to the present fable, the two being connected by
a belief, purpose, or ideal, which provides the point of view. In order for
an allegorical work of art to succeed, the artist derives his authority both
from personally creating a new structure and a new meaning, and from
an antecedent ideal which is in some way classical. That ideal is as a rule

absent from Happenings, which are concerned primarily (in a way that is perhaps understandable but nonetheless crippling) with nay-saying – or with a vague and general yea-saying which is equivalent to an absence (see 1.31).

Furthermore, to their contact-magic premise of human reorientation through "direct perception," I want to oppose two questions: (1) does this counter-magic mean playing the game of the opinion-manipulators, albeit in the contrary direction? (2) does this mean playing the game on the terrain of the establishment brainwashers, where they are much more powerful? One may discount the first question as liberal relativism. But the second one surely implies that Happenings techniques can be antidotal only if and when TV programming, newspaper and film financing and distribution, town planning, and so on are controlled by their producers and consumers – and that in the meantime the alienating powers of the system are such that "live" performances can do little to influence it.

I believe the greatest possibilities for Happenings techniques do in fact lie in a diffusion through media such as film and TV, which are already using some of them, e.g., in *Laugh-In*. Obviously, the exploration of such possibilities even now is at worst a worthwhile pursuit in avant-garde finger-exercises, and, at best, it might be of great influence as a laboratory experiment in new perception.

The foregoing discussion of Happenings may make clearer why they did not outlast their sociopolitical moment. A magico-religious stance is not able to cope with the world (or the U.S.) of today, and it cannot create a major spectacle form. Such a form can, I believe, arise only if it is steeped in and adopts the ideal of philosophical humanism. As Lukács, Merleau-Ponty, and many others have noted, present-day humanism no longer takes the side of man against his body, of his spirit against his language, of values against facts; man is not given, he *becomes* in the process by which the body becomes a gesture, the language a deed, and the facts a point of view (see Lukács 1969; Merleau-Ponty 1960). Adopting a humanist point of view, a new theatre coming after Happenings would have to face some basic dichotomies they left as legacy: between emotion and reason, facts and values, objects and persons, estrangement and cognition, wit and language. The new theatre would have to acknowledge openly that the nexus of the sensorium is, after all, the brain.[11] This means above all that Happenings have not faced the use of language as verbal poetry and not as noise. As Lukács pointed out, the spoken word, the conceptualized sound, is of paramount importance in establishing a continuity between past and present: "The loss of word means a loss of memory" (1968:78). Loss of contact with the past leads to a perpetual point-consciousness shifting with but never dilating beyond the fleeting point of the present: it is thus equivalent to the loss of contact with *future* too. An allegorical genre without memory of antecedent and without anticipation of posteriority must flounder in pure naturalism and phenomenology: the meaningful word seems to make the difference between nihilism and cognition. Its use would probably entail structural principles more sophisticated than simple permutation or quasi-circular repetition. In fact, this seems to be where we've been in the last few years.

Schechner believed that the delicate balance "between revitalization and fantasy, control and freedom, reflection and participation, complexity and simplification [...] can be maintained" (1969:155). Unfortunately, I think we must recognize that Happenings have achieved this balance only in exceptional cases. The failure to achieve it, because of subjectivity, imprecision, and dogmatic blindness to history, has prevented them from becoming more than a possibly fertile footnote in the history of theatrical spectacle. But then, as I remarked earlier, books and professional periodicals have been and are being devoted to less significant footnotes. And the dossier is not quite closed: the implications of this genre may hold some surprises yet.

NOTES

1. Apart from the classical approaches of Aristotle's *Poetics*, Diderot's *De la Poésie dramatique* and some other writings, Lessing's *Lakoon*, and Brecht's *Schriften zum Theatre*, the following secondary literature has been most useful in these "reflections" (and some of my conclusions and indeed terms are obviously indebted to them, whether I agree or disagree with them): Ay-o *et al.* (1966); Baxandall (1966); Eco (1967); Higgins (1969); Kaplan (1966); Kaprow (1966a, 1967); Kirby (1965a, 1965c); Lebel (1967); Schechner (1969); Sontag (1969); Tarrab (1968).

   Let me also make it clear that, though I have seen some performances billed as Happenings in Europe and America, I have worked basically from scenarios and descriptions, just as if discussing the commedia dell'arte, since my chief interest is in this case not that of a chronicler but that of a "socio-formalist" theoretician of spectacle.
2. See an account of it in Kirby (1965b:34–36 [and in this volume]), and of its direction by Judith Malina in Biner (1964:52–53).
3. Cp. Schechner on Ann Halprin's dance-Happening *Esposizione*: "the similarity of one human being to another and the ineluctable unity which comes from a group doing roughly the same thing together" (1969:149). Kaprow himself lucidly notes that his symbols "are so general and so archetypical that actually almost everyone knows vaguely about these things," since he tries to keep them "universal, simple, and basic" (in Kirby 1965a:50 [and in this volume]).
4. Oldenburg himself mentions that in *Fotodeath* "events repeated themselves in superimposed lines of movement," which seems a brief painterly

way of saying much the same thing I was trying to get at above.

5. The main works dealing with this theory are Shklovsky (1921, 1923a, 1923b); Tinyanov (1929); Tomashevsky (1925). Most quotations have been taken from the excellent study by Professor Victor Erlich (1955); see also Wellek and Warren (1956, Chapter 17). Another English-language book, *Russian Formalist Criticism: Four Essays* (Lemon and Reis 1965) has gaps and terminological difficulties.

6. Kirby developed the hypothesis of Happenings being defined by a performance nonmatrixed by time, place, or character in the introduction to his anthology *Happenings* (1965a [and in this volume]); Kaplan was referring to the restatement in Kirby's article "The New Theatre." I would like to stress that though I disagree with Kirby in some basic aspects, I found his notion and term of matrixing a really useful contribution to a not merely impressionistic discussion of the genre.

7. Souriau has enlarged on this score in several works, for example, in his presentation of the anthology *L'Univers filmique* (n.d), and in the well-known *Les Deux cent mille situations dramatiques* (1950).

8. See Block, *Mallarmé and the Symbolist Drama* (1963:86). I already mentioned affinities with Expressionist, Surrealist, and Futurist drama, and Kirby has gone much further in following *one* tradition behind the Happenings (the so-called Dadaist one) in the introduction to *Happenings* (1965a [and in this volume]).

9. This part of the essay owes much to Lee Baxandall's article "Beyond Brecht: the Happenings" (1966); though I am dubious about his basic stance, he had the perspicacity of first posing and problematizing the crucial comparison of the two estrangements – Brecht's and the Happenings'. It also owes much to discussions with Richard Schechner, before and after his quoted book.

10. See on the other hand Oldenburg's remarks on his *Gayety*, a very interesting manifestation of the tension which went into the making of that "civic spectacle":

> In *Gayety* I want to create a civic report on the community of Chicago, in the way I see it. [. . .] I think of O'Henry's or anyone else's municipal report, sociological studies etc. but that mine is poetic/ satiric/symbolic. The enigmatic portions may be taken to be the situation of the spirit in the community, often these have a violent turn. The relation of the incidents is fortuitous as is the case in real life. [. . .] Unfortunately I am limited to typicalities, but the spectator may imagine the numbers. The piece closes with a Finale, an apotheosis, in the form of a destruction which always seems appropriate in which the forces of the community are released functionlessly in relieving chaos.
>
> (in Kirby 1965a: 234–35)

11. I am indebted for this observation, as well as for stimulating my interest in a possible parallel between Masque and Happening, to Professor Donald F. Theall of McGill University, and to his unpublished manuscript of an address to McGill alumni from fall 1968 which he kindly allowed me to refer to.

REFERENCES

Ay-o *et al.* (1966) *Manifestos*. New York: Something Else Press.

Baxandall, Lee (1966) "Beyond Brecht: the Happenings." *Studies in the Left*, January–February.

Biner, Pierre (1964) *Le Living Theatre*. Lausanne: La Cité.

Block, Haskell (1963) *Mallarmé and the Symbolist Drama*. Detroit: Wayne State University Press.

Cunliffe, John W. (1907) "Italian Prototype of the Masque and Dumb Show." *PMLA* XXII.

Eco, Umberto (1967) *Opera aperta*. Milan: Bompiani.

Erlich, Victor (1955) *Russian Formalism*. The Hague.

Frye, Northrop (1957) *Anatomy of Criticism*. Princeton, NJ: Princeton University Press.

Hansen, Al (1965) *A Primer of Happenings & Time/Space Art*. New York: Something Else Press.

Hegel, Georg Wilhem (1963) [1862] *Lectures on the History of Philosophy*. London: Routledge and Kegan Paul.

Higgins, Dick (1965) *The Tart, or Miss America*. *TDR* 10, 2 (T30):133.

—— (1969) *FOEW&OMBWHNW*. New York: Something Else Press.

Kaplan, Donald M. (1966) "Character and Theatre." *TDR* 10, 4 (T32):93–108.

Kaprow Allan (1965) "*Calling*." *TDR* 10, 2 (T30):203–10.

—— (1966a) *Some Recent Happenings*. New York: Something Else Press.

—— (1966b) *Assemblages, Environments & Happenings*. New York: Harry N. Abrams.

—— (1967) *Untitled Essay and Other Works*. New York: Something Else Press.

Kirby, Michael (1965a) *Happenings*. New York: E.P. Dutton and Co., Inc.

—— (1965b) "Allan Kaprow's *Eat*." *TDR* 10, 2 (T30): 45–49.

—— (ed.) (1965c) *Tulane Drama Review* 10, 2 (T30). Special issue on Happenings.

Lebel; Jean-Jacques (1967) *Le Happening*. Paris: Donöel & Les Lettres Nouvelles.

Lemon, Lee T., and Marion J. Reis, (eds) (1965) *Russian Formalist Criticism: Four Essays*, Lincoln: University of Nebraska Press.

Lukács, Georg (1968) "Gedanken zú einer Aesthetik des Kinos." In *Schriften zur Literatursoziologie*. Neuwied: Luchterhand.

—— (1969) *Geschichte und Klassenbewusstsein*. Neuwied: Luchterhand.

Merleau-Ponty, Maurice (1960) *Signes*. Paris: Gallimard.

Oldenburg, Claes (1965) "*Fotodeath*." *TDR* 10, 2 (T30):85–93.

Rainer, Yvonne (1965) "Some retrospective notes on a dance for 10 people and 12 mattresses called *Parts of Some Sextets*, performed at the Wadsworth Atheneum, Hartford, Connecticut, and Judson Memorial Church, New York, in March, 1965." *TDR* 10, 2 (T30):168–78.

Schechner, Richard (1969) *Public Domain*. New York: Bobbs-Merrill.

Shklovsky, Viktor (1921) *Rozanov*. Petrograd.

———— (1923a) *Khod konya*. Berlin.

———— (1923b) *Literatura i kinematograf*. Berlin.

Sontag, Susan (1969) [1966] *Against Interpretation*. New York: Farrar, Straus & Giroux.

Souriau, Etienne (1950) *Les Deux cent mille situations dramatiques*. Paris: Flammarion.

———— (1962) *Les grands problèmes de l'esthétique théâtrale*. Paris.

———— (n.d.) *L'Univers filmique*. Paris.

Suvin, Darko (1967) "The Mirror and the Dynamo." *TDR* 12, 1 (T37):56–68.

Tarrab, Gilbert (1968) "Le happening." *Revue d'histoire du théâtre*. Special Issue.

Tinyanov, Yury (1929) *Arkhaisty i novatory*. Leningrad.

Tomashevsky, Boris (1925) *Teoriya literatury: Poetika*. Moscow-Leningrad.

Wellek, René, and Austin Warren (1956) *Theory of Literature*. New York: Harcourt Brace.

Welsford, Enid (1962) [1927] *The Court Masque*. New York: Russell and Russell.

31

HAPPENINGS IN EUROPE
Trends, Events, and Leading Figures

Günter Berghaus

INTRODUCTION

Pop Art, New Realism, and Proto-Happenings

After the restoration of peace on the European continent in 1945, artists turned their backs on figurative representation of reality. Abstract Expressionism, Art Informel, and Tachism became the dominant trends in the first postwar decade, assuming a position of virtual monopoly in Europe and the USA. In the mid-1950s a new development began to take shape – figurative paintings inspired by the new urban culture of the postwar period. What started off as a faint countertrend to high-modernist abstraction became a rising tide, for which Lawrence Alloway in 1958 coined the term "Pop Art" (1958:84–85). Artists as far afield as London, New York, Paris, Düsseldorf, and Milan turned toward a new form of realism without developing much of a group mentality or common program. Each possessed a recognizable, individual stance, yet all shared many concerns, which Henry Geldzahler defined at a symposium at the Museum of Modern Art in New York:

> The new art draws on everyday objects and images. They are isolated from their ordinary context, and typified and intensified. What we are left with is a heightened awareness of the object and image, *and* of the context from which they have been ripped.
>
> (Geldzahler 1963)

Pop Art was a reflection of postwar consumer society. The flood of new consumer products, the rising tide of images produced by a proliferating media industry, the bewildering barrage of sensations and visual stimuli assaulting people's nerves: all this was an experience abstract art could not adequately give expression to. The media-dominated urban culture offered untried themes and techniques to artists. Consequently, a new generation of figurative painters turned to recycling the motifs of advertisements, billboards, magazines, newspapers,

comics, photographs, television, and cinema. However, merely reproduc-
ing the current urban reality with painterly means was for some a rather
meaningless undertaking. "I think a picture is more like the real world
when it is made out of the real world," Robert Rauschenberg discovered
(in Tomkins [1965] 1976:193–94). Like many others, he began to work
with available material and included fragments of ordinary reality in his
pictures. Artists embraced the multiplicity and layered fragmentation of
media-duplicated imagery and transformed the ephemeral art of popular
magazines and pulp movies into works where the traditional opposition
of high and low art lost its significance. Andy Warhol neatly summed up
this attitude:

> The Pop artists did images that anybody walking down Broadway could
> recognize in a split second – comics, picnic tables, men's trousers,
> celebrities, shower curtains, refrigerators, Coke bottles – all the great
> modern things that the Abstract Expressionists tried so hard not to notice
> at all.
>
> (Warhol 1980:3)

While American artists embraced wholeheartedly the economic and
cultural changes of the postwar period, the attitude of European artists
toward their sources of inspiration was far more critical. Although it
would be simplistic to say that the American artists glorified the new
consumer culture, they can neither be regarded as politically engaged
critics of the "American way of life." Andy Warhol, for example,
consistently emphasized that his works were not intended as a social
comment (see Warhol 1989:458). American critics emphasized the
affirmative character of Pop Art: "Its social effect is simply to reconcile
us to a world of commodities, banalities and vulgarities" (Geldzahler
1963). Alan Solomon commented on this transformation of "trash" into
"art": "They [the artists] have done so not in a spirit of contempt or social
criticism or self-conscious snobbery, but out of an affirmative and
unqualified commitment to the present circumstance and to a fantastic
new wonderland, or, more properly, Disneyland" (1963:n.p.). Jim Dine,
when asked about the political dimension of his works, was slightly more
ambivalent:

> I'm certainly not changing the world. People confuse this social business
> with Pop Art – that it's a comment. Well, if it's art, who cares if it's a
> comment. [...] I'm involved with formal elements. You've got to be; I
> can't help it. But any work of art, if it's successful, is also going to be a
> comment on what it's about.
>
> (in Swenson 1963:62)

Given the diverse viewpoints expressed by artists and critics on the "meaning" of Pop Art, one might rightly assume that this evasion of clear political commentary was typical of the American branch of the movement. One can extrapolate from their paintings an attitude of humorous detachment or reverential embracement, tongue-in-cheek satire or detached neutrality. American Pop Art was certainly not didactic. The paintings were as ambivalent and contradictory as the individual reactions of artists and viewers toward the social reality depicted.

The European Pop artists, on the other hand, were far more outspoken in their critique of the brave new world of modern technology and mass-media culture. Their transformation of popular imagery involved devices that were similar to Brecht's *Verfremdungseffekt*. Without forcing one singular viewpoint on the recipient, they addressed a range of questions with an open-minded yet critical stance, inviting the viewer to participate in the reflective process and to develop an independent position on the subject matter presented. Rather than presenting the pure "spectacle" of mass culture, these artists raised questions on the persuasion techniques of advertising and TV culture. Images were not taken at face value; illusionary reality was revealed as fabricated. In fact, it became a major concern of European Pop artists to create an awareness of the dangers inherent in a popular culture where the "real" world is transformed into an image of reality that seems more perfect and desirable than the originary reality. The process-oriented nature of this transformation could of course be best captured in performance. Happenings[1] were a natural outcome of the Pop artists' concern with the problems of representation and with the connection between art and life.

Pop Art began in England, where the postwar economic depression, followed by a prolonged period of austerity, contrasted markedly with the consumer boom in the United States. Although Britain could boast some great painters in the immediate postwar era (e.g., Francis Bacon, Graham Sutherland, Lucian Freud), the art scene on the whole was rather unadventurous and was best characterized by the cozy landscape pictures of the St. Ives colony. Hence, a new generation of artists looked across the Atlantic for the kind of inspiration they had received in the past from Paris. The American society of abundance was regarded as a cultural alternative to declining postimperial Britain. American magazines, music, films, and literature were avidly received by intellectuals and artists. Soon, they turned their attention to prepackaged convenience food, brand-name consumer products, and streamline technology. Following the first meetings of the Independent Group at London's Institute of Contemporary Arts (ICA) in 1952 and the thematic exhibitions "Parallel of Art and Life" (1953) and "Man, Machine and Motion" (1955), the depiction of contemporary popular culture included sophisticated analyses of the conventions and implicit messages of modern mass-media culture.

Across the channel, a similar change in attitude toward the gap between high and low art, between reality and the representation of reality in art and popular culture had set in. The Continental-European equivalent to Pop Art is usually referred to as "New Realism" and was centered around a semiofficial "school" headed by the critic and theoretician, Pierre Restany (see Restany 1968, 1970, 1971, 1986). He founded the group on 26 October 1960 in the house of Yves Klein, together with Arman, François Dufrêne, Daniel Spoerri, Jean Tinguely, Klein, Martial Raysse, Jacques de la Villeglé, and Raymond Hains, later to be joined by Niki de Saint-Phalle, Christo, and Gérard Deschamps. He penned three influential manifestoes[2] and organized several exhibitions dedicated to the diverse trends of *Nouveau Réalisme*. It was largely through his organizational and publicity skills that the term New Realism began to be used as an umbrella covering the whole field of artists who sought inspiration from "modern nature" – the new realities of mass media, publicity, and popular imagery. They formed their collages or assemblages from found and processed fragments of reality and materials not commonly associated with high art. The appropriation of objective elements of the everyday world and their *presentation* in compressed objects that expressed the material poetics of reality followed a completely different philosophy from the *representation* of reality through the means of conventional realism. They elaborated a new methodology of perceiving and representing the objective quality of contemporary urban life.

In July 1961, Restany organized a First Festival of New Realism in Nice which, on the evening of 13 July, included a series of action-performances in the garden of Roseland Abbey. Arman presented *Anger*, where he destroyed a chair and table and fixed the debris on a panel in the exact position of their collapse. Tinguely gave a demonstration of his revolving water fountain, Mimmo Rotella recited phonetic poems, and Hains consumed a fenced-in pudding (*les entremets de la palissade*, an unusually shaped cake baked specially for this purpose). De Saint-Phalle performed *Surprise Shoots*, in which she aimed with her rifle at a panel containing glass objects, plastic bags of paint, and smoke bombs.[3] Even more spectacular was the second festival, held in February 1963 at the Neue Galerie im Künstlerhaus in Munich. Apart from Arman's *Anger* and de Saint-Phalle's *Surprise Shoot*, Rotella demonstrated his technique of poster tearing and Christo erected a temporary monument with metal beer-kegs.[4]

Although Restany had organized two immensely important joint exhibitions of French New Realists and American Pop artists (July 1961 at the Galerie Rive Droite in Paris, and in October 1962 at the Sydney Janis Gallery in New York), the beginnings of the Happenings genre in the work of Allan Kaprow were unknown to the Paris Action performers. Restany commented on this by calling the New Realism Festival a

> manifesto-gesture [which] finds a place on the royal road of those individual happenings with which the prehistory of the New Realism is marked. All the New Realists, moreover, have had this innate sense of the spectacle, of communicative extroversion, of the "event." [...] These action-performances are demonstrations, the purpose of which is to provoke the direct, spontaneous participation of the public in the process of group communication. Action is a labor, its result is a "work." In direct contrast to the Happening, New Realist action does not exhaust its meaning in the course of its unfolding. At the end of the performance the tangible trace remains. [...] The Paris public was incapable of reacting positively to what appeared to it to be a persistent provocation. It had to await the introduction in France in 1963 of the formula "Happening Made in USA" before rethinking the whole problem of the action-performance.
>
> (Restany 1971:247–48; see also 1983:49–58)

YVES KLEIN

A key figure in this movement toward performance was Yves Klein. Since 1949, he had experimented with paintings in pure color, and in 1955 he found the ideal pigment combination for this, the International Klein Blue. It was used not only for his paintings, but also to impregnate objects, sculptures, and sponges. In 1957/58 Klein developed a number of projects which translated his ideas from the materially based world of painting and sculpture into the world of immateriality and pure sensibility. In his "pneumatic period," Klein moved more and more into live Actions to stimulate human sensibility. One of them, called *Aerostatic Sculptures*, was performed on 10 May 1958 on Place Saint-Germain-de-Près. One thousand and one blue balloons were released into the Parisian sky to let the immaterial sensibility permeate and impregnate the world.[5]

Together with Tinguely, Klein constructed a painting machine, and in 1958 he experimented for the first time with "living brushes." A demonstration of his paint Actions employing human bodies to apply pigment to canvas was given in his Paris flat on 23 February 1960. His wife, Rotraut Uecker, covered a model's breasts, belly, and thighs with blue paint. Then, following Klein's instructions, she pressed the woman five times against a sheet of paper that had been pinned to the wall. Restany, who was present that evening, coined the term "Anthropometry" for this type of painting (see Restany 1974:93–94; 1982).

On 9 March 1960, at the Galerie Internationale d'Art Contemporain in Paris, Klein gave the first public presentation of his *Anthropometries of the Blue Epoch*. Twenty musicians and singers performed his *Monotonous Symphony* (consisting of twenty minutes of a single note and twenty minutes of silence), while Klein applied blue paint to the bodies of three nude models and directed them to create imprints on the canvases stretched out on the floor.

In the following years, more than 150 paintings of this kind were produced, using different methods for applying the pigments to canvas. They ranged from careful impressions of individual parts of the bodies, to full imprints created through dancing and rolling on the canvas, to the large *batailles*, or battlefields, of several models fighting with each other on a canvas.

On 27 November 1960, Klein announced a number of theatre, film, and ballet projects[6] in a one-off newspaper, *Dimanche: Le journal d'un seul jour*. One example of his *Théâtre du vide* (Theatre of Void) was his proposed *Sensibilité pure* (Pure Sensibility): The spectators enter the auditorium and take their seats. A man steps in front of the curtain and announces that all visitors will have to be gagged and chained to their seats. After this has been effected, the curtain rises and the lights go down. Pure void fills the space and a strange, monotonous sound pervades the theatre. A couple of nude women walk through the stalls to ensure that everybody is still safely tied up. After half an hour the sound fades and the audience is confronted with half an hour of pure silence. Then the lights go up and the spectators are released from their chains. The performance is over (Klein 1960:1–2).

PIERO MANZONI

Because of his untimely death at the age of 34, Klein did not realize his theatrical projects. The same, unfortunately, applies to his Italian friend Piero Manzoni, whose activities covered barely more than five years, 1957 to 1963. Manzoni came to art after having studied philosophy. His desire to overcome the limitations of abstractionism first led him to Informel paintings, where "art had abandoned representation to the delirium of gesture and to the jubilation of materials" (Celant 1991:13). Art Informel was a term coined in 1950 by the critic Michel Tapié. It was a late-modernist style of painting characterized by a spontaneous, intuitive treatment of the canvas that offered a seismographic reflection of the artist's subconscious states of mind and therefore stood in contrast to the intellectually controlled forms of abstraction employed in the previous period. After 1954, much of the same art was also referred to as *Tachism* because of the blots and patches this method of painting produced on the canvas.

Manzoni called his paintings *Achromes*. They were inspired by Lucio Fontana's method of treating the canvas with various tools and instruments in order to emphasize the material quality of its surface. While Fontana operated with the folds, seams, and creases of the "visual flesh" of the canvas, Manzoni covered his canvases with a support spread, molded them like a relief, and attached to them a variety of materials, such as cotton, fiber, felt, fur, and polystyrene.

Art Informel fostered Manzoni's wish to give up painting altogether and to express the ephemeral and transient gesture in pure event art. In his essay "The Concept of Painting," Manzoni asserted:

> Everything must be sacrificed to the possibility of discovering this need to assimilate one's own gestures. [. . . Painting] is no longer valid for what it recalls, explains or expresses (it is more a question of what it founds), and it neither requires nor is able to be explained as an allegory of a physical process: it is valid only insofar as it is: being.
>
> (Manzoni [1957] 1991:82)

In 1959, Manzoni moved away from his achromatic paintings and embarked on a line of research centered on conceptual and performative principles. In spring 1959, he mentioned for the first time his plan to sign the bodies of friends and fellow artists and to present them as artworks. Later that year he produced his *Bodies of Air*. They consisted of wooden boxes containing a balloon and a metallic base. The balloon could be inflated by the purchaser and exhibited on the base, thereby becoming a work of art. If Manzoni himself inflated the balloon (at a price of £300 per liter of breath) the work was called *The Artist's Breath*. In 1959, he published the first issue of the magazine *Azimuth* and later in the year opened a gallery in Milan with the same name. Both the magazine and the gallery served as a forum for his artistic ideas and as a link to the many international artists who sought to overcome the dominant abstractionist trends. His main collaborators in America were Rauschenberg and Jasper Johns; in Germany, the ZERO group; and in France, Yves Klein.

On 21 July 1960, Manzoni presented at the Azimut gallery *The Consumption of Dynamic Art by the Public Devouring Art*. He boiled a number of eggs and distributed them to the invited audience after having signed them with his thumb print. The exhibition lasted for seventy minutes and, by the end of it, all works had been consumed (see Manzoni [1961] 1973). The performance was an ironic statement on the role of the artist and of art in consumer society. But there were also many spiritual undertones: the symbolic significance of eggs as a source of life and germination was combined with references to the Last Supper and other mystical and Christian rituals.

On 22 April 1961, Manzoni presented in his gallery the first of his seventy-one *Living Sculptures*. He signed people on the arm or back and certified on a receipt that "X has been signed by my hand and is therefore, from this date on, to be considered an authentic and true work of art." He also designed plans for a new type of theatre building, the spherical Placentarium, which was originally planned for a production of one of Otto Piene's *Light Ballets*.[7] The project aimed at "placing the audience in a genuinely leading role" and providing them with a continuous supply of acoustical, visual, and tactile sensations. Spectators would enter a labyrinth composed of numerous cells controlled by a computer and, as the "subjects" of the performance, would determine the itinerary and the different sensations they would expose themselves to.

Manzoni's most famous and certainly most notorious Action came in May 1961 when he produced and packaged ninety tins of *Artist's Shit*. The conserves were sold by weight for the equivalent of the day's price of gold. Bernhard Aubertin happened to surprise Manzoni during the "production" of the shit cans and was told:

> I was in the toilet working, producing *Artist's Shit* to sell. If the potential buyer of one of my shit cans finds the price too high, I suggest he buys it in exactly the weight he wants, wrapped in a piece of toilet paper, after I have scooped it out of the toilet bowl with a spoon.
>
> (Aubertin 1968:n.p.)

Manzoni's revolutionary body of work was prescient of conceptual and performance art of the 1970s. He shared Duchamp's taste for irony and argued with him that there could not be a work of art that was not also a reflection on the myth of art and on the historical condition under which it was produced. Manzoni utilized the human figure and, in particular, his own body as a Readymade. It did not serve as a vessel for subjective expression, but was regarded as a valid artwork in itself. Manzoni deified himself in his corporeal and material existence. His own body was the focal point where art and life merged. Here, physicality asserted itself and did not need molding. The actuality of living and being mattered more to him than symbolic communication. In 1960, he wrote: "There is nothing to be said. There is only to be, there is only to live."

What's left behind of Manzoni's creations are nothing but traces of his existence: his blood, breath, feces, fingerprints. They are a reminder of a short life that *was* art. Manzoni did not deny the status of the artist as creative genius. There were, in fact, rather Platonic aspects in his work, which often went unnoticed under the witticism and humor contained in his creations. The shit cans were, of course, a gesture of protest against the commercialization of artistic production and its commodification on the art market. But not all of his works can simply be regarded as neo-Dadaist gestures. His *Breath Sculptures*, for example, underlined the Utopian and idealistic aspects contained in them: breath (*pneuma*) is the divine inspiration that connects the human and divine world. It is an expression of the most noble and spiritual part of the artist's soul and genius (see Celant 1991:21, 36). The process of creation relies on this "spiritual" element, which can only be given form in gestural actions or performances. The resulting traces are nothing but a reminder of the act of creation: "Once a gesture has been made, the work becomes thereafter a documentation on the advent of an artistic fact" (Manzoni [1956] 1975:73).

THE ZERO GROUP IN DÜSSELDORF

In 1957, Otto Piene, Heinz Mack, and Günther Uecker founded the group ZERO as an informal organization of young artists living and working in Düsseldorf and the Rhineland (see Piene and Barrett 1973). All of them were interested in an "expansion of art and the interpenetration of art and life" (Piene in Galerie Heseler 1972). They entertained close contacts with other artists who were similarly opposed to abstractionism and Art Informel, especially Manzoni, Klein, Tinguely, Arman, Spoerri, Fontana, and Max Bill. The name ZERO was chosen

> not as an expression of nihilism or a neo-Dada gag, but as a word indicating a zone of silence and of pure possibilities for a new beginning as at a countdown when rockets take off – ZERO is the incommensurable zone in which the old state turns into the new.
>
> (Piene 1964:812–13)

The ZERO group published the first two issues of its magazine, *ZERO* (April and October 1958), as catalogs accompanying the group's exhibitions. The format of these shows was rather unusual. Piene described them as "a vernissage at night without an exhibition lasting any longer" (1964:812). Later, he called them "Zero Happenings," where "the event structure permits an exchange of experience between artist and viewer, not possessions. The event as a work of art – as process art – is largely anti-materialistic" (Piene and Barret 1973:73). The first such Happening took the form of a demonstration: huge hot-air balloons and kites were carried through the streets and along the Rhine banks and finally set adrift, with searchlights following their paths up into the night sky.

In 1957 Piene had left his easel, paint, and canvas in the studio and created his first Light Paintings, trying to articulate light and making it perceptible as a source of energy. Instead of a brush he used hand-operated lamps and directed their beams through stencils and gels, in order to "transmit light as energy rather than, as in painting, to symbolize it by tonal gradients" (1964:812). In 1959 he produced his first *Light Ballet*, as an extension of his earlier Light Paintings. The movement of the light projections was now choreographed to the accompaniment of jazz music; in a second phase they turned into group performances where several people created an ensemble of different shapes and colors. The next stage was to mechanize the projections and to create whole *Light Environments*. Piene then developed *Light Theatre* (such as *The Fire Flower* at the Theater Diogenes in Berlin, 1964, and *The Proliferation of the Sun* in New York, 1966–67). Finally, he drew together the many strands of his early experiments in his *Sky Events* (see Claus 1974). Piene explained the concept of a light ballet:

> Light "dances" in a certain order and "choreographic" sequence. It's more or less improvised in accordance with the sound of the "guide beam." [...] The light is not restricted to the spatial section of the stage or the picture plane at the end of a long hall where the spectators are sitting in darkness. It can reach most parts of the space, thereby giving the viewer the impression of being the center of the event, of "being filled out by it" and "being part of the light." [...] His transformation will be more enduring than in traditional, representational performances, because he does not have to identify with a person who will always remain alien to him. He will only experience an agreement with the space. He shares its dimension, but here it is free, unencumbered space. He becomes part of a continuum that enables him to experience the pure sensation of his own steady dynamics.
>
> (Piene 1960; see also 1965:26–27)

WOLF VOSTELL

Wolf Vostell can be regarded as the father of the European Happening movement. He was certainly one of the most active Happeners, with a body of work that developed through the 1960s and 1970s, and a particularly active peak from 1964 to 1966. He had contacts with the Nouveau Réalisme group, but never fully converted to their philosophy.[8] He pursued an independent line, which resulted in a far more process-oriented conception of realist art.

Vostell's Happenings took place in real time. They were life, but also a commentary on it. He short-circuited life and art through the structure of the performance and allowed the audience to establish a feedback with reality. Vostell confronted the spectator with fragments of reality that had been reorganized according to the principles of collage, montage, assemblage, and décollage. The usual continuity of space and time was interrupted, just as modern life is discontinuous and fragmented. He broke through the normal context of the well-known, the habitual, the familiar. Elements of everyday existence were put into a new order so that the ordinary and commonplace assumed a new and strange face. This provoked spectators to take a fresh look at things. It pulled them out of their lethargy and passivity, mobilized their fantasy, and forced them to react creatively with their environment.

The materials Vostell selected for his Happenings were usually symbolic objects of the modern consumer society and/or modern apparatuses of communication: TVs, telephones, cars, trains. The environments were representative of mass society and pointed to the pervasive problem of anonymous and alienated existence in a modern, postindustrial world. But they also contained an aesthetic value: "The recreation and fixing of environment are the New Art" (in Becker and Vostell 1965a:68). The emphasis was, however, on the active, or rather *activating*, component in them. Happenings "present a do-it-yourself reality [...] and sharpen the consciousness for the inexplicable and for chance" (1966:1). Vostell used the spatial surroundings "to influence the participants through the environment, and the environment through the presence of human beings" (1965a:29). "Action," "Event," or "Happening" emphasized the process character of the artwork. The score established a framework, but the final form of the work could only unfold in the time–space continuum of the performance. Production and reception of the work of art became one. Spectators were drawn into the artwork and became coproducers.

Vostell's first move into the direction of Happenings took place in Paris in 1954, when he came to the realization that both abstract and Informel art "lacked essential categories & dimensions of our multi-material & multi-mixed technological existence [...]. The totality of phenomena of our changing & pulsating life was not in the least integrated in the art of that time in any way" (1968a:3).[9] The result was his first "dé-coll/age" paintings made up of layers of unstuck and decomposed posters. These works already dealt with constant change and openness, two ideas which characterized his later Happenings. Vostell commented: "Torn posters were my first dé-coll/ages, & as i was demonstrating the dé-coll/age principle in action it became an event, & out of these events grew my first dé-coll/age happenings" (1968a:4; see also Merkert 1974:195–204).

While the first décollage paintings were the *result* of an action, the décollage demonstrations turned the process into the artwork itself. In 1958, Vostell realized *The Theatre Takes Place on the Street*. He

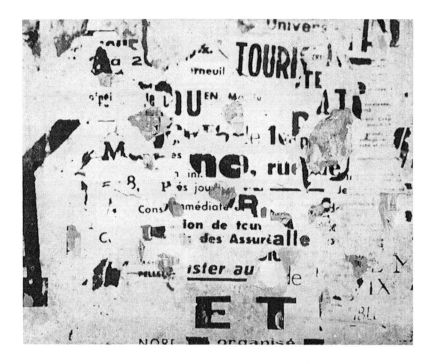

"Et ...," a dé-coll/age created with participants in Wolf Vostell's *Der theatre ist auf der strasse* (1958). (Photo courtesy of Dr. Thelen.)

prepared a score for the Action with concrete directions that transformed spectators into participants (1970a:327–28). The demonstration consisted of a group of people walking down Rue de Tour de Vanves and reading aloud text fragments they found on torn posters. The intention was to attract more and more passersby and to involve them in the reading of the texts. To create variations he instructed the performers to read the texts diagonally or to tear down more layers of the posters to create new texts. Apart from reading, the actors were encouraged to interpret the posters through gestures. The participants were able to go beyond the level of contemplating a work of art and to reflect critically on themselves and their relationship to reality by being involved in a change of their environment (see Vostell [1965] 1970a:198–200).

A more complex Action was *Cityrama* of 1961, a "permanent realistic demonstration at 26 places in Cologne, where life and reality, action and events are declared to be décollaged Total Works of Art."[10] Here, the spectators were encouraged to go to one of the twenty-six sites (a scrap yard, railway station, bomb sight, backyard, an entrance of an ordinary house, etc.) and to carry out actions such as: "listen to the noise of the railway and practice the art of love," "urinate into the debris and think of

Neun–nine dé-coll/agen (1968) took place in nine different sites throughout Wuppertal. (Photo courtesy of the Happening Archiv Vostell, Berlin.)

your best friends," "observe the children play, then take a fish in your mouth and take a walk," or "go into a laundry and ask which year we are living in."

A similar idea was *Mondlocog* of 1962, a décollage Action to be performed consecutively or simultaneously at nine different localities. Apart from the décollage proper ("Poster-board put up before the audience !political! !commercial! or !luxurious! Posters are pulled down. The act of pulling down /Décollage/ is stereophonically amplified and transmitted for the audience" [1970a:305]), spectators were given simple tasks such as playing with slot machines or household appliances, and more demanding ones such as "SMASH-IN of a RUIN or WALL by means of a crane with iron ball." Vostell left a number of gaps in the score for unforeseen incidents, thus allowing the spectators/performers to insert their own ideas and take control.

The first Action Vostell called a Happening was *Ligne PC Petite Ceinture*, performed on 3 July 1962 in Paris. The audience was asked to board a bus of the PC line, to ride around Paris, and to take note of their acoustical and visual impressions. The rationale behind the early Happenings was explained by Vostell:

> marcel duchamp has declared readymade objects as art, & the futurists declared noises as art – it is an important characteristic of my effort &

those of my colleagues to declare as art the *total* event, comprising noise / object / movement / color / & psychology – a merging of elements, so that life (man) can be art – [...] content & events in my happenings have to be ordered by the onlooker / participant himself – [...] a happening is *direct* art in a cathartic sense: realization of raw experiences & psychic recovery through conscious use of the inner freedom in man.

(Vostell 1968a:7–8)

In the following years, these open-air Happenings in a variety of city spaces became increasingly complex and large-scale. *No–Nine dé-coll/ ages* (14 September 1963) took place in nine different sites of the City of Wuppertal. The audience gathered at the Gallerie Parnass and were then taken "on a journey which equalled an indeterminate, open form of composition" (1970a:269). They were entertained in a bus that took them to a cinema. During the screening of *Sun in Your Head*, a décollaged TV program by Vostell, the artist carried out a number of simple actions, including brushing his teeth, pouring water into a glass, leafing through a book, vacuuming the floor. Then the spectators were driven to a switching yard surrounded by garden allotments. While one of the actors performed an everyday scene – selling sausages – the audience on the bus and the people working in the surrounding vegetable patches witnessed the spectacular destruction of a Mercedes 170 by two locomotives. Stage three of the journey was a garden center. Three large household mixers were used to grind a tabloid paper to pulp and to mix it with cologne, pepper, and flower seeds. The resulting paste was poured over the flower beds. Then, after being driven to a quarry where Vostell had set up a TV set, the audience settled down to watch a popular quiz show which Vostell, from the upper part of the quarry, constantly jammed or "décollaged." Finally, he blew up the television. The spectators were taken back to the city and driven down into a dark underground garage. They remained seated in the bus and watched through the windows as Vostell décollaged a number of objects. Next came a short interlude on the street – wrapping passersby in plastic foil. Sites seven and eight were situated in a factory: a cellar formerly used as an air-raid shelter and another room that looked like a prison. Twelve simultaneous actions unfolded among the spectators, including slide projections and trans- forming a TV set with the aid of barbed wire into a sculpture. The ninth and last stage was the same as the starting point, the Gallerie Parnass, where Vostell melted a number of plastic toys on an electric stove and sculpted them into a "décollage à la verticale."

The aim behind this and similar décollage Happenings was explained by Vostell: "I'm concerned with enlightening the audience through décollage. By taking everyday occurrences out of their context, it opens up for discussion the absurdities and demands of life, thereby shocking the audience and prompting them to reflect and react."[11]

Vostell's American Happenings, performed from 1964 to 1966 (*You*, New York, 19 April 1964; *Put a Tiger in Your Tank*, New York, March 1966; *Dogs and Chinese Not Allowed*, New York, 3 January 1966), followed more or less the established patterns of the earlier décollage Happenings. During the YAM Festival in New Brunswick, New Jersey, in May 1963, Vostell decided, in agreement with Allan Kaprow, "to call my décollage events from now on *Happenings*, in order to start an international movement" (1970a:273). Vostell's concept of a Happening differed from that of most American artists inasmuch as they were not staged in galleries or indoor locations, but consisted of

> planned or improvised events (incorporating already existing events plus phases & shocks of the environment) occurring either simultaneously or in linear succession in many parts of a city and not depending on closed rooms; [...] the spectator is actively engaged in a series of events that have not been rehearsed – his reactions & behavior determine the course of the happening [...]
>
> (Vostell 1968a:14)

Although Vostell repeatedly insisted on the difference between his Happenings and those of his American colleagues, he nevertheless collaborated with them on a number of events and festivals. In an "action lecture" given together with Allan Kaprow in the Cricket Theater in New York on 19 April 1964, he said:

> Principally, I'm interested in letting the décollage-events happen, so that they become events of change or decomposition of the life principles that surround us, whilst you [Kaprow] employ the principle of collage. You build up and construct your happenings.
>
> (Vostell 1965b:402)

Between 1961 and 1970 Vostell produced twenty-eight Happenings. Several of them must be regarded as milestones in the history of the genre: *Nie wieder – never – jamais* (Aachen, 20 July 1964); *In Ulm, um Ulm und um Ulm herum* (Ulm, 7 November 1964); *Phänomene* (Berlin, 27 March 1965); *24 Stunden* (Wuppertal, 5–6 June 1965); *Berlin 100 Ereignisse* (10 November 1965); *3 Kontinent H* (New York/Buenos Aires/Berlin, 24 October 1966); *Brotvermessung* (Cologne, 15 March 1969); *Salat* (between Cologne and Aachen, 7 November 1970–6 November 1971). Instead of describing the Actions in any detail[12] I should like to quote from a longer manifesto Vostell prepared for *In Ulm* and used during the Happening:

happening = life – life as art – no retreat from but *into* reality – making it possible to experience & live its essence – not to abandon the world but to find a new relation to it – to let the participant experience himself consciously in the happening – to shift the environment into new contexts – to create new meanings by breaking up the old – let the participant experience indeterminacy as a creative force – to uncover & let uncover nonsense in sense – lack of purpose as purpose – open form as form – eccentricity – participants & performers instead of spectators – simultaneousness through juxtaposition of contradictory elements – new combination & absurd use of everyday objects.[13]

(Vostell 1970a:231–32)

Apart from his Happening activities, Vostell engaged in the Fluxus movement following his first meeting with George Maciunas and Nam June Paik in 1962. He had already experimented with décollaging music, first in *Plakatphasen* in Barcelona (August 1960) and then in *Dé-coll/age Solo, Simultan*, and *Lemons* (all performed in Cologne in 1961), and so was inclined to participate in the famous *Neodada in der Musik* concert organized by Paik in Düsseldorf in 1962. Action music along the Fluxus model continued to occupy Vostell beyond the heyday of the Fluxus Festivals lasting roughly from 1962 to 1964. He gave more than twenty Fluxus concerts throughout the 1970s and 1980s.[14]

Vostell's interest in the fetishes of modern civilization and mass communication found an expression in his TV décollages, his video art, and his intermedia installations. The inner contradictions of the modern media of communication, the conflict between their positive potential and actual destructiveness was reflected upon in a large number of projects, beginning with *TV-Dé-coll/age Events and Actions For Millions* of 1959 and continuing through a particularly productive period in the 1970s and 1980s.

The *TV-Dé-coll/age Events and Actions for Millions* was intended for a broadcast by WDR.[15] The idea was to produce a TV broadcast with décollaged images that encouraged the viewer to act in response to the broadcast or to carry out actions suggested during the program (e.g., kiss the person on the TV screen; sit in front of the TV and brush your teeth; press your belly against the monitor; drink a can of Coca Cola, but think of the adverts of Pepsi Cola). In the introduction to the script, Vostell comments on the piece:

> The viewer who submits to the events or acts against them experiences the absurdity and the dubious quality of mass manipulation through the means of communication. The broadcast aims at revealing that TV has already reached our subconscious and has acted out all these actions or has stored them and carries them around everywhere. The absurd and critical game

ought to produce consciousness of these facts.

(Vostell 1970a:321)

Vostell tried to show the spectator that TV as a genre of the *tableau vivant* produces systems for the doubling of life and that the replica is fatally flawed: it is more real than real and therefore false. Vostell's manipulation of electronic images and his jamming of their perfect falsity draws our attention to the substance and the semblance of the medium. TV décollages use electronic images as a basis for a new generation of images which reveal the medium's ability to be manipulated. "Décollage" means stripping off the layers of falsity in the reality of electronically produced imagery. Destroying the images through electronic jamming or by shooting at the TV set (as in the *No–Nine* Happening in Wuppertal) or burying it (as at the YAM Festival in New York) is not just a destructive gesture. It shows the human being in control. It turns TV into an object which we can form, mold, structure, sculpt according to our will and desire.

This idea was probably best explored in Vostell's TV environments, for example the *Technological Happening Room* of 1966.[16] The room was conceived as a "visual-acoustic laboratory in which the media can be mixed / stored / blurred / & dé-coll/aged" in order to "generate an intense psychological and physiological period of experience by the availability of its media instruments & their information." A large number of electronic instruments (TV monitors, film projectors, videotapes, telephones, radios, Xerox machines, record players, epidiascope, computers, jukebox) were operated from a central control desk. Only individual visitors were allowed into the Happening room. Their initial function as object in a total network of information changed in the course of the visit. Their actions and reactions were recorded and immediately played back, so that the relation between object and subject became blurred. Sender and receiver of the information merged; (passive) watching of images turned into (active) producing of images. Instant reproduction and projection of reality broke down the traditional system of representation and the gap between art and life.

Vostell developed a large number of strategies and techniques to intervene, recast, manipulate, attack the antireality of modern mass media. His décollages transformed found imagery and converted the fragments into new gestalts. His Happenings allowed the audience to engage actively with their environment. His TV broadcasts and installations contrasted the potentially positive qualities of the electronic media with his own comments on and critique of the systems employed for the generation of images. These multifaceted aspects of his work made Vostell one of the most influential Happeners of the 1960s.

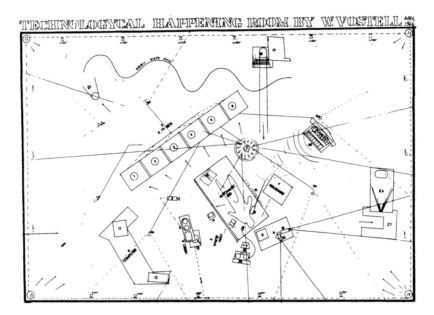

Individual visitors entered the *Technological Happening Room* (1966), becoming part of the work as their actions and reactions were recorded and immediately played back. (Groundplan courtesy of the Happening Archiv Vostell, Berlin.)

JOSEPH BEUYS

Far better known on the international art scene and more influential on the next generation of performance artists was Joseph Beuys. There could not be more of a contrast between these two key figures in the European Happenings movement: Vostell, the "new realist," who confronted the audience with clear and simple fragments of everyday reality, and Beuys, the "shaman," whose symbol-laden Actions exuded such a stark and mystical quality. Vostell guided his audiences through an external reality, while Beuys celebrated rituals aimed at channeling the energies of natural and supernatural worlds into the spiritual life of the audience.

Beuys' main aim was to unlock and mobilize people's latent creativity. He emphasized the role of intuition, empathy, and nonintellectualized thinking. The complex iconography of his Actions relied on the recurrent use of symbolic objects and materials, predominantly the cross, batteries, bones, fat, felt,[17] honey, and living creatures such as the hare, the horse, and bees. Beuys was extremely skeptical of modern science and felt that technology, in its present application, was reducing human creativity; people mechanized by machines and conditioned by the electronic media had become victims rather than masters of their environment. Beuys drew on the organic warmth of natural materials and used many metaphors of energy and transformation to indicate his desire for a return to a close and immediate contact with the earth.

Beuys' aesthetics were heavily influenced by his "Theory of Social Sculpture." His use of the term *Plastik* implied the molding of materials as well as ideas. For Beuys, any "form-giving process" that leads from chaos to structure can be considered *Plastik*. Development of human consciousness and spiritual awareness is the most important form of *Plastik*. For art to be a useful tool in this process it has to move beyond the static boundaries of traditional painting and sculpture. Happenings, or Actions as he preferred to call them, were works of art where everything was in a state of flux, of change and transformation.

In 1962, the Rhineland had become the center of the Fluxus movement. Beuys met Maciunas at the neo-Dada concert in Düsseldorf (16 June 1962) and agreed to stage his *Earth Piano* piece at the Fluxus Festival in Wiesbaden (1–23 September 1962; however, in the end he could not participate). From 1963 to 1965, Beuys was involved in a number of Fluxus concerts and events. He explained:

> The acoustic element and the sculptural quality of sounds have always been essential to me in art, and in terms of music maybe my background in piano and cello drew me to them [the Fluxus artists]. Then there was the use of sound as a sculptural material to enlarge the whole under-standing of sculpture from the point of view of using materials.
>
> (in Tisdall 1979:86)

Beuys' first Fluxus performance took place in 1963 at the Gallerie Parnass in Wuppertal. Dressed like a regular pianist he played the instrument with many pairs of old shoes until it fell apart. He invited his Fluxus friends to Düsseldorf and organized a Festum Fluxorum Fluxus at the State Academy of Fine Art, where he had been teaching as professor of sculpture since 1961. On 2 and 3 February 1963 the program of *Music and Anti-music: Instrumental Theatre* was performed by some fifteen to twenty artists. On the first evening, Beuys played *Composition for Two Musicians*. It lasted about twenty seconds and consisted of two wind-up toy drummers rattling their instruments on a grand piano. The next day he played *Siberian Symphony: Part One*. He prepared a piano with little clay hills and hung a dead hare from a blackboard. By means of wire and pine twigs he formed an energy channel between piano and hare. Beuys then played sections of Erik Satie's *Messe des pauvres* and *Sonnerie de la Rose + Croix*, dashing from time to time to the blackboard and writing phrases on it.

Another festival of "New Art Actions / Agit Prop / Dé-collage / Happening / Events / Anti-Art / Total Art / ReFluxus" took place on 20

July 1964 in the Technical College of Aachen. Beuys planned to perform *Kukei / Akopee-No / Brown Cross / Fat Corners / Model Fat Corners*. He began the performance by forming a sculpture with ultraviolet light beams. He then filled a grand piano with herbs, leaves, washing powder, and other things, just enough to alter the tone but still leaving the piano playable. For the second movement, a stove was heated up to melt the fat. Beuys raised a copper staff wrapped in felt and walked around the piano. He took an electric drill and bored holes into the piano, following the instructions on a musical note sheet covered with brown blots. By accident, a container of nitric acid (which Beuys had used for his introductory "light music") was tipped over and a few drops splashed onto a spectator's socks and trousers. The man was part of a group of right-wing students who had organized a protest action before and during the festival. Together with his friends, the student stormed the stage and punched Beuys in the face. In an emblematical gesture, Beuys – bleeding from his nose – held out a crucifix and raised his hand in a Nazi salute. The police intervened, Beuys distributed chocolate to the audience, and the concert was never completed. One may therefore doubt that his aims behind the concert were fulfilled: "The intention: Healing chaos and shapelessness, moving in a clear direction and enabling us to dissolve and warm up the frozen and rigid forms of the past and of social conventions, thereby making future forms becoming possible" (in Becker and Vostell 1965:327).

In 1963/64, Beuys participated in a number of other Fluxus events organized and scripted by other artists. But the Actions which he devised himself indicated that he was also moving beyond the provocation that characterized so many of the Fluxus concerts. *The Chief* was first presented in Copenhagen in 1963 and then again at the René Block Gallery in Berlin (1 December 1964). It was a nine-hour performance and emphasized the meditative and ritualistic aspect of Beuys' œuvre. The brightly lit gallery space was "decorated" with a strip of margarine, two fat corners, an assembly of hair and fingernails, a felt roll wrapped around a copper staff, and two dead hares. In the center of the room lay a large felt roll, with Beuys inside it. At irregular intervals he transmitted messages from the roll by chanting into a microphone. Contrasted to his "primary sounds" were electronic compositions played by Erik Andersen and Henning Christiansen. In New York, Robert Morris simultaneously executed the same performance, echoing Beuys' Action.

For Beuys, *The Chief* was "above all an important sound piece." His vocalizations were "taken consciously from animals" as a way of "coming into contact with other forms of existence, beyond the human one." The intense and meditative character of lying in the same position wrapped up in felt for nine hours was meant to have a consciousness-expanding effect on both spectators and performer: "Such an action, and indeed every action, changes me radically. In a way it's a death, a real action and not an interpretation" (in Tisdall 1979:95).

In 1965, Beuys separated from the Fluxus movement and began to perform far more structured Actions. On 15 June 1965, at the Parnass Gallery in Wuppertal during a collaborative twenty-four-hour Happening, he performed . . . *and in us . . . under us . . . land beneath*. The aim was to encourage the audience to develop a new, intuitive perception of time and space. For this, he mounted a crate, sometimes sitting with his legs stretched out over fat wedges or his head resting on a wedge placed on a stand, sometimes crouched with his hands extended over the fat. He "listened" to the fat and reached out for objects beyond his grasp.

In *How to Explain Pictures to a Dead Hare* at the Schmela Gallery in Düsseldorf (26 November 1965) Beuys spent three hours walking through an exhibition of his works. His head was covered with honey and gold leaf; attached to one foot was an iron sole, to the other, a felt sole. In his arms he cradled a dead hare and lifted its paw to touch the paintings. After the tour he sat down on a bench, mute, and "explained" the images to the hare. He commented on the Action:

> This was a complex tableau about the problem of language, and about the problems of thought, of human consciousness and of the consciousness of animals. [. . .] The hare incarnates himself into the earth, which is what we humans can only radically achieve with our thinking: he rubs, pushes, digs himself into materia (earth); finally penetrates (rabbit) its laws, and through this work his thinking is sharpened, then transformed, and becomes revolutionary.
>
> (Beuys 1972: 10)

In Beuys' symbolic language, the hare was also connected to birth, and the honey to organic productivity. Covering his head with honey indicated the contrast between intuitive sensibility and abstract intellectuality.

The ideas of energy, time, space, and language were explored in a number of pieces, including *Mainstream* at the Franz Dahlem Gallery in Darmstadt (20 March 1967). For ten hours Beuys inhabited a bare, whitewashed space with a rust-colored floor. The edges of the space were defined with a wall of fat. The audience was allowed to enter this space, but they kept a distance, either because of the unresponsiveness of the "fat-dweller" or because he cleaned up any area a spectator had entered. He repaired the boundaries that had been broken by the audience. He removed all traces of their presence and altered or rebuilt the fat walls that had been damaged. There was a recurring ritual of wiping and sliding on the fat-soaked floor. He played with lumps of fat and lay down on the floor, his limbs stretching beyond the demarcation lines that surrounded him. He then got up and held an antenna to his ear, listening intensely into space. Finally, as if imbued with superhuman power, he stood still with his hand placed in front of his brow. Throughout the Action, Henning Christiansen operated four tape recorders that issued sounds and word fragments. Beuys himself only produced his favorite "öö" sounds and spoke two sentences: "This is my axe and this is the axe of my mother" and "It is not your fault that you said that but that they asked you."

In 1969 Beuys was invited to design the sets for two theatre productions in Frankfurt, Goethe's *Iphigenia* and Shakespeare's *Titus Andronicus*. He decided to perform the two plays himself, simultaneously, at the Theater am Turm during the *Experimenta 3* theatre festival. The stage was divided into a Titus corner (empty) and an Iphigenia corner (with a microphone on a stand, chalk drawings and scores written on the floor, lumps of sugar, and blocks of fat distributed onstage). At the back of the performance area, a white horse was eating hay or stomping its hoofs on a resounding iron plank. Over the loudspeakers came fragments of both plays spoken by Claus Peymann and Wolfgang Wiens. Beuys himself, initially wrapped up in brilliant white fur, "played" Iphigenia. His movements echoed those of the horse as he spoke Goethe's text into the microphone. In between, he walked around the stage, patted the horse, squatted down and measured his head, made some guttural noises, spat fat into the Titus corner, played the cymbals. Some of the ritual actions were repeated; others were improvised and determined by the behavior of the horse.

The performance was far from a theatrical interpretation of the two plays. The texts were used to contrast humanist idealism and brutal realism. Between these two poles there was a field of interaction between Beuys and the horse. Beuys did not aim at making exact connections between the four elements, but rather established an intuitive field of associations between them. He sought to foster a prerational form of consciousness by contrasting the organic element of man and horse with the intellectual element of the play texts communicated via an electronic medium.

A last Action I want to mention is *I Like America and America Likes Me* (23–25 May 1974 at the René Block Gallery in New York). For three days, Beuys shared the gallery space with a coyote and demonstrated the possibilities of a harmonious coexistence of the human and animal worlds. This state of natural cohabitation was disturbed by the intrusion of capitalism, here indicated by fifty copies of the *Wall Street Journal*. Beuys covered himself with felt blankets and lived in a felt tent, always communicating with the coyote. He never took his eyes off the animal and performed a repertoire of movements that were subject to the coyote's responses and energy levels. He commented on the performance:

> Human Universality – a total contrast to the *Wall Street Journal*, the financial newspaper which embodies most symptomatically the ultimate rigor mortis inherent in the thinking about CAPITAL (in the sense of the tyranny exerted by money and power). A symptom of our time, where CAPITAL ought to have become an ARTISTIC CONCEPT.
>
> (in Tisdall 1976:16)

From about 1967 onwards, the political aspects of Beuys' Actions became more and more pronounced. He not only inserted references to contemporary political realities in his works, but he himself became actively engaged in the political arena. Despite his aversion to parties and organizations, he founded a number of groups based on nonhierarchical and free democratic principles, to pursue and publicize his political aims. He employed many channels to promote more participatory forms of government and the creation of a different society for the future.[18] However, his idealistic concepts of democracy were often derided by the Left and the Center, and the idiosyncratic forms he chose for his propaganda meant that outside the art world few people took him seriously as a politician. But in many ways, his work as a political activist was a logical extension of his attempts to bridge the gap between art and life in his Happenings and Actions:

> Art is now the only evolutionary-revolutionary power. Only art is capable of dismantling the repressive effects of a senile system that continues to totter along the deathline: to dismantle in order to build A SOCIAL ORGANISM AS A WORK OF ART. The most modern art discipline – Social Sculpture / Social Architecture – will only reach fruition when every living person becomes a creator, a sculptor or architect of the social organism. Only then would the insistence on participation of the action art of FLUXUS and Happening be fulfilled.[19]
>
> (in Tisdall 1979:268)

BAZON BROCK

One of the most ubiquitous artists on the German Happenings scene was Bazon Brock.[20] He began his career in the theatre, first as an assistant under Gustav Rudolf Sellner in Darmstadt (1958/59), then as dramaturg with Horst Gnekow in Luzern (1960/61). During that time he initiated, together with Claus Bremer, some of the most experimental theatre productions in the German-speaking countries. His attempts at overcoming the boundaries of theatrical performance led him more and more in the direction of Happenings:

> The emphasis in my work lies on social action, on the social processes, not on their results. I'm amazed with what clarity and directness I have always been interested in the aspect of reception, the moment of understanding, perception, appropriation. For fifty years, the history of art has revolved around altering production processes. Only recently did reception begin to play a certain role in the arts: Happenings discovered the spectator as coproducer. Without him the event could not take place.
>
> (Brock 1977:564)

Brock regarded himself as *Beweger*, a person who stirs and sets things in motion (see Brock 1960:2; 1977:551, 928). His method was derived from Pop Art and Nouveau Réalisme: fragments of everyday reality were framed or slightly altered or collaged in an unusual way to create an alienating effect. The aim was to focus spectators on the substance and character of a reality with which they have become too familiar and of which they have therefore lost a critical awareness. Brock's thinking was always scenic, theatrical, image bound. He examined to what extent a perception of reality is determined by the imagery of mass media, advertising, TV, and popular magazines. By confronting the viewer with the imagistic debris of modern consumer society, his Happenings became instruments for the production of resistance and the development of critical thinking. Brock explained the concept of realism behind his Happenings:

> New Realism meant that the artist gave up his existence in the ivory tower and stopped living in his artistic dream world. New Realism indicated a willingness of the artist to take his material from the living reality of the year 1961 or 1962 and to confront the problems of an industrial society and of the evolving mass consumer society.
>
> (Brock 1992).

Brock's first Action took place in Hamburg from 18–24 December 1959 when he and Fritz Hundertwasser painted a *Neverending Line* on the walls of the local art college. From 1960 to 1962, he performed his *Railway Poems* in various Frankfurt railway stations, painting slogans on the trains and reciting *Against the Moloch Technology*, based on texts by Nietzsche, to the sounds of the locomotives moving in and out of the stations. In 1962, he and his friend Hermann Goepfert carried out a number of public Actions in front of the Frankfurt police station. They consisted of rather idiosyncratic demonstrations – one against the persistent power of death, another against the exclusion of human beings from the Frankfurt zoological gardens. Another such event was *Gildening the Environment*, where volunteering passersby or any objects they carried were sprayed with bronze paint. In 1963 Brock painted the *Bloom-Zeitung*, a satirical copy of the tabloid *Bild-Zeitung*, and sold it on the main streets of various German cities. On 31 March 1964, he created a *Progressive Monument on Flat Ground*, in which a schoolboy was instructed to walk through Frankfurt with a photographic portrait of Brock attached to his back, while Brock followed closely behind. The idea of the Action was to satirize the ideology of the artist focusing only on himself. On 25 January 1965 he presented at the René Block Gallery in Berlin a program of what Brock called "Agit-Pop." The theme was *The Divided Germany as Seen by Our Beloved Mr. Springer*. The reactionary press czar's motto, "Always keep the German division in mind," was applied literally to the life of a normal German citizen. The Galerie Block was turned into a replica of a traditional, chintzy living room, the only difference being that in this "Room of German Reality" every piece of furniture, and every utensil was divided in half by means of barbed wire. With a Berlin city map on the floor under him, Brock stood on his head and performed his own version of "Front Theatre" (Brock's term referring to the Berlin Wall as a theatre of war), commenting on the everyday situation in the divided city. As a contrast, while standing on his head he read for two hours from his "postcard novel," trivial news which members of a French bourgeois family at the turn of the century had sent to each other. In the same year he exhibited himself in the display window of a Frankfurt department store while writing one of his literary masterpieces (*Art as Work*). Another Action was *The Street As Theatre*, which took place in Berlin in January 1965. He set up a row of chairs on the pavement of the busy Kurfürstendamm boulevard, sold tickets to passersby, led them to their seats, and then made them watch the "everyday theatre" around them.

In 1965 Brock became Professor of Nonconformative Aesthetics at the academy of art in Hamburg. He complemented his Happenings with "action lectures" and other didactic performances. He also experimented with more theatrical formats. At the first Frankfurt Experimenta Festival (June 1966) he produced his *Theatre of Positions*. This was a collage of hyperrealistic scenes that translated Pop Art into the language of performance and added a parodic touch. The scenes dealt with the banalities and coercions of everyday existence in modern consumer society, with technological and media culture, and with the fantasies conjured up by the advertising industry. There was also a strong connection with the aesthetics of Nouveau Réalisme: the roles in the piece were not performed by traditional actors, but by people who in real life occupied the same profession as their onstage characters. The audience could admire a revue of fashion models, rugby players discussing Plato's *Timaios*, a student offering Hegelian small talk, a woman with a washing compulsion showering off her frustrations and covering the stage with 150 bras. There were also actors portraying comic-strip figures such as Batman, Donald Duck, Goofy, and many other such characters. Scenes from old films were projected onto the walls of the auditorium, showing "life as we only know it from TV, but which nevertheless makes us feel how much it has determined our existence" (Brock 1966:62). Some of the scenes were directly inspired by English and American Pop Art paintings. Others copied German TV shows, well-known advertisements, or commercial theatre shows. The foyer of the theatre was a replica of a showroom for a Neckermann mail-order catalog, and the stage was flooded with Persil boxes, plastic baskets, and similar "piles of commodities, predominantly made of plastic, lightweight material ideal to be thrown away" (Brock 1966:60).

Brock himself introduced this "dramatic illustrated magazine" in the role of a *compère*. He presented a number of "guests" who were representing their real-life professions – a doctor, a nurse, an engineer, etc. When they went down into the auditorium to interact with spectators, the performers were able to relate to them as they did in their everyday jobs. One of the structural principles behind the main performance was to contrast the gestic repertoire of traditional theatre with the unpretentious world of commodities and everyday existence. For example, while a couple acted out a typical boulevard play with the routines of a clichéd adultery downstage, the upstage area was used to represent mundane actions such as crossing the street at a zebra crossing, boarding a tramway, or playing football.

The Nouveau Réalisme element continued to be a central feature of Brock's work in the late 1960s. In 1967, at the annual meeting of the German architects' association in Hanover, he transported the complete contents of his friend Werner Kliess' flat to the congress hall. Kliess and his wife continued to live and work as they were wont to, trying not to be disturbed by the people who kept walking through their relocated home (see Brock 1977:675, 745).

The didactic element in Brock's œuvre became most apparent in his *Besucherschulen* (Visitors' Schools), organized for the Kassel Dokumenta and the Frankfurt Theater am Turm. Just like the Happenings and theatre pieces, these schools were devised as "tools for the expansion of reception mechanisms." Brock regarded them as "schools of consumption. They are not schools where you learn about objective realities, but about how to liberate yourself from the objective constraints of reality" (1977:564). Brock understood aesthetic learning as "exemplary communicative action" (1987:1). It entailed not only the field of (high) art, but all aspects of social life and everyday existence. Learning was seen as a productive appropriation of reality, and "action teaching"' as a means to make the recipient understand that s/he is the real producer of an artwork, because only s/he can give "meaning" to reality.

DANIEL SPOERRI

In his early career in the theatre, Brock crossed paths several times with Daniel Spoerri, a Romanian-born artist employed between 1954 and 1957 as first dancer at the Opera House in Berne. Dissatisfied with the lowbrow repertoire he was appearing in, he began to study with the old Expressionist dancer, Max Terpis. Inspired by the abstract intermedia experiments of the early part of the century, he choreographed a *Suite en couleur* (performed at the Theater am Hirschgraben on 15 December 1955). The piece explored further the ideas of a *Ballet en couleur*, which he had written in 1954 in cooperation with Tinguely, who had devised a kinetic décor for the ballet. Spoerri also began to involve himself in experimental theatre productions at the Berner Kellertheater. He produced the world premiere of Picasso's *Desire Caught by The Tail*, Tardieu's *Sonata*, and Ionesco's *Bald Soprano*. The critical success of the productions resulted in an offer of work as assistant director at the Basle municipal theatre. Through his friend Claus Bremer, Spoerri became an assistant to Gustav Sellner in Darmstadt from 1957 to 1959. Unfortunately, Spoerri's plans for a production of Tzara's *Gas Heart* did not come to fruition,[21] nor did his plans for an abstract theatre which he had proposed to the Bauhaus-inspired art school in Ulm. Spoerri also edited, together with Bazon Brock, five issues of a magazine of concrete poetry, *Material*.

In 1959 Spoerri moved to Paris and was one of the founding members of the Nouveau Réalisme group. He involved himself in the Festival d'art d'avant-garde in Paris (18 November 1960) and produced one of his *tableaux-pièges*, where the leftovers of a meal were fixed on the table and presented to the spectator as

> a piece of information, a provocation, an indication for the eye to look at things which one usually does not look at. There is no other meaning behind it. After all, art, what is this? It is maybe a way, a possibility, to live.[22]
>
> (in Hahn 1990:33)

Spoerri wrote two manifestoes that presented the idea of a non-personal, physical form of theatre, where life and art merged and improvisation and chance played a key role. *Example of a Dynamic Theatre* (1959/60) describes a theatre where the elements of light, sound, and color are not used to serve any dramatic idea. They are not the vehicle of a message, they *are* the message; they have dramatic value in themselves. Their composition onstage is partly fixed by rules, partly left open to the intervention of the audience. The meaningless accumulation of sense impressions forces spectators to react and to create *their own* meaning from the elements offered to them. As an example of this principle, Spoerri cites his production of *The Sonata*, in which the fixed associations of words and movements were destroyed and offered to the audience as material for their own scenarios.

On the Auto-Theatre[23] describes in sixteen points a concrete way of forming a theatre space that offers opportunities for the audience to create their own "play" within it. The hall is divided into a multitude of rooms constructed from solid or flexible walls made of such materials as rubber, paper, or canvas. The brushing of the audience against these walls can be seen by other spectators in other rooms. There are also holes in the walls for the audience to observe the other spectators. By tripping over contacts they alter the illumination or trigger various sound mechanisms. At the entrance to this labyrinth the audience members are offered objects and instruments (e.g., balloons, typewriters, umbrellas) or masks which they can carry through the rooms and use to enjoy themselves or entertain each other. In some rooms they are asked to perform simple tasks, such as sawing apart a table and chair and nailing them together in a different form. They are also given texts which they can speak through a microphone, so that a steady stream of sounds coming from every direction fills the theatre. To augment the audience's sense impressions, the design of each room was to be handed over to different artists. Spectators would be able to experience contrasting sensations, such as cold–warm, straight–crooked, hard–soft, dry–wet. All rooms were to contain dynamic lighting effects produced by projections through stencils or prisms. Mirrors would reflect endlessly repeated optical effects. The constant change of the environment brought about by the audience's actions and interventions would ensure that no repetition set in and that every spectator would experience something different in the course of the visit.

There is no indication that Spoerri, when he wrote his manifesto, had any knowledge of Kaprow's *18 Happenings in 6 Parts*. The analogies between the two Happening rooms can only be explained by the fact that toward the late 1950s/early 1960s many artists were experimenting with similar ideas and arriving at similar conclusions. Once these correspondent results became publicized, many of them joined forces and created a multifaceted movement with many international cross-connections and joint activities.

In Spoerri's case this meant that he participated in the group activities of the Nouveaux Réalistes, the ZERO circle, the Fluxus movement, and the many European Happenings festivals. His play *Okay Mum, We Shall Do It*[24] was an attempt at translating the ideas of Nouveau Réalisme into theatrical language: A flow of nonpsychological, "concrete" word material, which had been taped in Ben Vautier's kitchen in Nice, was spoken by four actors onstage and was for a second time recorded. The new tape was then played back and the actors commented on the material and improvised with the situation they themselves had created earlier. Spoerri called this a "true *pièce-piège*, which through the mise-en-scène becomes a false *pièce-piège*, and then, in the second part of the show, becomes a true *pièce-piège* again." This "trap-play" was a further development from the "trap-pictures" Spoerri had created with kitchen leftovers (Spoerri in Bremer 1962:41–44). The idea of "trapping" a conversation, exhibiting it onstage, and then, through a *détrompe-l'œil* effect, drawing the audience's attention to the difference between art and life was nothing but a time-based extension of Spoerri's assemblages, whose function he described as "focusing attention on situations and areas of daily life that are little noticed" ([1961] 1973:217).

Spoerri's artistic production during the early 1960s oscillated between the poles of Nouveau Réalisme and Fluxus. He described his performances as "mini-pieces of auto-theatre" ([1961] 1973:50). At the October 1962 Festival of Misfits in London he constructed a dark room furnished with a labyrinth of mattresses, foam walls, and hanging objects. Visitors had to pass through the various corridors to reach the other end. Spoerri's *Homage to Germany* at the Festum Fluxorum Fluxus in Düsseldorf (2 February 1963) consisted of a rambling and confusing lecture given at the top of his voice while a number of other artists consistently disrupted him by walking in and out of the hall. At the same festival he also performed in a number of pieces by other artists, including Maciunas' *In memoriam Adriano Olivetti*.

In March 1963 at the opening of the restaurant at the Galerie J, Spoerri functioned as *metteur en cène*, serving a variety of specially formed and colored foodstuffs and transforming the unconsumed leftovers into a tableau-piège. Such gastronomic Happenings were repeated in different form at the Collection Hahn in Cologne (8 July 1964), the Frankfurt Book Fair in 1968, the Intermedia Festival in Heidelberg (1 May 1969), the Kunsthalle Basle (15 November 1969), the Kunsthalle Nuremberg (8 August 1970), and elsewhere. In 1964/65 he spent much of his time in New York with Kaprow and the American Fluxus group. On 13 March 1965 he organized with Arman, Christo, Warhol, Lichtenstein, and Kaprow the *Artists' Key Club: Gambling for Works of Art*, a lottery in the New York subway system. One hundred suitcases were placed in the unclaimed-baggage room. Thirteen of them contained an art work. For ten dollars, passersby could purchase a key and collect the appropriate suitcase, which may or may not contain a piece of art.

On 17 June 1968, Spoerri opened the Restaurant Spoerri in Düsseldorf, which became a favorite hangout for local artists and a popular eatery for the Rhenish bourgeoisie (who kept it going until 1982). Spoerri himself only cooked and served at the place until May 1969, but his Eat Art Banquets and exhibitions in the Eat Art Gallery ensured his regular return to Düsseldorf.

Spoerri's manifold activities as a dancer, choreographer, theatre director, playwright, designer, performer, sculptor, and painter were based on two central premises: creation as a performative process, and reality presented in its material concreteness. Spoerri operated with the dialectic correlation between the concrete quality of theatre and the theatrical quality of concrete reality. Art was not seen as a merely material substance; it was also energy, an active interchange with reality. During the performative process, the artist intervened into an unconscious state of material existence, just like the spectators interpolated themselves into the act of creation. Theatre performances or Happenings were therefore functioning at the same time as mental and material entities.

ROBERT FILLIOU

Nothing could be further removed from the concreteness of Spoerri's œuvre than the elusive and often unpalpable nature of the performance work of his friend Robert Filliou. Filliou shunned the traditional performance genres and theatre spaces and moved into the direction of purely conceptual art. While nearly all artists of the modern and postmodern period retained the idea of art as a metaphorical description or evocation of reality, he attacked the whole concept of the artist as a creative genius. Faced with a marketing system that judged art and the artist by their commodity value, Filliou refused to collaborate and produced concepts that had no chance to be marketed. He ran a shop that was never open, produced books that were too expensive to purchase or had such a small print run that they were not available to potential buyers. He opened a gallery in a hat and took to the streets to sell or simply give away the diminutive works it contained. His attacks on the art market were based on his idea that everyone is an artist and has the right to be creative. "To be a man or a woman means one is a genius, but most people have forgotten this; they are too busy exploiting their talents" (in Neue Galerie 1970b). Filliou regarded himself as an "arteur" and sought to provide people with a key to unlock their hidden genius[25] and to offer them the secret of the "Permanent Creation." His activities consisted of small and unusual gestures which encouraged the spectator to establish connections between seemingly unrelated elements of reality and to react with them according to their own desires. The performances were carried out with utmost simplicity. They did not impose any fixed ideas or structures on the audience, but only pointed them in the direction of *possibilities*.

> I speak a great deal of the Permanent Creation and try to make it available to others. There is something I think of as the relative secret of Permanent Creation, which is: Whatever you do, do something else, whatever you think, think something else. In French it's called the other-ism [*autrisme*].
>
> (Filliou 1984a:21)

Filliou's biography is as elusive as much of his performance work. His autobiographical statements contain little concrete information (see Filliou 1970a and 1970b). His friends knew little of what he did when he was not with them and the curators of some major retrospectives have been unable to document his activities. The few available facts about his life indicate that he was born in 1926 in the south of France, that he joined the *résistance* during the war and became a member of the Communist party. From 1949 to 1951 he studied economy at UCLA and became an American citizen. He then lived in Korea, Egypt, and Spain. In 1959 he returned to France with his Danish wife, Marianne, but throughout the 1960s he lived in various European cities, mainly Paris, Copenhagen, and Düsseldorf. Through Spoerri he was introduced to Maciunas and became involved with the Fluxus group (see Spoerri 1988:13). He participated in many of their festivals without, however, fully subscribing to the Fluxus ideas.

Since much of Filliou's work is classified as Fluxus, his own view on the matter needs stating:

> I have never joined any group. I dislike -isms. In art, in life I reject theories. Manifestos bore me. The spirit in which things are done interests me. So insofar as what I read in Fluxus did exist in Fluxus, Fluxus is the sort of non-group I've felt closest to, while keeping my own counsel and independence.
>
> (Filliou 1970c:n.p.)

The reason for his caution with regard to the Fluxus group was voiced in another letter written during the year when he was most actively involved in their festivals:

> Our main problems are, as I see it, to avoid: falling into mere slapstick, or into the trap of anti-art (neo-dadaism); being slack in the choice of works, by fear that the bad (the imitations) should drive out the good (the original contributions); becoming prisoners of a "system."
>
> (Filliou [1963] 1970d:n.p.)

Playfulness (*ludisme*) as a lifestyle forced Filliou to become a "man of the theatre outside the theatre." One of his key principles was: "I hate work which is not play." His *République Géniale* became the imaginary territory of his research aimed at "liberating the child in us" (in Cladders 1988:27). Although his performances were informed by a sophisticated aesthetic theory, they were never didactic or simply illustrations of his ideas. The elements of chance and improvisation prevented them from becoming mere realizations or preconceived scenarios. He relished the visual and sense-bound side of theatre; only later in his life did his work become overwhelmingly conceptual.

Filliou's earliest surviving play was *The Immortal Death of the World* (1960).[26] He defined the genre of the piece as "auto-theatre" and dedicated it to Daniel Spoerri, whose "theatre of colors" and "dynamic theatre" may have served as inspiration for the play. The score establishes a number of correspondences between colors, sounds, and emotions. However, the interaction between the performers is determined by chance and their spontaneous reactions. After they have come onstage, the first asks another: "What are you doing here?" According to random selection he may answer: "I'm here because I am a man. Man is good." He will then modify his explanation according to the five random sounds provided on tape. Each sound is associated with an emotion. The same happens in reaction to colors. The person to the right of the speaker may wear a blue costume and step forward. Then the speaker will alter his phrase to: "Man is not good." Instead of using words, the performers are free to express their emotions through gestures, movements, facial expressions, or sounds.[27]

Filliou wrote other plays with a strong improvisational element, such as *Total Submission, The Shepherd Dreams of Being a King, That's the Angel*, performed respectively at the Centre Americain in 1963, the Café Théâtre à la Vieille Grille in 1965, and the Comédie de Paris in 1966.[28]

Entirely different were his action poems, such as *Poi Poi*. The "Poi" signified the principle of reflective and active communication that can always be started, finished, started again, thereby giving expression to the process of Permanent Creation. *Poi Poi* was first performed at the Galerie du Fleuve in 1963 as a presentation of the Domaine Poétique, a society to promote a new form of poetry written for the stage. In the performance, Filliou arrived onstage with a suitcase full of pebbles and sand. While he threw the contents of his case bit by bit onto the floor, he recited in a monotonous voice a poem on the significance of emotions, juxtaposing the poi poi with an anti-poi poi, a post-poi poi, and after-poi poi (see Filliou 1970b:191–94, 197).[29] That same year Filliou planned, together with the architect Joachim Pfeuffer, the construction of a Poi

Poidrome as a meeting place for people with creative and communicative interests.

A similar type of action poem was *Kabou'inema 5*, performed in May 1963 with Emmett Williams and Jean-Loup Philippe. The first part is the Silent Kabou'inema. The performers sit onstage and A takes an object from his suitcase. He looks at it with surprise, then with indifference and passes it on to the next person. B looks at it with signs of anguish, disgust, and despair. C is an innocent and playful person. He handles the object with fantasy, plays with it and then rolls it into the auditorium. The second part is the Semi-silent Kabou'inema which "explains Zen Buddhism to those in the dark." B takes a candle out of the suitcase and breaks it in half. C comments: "First it is a candle." B takes a plastic elephant and breaks it. C comments: "Then it is not a candle." B breaks another candle. C comments: "Then once more it is a candle." The third part, or Spoken Kabou'inema, uses the names of well-known personalities, such as Picasso and de Gaulle. A says each name with surprise, B with anger, and C adds to each, "san." When the names have been circulated, C announces: "This was 'The name of some celebrities translated into Japanese'" (in Becker and Vostell 1965:170–171).

On 8 February 1965 at the Café au Go-Go in New York, Filliou and Alison Knowles performed *The Ideal Filliou*, an action poem he had written in 1964. The score reads: "not deciding – not choosing – not wanting – aware of self – wide awake – SITTING QUIETLY – DOING NOTHING." While Knowles read Filliou's "Yes," he sat cross-legged on a chair, emotionless and silent. Then he stood up, read out the text of "The Ideal Filliou" and returned to his former position. At the same time, Phillip Corner improvised an almost silent piece of music. They continued the performance until the audience left the café.[30]

At the Festival of Misfits at the Gallery One in London (23 October to 8 November 1962) Filliou announced a performance of a "fifty-three kilo poem,"[31] but in the end actually performed a "roulette poem." A bicycle wheel with a pointer attached to it was nailed to a board on which Filliou wrote the words of his poem. He then sat down at a table, spun the wheel, and read out the poem as determined by the pointer. In another version, two wheels were used for the same purpose and the audience was in charge of spinning the wheels and carrying out the instructions given to them by the poem, for example: "Pinch the bottom / of the third woman / on your right / but be aware / of the consequences." Filliou also performed a bowling piece, where he set up a number of pins with labels attached to them – "Think of Spoerri," "Think of Ben" – and then toppled them with balls on which he had written phrases such as, "When you see Filliou," "When you see Koepcke."

Collective Poem was performed in June 1963 in the Musée d'Arras together with Emmett Williams. The two opened a box that contained sixteen blank sheets of paper. They took one each and wrote on the paper a number of things – objects, emotions, memories – they were happy to get rid of: a wedding photograph, a pair of socks, rheumatism. The other sheets were given to members of the audience, who filled them in and finally read them out to the other visitors.

The principles of chance and audience participation that run through much of Filliou's performance work was complemented by another type of work which he called "No-Art." An example is "Poème des mots que l'on ne connait pas" (Poem of words one doesn't know, 1961), which reads:

> ?
> I don't know
> ?
> I don't know
> ?
> I don't know
> ?
> ....
> ?
> ....
> ?
> I don't know

(Filliou 1984b:129)

The poem forms part of a set of sixteen postcards. All the poems have missing lines, indicated by the rows of dots, which the reader is asked to complete according to her or his own whim and imagination. Another example is his *No-Play* of 1964. It begins: "This is a play nobody must come and see. That is, the not-coming of anyone makes the play." A variant, *No-Play #2*,

> consists of a performance during which no spectator becomes older. If the spectators become older from the time they come to the performance to the time they leave it, then there is no play. That is to say, there is a play, but it is a No-Play

(Filliou 1967b:14; see also Kostelanetz 1980:609)

Filliou explained the concept behind No-Art in an interview with Klaus Liebig (Liebig 1973): from the point of view of Permanent Creation a thing is of equal value if it is well made, badly made, or not made. The consequence of this is the Principle of Equivalence: Art is creation, and as such it has value. It does not matter if it is well made (like industrial production or art created for a market) or badly made (like

Filliou's pieces). Art is not only good art, but a principle. Art remains art even when it is bad art. The "badly-mades" are the best Filliou can produce. Therefore they are "well-mades" to him. From the concept of the "badly made" he then progressed to the concept of the "not made" (*bien fait, mal fait, pas fait*), which is not to be mistaken for Anti-Art. In its most radical form it can only take place in the mind: "The secret of absolute and permanent creation consists of: sitting there quietly, doing nothing." (It is worthwhile mentioning that Filliou was a Zen Buddhist and spent his final years in a monastery.)

To provide the audience with ideas of that kind and to restrict the purpose of the performance to passing on the impulse of creativity to the spectators and letting *them* go on with the performance falls outside the framework of theatre that can be documented. The same applies to Filliou's street Actions. He interacted as an individual with passersby. There were no critics or invited spectators. He moved into this field with *Performance Piece for a Lonely Person in a Public Place* of circa 1960 (Filliou 1967b:14; Kostalanetz 1980:610). The performer sits in a bar, a train, a park, or wherever, observes the people nearby, and chooses one who looks like what he or she might look like in twenty, thirty, forty years hence. If the performer happens to be old, the person chosen should look like what the performer had looked like twenty, thirty, forty years ago. By observing this person the performer will discover things about her or himself in the past or future.

From January 1962 onward, Filliou roamed the streets with his *Galerie légitime*, an art gallery contained in a cap, later on in a bowler hat. He offered little art works to people for five francs or a drink. Some of the works were simple questions, such as: "What do you do if you have meat but no teeth?"; "What do you do if you are afraid of death but have also no fun in life?"; "What do you do if you are happy with the color of your skin, but still preferred it were different?"

BEN VAUTIER

Ben Vautier's performances lend themselves to a discussion in conjunction with the work of Robert Filliou. They had a similar conceptual basis and are also largely undocumented (excepting his activities at the Fluxus festivals). Unable to offer any detailed analyses of Vautier's performances I shall at least offer an outline of his art theory and comment on some of the scripts and scenarios published in the 1960s.[32]

Vautier's biography is nearly as elusive as that of his friend Filliou: He was born of a Swiss-French father and an Irish mother in Naples in 1935. He received his education in Turkey, Egypt, and Greece. He had no formal art education and began his artistic career in Nice in the mid-

1950s. He established his own gallery, Laboratoire 32, later renamed Ben Doute de Tout (1958). He then moved into Actions and Happenings and became involved with the Fluxus movement.

Vautier concerned himself with the question of a post-Dadaist and, in particular, a post-Duchamp art. Overcoming the limits of what Dada had achieved and finding new forms of expression that went beyond Dada aesthetics and ideology informed Vautier's work of the 1960s and 1970s. He re-examined and verified the formula Art = Life and sought to find new proofs that met the conditions of a postmodern culture. Vautier applied himself to history: the history of artistic development since Duchamp's *Bottlerack* (1914) and the history of himself as a creative artist. Vautier's work was primarily concerned with a fundamental questioning of the mechanisms of the art market, the concept of the artist, the revalorization of simple and everyday activities as art. His work relied on thoughts and words, for example: "The reason I am in this box and that I am not eating is that everybody is eating and nobody is in a box–but when I think it over twice I think the whole thing is nonsense so I shall go to sleep. Ben" (text of a placard attached to the box exhibited at Quelques idées et gestes de Ben, Galerie Daniel Templon, Paris 1970).

He communicated his "work in progress" not through art objects but through linguistic and physical gestures. Vautier placed himself at the center of his works, not to put himself into the limelight but to express doubt. "To change art – to destroy ego" was the key phrase in his oeuvre. Other related ones, which he painted on canvas as artworks, include: Ben doute de tout; Prise de possession du tout; Art = Ben. Art Total; Ben = Rien. Ben = Tout; Théâtre d'Art Total: Regardez moi. Cela suffit; L'Art Total est d'abandonner l'Art; J'ai honte d'être artiste.

By exhibiting his ego and making it the center of his "exhibitions" he raised questions about the category of the "artist" and the demarcation line between the two assumed classes of human beings: artists and not-artists. Hence the banality of much of his work. To exhibit a banderole in the street saying "yesterday, 12.30, i ate a hard-boiled egg" has nothing to do with aesthetics, but everything to do with the ideology of art and the conditions of what constitutes an artist. By exhibiting himself, his doubts, his convictions, his problems with his role as an artist/not-artist, Vautier provoked more questions than he could answer.

Vautier's early performance work employed the conventional framework of institutionalized theatre. However, everything he devised to take place within that architecture was designed to break down the barriers between stage and auditorium. The key concept behind his work of the years 1960 to 1962 was the "Theatre of Shock," aimed primarily at abolishing the unspontaneous attitudes displayed by actors and audience alike. One of Vautier's first pronouncements on the theatre was a manifesto of 1962 entitled *Théâtre* in which he described theatre as a shock experience (see Stedelijk Museum 1973:10). Traditional anti-theatre is not able to achieve this any longer because the audience knows what to expect. The actors therefore have to aim at presenting a series of actions that are unforeseen and have unpredictable effects, for example, setting free eight cats and eight rats in the auditorium; instead of performing a play the actors sit onstage and listen to the radio.

Another manifesto/play, again entitled *Théâtre*, of January 1964 continued to propose unpredictable stage events that make the spectator ill at ease (see Stedelijk Museum 1973:22). The play part of the manifesto is called *Interrogation*. The stage set consists of a simple table, five chairs, a lamp, and several microphones. The five actors have to interrogate a person using questions that are on sale in the Centre d'Art Total. They are designed to embarrass, stun, or rattle the person questioned, for example: what would you do if you only had six hours left to live? What's your aim in life? Mention five things you regard as abnormal. Do you practice masturbation? Have you had homosexual experiences?

Most of Vautier's early plays fell into a similar category. In *Theatre. Proposals* he suggested a number of strategies to create a more active audience participation: declare unexpected news from the stage, for example, that the theatre is on fire; auction off the whole stage set; let the audience decide by vote if the play should continue or not (in Becker and Vostell 1965:253–57). The plays – or, rather, scenarios – read like this:

> *The Piece*. Knock three times – Curtain – No décor – Ben appears and says: This is my piece, find it – He throws a piece of money into the auditorium – Curtain.

> *Shower II*. Knock three times – Curtain – Décor: at the back of the stage a big French flag. An actor appears with the theatre's fire hose. He stands center stage (spotlight). He waits for four or ten or twenty minutes. When the audience gets restless he shouts "Now." Behind the stage the water is turned on and the actor sprays the audience with it. Curtain.

Not all suggestions were designed to take place in traditional theatre buildings. One of the pieces gets very close to the Happenings Vostell organized at that time:

> *Nice by Night*. When the theatre is full, it is announced that for the length of the play the audience is requested to leave the auditorium and to get into the buses waiting in front of the theatre. When everybody has boarded, they drive toward Mont Chauve. The petrol has to be calculated for the

distance between the theatre and Mont Chauve (bleak landscape without water or guest houses), so that the petrol runs out when they arrive. This is the curtain for the piece.

The plays and manifestoes mentioned above were justifiably called "theatre." But Vautier did not limit himself to those types of performances. During 1961 to 1962 he developed his first Actions, twenty of which he wrote down for the Becker/Vostell anthology of Happenings, including:

> Drink two liters of red wine in the morning. Walk into a restaurant and shout: "You're all pigs!" Try your utmost to seduce the wife of your best friend. Bite your mother in her arm. Shine your friends' shoes for a month in public.
>
> (Becker and Vostell 1965:257)

Breaking down the traditional notions of performance went hand-in-hand with breaking down the traditional concepts of art and anti-art. Vautier's discovery of non-art and of the fundamental role the artist played in the production of non-art led him to write plays like:

> *Not-doing* (1961). Project. Searching for a new expression for a kind of art that produces visible or tangible works has led me to the creation of inactivity.
>
> Constructing NOTHING, destroying NOTHING.
>
> This means that my inactive creation will become manifest only at the end of the month with the announcement of a crier. It's got nothing to do with Klein's "Immaterial," but it's a question of creative inactivity.

The concept behind the piece is explained in the following notes:

> Everything. If art is in everything and art is in nothing, then art is in emptiness and art is in everything. [...] The possession of EVERYTHING means the possession of the concept of EVERYTHING. It is the real consciousness that EVERYTHING is possible in art and in the personality of the artist. It is the will to be by wanting EVERYTHING, in relation to others. It is the immense desire to be EVERYTHING.
>
> (in Becker and Vostell 1965:259)

Many of these ideas Vautier tried out in his own performance work over the next couple of years. At the Festival of Misfits in London (23 October to 8 November 1962) he lived for the entire 15 days in the window of the Gallery One, declaring himself a work of art. His all-embracing sense of creativity went as far as turning himself into "God the Creator" and declaring everything he touched or looked at a work of art. Through his consciousness and power of appropriation he took "possession of the notion of WHOLE, as a work of art. I am a living and mobile sculpture in all my moments and all my gestures, to be purchased at £250."[33]

During the Misfit Festival Vautier met George Maciunas, to whom he explained his theory for a "Theatre of Shock." Maciunas liked his ideas, but found them too spectacular and sensationalist. He told Vautier about the simple Actions George Brecht was performing in New York, and Vautier understood that there could be radicalism and extremism without falling into the trap of showiness. He remembers his reaction to Maciunas' comments:

> Immediately after coming back to Nice I called together my friends Robert Erébo, Robert Bozzi, Pierre Pontani, etc., (later also Serge III) and we got the preparations for the Fluxus festival of 1963 under way. We started straight away doing Fluxus pieces in the street. I adapted many of my "Theatre of Shock" pieces to Fluxus. A the time, we had in Nice a very competitive theatre situation. There were many small groups, mainly friends. They were terribly pretentious, playing Beckett and Ionesco. And thinking they were innovative. That's why we, the Total Art Group, started playing Fluxus pieces as "real life" events. Our basic premise was: Fiction is dead. Today, theatre must be "real life" and involve audience participation. And to be honest, it was because of my ego-trip that I called the group *Art Total*, rather than Fluxus.
>
> (Vautier 1982:148–50)

The Festival d'Art Total took place in Nice in July 1963. Several Fluxus friends came to support the event. As far as Vautier's own performances were concerned, they did contain a certain Fluxus quality. But they also continued his line of thinking of the years 1959 to 1962. His Actions were a "Theatre of Appropriation," summed up in his placards "Ben = Art" and "Tout est Art." His earlier attempts at introducing surprise and improvisation into the conventional theatre format ("Theatre of Shock") were abandoned in favor of performances where everything could be appropriated and declared art, or anti-art, or non-art.

> The "gift to see" consists in the first instance of exhausting all possibilities and limits of the concept of "tout est art," and secondly of going beyond this "everything is art" to arrive at an attitude of non-art, anti-art. Thereby, Fluxus became interested in the content of art in order to combat it. On the level of the artist, this meant a new form of subjectivity. All this is difficult, if not impossible, because depersonalization is a new form of personality, and non-art a new form of art. However, the intention was there, and the honesty of that intention is one of the most fundamental characteristics of

As part of Jean-Jacques Lebel's 1964 First Festival of Free Expression in Paris, participants in Ben Vautier's *Total Theatre* are led out into the street with paper bags over their heads. (Photo by Cheney, courtesy of the Department of Rare Books and Special Collections, Princeton University Libraries.)

> Fluxus. Even if the question is impossible, it is still important to pose it.
>
> (Vautier 1980:270)

During the festival, Vautier again exhibited himself as a living sculpture:

> Ben the creator of Total Art, has given life to *Agui-gui*, god of the street, so that his actions are works of art. Ben will sign Agui-gui, the living and mobile sculpture in all instants of his life and all his gestures.[34]

He carried out a number of mundane actions in front of an invited audience and declared them works of art: on 26 July he ate some mysterious foodstuff on the Terrace of the Avenue Félix Faure and handed out guarantee cards to the spectators certifying that they had been presented with a work of art; on 4 August, "Agui-gui the Living Sculpture" invited people to a golf club for a bowl of salad and declared it a work of art; at the Centre d'Art Total Vautier presented himself as God the Creator, invited people to look at him, and if they desired, signed certificates of guarantee that they had "appropriated" a work of art at the price of 10 francs; on another day at the same Centre, he had "an artistic nervous breakdown" during which he accepted and signed "any kind of behavior by any kind of spectator" as works of art.

Over the next years, Vautier's Actions became more and more

conceptual. In 1966, the Venice Biennale invited him to exhibit/perform at the French pavilion. The audience was informed about the resulting creation on the following placard:

> 400 miles from Venise / In Nice / 32, Road Tondutti-de-l'Escarène / From the 18th of June 1966 / During the Biennale of Venise / BEN SHALL LIVE AS USUAL. / Everyday / He shall inscribe in a Fluxus copybook / Unimportant and important details / Of the day. / At the end of the Biennale of Venise / This copybook / Signed and dated / Will represent / *EVERYDAY LIFE.* / Ben's contribution to the Biennale of Venise 1966.

On 16 June 1966 he presented *Nobody,* a piece for which he sent out invitations that informed the potential audience that "the curtain will rise precisely at 21.30 and close at precisely 22.30. Absolutely nobody will be allowed to witness the performance." A photograph of the production shows Vautier and a group of ten friends sitting around a table on the stage. To the left of the proscenium arch on a chair stands a large placard saying *Personne.* The rows of seats in the auditorium are empty (Stedelijk Museum 1973:29).

In a manifesto of April 1966, *Le Happening de Ben,* Vautier distinguished between two types of Happenings: one that aims at a transformation of reality, the other at presenting reality through means taken from that reality (in Sohm 1970:n.p.; and in Dreyfus 1989:168). He sees himself operating in the latter category. Here, life is represented by simple and real actions which create an awareness of the fact that reality in all its aspects is a form of spectacle. That is why "EVERYTHING IS ART and ART IS LIFE." But this fact still needs to be communicated through the personality of the artist. The consequence is:

> If we all believe in this POSSIBLE WHOLE, everybody communicates it through his own personality. Therefore it is only the WHOLE of X, and Art is not life per se, but life as communicated by X. To me, the WHOLE is a WHOLE of sincerity and contradiction. It strives to be an unlimited WHOLE, which contains the WHOLE of all other WHOLES. It is therefore a work of ambition. My Happenings are concerned with communicating this claim. It is only possible within one frame: the acceptance of all reality. Its realization exists through my claim, which conditions and guarantees the reality which, whatever it may be, I communicate and authenticate through my signature.
>
> (Sohm 1970:n.p.)

JEAN-JACQUES LEBEL

In comparison to the highly complex aesthetics of some of the artists discussed above, the theoretical foundation and the artistic format of Jean-Jacques Lebel's Happenings were extremely simple to grasp and therefore had immediate impact on a whole generation of young artists. Lebel was a very active publicist, expressing his views in short statements, longer essays, and books. He was neither a sophisticated thinker, nor a particularly original visual artist. He did well to move away from painting and poetry into performance work.[35]

Lebel was instrumental in popularizing the Happenings genre, which he had studied firsthand in New York from November 1961 to February 1962, holding an exhibition at the March Gallery on 10th Street, giving poetry readings at the Living Theatre, and participating in Claes Oldenburg's *Store Days* at the Ray Gun Theatre. It was largely through Lebel's activism that Happenings became linked with hippie and Beat culture, antiestablishment sentiments, and leftist political convictions. His Festivals of Free Expression were major events reported by the national press in the most sensationalist manner. He revelled in shocking the bourgeois press with nudity, anarchical actionism, and radical political slogans. Even *Paris-Match* "reviewed" his Second Festival of Free Expression and declared the Happenings the "passe-temps favoris" of the Beatniks and "le dernier cri du pop art" (Hanoteau 1966). The American press took a belated interest in the event. Under the heading "Bacchanal of Nudity, Spaghetti and Poetry," *Life Magazine* reported that "the most admired of Europe's underground artists, Jean-Jacques Lebel put on a monstrous marathon of Happenings in Paris."[36] His Happenings in France, England, and Italy became a hallmark of the genre and inspired hundreds of other artists, writers, and performers to imitate his activities. Lebel himself, when watching some of these events, regarded their authors as second-rate "epigones" and declared with dismay:

> In the United States, Happenings are being turned out to order for Universities or smart parties. Certain playwrights and filmmakers have begun to plagiarize the finds uncovered by Happenings; needless to say they completely distort the significance of what they use.
>
> (Lebel 1967a:41)

Before describing some of Lebel's most significant Happenings, I want to summarize the key elements of his performances:[37]

1. Structure of Happenings

Happenings are an open and fluid art form with no beginning, middle, or end. The scenic actions are not mapped out in any detail and therefore allow plenty of room for improvisation. They only happen once and cannot be repeated (Lebel 1967a:30).

2. Audience Participation

Happenings are "the art of participation" and do not allow any voyeurism or exhibitionism. In a Happening, everybody involved acts out his or her relationship with their psycho-social environment. Happenings are not designed to be contemplated by spectators but to force them into active intervention (Lebel 1967a:34). They are not based on "unilateral processes, but propose an exchange and collaboration" (27). It is a central aim of Happenings to stir spectators out of their habitual passivity, which they have been conditioned to by literary theatre and the "alienating mechanism of an image industry" (36). Happenings are not unchangeable ceremonies. Paralysis is replaced by action. Happenings establish relations between subjects. Instead of monodirectional exchanges there is dialog and circulation of ideas (36–37).

3. Happenings and Life

Happenings are a means of breaking through the wall that separates art from life. The Happenings artist is not content with interpreting life, but offers a direct experience of life and allows us to participate in its unfolding in the reality of our existence (Lebel 1967a:21). In Happenings the participant finds "cosmogony in the action. He reinvents the world by coming into contact with it" (Lebel 1968a:98). Happenings are not "paintings" of the struggles of life, but intensive acts waging the battle of "overcoming art, of leaving theatre behind, and of arriving at life" (Lebel 1965b:359). They lead to a complete transformation of human beings by making them change "their old ways of seeing, of feeling, of being" (Lebel 1968a:89).

4. Theatre of Rebellion

Happenings are a protest against the power of State authority, the politics of the ruling class, the controlling of our actions through the police and of our mind through the censors. Happenings are a fighting method against "this exploiting society with its slave-owning mentality and its irremediable culture. Art is in full and fundamental dissidence with all regimes and all forms of coercion" (Lebel 1967a:19). It is a "combative art" and serves in "the struggle for liberty of expression on a political footing" (20, 21). Happenings are an expression of the "libertarian spirit" (76) and of "an artistic *and* political revolution" (40). They fight all forms of repression and coercion and "directly tackle political and sexual themes" (23). They launch the "advent of sexuality" in the performing arts and offer an alternative to "the adulterated chain-store eroticism" of today (29, 30).

5. A New Form of Communication

Happenings are a new form for communicating people's innermost feelings. "They give back to artistic activity something which has been torn away from it; the intensification of feeling, the play of instinct, a sense of festivity, social agitation. The Happening is above all a means of interior communication; then, and incidentally, a spectacle." (Lebel 1967a:40). Happenings bring us back into contact with our instincts, whose sexual basis has been sublimated for the sake of culture.[38] They give expression to our subconscious and turn dreams into actions (Lebel 1967a:27, 33). They produce "an intensely receptive state of mind" (39) akin to hallucinatory experiences after taking LSD or similar drugs (26) and "create a mood in which each person dreams the dreams of the others; the Happening is the concretization of a collective dream and a vehicle of intercommunication" (28).

6. Against the Capitalist At Market

More than any other art form, Happenings are created to fight "this mercantile, state-controlled conception of culture" (Lebel 1967a:18). The Happenings artist is no longer willing "to let himself be vampirized by the cultural industry" (Lebel 1966a:28). He is a counterimage to the old "clown of the ruling class," who has been "dispossessed of most of his intellectual resources, progressively depersonalized as he 'gets on' and 'succeeds' socially," and who in the end finds himself "on his knees before Authority and the Stock Market" (Lebel 1967a:18–19). "True creators," like the Happenings artists, have nothing in common with the artistic "civil servant or the street hawker" (22).

As far as I could gather from the various documents at my disposal, Lebel's most significant Happenings were:

L'anti-procès, Galerie de la Fontaine des Quatres Saisons, Paris, 29 April–9 May 1960 (repeated in Venice, 14 July 1960; and Milan, Galleria Brera, 5 June 1961).
Pour conjurer l'esprit de catastrophe, Galerie Raymond Cordier, Paris, 27 November 1962 (repeated in Boulogne, Studio de Cinéma, February 1963).
Incidents, Musée d'Art Moderne, Paris, 8 October 1963.
Tableaux-happenings, Galerie Raymond Cordier, Paris, 1963.
Collage Happening, Denison Hall, Paris, 8–9 June 1964.

(above and right) In Jean-Jacques Lebel's *Pour Conjurer l'Esprit de Catastrophe*, first performed in 1962, actions unfolded simultaneously throughout the Cordier Gallery. This 1963 version was done at the Boulogne Film Studios. (Photos by Francois Massal, courtesy of J.J. Lebel.)

1er Festival de la Libre Expression, American Center, Paris, 25–30 May 1964.

Mode d'emploi du Pseudo-kini, les vrais faux seins, et Play-tex, le soutien-gorge qui tient, Restaurant La Tour d'Argent, Paris, 11 March 1965.

2e Festival de la Libre Expression, American Center, Paris, 17–25 May 1965.

Déchirex, American Center, Paris, 25 May 1965.

Welsh Automative Salad with Yoghurt, Arts Festival at Reardon Smith Hall, Cardiff, 24 September 1965.

3e Festival de la Libre Expression, Théâtre de la Chimère, Paris, 4 April– 3 May 1966.

120 minutes dédiées au Divin Marquis, Paris, 27 April 1966.

Tant va la cruche a l'eau qu'a la fin elle s'enlace, Festival de Cassis, August 1966.

Distorted postcards, Destruction in Art Symposium at the Africa Centre, London, 12 September 1966.

Le Happening dans la rue, Festival Sigma, Bordeaux, 19 November 1966.

Fluxus: Une conférence-démonstration, Université, Nanterre, 12 February 1967.

Golden Duck Soup, Teatro Regio, Parma, 23 March 1967.

4e Festival de la Libre Expression, Papa Gayo, Saint-Tropez, 12 July–28 August 1967.

Homage à Lautréamont, Montevideo, 1967.

Conférence-Démonstration, Istituto di Tella, Buenos Aires, 1967.

Election de Miss Festival, Festival de Cinéma, Knokke-le-Zoute, 1967.

Lebel's debut as a performer took place in the *Anti-Process*, which he organized in 1960 with his friend Alain Jouffroy. Lebel himself described the event as "a hotchpotch of poetry, painting, jazz and very little theatre" (Lebel 1966a:81). It included a funeral for which they carried a coffin through the streets of Venice and at the end held a sumptuous ceremony. The poster for the event emphasized that it was directed against all forms of authority and for the absolute sovereignty of the artist from all moral or cultural dogmas.[39]

Lebel's first major Happening was *Catastrophe*, performed in the Cordier Gallery in front of a number of Surrealist and neo-Dadaist paintings and sculptures. Lebel had devised the event as a "collective exorcism" of a large number of contemporary problems:

> Blackmail by the market; war of nerves, sex, eye, and belly; coercion of the nuclear Santa Claus; nationalist terror; the moral crisis and its cultural exploitation; the physical crisis and its political exploitation; modern art praying to Wall Street.
>
> (Lebel 1966a:86–87)

In order to achieve his aims, he involved the visitors to the gallery in the whole event. Accompanied by the sounds of a frenetic jazz combo, a large number of simultaneous actions unfolded throughout the gallery: Lebel as President de Gaulle wheeled a toy baby carriage through the audience; abstract images were projected onto a nude female body; two naked women painted a collage on the walls of the gallery, had newspaper headlines stuck onto their bodies, then put on masks of Kennedy and Khrushchev and took a "blood-bath" in a tub filled with chicken blood; an erotic action painting was created under a row of penis-shaped objects hanging from the ceiling: the painter Ferrò, dressed as a sex priest, stuck a paintbrush in the form of a papier mâché phallus into paint pots which two women clasped between their legs, and finally collapsed in a "mystic orgasm"; Kudo demonstrated the "Impotence of Philosophy" by carrying a cupboard around the gallery, opening it and revealing a womb spiked with hypodermic needles; Jouffroy read a concrete poem; Lebel transformed himself into a TV set and declared that the revolution was on the march (signaling with his hands the union of a penis and vagina). Finally, Lebel and some members of the audience took off their clothes, danced, and produced an action painting. When it was completed, Lebel jumped through the canvas and walked out of the gallery to shouts of "Heil Art, Heil Sex."[40]

The *First Workshop of Free Expression* of 1964 lasted for six days and included an exhibition; a jazz evening; Happenings by Kudo, Ferrò, Brock, Daniel Pommereulle, Vautier; a performance of Carolee Schnee-mann's *Meat Joy*; a sociodrama on a theme by Duchamp; an evening with screenings of avant-garde films; and on the last day, a colloquium on experimental art.

The *Second Festival of Free Expression* (1965) lasted for eight days. It involved the participation of some sixty artists and was visited by over 2,000 people (according to *Time Magazine*, June 1965). There were again poetry readings, film screenings, and performances, this time by Filliou, Williams, Nam June Paik, Charlotte Moorman, Vautier, and others. Lebel's own contribution was *Déchirex*, the "Bacchanal of Nudity, Spaghetti and Poetry" mentioned above.[41] On the stage of the American Center, cast in penumbra, two women were playing badminton with fluorescent rackets. Two men with equally fluorescent helmets and spectacles joined them. Like snails, they glided toward the women and began to eat their costumes, which were made entirely out of cabbage. On the other side of the stage several films were being projected. Suddenly, a nude woman on a motorcycle roared into the auditorium. She was chased through the crowd until the lights suddenly went off. A spotlight focused on an old car that was being demolished with axes and hammers. A woman with a death mask kneeled on the crushed roof and a young man covered her body with spaghetti, which she then hurled into the jeering crowd. All the while one could hear a tape of Mayakovsky reading some of his poems, the noise of heavy gunfire and of screaming fire brigades, and finally a political speech by Fidel Castro. The badminton players, by now bereft of their vegetarian costumes, entered the auditorium and opened an auction of the demolished car. The Beat poet Lawrence Ferlinghetti read from his "The Great Chinese Dragon," while one woman shaved her groin, another woman tore off the arms and legs of a doll, and a naked couple made love in a vertically suspended bag. Finally, a huge plastic tube in the form of a serpent was inflated, the motorcycle left the hall, and the film screening came to an end. However, the audience carried on with the Happening for another one-and-a-half hours.

The *Third Festival of Free Expression* (1966) presented Happenings by Kudo, Vautier, and Filliou, and Lebel's homage to the Marquis de Sade, *120 Minutes Dedicated to the Divine Marquis*. A collage of Surrealist films was being screened to the sound of strident jazz music and a tape of the most obscene passages from *The 120 Days of Sodom*. Onstage, a nude woman wearing a mask of Charles de Gaulle was covered in cream and then gradually licked clean by volunteers from the audience.

Lebel staged his first open-air Happening for the Festival of Cassis under the title *The Pitcher Goes to the Well Until in the End it Makes Love*. Performed in the city's harbor, it involved a 300-meter-long Monster of Loch Ness, an apparition of Priap, Bernadette Lafont as Venus rising from the sea, a declaration of Free Love, and a lot of improvised actions carried out by members of the Living Theatre.

Far more unstructured was *Golden Duck Soup*, which Lebel organized at the Teatro Regio in Parma. Staging a Happening in a nineteenth-century proscenium arch theatre provided him with an opportunity to demonstrate how the traditional passivity of a bourgeois audience could be turned into an active experience of the forces of life.[42] Lebel began the evening with a speech, in which he reported how the mayor of the town had tried to prevent him from staging any indecent acts in the municipal theatre. He then asked the audience to join him onstage. To the diabolic sounds of the Musica Electronica Viva ensemble the first part of the Happening began: The spectators were bundled together by means of a rope, then blindfolded and led out of the theatre. When everybody had been guided back to the hall, Lebel repeated the play with the inflatable serpent that had proved so successful at the *Second Festival of Free Expression*. For the final part of the evening, the spectators were told: "We want to know what life is. We want to know what death is." This problem was debated until long after midnight. As the local reviewer reported, Lebel withdrew from the discussion after a while and left the theatre, knowing that the audience would continue the "performance" without his assistance.

In the course of the 1960s, there was little progression in Lebel's thinking. The only significant change took place in 1968 when, under the influence of the May Rebellion, he became a political activist and sought to integrate the performative expressions he had pioneered in the preceding years into the students' street actions. This last stage of Lebel's career as a Happenings artist he himself described as "Political Street Theatre" (Lebel 1969). A few examples of his Street Plays were printed in *TDR*, and he commented on the genre:

The May Revolution dynamited the limits of "art" and "culture" as it did all other social or political limits. The old avant-gardist dream of turning "life" into "art," into a collective creative experience, finally came true. [...] The May uprising was theatrical in that it was a gigantic fiesta, a revelatory and sensuous explosion outside the "normal" pattern of politics.

(Lebel 1969:112)

As Lebel declared to Vostell in a letter from October 1968:

I have ceased to be an artist. I'm still creative as much and as often as I can, especially producing collective, spontaneous, dangerous, consciousness-busting, empirical events (sometimes one can call them Happenings, sometimes, more often, they are simply life).

(in Vostell 1970b:n.p.)

However, this "permanent revolutionary process," as he called it in the letter, lasted only a short while and came to a halt very abruptly. Lebel withdrew from the art and theatre scene for nearly twenty years in a self-imposed "exile."

MILAN KNÍŽÁK

Lack of documentation precludes analysis of the many activities pursued in Poland, Czechoslovakia, Hungary, and other Eastern European countries. But I should like to present at least one artist who was generally regarded by the Happenings and Fluxus groups in the West to be their most significant representative in Eastern Europe: Milan Knížák. He studied at the Prague Art School (1958–1959) and Art Academy (1963–1964) and was expelled from both. His artistic output was extremely diverse: he worked in the fields of music, painting, sculpture, fashion design, and architecture. In 1964 he founded the group AKTUAL, with whom he carried out a significant number of Happenings and Events. In 1966 he was imprisoned and his activities were forcefully curtailed. He left the CSSR in 1968 and traveled in Europe and the USA, still pursuing his Happenings, Events, and Activities.[43]

Knížák's interest in live art began during his student years and was independent of anything that was happening in the West at that time. His "demonstrations" and "street actions" were very much a reaction against the dominant trends in postwar art and the mystic and Surrealist traditions in Czechoslovakia. Knížák's impulses for artistic creation were simple, practical, and direct in meaning. Hedonism and the enjoyment of positive life forces were combined with a sense for the poetic and sentimental. Knížák was a man of great optimism, sensuality, and *joie de vivre*. Spontaneity and immediacy meant more to him than aesthetic finesse. The demonstrations were designed to bring to the fore the inner forces that have been repressed or suffocated by social conditioning and material preoccupations. Knížák considered his Happenings to be a form of therapy. They were designed as concrete stimuli to evoke concrete responses and to bring about change in the life of the individual. He compared his Actions with a vitamin that stimulates energy and healthy activities. His Happenings had no hidden political messages, as was often assumed. Despite his many problems with the police, he never turned his art into a manifestation of political protest. He fought against tradition because it was an obstacle to the full enjoyment of life in all its manifold aspects. Art was for him an experience of life in a direct and immediate way.

Although Knížák tried to ensure that his creativity was not impeded by too many theoretical preoccupations and that his Actions preserved their improvised and fluid quality, he nevertheless operated with certain principles and concepts in mind, some of which he explained in the magazines *Aktual Art* (three issues, 1964–1966) and *Aktual Newspaper* (three issues 1966–1967). In the manifesto *Aktual: Another Life* (1965/66),[44] Knížák described his artistic program as overcoming the gap between rational and sensual thinking. Art was for him a "hygiene" that could liberate people from old ways of living:

> Create a game out of diverse, everyday life situations. Free humankind from its cramps and monstrosities. Influence them through movement, words, actions, looks, appearance, everything. Through simple, anonymous activities. There is no difference between provoked and spontaneous actions. Walking, having lunch, excursions, games, festivities, tram rides, shopping, talking, sports, fashion shows . . . – but everything in a slightly different way. Spontaneous street rituals. Conflicts. Conflicts that are there to be solved. It doesn't matter which means are employed for it.
>
> (Kunsthalle 1986:n.p.)

In another manifesto, *How My Actions Can Be Carried Out By Anyone* (1965) Knížák expands on this by saying:

> The Actions I have organized have no planned concept. They have only been sketched out, like Kaprow's Actions. [. . .] The realization of my present Actions depend to ninety-nine percent on the conditions and evolving circumstances at the moment of realization. [. . .] Some Actions demand an ability of the organizer to react sensitively to the development of the participants' behavior and an ability to recognize the necessity for an ineffectual intervention in order to achieve a maximum effect from the situation. [. . .] The Action gains momentum from the mental attitude of

the participants and planner, from confronting the existing reality with an evolving reality.

(Kunsthalle 1986:n.p.)

The first Happening Knížák organized in Prague took place in 1964 and was called *Demonstration for All the Senses* (see Oliva 1990:308; Kaprow 1966:305–09). It began with the organizer dressed up in unusual clothes handing out to the participants a number of objects, which they had to carry around during the whole action. They were led to a house and had to climb through a window. They entered a room where a lot of perfume had been sprinkled on the floor. The participants were locked up inside and left to their own devices in order to experience "a disturbance of their normal state of mind." Then they resumed their walk. On their way, there "happened" a number of unusual occurrences such as a man lying on the street playing a double bass, a chair falling down from a house. The participants assembled in a square and were asked to arrange a straight line with the various objects they had been carrying around. Then they were asked to collect the objects again and to form another row with them. When they walked back to the house, they encountered a woman lying on a mattress in the middle of the street. The participants were offered a book, from which each of them could tear out a page. Then they were told that this was the end of part one of the demonstration and that the follow-up would take place in two weeks' time. What happened in between these two dates was declared a Happening for which each participant was responsible.

Knížák distributed suggestions for such "individual Happenings" to people who participated in his activities or watched them in the streets. Other instructions he sent as letters to people he did not know at all, or he left them in doorways and mailboxes. Some of them read: "Destroy every picture in your flat and hang your dirty linen up in their place"; "Hand over your salary to the next person you meet on the street"; "Masturbate continuously for eight hours"; "Drink two quarts of rum every day."

The *Second Manifestation of Aktual Art* took place on 23 May 1965 in the middle of Prague and began with a lecture by Knížák on "The second atomic explosion in China and its influence on modern art" (see Kunsthalle 1986; Vostell 1982:129–31). He then took a book on Renaissance art, tore it apart and distributed the pictures among the participants. They were then led to a house, where many household objects were hanging outside on the wall. These objects fell onto the street and had to be collected by the participants and taken into the house. When they came out on the street again, thousands of pages torn out of telephone directories were littering the pavement. A (real) police officer appeared and ordered the Happening to be ended. The participants were forced to clear the debris off the street and were led to another house. Old pieces of furniture were lying everywhere and the participants were asked to demolish the whole installation. The third part took place in another square of the city. The participants were asked to paste together the next issue of the Aktual magazine. Then they were given a candle and led into a dark house. They were handed little pieces of paper with instructions written on them: "Ring telephone number 357 163 and speak with the person at the other end about the uselessness of art." Or: "Ring 887 259 and speak about the smile of Mona Lisa and the Third World War." After this, the participants were provided with a simple meal of baked potatoes. To avoid any further police intervention, they dispersed and met again outside the city center in a park. A young woman performed a striptease and asked everybody to join her. They lit a fire and a few pairs of underpants and stockings went up in flames. Everyone had great fun, and after eight hours the Happening came to a close.

VIENNESE ACTIONISM

The artists discussed above regarded themselves as part of a broad Happenings movement. Their participation in the many Happenings and Fluxus festivals created a certain group mentality, against which every individual artist guarded his or her own aesthetic stance and personal independence.

The case was slightly different with a rather special brand of Actions organized by a group of artists based in Vienna and known as the "Wiener Aktionsgruppe." They have rightly been called "a special feature within the context of the Fluxus and Happening movement" (Oberhuber 1989:17).[45] Although its individual members had been performing their works since 1962, the group was only formally constituted in July 1965. Otto Mühl once stated in an interview that he had heard of American Happenings "sometime before 1963" (Mühl 1981:35). But by that time both he and Hermann Nitsch had already developed the basic philosophy and aesthetics that informed their Actions. In their first group publication they placed themselves in a wider, international context and emphasized the parallels between their activities and those of the American Happenings artists.[46] And indeed, an American visitor who had seen several of Kaprow's performances reacted to one of their first public performances by exclaiming: "But this is a Happening!"[47] However, due to the unusual nature of the group's Actions they were rarely invited to present their works at other Happenings festivals in Europe.[48]

Viennese Actionism was the result of a continuous development that led from painting via collage, assemblage, installation, and action painting to time-based art, where the work with the material was exhibited in a performative process called *Materialaktion*. Hermann Nitsch progressed in 1960 from Expressionist religious painting to Tachism and then into action painting.[49] From the spraying, splashing, and smearing of dyes, he moved to working with blood, which he poured from a freshly slaughtered lamb onto the canvas. Before getting into action painting and actionism proper, Nitsch has been working on his idea of a *Theatre of Orgies and Mysteries* and had produced the first versions of a six-day drama that combined elements taken from the myths of Oedipus, Christ's passion, Parsifal, the Nibelungs, and other sources.[50] For Nitsch, the progression from ritual theatre to action painting to ritualistic Actionism was based on the "dionysic-dynamic" element entailed in all these forms of expression. The use of the vital substances of blood, viscera, and flesh in his paint actions of 1960 to 1963 led him quite naturally to his *Lammzerreißaktionen*, which formed the core of most of his over eighty performances in the past thirty years.

Most of these Actions contained a number of elements which were combined according to a standard formula: to the sound of loud music, Nitsch acted as a high priest and fastened a slaughtered lamb, head down, as if crucified. He gradually disemboweled it and let the blood and viscera fall onto a white cloth. The innards of other lambs were placed on the body of a nude human being, who was finally "crucified" like the lamb. The carcass of the eviscerated lamb was beaten and hurled against the wall. The actors tore out lumps of flesh with their teeth and stamped on the mutilated cadavers. In between the excessive actions there were quiet moments during which the carcasses were anointed with perfume and decorated with flowers. A chasuble, monstrance, or similar ecclesiastical garment was laid out on the floor. The objects were then discarded and a new cycle of ritual maltreatment set in. The Action usually ended with a totem meal that contained many reminiscences of the Eucharist.

The generic name Nitsch gave to these Actions was *Abreaktionsspiel* (abreaction play). The first of them was performed on 19 December 1962 in the flat of his friend Otto Mühl; the second was a public event at the Galerie Dvorak on 16 March 1963. By 1970 he had performed thirty-one of these rituals, mainly in private apartments or studios, some in galleries, in open-air spaces, in a restaurant, and in a meat market. His architectural plans for a specially constructed O.M. Theatre came finally to fruition when he acquired the Prinzendorf Castle in 1971. Ever since he has been perfecting his concept of a six day drama.

The origins of the abreaction plays go back to the year 1957, when Nitsch began to study systematically the available literature on ancient cults and rituals and the psychoanalytical writings of Freud, Rank, and

Jung. The most prominent myths to which he constantly refers in his texts are those of Dionysus Zagreus, Attis, Oedipus, and the Bacchae (see Stärk 1987:31–36). From these he developed his concept of a festival of orgies and mysteries with the sacrifice and crucifixion at its core. In *On the Essence of Tragedy* he wrote:

> Tragedy turned from its original state into something different, something that led far away from it: playful theatre. The innermost essence of tragedy was rooted in a natural desire to do justice to a collective human urge to ventilate our instincts. [. . .] The dramatic effect is caused by an instinctive attempt at using art as a means to rebel against the censorship of our Super Ego. Or better, it is an attempt at outwitting it. The intellectual and conscious control of our lower life energies is pushed aside in order to attain an insight into our subconscious, unbridled, chaotic libido. A short contact with these vital forces leads to their liberation. They are pushed to extreme satisfaction, ecstasy, joyful cruelty, sadomasochistic reactions, excess. Dionysus, in Greek mythology, provoked excess. He transcended into animality and chaos. He sacrificed himself and was torn apart. That's why tragedy is the beginning of excess. The Dionysian forces of the subconscious thrust out into the open gain form and become, to some extent, part of our conscious life. The result is psychic cleansing (catharsis). An effect is produced that hits the spectators and their psyche. Ancient drama, like the myths, was a reflection of a collective desire for abreaction, conditioned by the restrictive reality principle that has been imposed on all human beings.
>
> (Nitsch [1963] 1965)

Nitsch established a connection between the primitive cult of Dionysus – the tearing up of animals and the eating of raw flesh in a state of ecstasy and frenzy – with the transubstantiation rituals of the Catholic church. In the sacrifice of the god Dionysus he sees a prefiguration of the crucifixion of Christ. The totem meals are a counterpart of the Last Supper. Conquest of death, spiritual purification, redemption are as much a part of the cathartic abreaction plays as the liberation of stored-up aggression and the release of libidinal forces. Nitsch's abreaction plays are designed to have a therapeautic effect on their participants. Rather than letting out aggressive impulses in the barbarism of war, they are released through ritual acts of violence against a slaughtered animal. Thereby we gain insight into our aggressive instincts and can turn them into a form of art. Here, "erotic cruelty is overcome by aesthetic means" (Nitsch 1976b:n.p.). The performative process purifies us and, in the end, liberates us from the feelings of guilt.

If Nitsch, the Dionysian High Priest, attempted a return to the origins of tragedy, Otto Mühl, in a far more burlesque and hedonistic way, revived the tradition of the Greek Satyr play. Like his friend, Mühl arrived at Actionism through his work as a painter. His early "Material Actions" were dominated by a very painterly material aesthetics. In a way that was akin to Pop Art, he employed the everyday matter of foodstuffs, defunctionalized them, operated with them in an action-painting manner to create a material assemblage, and then let them degrade again into primal matter (*Versumpfung*). In the course of the early 1960s, the artist's body gained in importance over the concrete language of materials. The still lifes of bodies and materials (for example, *Still Life of a Male, A Female and a Bovine Head* of 1964, or *Penis Still Life* of 1964) turned into Actions where Mühl placed his and his assistants' bodies into the center of activity and arrived at a specific language of body gestures and improvised handling of the materials. For Mühl, the Action was a means of overcoming the representative in art and of establishing a direct, immediate contact with the substance of life. He saw the essence of existence in matter and energy. The improvised Material Action was a means of liberating vital (and especially sexual) impulses.

In 1965/66, Mühl's Actions gained in dramatic structure and theatrical appearance. The reckless and excessive orgies gave way to more controlled and precise psychomotoric exercises. His *First* and *Second Total Action* (1966) also allowed more interaction between the performers. With the founding of the Vienna Institute for Direct Art (June 1966), Mühl developed a sociopolitical action program under the name Zock. Together with a group of young colleagues he began to devise an alternative model to repressive, bourgeois society. Heavily inspired by the writings of Wilhelm Reich and the 1920s Sexpol movement, he founded, in 1972, the Action-Analytical Commune.[51] Mühl performed his last Action in 1970, declaring: "We from the Institute of Direct Art see in Happenings a thoroughly bourgeois art, just art. We want to overcome this idiotic art."[52]

Two other artists from the Vienna Actionist group, the two youngest, built on what Nitsch and Mühl had already established as a conceptual framework for "Action Happenings" or "Direct Art Happenings," as they often called their performances. From 1966 onward, Günter Brus and Rudolf Schwarzkogler transcended the Happening format and moved into pure body art.

Between 1964 and 1970, Brus created forty-three Actions. His first work, *Ana*, while still painting, extended into the third dimension. After that, he concentrated on using his own body as a medium of expression:

> Self-painting is a further development of painting. The pictorial surface

has lost its function as the sole expressive support. It was led back to its origins, the wall, the object, the living being, the human body. By incorporating my body as expressive support, occurrences arise as a result.

(in Mühl 1986)

Brus not only used his body as a painterly surface, but with increasing rigor also attempted to penetrate the exterior shell of the human body, incorporating razor blades, nails, scissors, and a saw into his performances. The dividing, violating line, which was present in his early paintings, was now literally applied to his own body. The seventh Action – *Painting, Self-Painting, Self-Mutilation* (6 July 1965) – was his first in front of a general audience. The performance itself was less shocking than what Brus announced in the catalog as his ultimate aim:

I dissever my left hand. Somewhere lies a foot. A suture on my wrist joint bone. I press a drawing pin into my spinal cord. I nail my large toe to my forefinger. Pubic, underarm, and head hairs lie on a white plate. I slit open the aorta with a razor blade. I slam a wire-tack into my ear. I split my head lengthwise into two halves. I insert barbed wire into my urethra and by turning it slightly try to cut the nerve.

(Brus 1965: n.p.)

In 1967, Brus created a new type of performance, which he called Body Analysis. He gave up all theatrically staged Direct Art Happenings and discarded the material symbolism of props and costumes. The body itself with its functions, reactions, and secretions became the sole medium of expression. However, the masochistic element employed in these performances became increasingly dangerous. After his last and most extreme Action, *Breaking Test* (19 June 1970) – a test of nerves for the audience who watched as he mutilated himself – Brus came so close to self-destruction that he was forced to abandon all further performance work.

Even more masochistic and, ultimately, fatal was the body art of Rudolf Schwarzkogler (see Cibulka 1977). He was only twenty years old when he met Hermann Nitsch in 1960. The problem of overcoming Informel Art meant little to him. He derived his inspiration from the paintings of Schiele, Kokoschka, Mondrian, and Klein, and the theatrical ideas of Artaud. Between 1965 and 1968 he created five solo performances, devoid of any expressive-gestural drama and presented in private spaces to a small, invited audience. Parallel to that, in a process of extreme intensity, he carried out a series of auto-performances without an audience, fully concentrating on his own experience of the work and transposing it onto photographic plates. Already his early solo Actions were monologs without any interaction with the audience; but now, in his solipsistic auto-performances, which were also conceived as a "school of experience," actor and spectator merged (see Schwarzkogler 1970). After his last Action in the spring of 1968, which was a collaboration with Brus and Mühl, he occupied himself solely with performance ideas without bringing any of them to realization. Schwarzkogler's work became pure concept art. His desire for absolute perfection did not permit him to execute any of his scores. The study of Eastern mysticism and philosophy compelled him to find an ultimate solution in the complete suspension of corporeality: "All bodies are only appearances, images of the imagination, states of mind created out of its own volition" (in Klocker 1989:381; see also Badura-Triske and Klocker 1992). He withdrew more and more into an internal world, which he finally dissolved by committing suicide:

> The distinction between the mortal and the immortal. The strength to be able to renounce enjoying the fruit of the works. The ability to keep calm (reserved, self-controlled, resigned, collected, confident, and concentrated in thought and desire). The determination to be free . . .
>
> (Schwarzkogler 1970)

Viennese Actionism undoubtedly occupies a special position within the panorama of the European Happenings movement. It was firmly rooted in the Austrian tradition of introspection and psychoanalytical inquiry which investigated the existential condition under the surface of repressive social structures. The specific context of Austrian Catholicism, the heathen rituals and festivities of the peasant communities, the oppressiveness of Viennese bourgeois society, the brutality of Austro-fascism in its various guises: all these served as reference points for the Actionists and their extreme attempts at breaking down taboos and inhibitions. All Happenings artists were concerned with overcoming the gap between art and life. In Vienna it took on a far more specific form: breaking down the barriers between Super-Ego and Id, between social/cultural conventions and the libidinal forces. Unveiling the psychic condition of the human race was a process of sociopolitical critique and brought the Actionists into permanent conflict with the representatives of state power. The extreme unpleasantness of their performances led to exclusion from most "official" Happenings festivals.[53] However, the Viennese "aesthetics of ugliness"[54] cannot be fully understood without acknowledging its counterpoint, the emphasis on form and ritual perfection. Nitsch's idea of "form as the innermost essence of art" (1979 and 1986, II:16–19), Brus' concern with the perfect spatial surroundings for his performances, or Schwarzkogler's absolute purism and minute

determination even of the temperature and light quality of the performance space: all this seems to reflect what another Viennese writer,
Hermann Bahr, characterized as the essence of tragedy: "extracting
beauty from ugliness" (Bahr 1907:276).

HAPPENINGS IN GREAT BRITAIN

There were many other individuals and groups working within the
Happenings format all over the European continent. From Scandinavia
to Italy, from Spain to Hungary: everywhere there existed a rich field of
activity and experimentation, which has been chronicled by Hanns Sohm
in the catalog *Happening & Fluxus*, published on the occasion of the
1970 retrospective exhibition at the Cologne Kunstverein. There appears
to be only one major gap in Sohm's documentation: the Happenings
scene in Great Britain. Apart from a few major and well-known events
(the Festival of Misfits, 23 October–8 November 1962; the Edinburgh
Theatre of the Future Conference, 7 September 1963; the Destruction in
Art Symposium, 31 August–30 September 1966) there was a plethora of
similar activities which have never been systematically investigated and
recorded.[55] Given the lack of documentation I can only offer a few
general comments on some of the dominant trends in Britain.

The first Happenings took place in 1962 during the Merseyside Arts
Festival. They were directly inspired by Allan Kaprow's work and the
reports on the American Happenings movement, which slowly filtered
through into the British arts community. There had been a strong interest
in assemblage and environment art among British Pop artists. The
extension of this into the fourth dimension seemed logical to them, and
many followed the example given by their American colleagues. Mixed-
media artists such as Mark Boyle, John Latham, Jeff Nuttall, Bruce
Lacey, and Roger Ruskin Spear began to experiment with the Happenings genre. The form and content of their performances initially did not
differ a great deal from what had been developed in the USA. But given
the specific structure of the British art scene, an entirely different form
of presentation had to be found, which eventually led to many special
traits that distinguished British from American or Continental-European
Happenings.

First of all, Britain was nearly devoid of art galleries with a serious
interest in contemporary and experimental art. Victor Musgrave's
Gallery One in London was a rare exception, and it was here that the
Festival of Misfits was held.[56] However, the recent institution of the Arts
Council with its many regional branches created for the first time a
noncommercial base for young and enterprising artists. This shift away
from London to the provinces was strengthened by the many art schools

that gave the youngest generation an outlet for their interest in time-based art. The colleges of art in Leeds, Bradford, Wolverhampton, Newcastle, and Nottingham became a hub of experimentation with the Happenings genre.

The Happenings at the 1963 Edinburgh six-day conference on the future of the theatre was considered a major disturbance of a "serious" international event and a scandalous provocation that brought disrepute to the Scottish capital (see Calder 1967:57–79). Charles Marowitz remembered that the organizer of the Happening, Ken Dewey, "was called up before the conference like a kid who had thrown an inkwell into the electric fan, and asked to explain" (in Calder 1967:61). When, the following day, Allan Kaprow staged an open-air Happening outside the city center, the honor of the town was deemed to have been tarnished by the "barbarians" and "bohemians," as they were called in the local press. The Lord Provost (the Scottish equivalent to a mayor) declared that "it is a very great pity, indeed in a way it is quite a tragedy, that three weeks of glorious festival should have been smeared by a piece of pointless vulgarity."

The Edinburgh "scandal" brought the potential of Happenings as a means of protest and provocation to the attention of many nonconformist writers and dramatists. It inspired John Arden in 1963 to organize a Festival of Anarchy in the Yorkshire village of Kirkbymoorshire. The next years saw a mushrooming of groups who combined the inspiration they had received from the Happenings genre with their artistic training and/or literary and dramatic interests. Marowitz became instrumental in establishing the "Fringe" theatre scene in London. Welfare State, The People Show, John Bull's Puncture Repair Kit, the Yorkshire Gnomes, Cyclamen Cyclists, New Fol-de-Rols: a large number of early British fringe and experimental touring companies evolved from the Happenings scene.

As Adrian Henri has pointed out, one of the key centers for this activity was Liverpool, home of the Beatles and many other pop groups. The music clubs, with their regular supply of jazz, folk, pop, Beat, and rock groups were favored venues for Happenings performances. Together with the poetry clubs and certain bookshops (such as Better Books in London) they offered an alternative network to the overwhelmingly conservative theatres and exhibition spaces. Apart from that, there were some small studio theatres, rehearsal spaces, or foyers that were occasionally used for Happenings. And some art colleges had performance studios where time-based presentations were possible.

The close connection between the Happenings and music scenes meant that in Britain a quite different performance aesthetic developed in comparison to the USA and to Continental Europe. Many Happenings were featured as surprise elements in rock concerts. They were often organized by members of the pop group, who changed the musical and theatrical style of their performances in order to accommodate these "interludes" in their stage shows or even to make them an integral element of them. Henri described the typical visitors to these "Happening concerts" as "discriminating pop music fans." They were young people with a high school education or a university degree, but rarely with any art-college training. As a consequence, the performances made little intellectual demand on the club visitors. Many Happenings resembled a vaudeville show, a Monty Python sketch, or a scene from a *Beano* comic. A sense of fun was more important than straining one's brain muscles. The proverbial British reserve may explain why audience participation was relatively limited. Happenings were always loosely structured, but they depended to a large degree on the script, the score, and the prerecorded soundtracks. These Happenings were primarily performed to or for an audience. The spectators were activated and prompted to respond, but the degree of involvement in the unfolding of the event was far more restricted than in America. The Happeners knew their audiences and were fully aware that, primarily, they wanted to enjoy themselves and have a "fab" evening out with a slightly different note attached to it. They might be amused by the strange things that were "happening" onstage, and sometimes irritated by them. Even when provoked to anger, the audiences never revolted with outrage or physical reactions against the artists.

The music and poetry clubs became the favorite venues for musicians, artists, writers, and dramatists who had turned to Happenings as a contemporary art form. The relaxed liveliness that could be found in these clubs offered a welcome contrast to the staid art and theatre scene in London. Among the exceptions to this rule one must count the Institute of Contemporary Arts in London, a subsidized venue that hosted several Pop Art exhibitions and related activities. Otherwise, the capital offered Musgrave's Gallery One and the Better Books store. Some of the London Happenings took place in private lofts, warehouses, or apartments, or simply on the street. In Mark Boyle and Joan Hill's *Theatre* (1964), for example, a group of people was led down Potter's Lane into a derelict building that was marked on the outside with a sign saying: "Theatre." The spectators were seated in the kitchen in front of a plush curtain. When it was drawn aside, the "performance" began: the audience was looking out of the window onto the street, where nothing except everyday hustle and bustle could be observed.

Most British Happenings formed part of a carnivalesque celebration of oppositional values (see Nuttal 1968). The development of a youth culture, from the Liverpool Beat scene via the hippie festival on the Isle of Wight to the punk shows at the Roxy Club,[57] was accompanied by a stream of semi-improvised performances based on the model of American Happenings. To classify a pop group such as Bonzo Dog Doodah Band or a theatre company such as The People Show as belonging to the subject matter of this publication may stretch the term Happenings beyond its accepted limits. But the performances of such groups were more typical of the British Happenings scene than, say, Boyle's *Suddenly The Last Supper* (1964), a piece presented in his own flat, in which spectators watched slides of Botticelli's *Birth of Venus* projected onto a nude woman as Boyle and some friends quietly removed the contents of the apartment (Henri 1974:112–14). As to the many performances "in streets, public squares, boiler rooms, basements, department stores, forests; on buses, building sites, bridges, rooftops" to which Marowitz refers in his attempt at disproving the popular notion that, "for many people a Happening is a nude lady at the Edinburgh drama conference" (1965:21) – I have not been able to find any detailed descriptions.

SUMMARY

Comparing the wide spectrum of performance modes explored by American and European Happenings artists, one may find that the general characteristics outlined by Darko Suvin in this volume apply equally to the activities pursued on both continents. However, within this spectrum, there were certain shifts of emphasis that point toward a different mentality as well as a contrasting attitude toward the artistic developments in the postwar period.

The main reference point for all Happenings artists was Dada. But whereas in America the theories and artistic practices of the likes of Tzara, Duchamp, and Schwitters had to be (re)discovered in the 1950s and made generally available through translations and monographs (namely Robert Motherwell's *Dada Painters and Poets*, 1951), the European artists had easy access to this material and were therefore well-acquainted with the tradition of anti-art and nonmatrixed performances before the Second World War. All artists mentioned in this essay displayed in their statements an intimate knowledge of Dada art. Therefore, it is not astonishing that their reasoning on how to overcome the limits set by their forebears was far more profound than the aesthetics and philosophical presumptions of their American colleagues.

Secondly, there prevailed a political dimension to European Happenings which because of its depth, breadth, and pervasiveness did not possess an equivalent in the United States. Most American Happenings artists regarded their activity as an apolitical means of changing people's attitudes toward life. In some cases, this may have implied a sociocritical attitude. But more often it was restricted to altering the process of perception. Explicit political activism was generally shunned and deprecated:

> I'm not a social critic, neither am I simply an uncritical acceptor of the status quo [...]. Sometimes I'm quite political, but then I change my mind [...]. For me to see people wasting their time in the arts if they want to do social action, it almost makes me laugh.
>
> (Kaprow in Wick 1975:148)[58]

By contrast, both Happenings and Pop Art in Europe contained a conscious sociopolitical critique of affluent consumer society as it had developed after the Second World War. The affirmative attitude toward the artifacts of modern mass media that can be found among so many of the American artists was rarely shared by their European colleagues. Their standpoint ranged from open critique to subtle satire. Performances were conceived as a means of stimulating a critical consciousness in the viewer/spectator and, in that respect, the formula Art = Life possessed a far more concrete significance. Life as experienced in a Happening was no longer a mere reproduction or symbolic interpretation of our existential reality. It was rather a confrontation with our alienated existence in late-capitalist society, a discourse on the conflict between our real self and its alienated state. Through the performance the audience was encouraged to experience the authenticity of their exist-ence in opposition to "life unlived." The advantage of performance over painting/sculpture/environment was that it could draw the audience into a live experience of their social surroundings. It could eschew the pitfalls of didactic theatre, because it did not demonstrate political beliefs but rather arranged the conditions for an active experience of reality. Knowledge of the Brechtian *Verfremdungseffekt* can be presumed in all artists discussed in this essay. Alienating through artistic means an alienating existence (reality) approximates the Hegelian triad of negation of negation. Dialectics as "the mother of progress" lies at the basis of many Happenings discussed above. Happenings as a method of social change were far more effective in the eyes of many European Happeners than the traditional political theatre.

However, as to the application of this method there prevailed a great divergence of opinion. Lebel operated with a very simple, semi-Marxist model in mind. Vostell led his spectators/performers into a prearranged frame, where individual experiences were to inform individual respon-ses. The outcome was never predetermined; it was left to the audience to draw their own conclusions from what they had experienced. Beuys' anthropological and anthroposophical Utopia of a nonalienated society formed an ideological background that influenced the specific character of his "shamanistic" performances. He saw himself as a medium who could put the audience into contact with their "true nature." The use of myth and of archetypal symbols was a regression into a prehistoric state of human development and an attempt at employing this ancient knowledge for a regeneration of modern society. Art as "social sculpture" was to mold an ecological, free community of creative and autonomous individuals. Filliou and Vautier, on the other hand, reverted to French Existentialism in their concepts of creativity. In their theory, the epistemological differentiation between art and non-art was sublated in the creative process, which was seen as a purely individual act of self-realization and as such could transcend all social barriers and restrictions. A rather more psychological existentialism formed the basis of Viennese Actionism. For Mühl and Nitsch, perversion was seen as a rebellion of pleasure principle against reality principle, a protest against the functional use of sexuality in the service of procreation. Sublimating the infantile partial desires for the sake of cultural and social achievement was believed to lead to the formation of "authoritarian characters" (Horkheimer) and fascist social structures. Mühl's statement, "I'm in favor of fornication, of demythologization of sexuality. Intercourse is not a state-supportive sacrament, but a purely bodily function" (Mühl 1969: 9), was complemented by Nitsch's therapeutic definition of his abreaction plays as "aesthetic means for the mastering of cruelty" (Nitsch 1976b:n.p.) and "sadomasochistic destructiveness" (1986:62).[59] Freud's message in *Totem and Taboo* and *Studies on Hysteria* was combined with the sociopolitical analyses of the Frankfurt School, especially Marcuse's *Eros and Civilization*, a key text for many European Happenings artists.[60]

Marcuse's opposition of genuine eroticism on the one hand and pseudo-liberated sexuality harmonized with profitable conformity ("repressive desublimation") on the other was echoed in Mühl's and Lebel's repeated characterization of their actions as antipornography. They shared Marcuse's thesis that sexual repression is inextricably intertwined with political oppression. Therefore, the breaking of taboos in a Happening prepares the participant's disposition for abolishing all forms of despotism: political, social, economic, artistic, and sexual. Marcuse's theory of transformation of the libido (from sexuality constrained under genital supremacy to eroticization of the entire personality) was combined with an aesthetic theory, where the liberation of a person's inborn creativity leads to a change in her or his whole existence: the alienated experience of our self in capitalist society is transformed into self-realization through unrestrained, creative activity in a classless society.

This social-critical and sexual-political dimension of many European

Happenings became even more accentuated in the late 1960s. The development of an alternative youth culture based on an open critique of the value system of the bourgeois "establishment" filtered through into the artistic and intellectual domain and became a concern for many performance artists. Even before the Vietnam War broke out, criticism of American imperialism and capitalism complemented the critique of the "American Way of Life" and its adaptation in European consumer society. But it was the 1967/68 rebellion that brought about a profound and pervasive politicization of the Happenings genre. Vostell's *Miss Vietnam* (1967) for example combined images of

> somebody burning himself in saigon – close combat – school for mannequins – child's doll – dead vietcong hooked up to a tank – bra ad – dummy with cameras – dummy with bomb – dummy with machinegun bullets – irons – napalm bombardment – candy box – US soldier with machinegun belts in hand – dolls on conveyor belt – close combat with bayonets

(Vostell 1968b:33).[61]

One of the most spectacular political Happenings was *Art and Revolution*, organized jointly by the Austrian Socialist Students' Union (SÖS) and the Viennese Actionists and presented on 7 June 1968 in the University of Vienna (see Weibel and Export 1970; Stumpfl in Engerth 1970:167–68). After an introductory lecture by an SÖS member on "The Function of Art in Late-Capitalist Society," Mühl read out a defamatory obituary on Robert Kennedy and a string of insults against the ruling political élites in America; Peter Weibel reviled the Austrian institutions of parliamentarianism and pluralistic democracy; Franz Kaltenbeck declared at the top of his voice: "Abolish the madness of everyday life!! Away with the labor camp of the State!! Redeploy the billions spent on the army for the construction of lust machines! Psychotherapy for all artists! Liberation of all slaves of marriage! End reality!!!" At the same time, the shocked audience in the lecture theatre could observe the Actionists defecating from a table, holding a urinating competition, whipping a naked masochist, vomiting, masturbating, reading excerpts from a pornographic novel, and all along singing the Austrian national anthem. At the end, they invited the spectators for a repeat performance in the Saint-Stephan cathedral. The event created a major scandal and was widely reported in Austrian and German newspapers. The organizers were taken to court and charged with debasing the Austrian state symbols, causing a public nuisance, gross disorderly conduct and violation of the laws of decency and morality, causing actual bodily harm, debasing the institution of marriage and family, sanctioning unlawful and indecent behavior. They were condemned to six months'

(Brus) and four weeks' imprisonment (Mühl), and a penalty of fourteen (Weibel) and twenty days' community service (Stumpfl).

The student rebellion of 1967/68 was accompanied by a flood of books, brochures, and pamphlets on the topic of sexual liberation and class struggle. Love-ins and sit-ins turned into veritable Happenings and elicited enthusiastic responses from artists who had spent many years establishing exactly such a link between art and life. Lebel regarded his participation in the burning down of the Paris stock exchange on 24 May 1968 as the pinnacle of his career as a Happenings artist. In a letter of August 1970 to Vostell he declared:

> There is truly no longer any separation between "art" and "life": the permanent creative process of life as art is taking form on a *mass basis* and has become a *collective* movement. [...] have always admired Courbet because of his paintings, but even more so because he participated in the Paris Commune and the destruction of the Vendome Column. [...] There is more honor in being a street guerilla than being an artist – and it is more useful. The ideal, of course, is to be *both*, and in May there were millions of them on the streets of Paris creating and living the revolution.
>
> (in Vostell 1970b:n.p.)

NOTES

1. I have operated throughout with a rather loose definition of the term "Happening" and have regularly employed other expressions such as Action, Event, and Activity. It is not the aim of this essay to arrive at a clear-cut answer to what constitutes a Happening and what distinguishes it from other performance genres.

2. The texts have been reprinted in the Musée d'Art Moderne catalog *Nouveau réalisme* (Restany 1986).

3. De Saint-Phalle started her shooting paintings in 1960 and presented them for the first time to a general public in Stockholm at the Moderna Museet in 1961. On 30 June 1961 she arranged *Feu à volonté* at the Galerie J. The visitors were handed rifles and were asked to aim at the gypsum sculptures, behind which bags of paint were hidden. With every bullet that lacerated the pouches, splashes of paint ran down the reliefs and turned them into "paintings." On 4 May 1962 she performed *Shooting the Venus of Milo* at the Maidman Playhouse in New York, turning a replica of the famous statue into a colorful stage object. The same year, she presented a shooting Action at the Dwan Gallery in Los Angeles. See the catalog *Niki de Saint-Phalle* (Musée national d'art moderne 1980) and the extensive monograph *Niki de Saint-Phalle* (Hulten 1993).

4. A forerunner of this had been *Mur de tonneaux*, which Christo had erected on 27 June 1962 in the Rue Visconti in Paris. See the exhibition catalog, *Ubi Fluxus ibi motus*, 1990–1962 (Oliva 1990:50–51).

5. Klein's larger projects, which aimed at stimulating the "Blue Revolution" and leading the human being back to an authentic spiritual existence, were never realized. Many of these projects, together with documents and Klein's theoretical statements, have been described in the catalog of the 1976 Yves Klein exhibition at the Nationalgalerie Berlin (Hönisch 1976).

6. According to Pierre Restany, some of these projects date back as far as 1954 (1974:145).

7. The designs were published in the July 1961 issue of Piene's magazine, *ZERO* (Piene and Barret 1973: see also Manzoni 1991:106–08).

8. Restany in *Une vie dans l'art* reports on Vostell's activities in Paris and his fraught relationship with the New Realists (1983:55–57).

9. The text of this "action-lecture," given at the University of Heidelberg on 11 June 1967, was originally published in a newsletter of the Heidelberg student's residence (Vostell 1967:3–6).

10. The score is reprinted in Vostell's *Happening und Leben* (1970a:308–15). For an English translation see Kaprow (1966:244–45).

11. From "Neun Nein Decollagen von Wolf Vostell" in Vostell ([1965] 1970:270). An English translation is printed in Kaprow (1966:248–253).

12. Apart from the scores in *Happening und Leben* (Vostell [1965] 1970a) there are many photographs that help reconstruct the performances. More material can be found in Vostell's anthologies, *Happenings, Fluxus, Pop Art, Nouveau Réalisme* (Becker and Vostell 1965) and *Aktionen, Happenings und Demonstrationen seit 1965* (1970b), and the many exhibition catalogs, of which the following are particularly useful: *Vostell: Bilder, Verwischungen, Happening-Notate* (Kunstverein 1966); *Wolf Vostell Elektronisch* (Neue Galerie 1970a); *Vostell:Retrospektive 1958–1974* (Nationalgalerie 1975); *Wolf Vostell: Dé-coll/agen, Verwischungen, Schichtenbilder, Bleibilder, Objektbilder 1955–1979* (Kunstverein 1980); *Vostell und Berlin: Leben und Werk 1971–1981* (DAAD Galerie 1982).

13. "Was ich will" was published in *Ulmer Theater 64/22*, the program for *In Ulm um Ulm und um Ulm herum*, and reprinted in *Happening und Leben* (Vostell 1970a).

14. On his Fluxus activities see Michael Euler-Schmidt (1992:87–101); Vostell (1990:275–78; the German original published in 1982:235–42); Gabriele Lueg (1986:264–85).

15. See Vostell (1970a:321–22). The score was rejected by the WDR programmers and then performed as a live event in Cologne. For a similar work see *TV-Dé-coll/age and Morning Glory: 2 Pieces by Wolf Vostell* (1963).

16. See *Happening und Leben* (Vostell 1970a:170–72). The score for the Happening has been translated in *Miss Vietnam* (Vostell 1968a:8–9).

17. The paramount importance of felt and fat in Beuys' œuvre has a fairly simple explanation: As a pilot during the second World War he was shot down in the Crimea. He was nearly frozen to death when some nomadic Tatars found him in the snow. They rescued him by covering his body in fat and wrapping him up in felt. He was then nursed back to life in their felt tents and fed on butter, milk, and cheese. Consequently, all these materials had a powerful emotional resonance for Beuys.

18. In the period of the student rebellion he founded the German Student Party

(1967), followed by the Organization of Non-Voters/Free Referendums (1970), Organization for Direct Democracy (1971), and the Free International School for Creativity and Interdisciplinary Research (1973). He became a candidate for the ecological Green Party in the European Parliament election in 1979.

19. From a description of the aims of the Organization for Direct Democracy, translated in Tisdall (1979).

20. His aesthetics can best be gleaned from his two collections of theoretical writings: *Ästhetik als Vermittlung: Arbeitsbiographie eines Generalisten* (1977) and *Ästhetik gegen erzwungene Unmittelbarkeit: Schriften 1978–1986* (1986). For a documentation of his Happenings see *Was machen Sie jetzt so* (1968).

21. He produced it, much later in 1972, at the Düsseldorfer Schauspielhaus.

22. From a manifesto written during the festival.

23. The manifesto was the result of a first attempt at producing a piece of sculpture that extended into the environment and involved the spectator in an active response mechanism. Spoerri had organized this "sculpture" with Yves Klein at the Hessenhuis in Antwerp in June 1959. He described it as

> *Auto-théâtre*: Three flexible mirrors deformed by a mechanism reflect the image of the spectators. Underneath the distortions, on the frame, there were inscriptions indicating the attitude the audience was supposed to assume: stretch out your tongue, bend your head forward, etc. Tinguely had helped me to realize this piece which mixes theatre, happening, concrete poetry, transformable art and audience participation.
>
> (in Hahn 1990:20)

24. *Ja, Mama, das machen wir*, performed in 1962 in Ulm and published in *Modernes Schweizer Theater* (Hilty and Schmid 1964).

25. Filliou sometimes used the metaphorical term "mind-opener" for this. Art was for him a tool just as a can opener is a tool for more mundane purposes.

26. *The Immortal Death of the World* was published in 1967. *A Filliou Sampler*, also published in 1967, contains *A Play Called FALSE!*, which despite the three-act division must be regarded as a prose text rather than a performance piece.

27. In 1967, during his stay in New York, Filliou tried to persuade Earle Brown to set the piece to music and Merce Cunningham to turn it into a ballet.

28. The actor Jean-Loup Philippe describes *Soumission au possible, Le berger révant qu'il était roi*, and *C'est l'ange* in Dreyfus (1989:63–64).

29. A variant that relates the sounds to colors and emotions is *Symphonie Poi Poi No. 4*, printed in Becker and Vostell (1965:172–73).

30. The texts of "Yes" and "Le Filliou idéal" are reprinted in *A Filliou Sampler* (1967b:5–10) and in the Sprengel-Museum catalog (1984b:88, 70).

31. *Père Lachaise no. 1*, which he had performed in Copenhagen in September 1961. The text has been printed in *Phantomas* (Filliou 1963).

32. For Vautier's aesthetics see *L'esthetique de Ben* (1960); *Ecrit pour la goire à force de tourner en rond et d'être jaloux* (1970), parts of which have been translated in *Me Ben I Sign* (1975); *Ecritures de Ben* (1972); *Textes théoriques: Tracts 1960–74* (1974); *Théorie, 1965–1979* (1979a), which also comprises vol. 8 of *My Berlin Inventory* (1979b). Some of his

performance scripts have been published in Becker and Vostell (1965:253–60) and the catalog *Art = Ben* (Stedelijk Museum 1973). References to his performance work can be found in C. Millet (1970); *Flash Art*, Special Issue on Ben (1971); R. Nabakowski (1971); David Briers (1972).

33. Statement on a handout distributed at the Festival.

34. Statement on a poster distributed in the streets of Nice.

35. In an interview with an Italian journalist he described his motives for this change of directions:

> Before making Happenings I was a painter. At a certain moment I felt a violent disgust for painting. I became aware that it had become a consumer object, an industry. [. . .] I had a very bad crisis, then I began to see a bit clearer: [. . .] Man is no longer just an artist, but a work of art himself. [. . .] Art invades life.
>
> (Lebel 1967b)

36. Barry Farrel filed his report in May 1965, but it was not printed until 7 February 1967.

37. Nearly all of these ideas can be found in Lebel's *Le happening* (1966a). An edited and slightly shortened version of this is the long essay "Theory and Practice" (1967a), partly reprinted as "On the Necessity of Violation" in *TDR* (1968a [and in this volume]). Large sections of this are literal translations of *Le happening*, to which I shall only refer when the respective passages are missing in the English version. Other theoretical statements include: "A l'œil: note sur les happenings" (1962; reprinted in Sohm 1970); "Happenings" (1963); "A Point of View on Happenings from Paris" (1965a); "Umsonst. Bemerkungen zu den Happenings" and "Grundsätzliches zum Thema Happening" (1965b:355–59); "Le happening" (1966b; reprinted in Sohm 1970); *Lettre ouverte au regardeur* (1966c); "Qu'est-ce qu'un happening? Dialogue avec Francis Leroi" (1966d); "Parler du happening" (1966e); "Intervista-collage" (1967b); "Happenings" (1968b); "Notes on Political Street Theatre" (1969). The most informative publication on Lebel, which also includes many reprints of reviews and statements, is the exhibition catalog *Jean Jacques Lebel: Retour d'exil* (Galerie 1900–2000 1988).

38. Lebel draws heavily on Herbert Marcuse's theory of sublimation expressed in his *Eros and Civilization* (1955) which was translated as *Eros et civilisation* and published in France in 1963 and again in 1968 (see Lebel 1966a:16, 40).

39. The poster has been reproduced in *Retour d'exil* (Galerie 1900–2000 1988:59). There are several photographs in Allan Kaprow's *Assemblages, Environments & Happenings* (1966:228–32). The text of the funeral ceremony can also be found in *Ubi fluxus ibi motus* (Oliva 1990:76).

40. See the detailed description of the Happening by E.C. Nimmo in *New Writers IV* (Calder 1967:50–52), the review by Elena Guicciardi (1962), reprinted in *Retour d'exil* (Galerie 1900–2000 1988:66–67). The report in Kaprow (1966:234) relates to the Boulogne performance. There are several photographs in *Le happening* (Lebel 1966a:plates 27–28), and Kaprow (1966:235–40).

41. For other descriptions of the Happening see Lebel (1966a:71–73); *Retour d'exil* (Galerie 1900–2000 1988:68, 70, 72, 73–74). There is a set

of five photographs of the show in Dreyfus (1989:6), another one in "On the Necessity of Violation" (Lebel 1968a:92) and in *Le happening* (1966a:plate 32).

42. See the review in *La Gazzetta di Parma* (1968), reprinted in *Retour d'exil* (Galerie 1900-2000 1988:78-79).

43. Some of these activities have been described by Knížák in his essay, "Aktual in Czechoslovakia" (Knížák 1972:40-43). There is a monograph on him by Dietrich Albrecht, Wolfgang Feelisch, and Hanns Sohm (1973), and a number of informative exhibition catalogs: (DAAD 1980; Kunstverein 1980; Kunsthalle 1986; Sprengel 1986).

44. I use the German edition of the exhibition catalog *Milan Knížák, Action is a Life Style: Auswahl der Aktivitäten, 1953-1985* (Kunsthalle 1986).

45. The Oberhuber essay is in the second part of an exhibition catalog edited by Huber Klocker (1989). It contains the most complete documentation of the group's activities. For an earlier compendium see Peter Weibel and Valie Export (1970).

46. See in particular Udo Kultermann's "Introduction" to the special issue *Le Marais: Sondernummer zur Aktion und Ausstellung Günter Brus*, which served as a catalog to the Günter Brus exhibition, "Malerei, Selbstbemalung, Selbstverstümmelung" (1965).

47. Kiki Kogelnik's reaction after the "Festival of Psychophysical Naturalism" (28 March 1963) has been reported in Peter Gorsen's *Sexualästhetik* (1972:162).

48. A rare exception was the Destruction in Arts Symposium in London, where they gave several performances at the Africa Centre (10 and 15 September 1966), the Conway Hall (12 September) and the St. Bride's Institute (13 and 16 September).

49. Tachism had become known in Vienna around 1951 and can be found in the work of many Austrian painters from 1955 onwards. Nitsch saw an exhibition of works by Jackson Pollock, Franz Kline, and Willem de Kooning in 1959 (see Feuerstein *et al.* 1965; Stärk 1987:25).

50. See Nitsch (1982) and the excerpts in (1981:79-85). For the scores of his later actions see Nitsch (1979 & 1986; and 1987). His theoretical writings have been collected in Nitsch (1976a). A few texts have been translated in the bilingual edition *Orgien Mysterien Theater. Orgies Mysteries Theatre*.

51. On Reich and the history of the National Union for Proletarian Sexual Politics see the volume edited by Hans-Peter Gente, *Marxismus, Psychoanalyse, Sexpol* (1970). (There is also a second volume, printed in March 1972, analyzing the influence of the Sexpol movement on the "antiauthoritarian rebellion" of the late 1960s). The Action-Analytical Commune understood itself as "a therapeutic group with the mission of making the group members damaged by being brought up in small families healthy again and enabling them to get into social communication with others. Free sexuality and collective ownership, mutual child rearing, promotion of creative activity and further development of the action analysis for the analytical self-representation are the basic structures of the commune" (in Klocker 1989:214-15). However, in the 1980s, these ideals became more and more perverted until, in 1991, "Great Pan Otto" was taken to court for sexual child abuse and the commune was forced to dissolve.

52. From a manifesto published and distributed on the occasion of Mühl's

performance at the 1970 exhibition *Happening and Fluxus* in Cologne; also quoted in Klocker (1989:213–14).

53. However, they were represented in one of the first anthologies of Happening documents, Becker and Vostell's *Happenings, Fluxus, Pop Art, Nouveau Réalisme* of 1965 and the first major retrospective of Happenings art, held in Cologne in 1970.

54. Karl Rosenkranz' *Ästhetik des Häßlichen* (1853) reads in part like a philosophical comment on Viennese Actionism.

55. For a brief survey of the activities in Britain see Adrian Henri's *Environments and Happenings* (1974:111–28). I am most grateful to Mr. Henri for sharing his rich experience as a Happenings artist with me. British newspapers did not have at that time any critics with a special responsibility for covering these kinds of performances. The arts and theatre journals did not recognize Happenings as a legitimate art form and rarely mentioned them at all. A rather tame protest against this kind of affairs was Charles Marowitz' essay, "Whatever Happened to Happenings" (1965:21, 50).

56. Victor Musgrave began his career as a Surrealist painter in Cairo in the 1940s. He then became a poet and filmmaker. He ran the Gallery One for twelve years and organized several other performance events. See his essay "The Unknown Art Movement" (1972:12–14).

57. On the connection between punk and 1970s performance art see Roselee Goldberg's *Performance Art: Live Art 1909 to the Present* (1979:117–22).

58. Allan Kaprow in a 1973 interview with Reiner Wick (in Wick 1975:148).

59. See also the section "zur theorie des grundexzess-erlebnisses" in his essay, *Vom Wesen der Tragödie* (Nitsch 1965).

60. The Marcuse book was first published in English and ran through a number of American and British editions (1955, 1956, 1961, 1962, 1966, 1969, 1970, 1972). There were three German editions (1957, 1965, 1968), two in French (1963 and 1968), and three in Spanish (1968, 1969, 1970).

61. See also his earlier *Vietnam Symphony* (1966) in *Happening und Leben* (Vostell 1970a:148–51).

REFERENCES

Albrecht, Dietrich, Wolfgang Feelisch, and Hanns Sohm (1973) *Milan Knížák*. Stuttgart: Reflection Press.

Alloway, Lawrence (1958) "The Arts and the Mass Media." *Architectural Design 28*, 2 (February):84–85.

Aubertin, B. (1968) "Sur Piero Manzoni." *Robho*, no. 3 (Spring).

Aue, Walker (1971) *P.C.A.: Projecte, Concepte and Actionen*. Cologne: DuMont.

Badura-Triske, Eva, and Hubert Klocker (1992) *Rudolf Schwarzkogler: Leben und Werk*. Klagenfurt: Ritter.

Bahr, Hermann (1907) "Elektra." In *Glossen zum Wiener Theater (1903–1907)*. Berlin: S. Fischer Verlag.

Becker, Jürgen, and Wolf Vostell, eds (1965) *Happenings, Fluxus, Pop Art, Nouveau Réalisme*. Reinbek: Rowohlt.

Beuys, Joseph (1972) *Zeichnungen von 1947–69*. Exhibition catalog. Galerie Schmela, Düsseldorf. Munich: Schirmer Mosel.

Bremer, Claus (1962) *Theater ohne Vorhang*. St. Gallen und Stuttgart: Tschudy-Verlag.

Briers, David (1972) "Ben doute de tout: David Briers looks at the career of Ben Vautier." *Art and Artist*, April: 25–7.

Brock, Bazon (1960) D.A.S.E.R.S.C.H.R.E.C.K.E.N.A.M.S. Basle: Panderma-Verlag.

—— (1966) "Theater der Positionen." *Theater Heute*, July:62.

—— (1968) *Was machen Sie jetzt so*. Darmstadt: Melzer.

—— (1977) *Ästhetik als Vermittlung. Arbeitsbiographie eines Generalisten*. Cologne: DuMont.

—— (1986) *Ästhetik gegen erzwungene Unmittelbarkeit: Schriften 1978–1986*. Cologne: DuMont.

—— (1987) "Die utopische Vergangenheit ist für uns inzwischen wichtiger als die utopische Zukunft." *Basler Magazin. Beilage der Basler Zeitung*, 3 January:1.

—— (1992) Interview with author. Wuppertal, Germany, April.

Brus, Günter (1965) "Malerei, Selbstbemalung, Selbstverstümmelung." *Le Marais*, special issue on the action (Aktionen von Brus) and exhibition at the Galerie Junge Generation, Vienna.

Calder, John, ed. (1967) *New Writers IV: Plays and Happenings*. London: John Calder.

Celant, Germano (1991) "Piero Manzoni, an Artist of the Present." In *Piero Manzoni*, edited by G. Celant. Exhibition catalog. Paris: Musée d'Art moderne de la Ville de Paris.

Cibulka, Heinz (1977) *Mein Körper bei den Aktionen von Nitsch und Schwarzkogler*. Naples: Morra.

Cladders, Johannes (1988) "Fröhliche Einsamkeit." In *Robert Filliou 1926–1987 zum Gedächtnis*. Exhibition catalog. Düsseldorf: Städtische Kunsthalle Düsseldorf.

Claus, Jürgen, ed. (1974) *Otto Piene–Sky Art*. Exhibition catalog. Ingolstadt: Kunstverein.

DAAD Galerie (1980) *Milan Knížák*. Berlin: DAAD Galerie.

—— (1982) *Vostell und Berlin: Leben und Werk 1971–1981*. Berlin: DAAD Galerie.

Dreyfus, Charles (1989) *Happenings and Fluxus*. Paris: Galerie 1900–2000.

Engerth, Rüdiger (1970) "Der Wiener Aktionismus." *Protokolle 1:152–69*.

Euler-Schmidt, Michael (1992) "In Köln und von Köln aus." In *Vostell*, ed. Rolf

Wedewer, 87–101. Exhibition catalog. Heidelberg: Edition Braus.

Farrel, Barry (1967) "Bacchanal of Nudity, Spaghetti and Poetry." *Life Magazine* 7 February.

Feuerstein, G., *et al.* (1965) *Moderne Kunst in Österreich*. Vienna: Forum Verlag.

Filliou, Robert (1963) *Père Lachaise no. 1. Phantomas*, nos. 38–40 (May). (Brussels).

——— (1967a) *L'immortelle mort du monde*. New York: Something Else Press.

——— (1967b) *A Filliou Sampler*. New York: Something Else Press.

——— (1970a) *Filliou Autobiography*. New York: Vague TREasure Edition Fluxus.

——— (1970b) *Teaching and Learning as Performing Arts*. Cologne: Koenig.

——— (1970c) Letter to George Maciunas, 27 May 1970. In *Happening & Fluxus*, ed. Hanns Sohm. Exhibition catalog. Cologne: Kunstverein.

——— (1970d) Letter to Berlinske Tidende, 21 December 1963. In *Happening & Fluxus*, ed. Hanns Sohm. Exhibition catalog. Cologne: Kunstverein.

——— (1984a) "L'autrisme." In *Das immerwährende Ereignis zeigt: Robert Filliou*. Exhibition catalog. Hanover: Sprengel-Museum.

——— (1984b) *Longs poèmes courts a terminer chez soi*. In *Das immerwährende Ereignis zeigt: Robert Filliou*. Exhibition catalog. Hanover: Sprengel-Museum.

Flash Art (1971) Special Issue on Ben. *Flash Art*, no. 23 (April).

Galerie 1900–2000 (1988) *Jean Jacques Lebel: Retour d'exil*. Paris: Galerie 1900–2000.

Galerie Heseler (1972) *Otto Piene – Lichtballett und Künstler der Gruppe Zero*. Exhibition catalog. Munich: Galerie Heseler.

La Gazzetta di Parma (1968) "Il Regio transformato in una bolgia durante la recita 'Happening.'" *La Gazzetta di Parma*, 24 March.

Geldzahler, Henry (1963) "A Symposium on Pop Art." *Arts Magazine*, April:37–42.

Gente, Hans-Peter, ed. (1970) *Marxismus, Psychoanalyse, Sexpol*. Frankfurt: Fischer Verlag.

Goldberg, Roselee (1979) *Performance Art: Live Art 1909 to the Present*. New York: Harry N. Abrams.

Gorsen, Peter (1972) *Sexualästhetik*. Reinbek: Rowohlt.

Guicciardi, Elena (1962) "L'uomo-televisore annuncia la rivoluzione." *Il Giorno*, 18 December.

Hahn Otto (1990) *Daniel Spoerri*. Paris: Flammarion.

Hanoteau, Guillaume (1966) "A-t-on le droit de condamner le 'Happening'?" *Paris-Match*, 18 June.

Henri, Adrian (1974) *Environments and Happenings*. London: Thames & Hudson.

Hilty, M.R., and M. Schmid, eds (1964) *Modernes Schweizer Theater*. Egnach: Clou Verlag.

Hönisch, Dieter, ed. (1976) *Yves Klein*. Exhibition catalog. Berlin: National-galerie.

Hulten, Pontus (1993) *Niki de Saint-Phalle*. Stuttgart: Hatje.

Kaprow, Allan (1966) *Assemblages, Environments & Happenings*. New York: Harry N. Abrams.

Klein, Yves (1960) *Sensibilité pure*. In *Dimanche: Le journal d'un seul jour*, 27 November:1–2.

Klocker, Huber (1989) *Wiener Aktionismus/Viennese Aktionism* [sic] *Wien/Vienna 1960–1971: Der zertrümmerte Spiegel/The Shattered Mirror*. Klagenfurt: Ritter Verlag.

Knížák, Milan (1972) "Aktual in Czechoslovakia." *Art and Artists*, October: 40–43.

Kostelanetz, Richard (ed.) (1980) *Scenarios: Scripts to Perform*. New York: Assembling Press.

Kultermann, Udo (1965) "Introduction." *Le Marais: Sondernummer zur Aktion und Ausstellung Günter Brus*. Exhibition catalog. Vienna: Galerie Junge Generation.

Kunsthalle (1986) *Milan Knížák, Action is a Life Style: Auswahl der Aktivitäten, 1953–1985*. Hamburg: Kunsthalle.

Kunstverein (Braunschweig) (1980) *Wolf Vostell:Dé-coll/agen, Verwischungen, Schichtenbilder, Bleibilder, Objektbilder 1955–1979*. Braunschweig: Kunst-verein.

Kunstverein (Cologne) (1966) *Vostell: Bilder, Verwischungen, Happening-Notate*. Cologne: Kunstverein.

Kunstverein (Oldenburg) (1980) *Milan Knížák*. Oldenburg: Kunstverein.

Lebel, Jean-Jacques (1962) "A l'œil: note sur les happenings." Program for *Catastrophe*. Paris: Galerie Cordier.

——— (1963) "Happenings." *City Lights Journal*, no. 1.

——— (1965a) "A Point of View on Happenings from Paris." In *ICA Bulletin*. London: Institute of Contemporary Arts.

——— (1965b) "Umsonst. Bemerkungen zu den Happenings" and "Grundsätz-liches zum Thema Happening." In *Happenings, Fluxus, Pop Art, Nouveau Réalisme*, edited by J. Becker and W. Vostell, 355–59. Reinbek: Rowohlt.

────── (1966a) *Le happening*. Paris: Donoël & Les Lettres Nouvelles.

────── (1966b) "Le happening." Manifesto distributed at SIGMA Art Festival, Bordeaux.

────── (1966c) *Lettre ouverte au regardeur*. (Paris).

────── (1966d) "Qu'est-ce qu'un happening? Dialogue avec Francis Leroi." *Combat*, June.

────── (1966e) "Parler du happening." *Cité Panorama*, no. 10. (Villeurbanne).

────── (1967a) "Theory and Practice." In *New Writers IV: Plays and Happenings*, edited by John Calder: 11–45. London: John Calder.

────── (1967b) "Intervista-collage." In the program of the International Theatre Festival in Parma.

────── (1968a) "On the Necessity of Violation." *TDR* 13, 1 (T41):89–105.

────── (1968b) "Happenings." *The San Francisco Earthquake*.

────── (1969) "Notes on Political Street Theatre, Paris: 1968, 1969." *TDR* 13, 4 (T44):111–18.

────── (1970) "Le happening." In *Happening & Fluxus*, edited by Hanns Sohm. Exhibition catalog. Cologne: Kunstverein.

Liebig, Klaus (1973) *Robert Filliou*. Exhibition catalog. Munich: Galerie Buchholz.

Lueg, Gabriele (1986) "Gabriele Lueg: Gespräch mit Wolf Vostell." In *Die 60er Jahre: Kölns Weg zur Kunstmetropole*, 264–85. Exhibition catalog. Cologne: Kunstverein.

Manzoni, Piero (1960) "Libera dimensione." *Azimuth*, no. 2. (Milan).

────── (1973) [1961] "Progetti immediati." In *ZERO* reprint, ed. O. Piene and C. Barret. Cambridge, MA: M.I.T. Press.

────── (1975) [1956] "Per la scoperta di una zona di immagini." In *Piero Manzoni: Catalogo generale*, ed. G. Celant. Milan: Prearo Editore.

────── (1991) [1957] "Oggi il concetto di quadro." *Corriere della Provincia di Como*, December. Reprinted in *Piero Manzoni*, ed. G. Celant. Paris: Musée d'Art moderne de la Ville de Paris.

────── (1991) "Placentarium." In *Piero Manzoni*, ed. G. Celant, 106–08. Exhibition catalog. Paris: Musée d'Art moderne de la Ville de Paris.

Marcuse, Herbert (1955) *Eros and Civilization*. Boston: Beacon Press.

Marowitz, Charles (1965) "Whatever Happened to Happenings." *Plays and Players*, March:21, 50.

Merkert, Jörn (1974) "Pre-Fluxus-Vostell." *Kunstforum 2*, 10:195–204.

Millet, C. (1970) "Ben entre Duchamp et l'art conceptuel." *Chroniques de l'art vivant*, no. 14 (October).

Motherwell, Robert, ed. (1951) *The Dada Painters and Poets*. New York: George Wittenborn, Inc.

Mühl, Otto (1969) *Papa und Mama: Materialaktion 63–69*. Frankfurt: Kohlkunst-Verlag.

———— (1981) "Gespräch mit Otto Mühl." *Die Stadtillustrierte Wiener. Sonderdruck Wiener Aktionismus.* (Vienna).

———— (1986) *Ausgewählte Arbeiten 1963–1986*. Zurndorf: Archiv des Wiener Aktionismus.

Musée national d'art moderne (1980) *Niki de Saint-Phalle*. Paris: Musée national d'art moderne.

Musgrave, Victor (1972) "The Unknown Art Movement." *Art and Artists*, October: 12–14.

Nabakowski, R. (1971) "Zu den Arbeiten von Ben Vautier: 'To change art – destroy ego.'" *Kunst Nachrichten* 7, no. 8 (April).

Nationalgalerie (1975) *Vostell: Retrospektive 1958–1974*. Berlin: Nationalgalerie.

Neue Galerie (1970a) *Wolf Vostell Elektronisch*. Aachen: Neue Galerie im Alten Kulturhaus.

———— (1970b) *Robert Filliou – Commemor*. Exhibition catalog. Aachen: Neue Galerie im Alten Kulturhaus.

Nitsch, Hermann (1965) [1963] "Vom Wesen der Tragödie" (On the Essence of Tragedy). In *Le Marais: Sondernummer zur Aktion und Ausstellung Günter Brus*. Exhibition catalog. Vienna: Galerie Junge Generation.

———— (1969) *Orgien Mysterien Theater. Orgies Mysteries Theatre*. Darmstadt: März Verlag.

———— (1976a) *das orgien mysterien theater 2: theoretische schriften*. Naples: Chiessi & Morra.

———— (1976b) "Rudolf Schwarzkogler." In *Rudolf Schwarzkogler*, Exhibition catalog. Innsbruck: Galerie Krinzinger.

———— (1981) *Excerpts from die wortdichtung des orgien mysterien theater.* Protokolle, no. 2:79–85.

———— (1982) *Die Wortdichtung des Orgien Mysterien Theaters*. Private edition.

———— (1979 and 1986) *Das Orgien Mysterien Theater: Die Partituren aller aufgeführten Aktionen, 1960–1979*. 2 vols. Naples, Munich, Vienna: Edizione Morra & Edition Freibord.

———— (1986) König Oedipus. *Eine spielbare Theorie des Dramas (1964) Neu verlegt in der Edition Kalter*. Berlin: Schweiß Verlag Jochen Knoblauch.
———— (1987) *Das Orgien Mysterien Theater 1960–1987*. Naples: Morra.

Nuttal, Jeff (1968) *Bomb Culture*. London: MacGibbon & Kee.

Oberhuber, Konrad (1989) "Thoughts on Viennese Actionism." in *Wiener Aktionismus/Viennese Aktionism* [sic] *Wien / Vienna 1960–1971*, ed. Huber Klockner. Klagenfurt: Ritter Verlag.

Oliva, Achille Bonito, ed. (1990) *Ubi Fluxus ibi motus, 1990–1962.* Exhibition catalog. Venice: Ex Granai della Repubblica alle Zitelle (Giudecca).

Piene, Otto (1960) *Otto Piene.* Exhibition catalog. Berlin: Galerie Diogenes.

—— (1964) "The Development of the Group Zero." *Times Literary Supplement*, 3 September: 812–13.

—— (1965) "Lichtballet." *Theater Heute*, May:26–27.

—— (1974) *More Sky.* Cambridge, MA: M.I.T. Press.

Piene, Otto, and Cyril Barret, eds (1973) *ZERO.* Reprint of the three issues, with an introduction by Lawrence Alloway. Cambridge, MA: M.I.T. Press.

Restany, Pierre (1968) *Les Nouveaux Réalistes.* Paris: Editions Planète. Second, enlarged edition: *Le Nouveau Réalisme*, Paris: Union générale d'éditions, 1978.

—— (1970) *Nouveau Réalisme 1960/70.* Exhibition catalog. Paris: Galerie Mathias Fels.

—— (1971) "The New Realism." In *Art Since Mid-century, vol. 2: Figurative Art*, 242–71. Greenwich, CT: New York Graphic Society.

—— (1974) *Yves Klein: Le Monochrome.* Paris: Hachette-Littérature.

—— (1982) *Yves Klein.* Paris: Chêne. English translation published simultaneously by Harry N. Abrams under the same title.

—— (1983) *Une vie dans l'art.* Neuchâtel: Ides et Calendes.

—— (1986) *1960: Les Nouveaux Réalistes.* Exhibition catalog. Paris: Musée d'Art Moderne.

Rosenkranz, Karl (1853) *Ästhetik des Häßlichen.* Königsberg: Bornträger.

Sandberg, J.H. (1991) "Søren Kirkegard is My Father: His Goal Was to Clarify the Concept." In *Piero Manzoni*, ed. G. Celant, 31. Exhibition catalog. Paris: Musée d'Art moderne de la Ville de Paris.

Schwarzkogler, Rudolf (1970) "Das ästhetische Panorama." *Die Schastrommel*, no. 3 (October).

Sohm, Hanns, ed. (1970) *Happening & Fluxus.* Exhibition catalog. Cologne: Kunstverein.

Solomon, Alan (1963) *The Popular Image Exhibition.* Exhibition catalog. Washington, DC: Gallery of Modern Art.

Spoerri, Daniel (1959/60) *Beispiel für das dynamische Theater. Das Neue Forum*, no. 7:109–12.

—— (1973) [1961] "Über das Autotheater" and "Fallenbilder." In *ZERO* reprint, edited by O. Piene and C. Barret. Cambridge, MA: M.I.T. Press.

—— (1988) "Filliou ist mein großer Bruder, aber ich bin seine Mutter: Ein Interview mit Daniel Spoerri von Hans-Werner Schmidt, München, 21. Juni 1988." In *Robert Filliou 1926–1987 zum Gedächtnis*. Exhibition catalog. Düsseldorf: Städtische Kunsthalle Düsseldorf.

Sprengel (1986) *Milan Knížák*. Hanover: Sprengel.

Staatliche Museen Preußischer Kulturbesitz (1976) *Yves Klein*. Exhibition catalog. Nationalgalerie, Berlin. Berlin: Staatliche Museen Preußischer Kulturbesitz.

Stärk, Ekkehard (1987) *Hermann Nitschs "Orgien Mysterien Theater" und die "Hysterie der Griechen."* Munich: Wilhelm Fink Verlag.

Stedelijk Museum (1973) *Art = Ben*. Exhibition catalog. Amsterdam: Stedelijk Museum.

Swenson, G.R. (1963) "What is Pop Art." *ARTnews*, November.

Tisdall, Caroline (1976) *Joseph Beuys: Coyote*. Munich: Schirmer Mosel.

—— (1979) *Joseph Beuys*. London: Thames & Hudson.

Tomkins, Calvin (1976) [1965] *The Bride and the Bachelor*. New York: Penguin.

Vautier, Ben (1960) *L'esthétique de Ben*. Nice.

—— (1970) *Ecrit pour la goire à force de tourner en rond et d'être jaloux*. Paris.

—— (1972) *Ecritures de Ben*. Paris.

—— (1974) *Textes théoriques: Tracts 1960–74*. Milan.

—— (1975) *Me Ben I Sign*. Translated by David Mayor. Cranleigh: Beau Geste Press.

—— (1979a) *Théorie, 1965–1979*. Berlin.

—— (1979b) *My Berlin Inventory*. Berlin: DAAD Galerie.

—— (1980) "Tout cela est difficile." In *Ubi Fluxus ibi motus, 1990–1962*, ed. Achille Bonito Oliva, 270. Exhibition catalog. Venice: Ex Granai della Repubblica alle Zitelle (Giudecca).

—— (1982) *"Dies ist die Geschichte von Fluxus in Nizza."* In *Fluxus*. Exhibition catalog. Wiesbaden.

Vostell, Wolf (1963) *TV-Dé-coll/age and Morning Glory: 2 Pieces by Wolf Vostell*. New York: Third Rail Gallery.

—— (1965a) "Happening." *Theater Heute*, May: 29.

—— (1965b) "Die Kunst des Happenings: Aktionsvortrag von Allan Kaprow und Wolf Vostell, Cricket Theatre, New York City 19/4/64." In *Happenings, Fluxus, Pop Art, Nouveau Réalisme*, eds J. Becker and W. Vostell, 399–409. Reinbek: Rowohlt.

—— (1966) "Statement." *da-a/u delà*, October:2. (Milan).

———— (1967) "Genesis und Ikonographie meiner Happenings." *Folia. Blätter aus dem Studentenwohnheim* 1, 15:3–6.

———— (1968a) "Genesis and Iconography of My Happenings." In *Miss Vietnam* 1–19. San Francisco: The Nova Broadcast Press.

———— (1968b) *Miss Vietnam and Texts of Other Happenings*. Transl. Carl Weissner. San Francisco: The Nova Broadcast Press.

———— (1970a) [1965] *Happening und Leben*. Neuwied: Luchterhand.

———— (1970b) *Aktionen, Happenings und Demonstrationen seit 1965*. Reinbek: Rowohlt.

———— (1982) *Fluxus: Aspekte eines Phänomens*. Exhibition catalog. Wuppertal: Kunst- und Museumsverein.

———— (1990) "Fluxus." In *Ubi Fluxus, ibi motus*. Exhibition catalog, 275–78. Venice: Biennale.

Warhol, Andy (1980) *POPism: The Warhol '60s*. New York: Harcourt Brace Jovanovich.

———— (1989) *Andy Warhol: A Retrospective*. New York: Museum of Modern Art.

Weibel, Peter, and Valie Export, eds (1970) *Wien: Bildkompendium Wiener Aktionismus*. Frankfurt/M: Kohlkunst Verlag.

Wick, Reiner (1975) *Zur Soziologie intermediärer Kunstpraxis: Happening, Fluxus*, Aktionen. Ph.D. diss. Faculty of Philosophy, Cologne.

INDEX